Britain 1815–1895
and Ireland 1798–1922

Derrick Murphy ■ **Patrick Walsh Atkins** ■ **Neil Whiskerd**

Published by Collins
An imprint of
HarperCollinsPublishers
77–85 Fulham Palace Road
Hammersmith
London
W6 8JB

Browse the complete Collins
catalogue at
www.collinseducation.com

10 9 8 7 6 5 4 3

ISBN-13 978 0 00 726868 9

British Library Cataloguing in
Publication Data
A Catalogue record for this
publication is available from the
British Library

Edited by Graham Bradbury
Commissioned by Michael
Upchurch
Design and typesetting by Derek Lee
Cover design by Joerg
Hartmannsgruber, White-card
Map Artwork by Tony Richardson
Picture research by Celia Dearing
and Michael Upchurch
Production by Simon Moore
Indexed by Lisa Footit

ACKNOWLEDGEMENTS
Every effort had been made to
contact the holders of copyright
material, but if any have been
inadvertently overlooked the
publishers will be pleased to make
the necessary arrangements at the
first opportunity.

Blackwell Publishers for the extract
from *The Making of Modern British
Politics 1867 to 1939* by Martin Pugh
(1982). Cambridge University Press
for extracts from *1848: The British
State and the Chartist Movement* by
John Saville (1987). The Historical
Association for the extract from
*Reformed Electoral System in Great
Britain 1832–1914* by H.J. Hanham
(1968). Hodder Headline for the
extracts from *Aristocracy and People,
Britain 1815–1865* by Norman Gash
(Hodder Arnold, 1987); *A Social
History of the English Working
Classes, 1815–1945* by E. Hopkins
(Hodder Arnold, 1979); *Government
and Reform* by Robert Pearce (1994);
Victorian Imperialism by C.C.
Eldridge (Hodder and Stoughton,
1978); *Britain and the European
Powers 1865 to 1914* by Robert
Pearce (1996); *The Climax of Liberal
Politics, 1868–1916: British
Liberalism in Theory and Practice* by
Michael Bentley (Hodder Arnold,
1987); *Democracy and Empire:
British History 1865 to 1914* by E. J.
Feuchtwanger (Arnold, 1985) and
*Conservatism and the Conservative
Party in Nineteenth Century Britain*
by Bruce Coleman (Hodder Arnold,
1988). Longman for the extracts
from *Nineteenth-Century Britain
1815–1914* by Anthony Wood
(1984); *The Age of Improvement
1783–1867* by Asa Briggs (1979);
*'Pax Britannica?' British Foreign
Policy 1789–1914* by Muriel
Chamberlain (1988); *Home Rule and
the Irish Question* by Grenfell Morton
(Seminar Studies, 1980) and *The
Theory of Capitalist Imperialism* by
D. Fieldhouse (1967). Macmillan for
the extracts from *Party and Politics
1830–1852* by Robert Stewart
(1989). Orion Publishers for the
extracts from *Ireland Since the
Famine* by F.S.L. Lyons (Weidenfeld,
1971). Penguin for extracts from
*The Formation of the Liberal Party,
1857–68* (Pelican, 1972) and *Lord
Salisbury* by Robert by Robert Taylor
(Allen Lane, 1975). Temple Smith
for the extract from *Conservatives
and conservatism* by Philip Norton
(1981) and *The Chartists* by Dorothy
Thompson (1984). A P Watt Ltd for
the extracts from *Gladstone* by E.J.
Feuchtwanger (1975).

The publishers would like to thank
the following for permission to
reproduce pictures on these pages.
T=Top, B=Bottom, L=Left, R=Right,
C=Centre

The Bridgeman Art Library 80(T);
Illustrated London News 197; Mary
Evans Picture Library 39, 40, 51, 65,
76, 80 (B), 93, 149; © Museum of
London /HIP 109; National Portrait
Gallery 91 (T); © Punch Limited
191; HIP / TopFoto 118, 152;
© World History Archive / TopFoto
182; © Print Collector / HIP
/TopFoto 44, 91 (B); Trustees of the
Ulster Museum, Belfast 219;
Unknown 38, 73, 82, 84, 105, 130,
135, 169, 183, 185, 213, 227.

Printed and bound by CPI Group (UK)
Ltd, Croydon, CR0 4YY

Contents

Study and examination skills

This section of the book is designed to aid Sixth Form students in their preparation for public examinations in History.

- Differences between GCSE and Sixth Form History
- Extended writing: the structured question and the essay
- How to handle sources in Sixth Form History
- Historical interpretation
- Progression in Sixth Form History
- Examination technique

Differences between GCSE and Sixth Form History

- The amount of factual knowledge required for answers to Sixth Form History questions is more detailed than at GCSE. Factual knowledge in the Sixth Form is used as supporting evidence to help answer historical questions. Knowing the facts is important, but not as important as knowing that factual knowledge supports historical analysis.

- Extended writing is more important in Sixth Form History. Students will be expected to answer either structured questions or essays.

Structured questions require students to answer more than one question on a given topic. They usually involve studying information from sources.

The first sub-question (a) requires you to engage in source analysis.

This may involve comparing two sources or assessing the value of two sources from a set of four or five sources.

The second sub-question (b) requires you to integrate information from the sources and your own knowledge to answer a specific question.

Each part of the structured question demands a different approach.

An example of this type of question from AQA AS Unit 1 on Britain 1815–1865:

(a) Explain why there was widespread support for electoral reform in the years 1830–1832. (12 marks)

(b) How important was disappointment with the Great Reform Act in explaining the rise of Chartism? (24 marks)

Essay questions require students to produce one answer to a given question.

An example from OCR 'A' Unit F961, Option B:

How liberal were the reforms of Gladstone's first ministry (1868–1874)? Explain your answer.

Similarities with GCSE

● Source analysis and evaluation

The skills in handling historical sources, which were acquired at GCSE, are developed in Sixth Form History. In the Sixth Form, sources have to be analysed in their historical context, so a good factual knowledge of the subject is important.

● Historical interpretations

Skills in historical interpretation at GCSE are also developed in Sixth Form History. The ability to put forward different historical interpretations is important. Students will also be expected to explain why different historical interpretations have occurred.

Extended writing: the structured question and the essay

When faced with extended writing in Sixth Form History students can improve their performance by following a simple routine that attempts to ensure they achieve their best performance.

Answering the question

What are the command instructions?

Different questions require different types of response. For instance, 'In what ways' requires students to point out the various ways something took place in History; 'Why' questions expect students to deal with the causes or consequences of an historical event.

'How far' or 'To what extent' questions require students to produce a balanced, analytical answer. Usually, this will take the form of the case for and case against an historical question.

Are there key words or phrases that require definition or explanation?

It is important for students to show that they understand the meaning of the question. To do this, certain historical terms or words require explanation. For instance, if a question asked 'how far' a politician was an 'innovator', an explanation of the word 'innovator' would be required.

Does the question have specific dates or issues that require coverage?

If the question mentions specific dates, these must be adhered to. For instance, if you are asked to answer a question on Gladstone and the Irish Question it may state clear date limits, such as 1868 to 1886. Also questions may mention a specific aspect such as 'domestic policy' or 'foreign affairs'.

Planning your answer

Once you have decided on what the question requires, write a brief plan. For structured questions this may be brief. This is a useful procedure to make sure that you have ordered the information you require for your answer in the most effective way. For instance, in a balanced, analytical answer this may take the form of jotting down the main points for and against an historical issue raised in the question.

Writing the answer

Communication skills

The quality of written English is important in Sixth Form History. The way you present your ideas on paper can affect the quality of your answer. Therefore, punctuation, spelling and grammar, which were awarded marks at GCSE, require close attention. Use a dictionary if you are unsure of a word's meaning or spelling. Use the glossary of terms you will find in this book to help you.

The quality of your written English will not determine the Level of Response you receive for your answer. It may well determine what mark you may receive within a level. To help you understand this point ask your teacher to see a mark scheme published by your examination board. For instance, you may be awarded Level 2 (10–15 marks) by an examiner. The quality of written English may be a factor in deciding which mark you receive in that level. Will it be 10 or 15 or a mark in between?

The introduction

For structured questions you may wish to dispense with an introduction altogether and begin writing reasons to support an answer straight away. However, essay answers should begin with an introduction. These should be both concise and precise. Introductions help 'concentrate the mind' on the question you are about to answer. Remember, do not try to write a conclusion as your opening sentence. Instead, outline briefly the areas you intend to discuss in your answer.

Balancing analysis with factual evidence

It is important to remember that factual knowledge should be used to support analysis. Merely 'telling the story' of an historical event is not enough. A structured question or essay should contain separate paragraphs, each addressing an analytical point that helps to answer the question. If, for example, the question asks for reasons why Disraeli won the 1874 election, each paragraph should provide a reason for his electoral success. In order to support and sustain the analysis evidence is required. Therefore, your factual knowledge should be used to substantiate analysis. Good structured question and essay answers integrate analysis and factual knowledge.

Seeing connections between reasons

In dealing with 'why'-type questions it is important to remember that the reasons for an historical event might be interconnected. Therefore, it is important to mention the connections between reasons. Also, it might be important to identify a hierarchy of reasons – that is, are some reasons more important than others in explaining an historical event?

Using quotations and statistical data

One aspect of supporting evidence that sustains analysis is the use of quotations. These can be from either a historian or a contemporary. However, unless these quotations are linked with analysis and supporting evidence, they tend to be of little value.

It can also be useful to support analysis with statistical data. In questions that deal with social and economic change, precise statistics that support your argument can be very persuasive.

The conclusion

All structured questions and essays require conclusions. If, for example, a question requires a discussion of 'how far' you agree with a question, you should offer a judgement in your conclusion. Don't be afraid of this – say what you think. If you write an analytical answer, ably supported by factual evidence, you may under-perform because you have not provided a conclusion that deals directly with the question.

Source analysis

Source analysis forms an integral part of the study of History.

In dealing with sources you should be aware that historical sources must be used 'in historical context' in Sixth Form History. This means you must understand the historical topic to which the source refers. Therefore, in this book sources are used with the factual information in each chapter. Also, specific source analysis questions are included at the end of most chapters.

How to handle sources in Sixth Form History

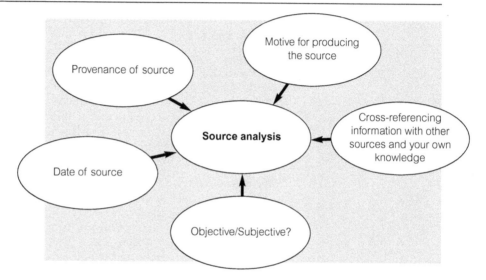

In dealing with sources, a number of basic hints will allow you to deal effectively with source-based questions and to build on your knowledge and skill in using sources at GCSE.

Written sources

Attribution or Provenance and date
It is important to identify who has written the source and when it was written. This information can be very important. If, for instance, a source was written by Benjamin Disraeli during the General Election campaign of 1874, this information will be of considerable importance if you are asked about the usefulness (utility) or reliability of the source as evidence of Conservative election policy in 1874.

It is important to note that just because a source is a primary source does not mean it is more useful or less reliable than a secondary source. Both primary and secondary sources need to be analysed to decide how useful and reliable they are. This can be determined by studying other issues.

Is the content factual or opinionated?
Once you have identified the author and date of the source, it is important to study its content. The content may be factual, stating what has happened or what may happen. On the other hand, it may contain opinions that should be handled with caution. These may contain bias. Even if a source is mainly factual, there might be important and deliberate gaps in factual evidence that can make a source biased and unreliable.

Usually, written sources contain elements of both opinion and factual evidence. It is important to judge the balance between these two parts.

Has the source been written for a particular audience?
To determine the reliability of a source it is important to know to whom it is directed. For instance, a public speech may be made to achieve a particular purpose and may not contain the author's true beliefs or feelings. In contrast, a private diary entry may be much more reliable in this respect.

Corroborative evidence
To test whether or not a source is reliable, the use of other evidence to support or corroborate the information it contains is important. Cross-referencing with other sources is a way of achieving this; so is cross-referencing with historical information contained within a chapter.

Visual sources

Cartoons
Cartoons are a popular form of source used at both GCSE and in Sixth Form History. However, analysing cartoons can be a demanding exercise. Not only will you be expected to understand the content of the cartoon, you may also have to explain a written caption – which appears usually at the bottom of the cartoon. In addition, cartoons will need placing in historical context. Therefore, a good knowledge of the subject matter of the topic of the cartoon will be important.

Photographs
'The camera never lies'! This phrase is not always true. When analysing photographs, study the attribution/provenance and date. Photographs can be changed so they are not always an accurate visual representation of events. Also, to test whether or not a photograph is a good representation of events you will need corroborative evidence.

Maps
Maps which appear in Sixth Form History are predominantly secondary sources. These are used to support factual coverage in the text by providing information in a different medium. Therefore, to assess whether or not information contained in maps is accurate or useful, reference should be made to other information. It is also important with written sources to check the attribution and date. These could be significant.

Statistical data and graphs
It is important when dealing with this type of source to check carefully the nature of the information contained in data or in a graph. It might state that the information is in tons (tonnes) or another measurement. Be careful to check if the information is in index numbers. These are a statistical device where a base year is chosen and given the figure 100. All other figures are based on a percentage difference from that base year.

An important point to remember when dealing with data and graphs over a period of time is to identify trends and patterns in the information. Merely describing the information in written form is not enough.

Historical interpretation

An important feature of both GCSE and Sixth Form History is the issue of historical interpretation. In Sixth Form History it is important for students to be able to explain why historians differ, or have differed, in their interpretation of the past.

Availability of evidence

An important reason is the availability of evidence on which to base historical judgements. As new evidence comes to light, an historian today may have more information on which to base judgements than historians in the past. For instance, a major source of information about 19th-century political history is the National Archive (Public Record Office) in Kew, London. Some of the information held at the PRO has remained confidential, in some cases for 50 to 100 years. Therefore, it is only recently that historians have been able to analyse and assess this evidence.

'A philosophy of history?'

Many historians have a specific view of history that will affect the way they make their historical judgements. For instance, Marxist historians – who take the view from the writings of Karl Marx the founder of modern socialism – believe that society has been made up of competing economic and social classes. They also place considerable importance on economic reasons in human decision making. Therefore, a Marxist historian of Chartism may take a completely different viewpoint to a non-Marxist historian.

The role of the individual

Some historians have seen past history as being moulded by the acts of specific individuals who have changed history. Gladstone, Disraeli and Lord Palmerston are seen as individuals whose personality and beliefs changed the course of 19th-century British history. Other historians have tended to 'downplay' the role of individuals; instead, they highlight the importance of more general social, economic and political change. Rather than seeing Joseph Chamberlain as an individual who changed the course of political history, these historians tend to see him as representing the views of a broader group of individuals, such as the industrial middle class of late Victorian Britain.

Placing different emphasis on the same historical evidence

Even if historians do not possess different philosophies of history or place different emphasis on the role of the individual, it is still possible for them to disagree because they place different emphases on aspects of the same factual evidence. As a result, Sixth Form History should be seen as a subject that encourages debate about the past based on historical evidence.

Progression in Sixth Form History

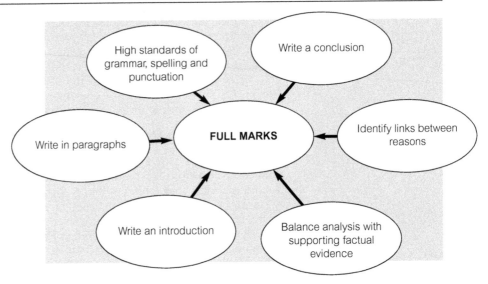

The ability to achieve high standards in Sixth Form History involves the acquisition of a number of skills:

- Good written communication skills

- Acquiring a sound factual knowledge

- Evaluating factual evidence and making historical conclusions based on that evidence

- Source analysis

- Understanding the nature of historical interpretation

- Understanding the causes and consequences of historical events

- Understanding themes in history which will involve a study of a specific topic over a long period of time

- Understanding the ideas of change and continuity associated with themes.

Students should be aware that the acquisition of these skills will take place gradually over the time spent in the Sixth Form. At the beginning of the course, the main emphasis may be on the acquisition of factual knowledge, particularly when the body of knowledge studied at GCSE was different.

When dealing with causation, students will have to build on their skills from GCSE. They will not only be expected to identify reasons for an historical event but also to provide a hierarchy of causes. They should identify the main causes and less important causes. They may also identify that causes may be interconnected and linked. Progression in Sixth Form History will come with answering the questions at the end of each sub-section in this book and practising the skills outlined through the use of the factual knowledge contained in the book.

Examination technique

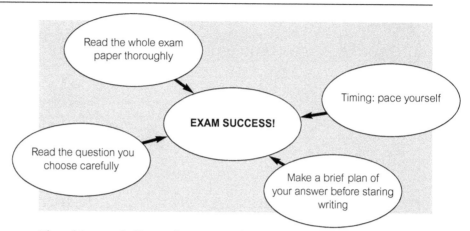

The ultimate challenge for any Sixth Form historian is the ability to produce quality work under examination conditions. Examinations will take the form of either modular examinations taken in January and June or an 'end of course' set of examinations.

Here is some advice on how to improve your performance in an examination.

- Read the whole examination paper thoroughly
  Make sure that the questions you choose are those for which you can produce a good answer. Don't rush – allow time to decide which questions to choose. It is probably too late to change your mind half way through answering a question.

- Read the question very carefully
  Once you have made the decision to answer a specific question, read it very carefully. Make sure you understand the precise demands of the question. Think about what is required in your answer. It is much better to think about this before you start writing, rather than trying to steer your essay in a different direction half way through.

- Make a brief plan
  Sketch out what you intend to include in your answer. Order the points you want to make. Examiners are not impressed with additional information included at the end of the essay, with indicators such as arrows or asterisks.

- Pace yourself as you write
  Success in examinations has a lot to do with successful time management. If, for instance, you have to answer an essay question in approximately 45 minutes, then you should be one-third of the way through after 15 minutes. With 30 minutes gone, you should start writing the last third of your answer.

Where a question is divided into sub-questions, make sure you look at the mark tariff for each question. If in a 20-mark question a sub-question is worth a maximum of 5 marks, then you should spend approximately one-quarter of the time allocated for the whole question on this sub-question.

1 Britain 1815–1895: A synoptic overview

Key Issues

- Why did the British political system change from rule by the monarchy and aristocracy in 1815 towards a more parliamentary form of government by 1895?

- Why did Britain experience rapid economic growth, and then relative economic decline, in the years 1815–1895?

- Why did Britain become the world's major imperial power in the years 1815–1895?

1.1 How did British society change in the years 1815–1895?

1.2 Why was the extension of the right to vote an important issue in the British political system in the period 1815 to 1895?

1.3 How did political parties develop in the years 1815–1895?

1.4 Why did Britain experience rapid economic growth in the years 1815 to 1873?

1.5 What impact did relative economic decline have on Britain in the years 1873 to 1895?

1.6 What were the main aims of British foreign policy in the years 1815 to 1895?

1.7 Were the British 'reluctant imperialists'?

BRITAIN underwent considerable political, social and economic change in the period from 1815 to 1895. It began and ended with a major war. In 1815, Britain had just won the Battle of Waterloo against Napoleon's France. The victory confirmed Britain's position as a European Great Power. In fact, Nelson's naval victories, culminating in Trafalgar, ensured that Britain also became the world's major naval power throughout the 19th century.

In political terms, Britain was a constitutional monarchy in 1815, where the monarch could exercise considerable political influence. In 1800, George III intervened to prevent Catholic emancipation. In 1834 William IV was able to dismiss the Prime Minister, Lord Melbourne. By 1895, however, the role of the monarchy had changed considerably. In 1895, Queen Victoria reigned but did not rule. The monarchy had become the ceremonial head of nation and Empire.

This change took place alongside the growth and development of political parties as the real power base in the formation and dismissal of governments. Although political parties had existed in Britain since the reign of Charles II (1649–85), their growth as nationwide institutions capable of gaining electoral support in their quest for government office only occurred during the 19th century. The need to become national organisations was a response to the extension of the right to vote. In 1815, only 3% of adult males could vote. Through parliamentary reform acts in 1832, 1867, and 1884 the right to vote was extended to include the vast majority of adult males over the age of 21. Woman still did not have the right to vote. The British political system had been transformed from rule by a few towards a parliamentary democracy.

This political transformation had taken place during a period of dramatic social

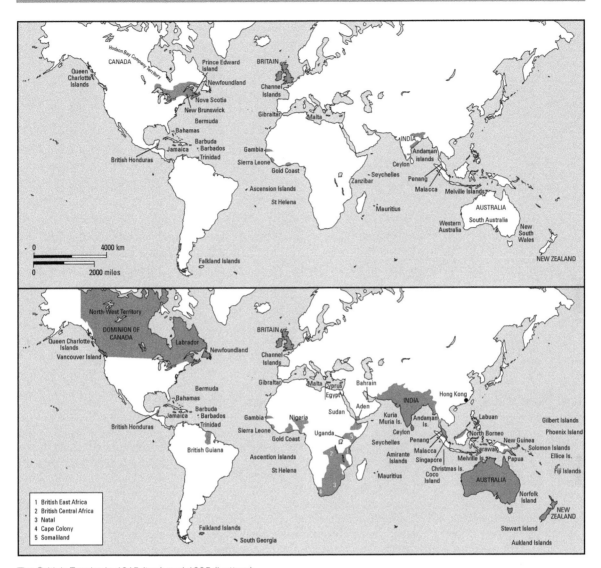

The British Empire in 1815 (top) and 1895 (bottom)

Industrial Revolution: A term meaning that the majority of the working population became involved in manufacturing industry (the secondary sector of the economy) rather than agriculture (the primary sector of the economy). This took place relatively rapidly from the mid-18th century onwards. It also involved the idea of 'self-sustaining growth', an idea associated with the American economist Walt Rostow. This meant the economy was able to grow using wealth it had created through manufacturing. Such a change would then be irreversible.

and economic change. By 1815 Britain had already undergone the first stages of an **Industrial Revolution**. Britain was alone in the world as the only country to have experienced such economic and social change. In the years 1815 to 1873 the British economy grew rapidly, making Britain 'the workshop of the world', the centre for world manufacturing, finance and trade. After 1873, however, Britain's position as the world's major economic power came under threat. The growth in economic power of the United States and Germany led many in Britain to question why Britain had lost its economic lead.

Britain's economic development was accompanied by major social change. Although new industrial towns had been created by the Industrial Revolution, Britain was still a mainly agricultural country in 1815, with most of the population living and working in the countryside. By 1895, Britain had a mainly urban population, with the majority of the population employed in manufacturing and commerce rather than farming. With the rise of industry and commerce came the rise in the number and importance of new social classes: the industrial middle

Aristocracy: A Greek word meaning, literally, 'the government of a state by its best citizens'. In the period covered by this book, the aristocracy comprised titled families whose wealth was passed down the generations by inheritance. About 200 or so families controlled most of the nation's land and dominated the political and social leadership.

class and the industrial working class. The traditional wealthy elite, the **aristocracy**, was now faced with an economic and a political challenge from these groups. The campaigns for the extension of the right to vote are interconnected with these social developments. The rise in political power of the House of Commons and the decline in power of the House of Lords reflected the decline in political power of the aristocracy.

While British economic power was under challenge in the years after 1873, Britain's imperial power reached its height. Although Britain had acquired a large empire in the 18th century, the loss of the American colonies in 1783 marked the end of this first empire. However, during the 19th century, and in particular after 1880, Britain acquired the largest empire in world history. By 1895 the British Empire covered one-quarter of the world's land area and encompassed one-third of the world's population. The centre of British imperial power throughout the period 1815 to 1895 was India. The focus of British foreign policy throughout the period was to preserve Britain's economic and imperial position. For this reason, Britain was an enthusiastic supporter of the preservation of European peace through the balance of power.

On three occasions between 1783 and 1918 Britain went to war with another Great Power, 1793–1815, 1854 and 1914. On these occasions, the prime concern was to maintain the European balance of power.

1.1 How did British society change in the years 1815–1895?

Established Church: The religion recognised officially as the State religion – the Anglican Church in England, Wales and Ireland, and the Church of Scotland in Scotland. The monarch was Supreme Governor and the religion had special privileges and received financial support from the government.

Veto (Latin for 'I forbid'): A negative vote exercised constitutionally by an individual, an institution or a state. It has the effect of automatically defeating the motion against which it is cast.

In 1815, British society was dominated by the monarchy, the landowning class (in particular the aristocracy), and the **Established Church**. In England, Ireland and Wales, the Established Church was the Anglican Church. In Scotland, it was the Presbyterian Church of Scotland. These institutions formed the ruling elite of the State. They dominated the House of Lords which, until 1911, possessed an absolute **veto** on all legislation passed by Parliament. They also dominated government. Nearly every prime minister between 1815 and 1895 came from this group. The most notable exception was Benjamin Disraeli . It was not until 1868 that the first non-Anglican Cabinet minister was appointed, John Bright, a Quaker.

In England, Wales and Ireland, education was also dominated by the Anglican establishment. Oxford, Cambridge and Trinity College, Dublin were all Anglican foundations. So were the major public schools: Eton, Harrow and Winchester.

Religion and the Established Church

Nonconformity: Religious groups who were Protestant but not Anglican. These included Quakers, Methodists, Baptists and Unitarians. They wished to have political, social and religious equality with Anglicans.

In the years after 1815, however, the Anglican landowning establishment came under attack. First, within England and Wales, the Church of England was challenged by the rise in popularity of **Nonconformity**. The development of Methodism in the 18th century and the growth of churches such as the Baptists, Unitarians and Congregationalists meant that 19th-century Britain was affected by intense religious rivalry between nonconformists and Anglicans. This rivalry was given a boost when, in 1851, the American Horace Mann took the only religious census in British history. The census revealed that the nonconformist and Anglican churches had approximately the same number of followers. (According to the census, of the 6.3 million who attended church on Easter Sunday 49% were nonconformists, 47% were Anglicans and 4% were Catholics.) This religious rivalry took place in many areas. In politics, the repeal of the Test and Corporation Acts in 1828 gave the nonconformists equal political rights with Anglicans. The rise of political nonconformity was an important factor in the formation of the Liberal Party during the 1850s. Conflict also took place in education, which proved to be a major issue dividing Anglicans from nonconformists throughout the period. Finally, many nonconformists wished to see an end to the Anglican Church's established status. In this, they were partly successful. In 1869, the Anglican Church was disestablished in Ireland.

Catholic emancipation: The right of Catholics to sit as Members of Parliament (MPs). Although before 1829 Catholics could vote in elections, if they possessed the necessary voting qualifications, the oath of allegiance all MPs had to take before sitting in the House of Commons was anti-Catholic. After the passage of the Catholic Relief Act in 1829, the oath was altered.

The other major religious group in the United Kingdom was Roman Catholics. Although they comprised a small minority of the populations of England, Wales and Scotland, they constituted 80% of the population of Ireland in 1815. Before 1829, Catholics were prevented from sitting as MPs, and getting this situation reversed – **Catholic emancipation** – was a dominant issue in British politics from 1801 to 1829, when it was eventually achieved. From 1829 onwards, the House of Commons contained a group of Irish Catholic MPs who supported the idea of greater self-government for Ireland. In the 1830s and 1840s, this group was led by Daniel O'Connell. Later in the century, after 1870, many Irish MPs belonged to the Home Rule Party, which became Britain's third largest party.

Although Catholics formed a small part of the population of Britain in 1783, this situation changed dramatically after 1845 with the onset of the Great Irish Potato Famine. Over 1.5 million Irish emigrated, many going to Britain. Regions such as Clydeside in Scotland and South Lancashire in England received large numbers of Irish Catholic immigrants. In fact, so large were the numbers that the Liverpool Scotland Road Division constituency returned an Irish Home Rule MP from 1885 to 1924.

Catholicism also had an important impact on the Church of England. Beginning in Oxford in the 1830s and 1840s, many Anglican academics supported the idea that the Anglican church should adopt Roman Catholic religious practices while maintaining the Church of England's independence from Rome. The Oxford Movement, led by Henry Newman and John Keble, established Anglo-Catholicism which became an important and divisive force within the 19th-century Anglican Church. Newman eventually left the Anglican Church and became a Roman Catholic cardinal.

The decline of the landowning class

Franchise: The right to vote. Also known as suffrage.

Perhaps the most important challenge to the Anglican-landowning establishment were the social changes brought about by the Industrial Revolution. The growth in size and economic importance of the industrial middle class meant that wealth was no longer centred on the land. The most dramatic examples of this challenge to the landowning class came in 1830–32 and in 1846. In 1830–32 middle-class agitation was an important factor in the extension of the **franchise** which broke the landowning monopoly on political power. In 1846, partly as a result of agitation by the Anti-Corn Law League, the economic basis of landowning power was threatened with the repeal of the Corn Laws. Although landowners did not face financial ruin immediately after the repeal of the Corn Law in 1846, this event marked a turning point in the decline of landowner power in Britain. It was not until the 1870s that agricultural Britain faced a major economic depression that lasted until the outbreak of the First World War.

Although the landowning classes' dominant position in politics and the economy declined during the 19th century, it did not disappear. Aristocrats continued to be important members of every government, including prime minister. The last aristocrat to hold the position of Prime Minister was Lord Salisbury, who retired in 1902.

By 1895, the aristocracy may have lost political and economic power but they maintained their social prestige. Many members of the industrial middle class wished to emulate the aristocracy by sending their sons to Eton and Harrow, and Oxford and Cambridge.

The decline of the monarchy's political power

The decline in the political power of the aristocracy was mirrored by a decline in the political power of the monarchy. In 1815, the monarchy still possessed considerable political power. The monarch could create peers and had considerable influence over many parliamentary constituencies. Up until 1867, a general election had to be held on the occasion of a monarch's death. With the reform of the electoral system and the decline in power of the aristocracy, monarchic power was almost inevitably going to decline as well. However, the decline was accelerated by the nature of the monarchy. In 1815, George III was regarded as insane and his son acted as **regent**. His successor, George IV, was deeply unpopular, and in 1837 an 18-year-old girl, Victoria, occupied the throne.

Regent: Person who is given royal authority on behalf of another. It usually applies when the monarch is a minor (under age).

William IV, in 1834, may have been the last monarch to dismiss a prime minister but it did not mean the monarch was without political influence. Victoria's consort, Prince Albert, worked closely with many prime ministers, in particular Robert Peel. In 1861, his intervention in the 'Trent Incident' helped prevent war breaking out between Britain and the United States. In 1880, Victoria refused to read out in the Queen's Speech that British troops were to be withdrawn from Afghanistan. But this did not prevent Gladstone from doing so. However, in 1894, Victoria ignored Gladstone's advice concerning his successor as Liberal Prime Minister and chose Lord Rosebery instead.

The changing role of women

An important social change that occurred during the 19th century was the position of women within society. The Industrial Revolution had brought about new opportunities for women in the economy. Women were able to obtain employment in textile mills and factories. But the most likely occupation for a woman in Victorian Britain was in domestic service. The change in the economic position of women acted as a catalyst to the move for women's political rights. Votes for women was discussed seriously for the first time during the Reform Bill debates of 1867. However, it was not until 1894 that women could vote for parochial councils and in 1907 for county councils. In 1870, 1882 and 1884, Married Women's Acts gave married women considerable financial independence.

1.2 Why was the extension of the right to vote an important issue in the British political system in the period 1815 to 1895?

One of the most significant political developments between 1815 and 1895 was the transformation of Britain from a state ruled by the monarchy and aristocracy into a parliamentary democracy. This transformation occurred through the passage of a number of Acts of Parliament in 1832, 1867 and 1884. Although the passage of the first two acts was associated with rioting and demonstrations, the process took place relatively peacefully.

Why did the aristocracy, who dominated the political system and Parliament, allow the extension of the right to vote? One major factor was the tremendous social and economic change that occurred in Britain during the Industrial Revolution. Before the beginning of the Industrial

TABLE 1: The population and electorate of the UK, 1831–1885

	Population	Electorate
1831	24 million	435,000*
1833	24 million	813,000 (1 in 7 adult males)
1865	30 million	1,430,000
1868	30 million	2,500,000 (1 in 3 adult males)
1883	35 million	3,000,000
1885	36 million	4,900,000 (2 in 3 adult males)

* = estimate

Revolution (about 1760–1914), the main source of economic wealth in Britain had been land and agriculture. As the largest landowners, the aristocracy were the wealthiest members of society. They dominated the House of Lords. They also dominated the electoral system: without the secret ballot, and with very small electorates, the landowning class were able to 'buy' seats, and thus have a dominant role in the House of Commons. According to Patrick Colquhoun's estimate, in 1815 the aristocracy and nobility comprised only 53,000 out of an estimated population of 20 million.

With the Industrial Revolution the industrial middle class (factory owners and merchants) and the industrial working class (factory workers and **artisans**) grew rapidly in number. As these social classes gained increased economic wealth, they also wished to gain political power through securing access to the political system through the electoral system and, thence, to the House of Commons.

Artisans: A term to describe members of the working class. They usually acquired a trade after a lengthy period of apprenticeship (e.g. carpenters, mechanics and boilermakers).

By 1815 the electoral system, which had been based on a pre-industrial society, was out of date. Throughout the period 1815–1830, parliamentary reform was an important political issue among radical elements in society. By 1830, it was also an important issue within the Whig Party, which regarded the unreformed electoral system as favouring the Tory Party. Thanks to a split in the Tory Party and fear of rioting and unrest, the Whig Government was able to pass the Great Reform Act of 1832. Although regarded at the time as a final settlement in the electoral system, it in fact paved the way for moves towards further reform. In 1835, the electoral system for local government in towns was reformed and the size of the electorate was increased dramatically. (Further reform in 1888 and 1894 brought **democracy** to local government.) It also provided the unifying focus for the world's first working-class political movement – Chartism – which from 1836 to 1850 demanded major parliamentary reform.

Democracy: A system of running organisations, businesses, government, etc. in which each member is entitled to vote and participate in management decisions.

Between 1865 and 1867, extra-parliamentary agitation, again, helped

TABLE 2: Parliamentary and electoral reform, 1832–1895

1832	Reform Act
1835	Municipal Corporations Act created elected town government
1858	Abolition of Property Qualification for MPs
1867	Second Reform Act
1872	Secret Ballot Act
1883	Corrupt and Illegal Practices Act aimed at preventing corruption at elections
1884	Third Reform Act
1885	Redistribution of Seats Act creates equal electoral districts and single-member constituencies
1888	County Councils Act creates elected county government
1894	Parish Councils Act creates elected village government

force an extension of the franchise. The 1867 Reform Act gave the franchise to artisans. In 1884, agricultural labourers were added and, in 1918, most adult males and women over 30 joined the electoral system.

These changes meant that Britain was able to modernise its electoral system peacefully. The terms of the 1832, 1867 and 1884 Reform Acts were phrased in such a way as to allow a specific social class to enter the political process. In 1832 it was the industrial middle class, in 1867 the skilled working class and in 1884 the agricultural workers. (But it was not until 1918 that universal male suffrage – one of the Chartist demands of the 1830s and 1840s – was achieved.)

1.3 How did political parties develop in the years 1815–1895?

The move towards a parliamentary democracy by 1895 is closely associated with the development of political parties. As the 19th century progressed, these institutions became the base for political power. In the 18th century, it was unlikely that any prime minister would survive in office if he lacked the support of the monarch. In the 19th century, prime ministers had to ensure they had majority support in the House of Commons. Although many MPs were independent of party allegiance in 1815, by the end of the century the political system was in the hands of political parties.

The 19th-century political system was dominated by the Whig/Liberal Party and the Tory/Conservative Party. The change in name of these political groupings reflects a change in aims, composition and organisation, which was associated with the extension of the franchise. Throughout the century, the Tory/Conservative Party was associated with defending the Anglican landowning establishment. The Whig/Liberal Party was associated with gaining religious and political equality for nonconformists and free trade.

In organisational terms, the parliamentary reform acts were important milestones. Until 1832, political parties were organised as groups within parliament. Outside parliament, party organisation was limited to a number of select gentlemen's clubs in London, such as Whites and Boodles. After 1832, both major parties began to set up registration associations to gain support from the newly enfranchised electorate. After the 1867 Reform Act, first the Conservatives and then the Liberals set up a nationwide network of party organisations. In 1867, the National Union of Conservative Associations was formed, followed three years later by the creation of Conservative Central Office. In 1877, the National Liberal Federation was formed. As the electorate became ever larger, leading politicians realised they had to engage in nationwide campaigning to gain votes. Peel's 'Tamworth Manifesto' in 1835 was the first example of this development. For the general election campaign of that year, the party's name was officially changed from Tory to Conservative. Later in the century, Disraeli's speeches at Manchester and the Crystal Palace in 1872, and Gladstone's Midlothian campaigns of 1879 and 1880 are further examples.

The development of political parties in the years 1815 to 1895 was far from smooth. Between 1828 and 1830, and again in 1846, the Tory/Conservative Party split. In 1846, the landowning and industrial middle-class wings of the party split over the repeal of the Corn Laws. The industrial middle-class wing became known as 'Peelites', and subsequently joined the Liberal Party in 1859. The Whig/Liberal Party was also prone to splits and divisions. The Whigs, along with Peelites and Radicals, formed the Liberal Party in 1859. However, from its creation the party was in danger of splitting apart. In 1866, the Party split over parliamentary reform, Robert Lowe leading an 'Adullamite' faction against the Liberal plan for reform. In 1874, the Liberal Party's internal divisions led to its electoral defeat. However, the most spectacular split was in 1886 over Irish Home Rule. The party split between Gladstonian Liberals and Liberal Unionists, the latter joining the Conservatives in 1895. Although the period is dominated by these parties, two other political parties did make a significant impact. Between 1870 and 1895, the Irish Home Rule Party acted as a third party. From the mid-1880s to 1895, it consistently won three-quarters of the Irish seats and, between 1892 and 1895 Irish Home Rule support kept the Liberal Party in power.

The influence of pressure groups

Pressure groups: Organisations that wish to influence political decision making but do not wish to gain political power.

Apart from political parties, **pressure groups** were another major force for change. These organisations did not want to win political power. Instead, they wished to influence government in favour of a particular issue or group in society. In Ireland, in 1823, Daniel O'Connell helped create the Catholic Association which supported the idea of Catholic emancipation. It was this pressure group that forced the Government to pass the Catholic Relief Act of 1829. In parliamentary reform, the Birmingham Political Union in 1830–32 and the Reform League and Reform Union in 1865–67 kept up pressure on Parliament to push through electoral reform.

Perhaps the most famous early Victorian pressure group was the Anti-Corn Law League. Under the leadership of Richard Cobden, John Bright and George Wilson, this group pressured Sir Robert Peel into repealing the Corn Law. When repeal came in 1846, this development not only split the Conservative Party but also was a milestone on Britain's road to becoming a free trade nation.

The political party most closely associated with pressure groups was the Liberal Party. In fact, the party could be regarded as a coalition of pressure groups. The United Kingdom Alliance and the Band of Hope Union wished to see changes in laws relating to alcohol drinking. The Liberation Society wanted to disestablish the Church of England, while the National Education League wanted free, compulsory state elementary education. These competing interests were one of the reasons why it was difficult to keep the Liberal Party united.

A set of pressure groups which represented a section of society was trade unions. Throughout the period 1815–1895 trade unions attempted to improve the pay and working conditions of their members. Groups of workers had been formed in the 18th century for this purpose. However, with the passing of the Combination Acts of 1799 and 1800, trade unions were made illegal. These Acts were passed because the Government feared links between trade unions and ideas associated with the French Revolution. Although legalised in 1824, trade unions found it difficult to organise and develop due to opposition from Parliament and the courts. The Tolpuddle Martyrs and the collapse of the Grand National Consolidated Trades Union, both in 1834, are examples of this problem. It was not until the formation of New Model Unions after 1850 that trade unions began to wield some economic and political power. However, trade unions were limited to only the skilled element of the workforce. Only between 1871 and 1875 did trade unions gain full legal protection and the right to picket peacefully.

Although closely associated with the Liberal Party from the 1850s to the 1890s, the trade unions eventually decided in 1900 to found their own political party, the Labour Representation Committee, which became the Labour Party.

1. In what ways was the organisation of political parties different by 1895 from 1815?

2. The period 1815–1895 saw many turning points in the development of political parties.

Using the information contained above, find out when these turning points occurred.

3. Which turning points in the development of political parties do you regard as the most important?

Give reasons for your answer.

1.4 Why did Britain experience rapid economic growth in the years 1815 to 1873?

City of London: General name given to the banks, insurance companies and financial institutions in the old centre of London.

The political changes that occurred during the 19th century took place against a background of major economic change. In the period 1815 to 1873, Britain could rightly claim to be the 'workshop of the world'. Britain was the leading country in the manufacture of textiles – cotton in particular, and iron and coal. In addition, Britain was the world's major shipbuilding nation, with British merchant shipping dominating world trade. To help finance these developments the **City of London** was the world's financial centre for banking, insurance and financial trading in shares and commodities. Why was Britain so prosperous compared to other countries at this time?

- First, Britain had acquired sufficient financial wealth during the 18th century to finance industrial and commercial growth. The growth of the British Empire in the Caribbean and North America and the development of the Atlantic slave trade had provided the wealth that could then be invested in the development of industries such as cotton textile production.

- Secondly, this acquisition of wealth took place at a time of rapid population growth. In 1711, the population of England and Wales was estimated at 6 million. By 1791, it had risen to 8.3 million and by 1821 to 13.9 million. This increased population provided both a source of labour and a market for manufactured goods.

Technological innovation: The practical application of inventions that improve the production process.

- Thirdly, **technological innovation** enabled manufacturing production to increase rapidly. In cotton textile production Hargreaves' 'spinning jenny' in 1764, Crompton's mule in 1779 and Cartwright's power loom in 1785 all helped to increase the output per worker. These changes also took place at a time when manufacturing was being relocated from cottage-based domestic industry to factories located near sources of power, such as rivers for water power or coalfields for steam power. Therefore, in the years after 1760 to the mid-19th century industrial towns in east Lancashire and west Yorkshire – such as Blackburn, Manchester, Leeds and Bradford – developed rapidly. Leeds and Bradford were involved in woollen textile production. In Scotland the Clyde valley towns of Coatbridge, Hamilton and Motherwell developed due to the coal and iron industries.

To allow the easy movement of raw materials and finished goods, a cheap and extensive transportation system was required. Canals provided the basis of the late 18th-century transport network, linking industrial towns like Birmingham to seaports and sources of raw materials. However, from 1830 onwards, railways had superseded canals. By 1870, Britain had the most extensive railway system in the world. In that year, it carried 490 million passengers on 13,500 miles of track.

A stimulus to economic growth in the late 18th and early 19th centuries was the demand for goods associated with warfare. From 1793 to 1815, Britain was almost continually at war with France. This led to government demand for shipping, uniforms and armaments.

After 1815, economic growth was sustained by the gradual adoption of a free trade policy. In the years 1823–63, Britain abolished virtually all taxes on imported and exported goods. As Britain had the most advanced, competitive economy in the world, British businessmen were able to acquire new markets for their goods. The British Indian Empire and China provided huge potential markets in Asia, while a free trade treaty with the

Turkish Empire in 1838, and with France in 1860 (the Cobden Treaty) allowed the economic exploitation of Middle-eastern and European markets.

Government policy also aided the development of the economy internally. Acts passed in the 1830s and 1840s allowed the creation of joint stock, limited liability companies. In 1844, the Bank Charter Act placed British banking on a sound financial footing. Low taxation and the avoidance of major war, except in 1854–56, provided economic stability. Britain's political stability in the years 1815 to 1873 stood in marked contrast to some of its potential economic rivals in Europe. For example, France was affected by revolution in 1830 and 1848, followed by a political coup in 1851, and then military defeat in 1870–71 by Prussia.

1. What were the main reasons for the rapid economic growth of the period 1815–1873?

2. How far was government policy responsible for this growth?

TABLE 3: Output of selected British industries (in thousands of tonnes)

	1800	1880
coal	10,000 tonnes	147,000 tonnes
iron	200 tonnes	7,700 tonnes
cotton imported	22 tonnes	650 tonnes
shipping launched	50 tonnes	660 tonnes

1.5 What impact did relative economic decline have on Britain in the years 1873 to 1895?

Some historians have regarded the years after 1873 as the 'Great Depression'. Although the British economy continued to grow each year, the rate of growth was smaller. What was more worrying was the increased economic rivalry Britain was facing from other countries, in particular the United States of America and Germany. Table 4 shows the share of the world's manufacturing output in the years 1870–1885.

TABLE 4: Percentage share of the world's manufacturing output

	Britain	USA	Germany
1870	31.8	23.3	13.2
1881–85	26.6	28.6	13.9

The relative decline of Britain's economic position in the world had several important repercussions. First, the need to maintain markets for British goods helps to explain why Britain obtained colonies during the last quarter of the 19th century. In west Africa, the need to defend British markets was the main reason for the growth of the Empire.

In what ways did Britain's relative economic decline after 1873 affect British politics and British political parties?

Secondly, as the Great Depression developed, all of Britain's main economic rivals placed taxes (tariffs) on imported goods in order to protect their own industries. This meant that by 1900 Britain was the only major economic power which still had a free trade policy. Demands for Britain to abandon free trade had begun to grow in the 1880s. A Fair Trade League pressured the government to introduce tariffs.

1.6 What were the main aims of British foreign policy in the years 1815 to 1895?

In 1815, Britain, along with its European allies such as Prussia, Russia and Austria, had defeated the French. Britain was one of the major European countries that produced the Treaty of Vienna which redrew the map of Europe in 1814–15.

Throughout the period 1815 to 1895, Britain was regarded as a European **Great Power**. The other Great Powers were Russia, France, Austria and Prussia (after 1871 Prussia was absorbed into the German Empire). Britain's claim to be a Great Power rested on British sea power, trade and industry, and its imperial possessions across the globe. Although British foreign policy was conducted by a large number of individuals from several different political parties in the years 1815 to 1895, there were a number of aims that remained constant for much of the period.

Great Power: A term used to describe the major military powers of Europe. Between 1815 and 1846 there were five Great Powers: Britain, France, Russia, Austria and Prussia.

The Concert of Europe

One of the most important aims in foreign policy was the need to maintain the European balance of power. Following the defeat of Napoleon, the peacemakers at Vienna tried to prevent future European war through an international system where no one European power had sufficient military strength to dominate the rest of Europe. From 1815 to 1895, Britain supported this idea. The main method used by the Great Powers to solve international disputes was the 'Concert of Europe'. This idea involved the Great Powers working together (in concert) to solve disputes. Between 1815 and 1823, the Concert of Europe took the form of the Congress System. After 1823, when international disputes occurred, meetings of the Great Powers helped to maintain European peace. The issues of Greek and Belgian independence (1820s and 1830s), the issue of the Straits (1841) and the Great Balkan Crisis (1878) were all solved by this method.

However, on a number of occasions the Concert of Europe failed to maintain European peace. In 1853–54, a crisis in south-eastern Europe led to a Great Power war involving Britain – the Crimean War. Britain went to war to preserve the European balance of power.

The defence and promotion of trade

de facto: In actual fact. A de facto government is a government that is in actual control of a country, as opposed to a *de jure* government which is legally recognised but may have lost control.

Another aim of most British foreign secretaries was support for British trade across the globe. This involved the recognition of **de facto** governments. For instance, in the 1820s Canning recognised the new republics of Latin America. In December 1851, Palmerston recognised Louis Napoleon's coup d'état in France. On both occasions, decisions were made with the aim of furthering British trading opportunities. From 1880 to 1895, Britain was involved in the partition of Africa. This was due, at least in part, to the desire to assist British trade.

In some cases, British foreign secretaries actively promoted the growth of British trade. The most notable was Lord Palmerston, who had considerable influence on British foreign policy from 1830 until his death in 1865. In China in 1839–42, and again in 1857–60, Palmerston helped to force the Chinese government to open up their Empire to British trade. Palmerston was also able to aid British trade in the Anglo-Turkish Convention of 1838. On several occasions, he came to the defence of British subjects abroad when they faced problems with foreign governments. In 1850, he came to the aid of Don Pacifico in his dispute with the Greek government. In 1863, he used the Navy to bombard the Japanese town of Kagoshima after a conflict between the local ruler and British traders.

In the period 1815 to the 1860s, another aim followed by successive foreign secretaries was the opposition to the Atlantic slave trade. Britain had abolished the slave trade in 1807 and for the next 50 years attempted to prevent any other country participating in the trade. The main method used was the 'right of search', where British warships searched any foreign ship on the high seas for slaves. In addition, Palmerston's recognition of the Texas Republic in 1836, as an independent state, was only on the basis that Texas accepted the end of the Atlantic slave trade.

'Splendid isolation'

Another feature of foreign policy during this period was the desire of Britain not to be allied to other countries, if at all possible. Between 1815 and 1823, Britain was a part of the Congress System. However, for much of the century Britain stayed isolated from the other European powers. Britain did make some agreements, but these were for specific reasons and for a short period of time. In 1834, Britain signed the Quadruple Alliance with France, Spain and Portugal as a counter to the Holy Alliance of Russia, Prussia and Austria. In 1854, Britain signed an alliance with France against Russia in the Crimean War. Then in 1878 Disraeli signed secret agreements with Austria and Turkey shortly before the Congress of Berlin.

Britain was able to remain aloof from European alliances partly because of the success of the Concert of Europe but also because Britain's main foreign policy interest lay outside Europe. Throughout the 19th century, Britain possessed the largest Empire of any European state. In particular, Britain had major interests in India. Up to 1858, the East India Company handled British interests in India. After that date, the British Indian Empire was proclaimed under the responsibility of a cabinet minister.

Foreign affairs were not an isolated aspect of government policy. On a number of occasions there was a direct link between political developments in Britain and the foreign policy pursued by the Government. On several occasions, George Canning (Foreign Secretary 1822–27) and Lord Palmerston used foreign policy issues to gain political popularity at home. Canning's opposition to the Congress System in 1822–23, and the Don Pacifico Affair of 1850 were two examples. In 1868, Disraeli sought popular support with his expedition to Abyssinia. In 1876, Gladstone came out of retirement to lead a campaign against Disraeli's handling of the Eastern Question. During the period 1815 to 1895, the Great Power most distrusted by Britain was Russia. From 1815 to 1848, Russia acted as a force for conservatism and reaction in Europe, which was opposed by foreign ministers such as Canning and Palmerston. However, the main reason for hostility towards Russia was fear of Russian ambitions in south-eastern Europe. The danger of Russian expansion at the expense of the Ottoman Empire and the possibility of Russian warships entering the Mediterranean Sea were major worries for British governments from the 1820s to the 1880s. Britain's involvement in the Crimean War was associated with these issues. After 1860, Russia posed a threat to British interests in Central Asia and India. From 1880 to 1895, Russia posed a threat to British interests in China and the Far East.

In contrast, Britain's relations with the German powers, Prussia and Austria, were more cordial. Hostility with the German Empire began as economic rivalry from the 1870s.

Relations with France varied considerably during the period 1815 to 1895. On occasion Britain and France came close to war, in 1840 over the Eastern Question. However, for large parts of the century Britain and France were on good terms. In the 1830s Britain and France stood together against the Holy Alliance Powers and between 1854 and 1856 Britain and France fought together against Russia in the Crimea.

The Irish Question

The Irish Question is the name given to the series of issues which affected British–Irish relations. It involved political, economic, religious and strategic issues. On several occasions, Irish issues caused the resignation of prime ministers. In 1801, Pitt the Younger resigned because of George III's opposition to Catholic emancipation. Peel fell from power in 1846 over the repeal of the Corn Laws. Gladstone split the Liberal Party in 1886 with his conversion to Irish Home Rule. The Liberal governments from 1912 to 1914 faced a serious crisis over Ulster which was brought to a temporary conclusion by the outbreak of the First World War. Finally, Lloyd George's fall from power, in 1922, was due at least in part to his handling of the Irish Question in 1921.

Therefore, as a theme the Irish Question must be regarded as an important, if not the most important, aspect of British domestic history (see Chapter 10).

1. In what ways did British foreign policy change during the years 1815–1895?

2. In what ways did British foreign policy remain the same during the years 1815–1895?

3. How far do you think British foreign policy changed during the years 1815–1895? Give reasons for your answer.

1.7 Were the British 'reluctant imperialists'?

During the 19th and early 20th centuries, Britain expanded its political control across the world. By the conclusion of the First World War, the British Empire covered 25% of the world's land surface and included one-third of the world's population. British imperial possessions could be found on every continent.

However, British imperial expansion was not an even process. For much of the period 1815 to 1880, Britain seemed to be uninterested in acquiring colonial possessions. Then, from 1880 to 1895, Britain expanded its empire rapidly, mainly in Africa.

Was there a sudden change in thinking in government circles around 1880 towards the Empire or was there a continuity of approach?

Although the first half of the 19th century was not noted for imperial expansion, Britain did acquire colonial possessions: Hong Kong in 1842, British Columbia in 1846 and, most notably, in India where the East India Company expanded its control over northern India from the River Indus to the Ganges.

However, for most of this period British governments did not feel the need to acquire overseas territory formally. This period was seen as an era of 'informal' empire where Britain controlled the trade of overseas areas without the need to control regions politically. In South America and much of Africa, British traders dominated international trade.

It has been claimed that Britain's decision to acquire colonies after 1880 had a lot to do with the increasing economic challenge of other countries in a period of economic depression. Britain's acquisition of territories in west Africa had much to do with the protection of British trade.

Also of importance in the acquisition of colonies was the desire to protect Britain's position in India, the 'jewel in the crown' of the British Empire. The decision to expand colonial control in southern Africa from 1870 to the end of the century and the decision to invade and occupy Egypt in 1882 had a lot to do with protecting the sea routes to India. In order to protect these areas British governments, reluctantly, were forced to take control of other parts of Africa, such as the Sudan and Uganda, to

1. Why did Britain abandon informal control and replace it with formal political control, in areas such as Africa, after 1880?

2. 'Britain went through a period of major political, social and economic change in the years 1815–1895.'

Using the information in this chapter, assess the accuracy of this statement.

3. In what ways can it be argued that in spite of considerable change there were elements of continuity in Britain's political, social and economic development and Britain's relations with Europe and the world?

protect the River Nile and Egypt, and the Transvaal and Orange Free State, to protect the Cape of Good Hope.

The main instrument British governments possessed to defend this large empire was the Royal Navy. Throughout the 19th century, Britain possessed the world's largest navy. To maintain a naval presence around the globe, harbours and coaling stations were required. Territories such as Malta, Labuan and Mauritius were acquired as strategically placed naval bases to defend the world's sea routes.

There were many reasons for the expansion of the British Empire. Trade, strategic reasons and the defence of India were the most important. Throughout the 19th century Britain acquired colonies, with the most rapid expansion taking place during the 1880s in Africa.

2 The Tories in government, 1815–1830

Key Issues

- How successfully did Tory governments deal with the problems they faced?

- How far did Tory policy change in the period 1815 to 1830?

- Did the Tory governments successfully defend British interests abroad?

2.1 Britain in 1815
2.2 What problems faced Liverpool's government in 1815?
2.3 How serious was the threat of revolution in the years 1815 to 1822?
2.4 Why was the Tory government able to survive the problems it faced in the period 1815 to 1822?
2.5 Historical Interpretation: To what extent did the Cabinet changes of 1821–22 bring about a change in government policy?
2.6 How 'liberal' were the Tory governments between 1822 and 1827?
2.7 Liberal Tory reforms
2.8 Why did the Tory Party collapse between 1827 and 1830?
2.9 How successful was Castlereagh as Foreign Secretary, from 1812 to 1822?
2.10 What problems did Canning face as Foreign Secretary in the years 1822–1827?

Framework of Events

1812	Lord Liverpool becomes Prime Minister
	Viscount Castlereagh becomes Foreign Secretary
1815	French Wars (1793–1815) come to an end with the defeat of Napoleon at Waterloo
	Congress of Vienna (1814–15) ends
	Treaty of Vienna and Second Treaty of Paris
	Quadruple Alliance between Britain, Austria, Russia and Prussia
	Holy Alliance between Austria, Russia and Prussia
	Corn Law introduced
1816	Income tax repealed
	Spa Field riots
1817	Suspension of Habeas Corpus
	Seditious Meetings Act
	Pentrich 'uprising'
	March of the Blanketeers
1818	Congress of Aix la Chapelle
1819	Peterloo Massacre
	Six Acts
	Rush–Bagot Agreement with USA
1820	Queen Caroline Affair
	Revolutions in Spain, the Italian states and Portugal
	Congress of Troppau
	State Paper issued by Castlereagh
	George IV becomes king on death of George III
1821	Congress of Laibach

1822	Congress of Verona
	Castlereagh commits suicide. Replaced by Canning as Foreign Secretary
1822/23	Cabinet changes made. Beginning of the 'liberal' Tory era
1823	Changes in trade regulations
1824	Repeal of Combination Acts of 1799 and 1800
1825	Amending Act on combinations
1825	Peel begins work on changing the criminal code
1826	St Petersburg Protocol
1827	Treaty of London on Greece
	Lord Liverpool resigns, due to ill health
	Canning become Prime Minister
	Canning dies
1827	Viscount Goderich becomes Prime Minister until January 1828
1828	The Duke of Wellington becomes Prime Minister
	Russo-Turkish War begins
	County Clare by-election
	Catholic emancipation crisis begins
1829	Catholic Relief Act passed
	Treaty of Adrianople ends Russo-Turkish War
1830	George IV dies and William IV becomes king
	Duke of Wellington loses general election

Overview

Reactionary: A person opposed to political change.

THE Tory Party dominated politics from 1815 to 1830 to such an extent that the Whig opposition failed to occupy office at all during the period. The Prime Minister from 1812 to 1827 was Lord Liverpool and he presided over a number of important developments, such as the defeat of Napoleonic France in 1815. There is considerable controversy over Liverpool's administration and the place it occupies in history. People at the time tended to dismiss it as being **reactionary**. Recently however, historians such as John Derry have produced a far more positive view of his achievements. By comparison his successors – George Canning, Lord Goderich and the Duke of Wellington – proved to be much less successful. The collapse of Tory rule in 1830 meant a period in the political wilderness that would eventually come to an end in 1841 under Peel.

Britain in 1815 was a society undergoing considerable change as a result of the Industrial Revolution. The urbanisation of society led to the growth of major industrial cities such as Manchester, Leeds and Sheffield which all experienced massive population growth that required a change in working patterns and living conditions. The predominantly rural society that had been a major feature of the 18th century was now changing at a rapid rate, but the agricultural changes that had been a major feature of the Agricultural Revolution helped feed a growing population.

Since 1793, Britain had been almost continuously at war with France. The eventual victory in 1815 should have led to celebration, but the aftermath of the war caused many problems as Britain failed to come to terms. For example, around 400,000 demobilised soldiers and sailors entered an already depressed labour market. The resentment and sense of not belonging to this new society produced radical movements that threatened to undermine it and increase demands for a republic and an extension of the right to vote. Up to 1821, the Tory Government was forced to introduce some drastic measures in order to maintain law and order. However, once economic conditions improved, from 1821, the Tories were able to govern more sympathetically and introduce a series of measures that some have labelled Enlightened Tory.

Politics in the latter half of the 1820s was dominated by the issues of Catholic emancipation and the demands of the Radicals and the Whig opposition for more people to have the vote. It was these two issues, and the splits within the party they revealed, that led to the collapse of Tory rule in 1830.

1. What do you regard as the most important reform passed by the Tory governments in the period from 1815 to 1830? Explain your answer.

2. What do you regard as the most controversial reform passed by the Tory governments in the period from 1815 to 1830?

3. Using information from this mind map, put down what you think were the successes of the Tory governments in one column, and what you think were its failures in another column. On balance, were the Tory governments a success or failure?

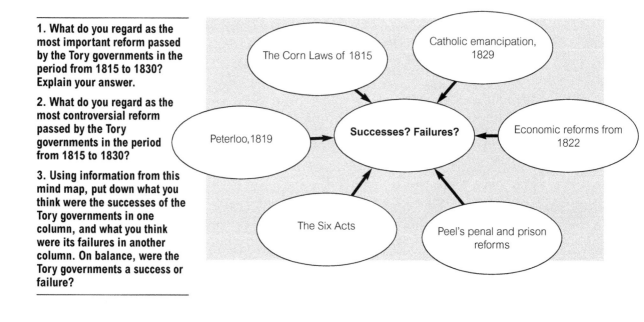

2.1 Britain in 1815

How did the political system work?

Parliamentary democracy: Term used to describe today's political system in Britain with its emphasis on the use of elections, a free press and full participation in the political process by anyone over the age of 18 who possesses the vote.

At the end of the Napoleonic War the political system in Britain had changed little from the 17th century. Our modern political system is based on **parliamentary democracy**. The main features of our modern political system are contrasted with that of the early 19th century system in the table below.

The system in place in the early 19th century had lasted a long time because it served a useful purpose. It had reflected the social and economic system of pre-industrial Britain. Most power lay with the majority in Parliament and the men who controlled it, but it was never seriously understood that this body represented the people. Those who defended the system stated that it defended the landowning majority. In 1815, the authority of the Cabinet was a recent development and the principle of collective responsibility was not yet accepted. The office of Prime Minister was undefined, for all ministers were servants of the King and his support was vital if any government was to survive. Political parties as we understand them today did not exist, as there was no party discipline or organisation on voting. Many Independents (non-party MPs) were quick to change sides over issues that affected their personal interests, regardless of political loyalties. At the beginning of the period, the position of Lord

Liverpool's ministry was made even more difficult by the monarchy's weaknesses. George III ceased to be important as a king after 1810 due to mental illness and George IV was unable to support or strengthen the position of his ministers. Yet to underestimate the power of the monarchy was fatal as it had the power to bring down a government. Up to 1830, the King was the most important political figure.

Today	1815
Adults over 18 have the right to vote	The electorate is very small. One in 24 adults over 21 have the right to vote
Elections every 5 years	Elections every 7 years
Secret ballot	Open ballot (which allows bribery, corruption and intimidation)
Party competition	Parties are factions of one small social group – the upper class
Even distribution of seats	Towns under-represented
Monarch acts as a figurehead	Monarch possesses political power

British society in 1815

Most British institutions had been operated for, and on behalf of, the landowning class, headed by the aristocracy. The basis of their social power was the amount of land they owned. These leading landowners dominated the House of Lords and the Commons was filled with their supporters. It was claimed that men who had no property were unfit to govern and could be indirectly represented by these men of property on whose behalf they were elected. As Anthony Wood has written, in *Nineteenth-Century Britain* (1981), 'whether Whig or Tory, either would be likely to uphold the interests of landowners and farmer'. Government service, the Church and the powerful positions in the armed forces helped to provide for their families. In the 18th century, **patronage** and corruption were natural, and acceptable, as the central government's role in life was so limited.

It was local government that affected people more directly and not surprisingly the bulk of this was left to the nobility in the counties. The key people were the **Justices of the Peace (JPs)**, appointed from the prominent landowners in the district on the recommendation of the Lord Lieutenant of the county (normally the greatest landowner).

Patronage: The right of giving offices and privileges on the basis of favour and not as a result of merit. The monarch at this time was said to be a great political patron.

Justices of the Peace (JPs): Officials who bore the brunt of English local government. JPs were the key officials responsible for maintaining law and order and for exercising criminal jurisdiction. In addition, JPs were responsible for carrying out much of the legislation concerning poor relief, vagrancy, apprenticeship and other social laws.

Agrarian: Relating to the ownership and use of land, especially farmland.

How far did the Agricultural Revolution change Britain?

Society was predominantly rural, **agrarian** and based on 18th-century values but there were dramatic forces at work. These threatened not only to change the economic system but, as a result, would have serious political consequences.

The massive scale and pace of agrarian and industrial change brought painful consequences. The countryside faced an agrarian revolution. This resulted in a more efficient use of the land but, by around 1780, it also created a new class of landless agricultural workers. Cottagers lost their old rights to the common land and the fuel they once gathered from the wastelands. This compact society was under siege from increased commercialisation: farming for profit rather than just making a living. These trends increased pressure on the land to feed a growing population and these difficulties were made even worse by the Game Laws of 1816.

Why was the Industrial Revolution so important?

Together with great changes in the countryside, there were even bigger developments in the scale of the workplace. The historian Anthony Wood describes it, in *Nineteenth-Century Britain*, as 'A momentous change from an agrarian to an industrial society'. What is meant by this? The demands to feed and clothe a growing population led the pressure to move from a predominantly domestic (cottage based) industry. Cottage industry was carried out usually at home on a small scale for a small market. With a growing population, industry moved to a larger site usually in an urban area and for a larger market. Urban growth and the Industrial Revolution went hand in hand (e.g. Manchester, Sheffield). There were many positive aspects such as large-scale production; but equally there were as many drawbacks:

● Manual skills – work carried out by hand in the home was replaced by the new machines located in factories. Eric Hobsbawm, a well-respected left-wing historian, writing in support of the new working classes, has described the machine breaking carried out by the **Luddites** as 'collective bargaining by riot'. Serious outbreaks of machine breaking in the East Midlands were commonplace because of the resentment produced.

● The social consequences of industrialisation tended to widen the differences between rich and poor and to create 'slum' conditions. This produced a group of workers who felt hatred towards the establishment which they blamed for their distress. Added to this were:

  – the discipline and rigour of factory work;

  – the physical conditions and long hours;

  – the employment of young women and children denied legal protection against industrial exploitation and banned from joining trade unions (which had been the case from 1799).

Now you can begin to get the picture. Wage reductions and the threat of imprisonment hung over them if they refused rates of pay.

What were the effects of a rising population at this time?

To make these massive socio-economic changes seem worse, add a rising population. This process had begun in the middle of the 18th century but reached its height at the start of our period.

Population growth in Britain 1801–1821

1801	10.5 million	
1811	12 million	an increase of 25.5%
1821	14.1 million	

It was the speed of this change more than anything else that destabilised society. A rising population had a number of implications for Britain after 1815:

● There was a need to feed more mouths, therefore greater pressure on the land. The system of farming in the early 19th century was unable to cope with that increased demand.

● A rising population placed greater strain on the system of poor relief, especially the **Speenhamland system**. It was always assumed that these payments were in proportion to family size and it was argued that a large family made one idle and employers knew they could underpay

Luddites: Those who objected to the machines needed to equip the new factories during the Industrial Revolution. They developed as a movement between 1811 and 1817 as a reaction against what they saw as a threat to their livelihood and what was obviously an inferior product mass produced by workers in the factories who did not have their technical skill.

Speenhamland system: A system of poor relief devised in 1795 that attempted to help the large numbers of unemployed. Extra money was made available to the needy from parish funds depending on the size of the recipient's family and the price of bread. Initially used in the south of England, it became more widespread as the 19th century progressed. This was the 19th-century equivalent to a welfare system.

because the difference would be made up by the poor rate. The historian John Plowright argues that the burden on taxpayers increased fourfold between 1775 and 1817 as a result of these developments.

What were the consequences of the French Revolution for Britain?

Ancien régime: A term first used to describe the regime in France that was overthrown by the French Revolution. It is now used more generally to describe any regime that has been replaced by another.

Arguably the most important political event in modern history, the French Revolution broke out in July 1789 and was a protest against privilege, patronage and inequality. The *ancien régime* (old order) collapsed quickly as a result of the pressures imposed by the 'have nots' in French society. The ultimate expression of their hatred was the execution of the French king, Louis XVI, in 1793. The shock waves of these events soon spread across the Channel and divided political opinion. These events also helped to intensify existing radical grievances and produced an extreme reaction on the part of the Government. The leading writer supporting the rights of the French revolutionaries was Thomas Paine, in his book *The Rights of Man* (published in 1791). Paine advocated an impassioned defence of people in France displaying their natural rights to freedom, equality and brotherhood. The conservative response to the French Revolution was voiced by Edmund Burke in his *Reflections on the Revolution in France* (1790) – a strong critic of the violence, bloodshed and disregard for property. Burke argued that the gradual and peaceful nature of the British political system was its greatest defence. Radicalism developed at first among skilled artisan groups in London but spread rapidly during the Napoleonic Wars, centring on the northern industrial towns. An increasingly literate workforce read the latest publications with enthusiasm and formed their own political organisations. They were demanding a more open debate on the existing political and social system, which deprived them of their rights.

1. What do you regard as the main features of British society in 1815?

2. How far was Britain a society undergoing major social and economic change?

2.2 What problems faced Liverpool's Government in 1815?

How did war affect Britain between 1793 and 1815?

Britain declared war on France in 1793. The war was to last almost continually until Napoleon's defeat at Waterloo in June 1815. How did war speed up change in society?

- The war gave a boost to the enclosure movement in the countryside as pressure on the land grew to feed a growing population. More land was needed for cultivation at a time of great national crisis.

- The demand for more industrial (heavy) goods brought more squalor to the working classes, especially in the major cities, as working conditions worsened and ruthless employers were able to get away with lower pay rates. The terrible social consequences of industrialisation were felt by those in society unable to defend themselves against its worst effects.

- The war brought dear food as farmers benefited from inflated prices (which workers' wages never matched). War kept prices high due to the breakdown of trade between nations in Europe, helping home producers make large profits at the expense of those for whom bread was their staple diet.

- More expensive timber, bricks and glass meant inferior housing which further deteriorated the social living conditions of the poor.

Income tax: A tax introduced in 1797 at the height of the Napoleonic War. It was based on how much a person earned and, therefore, was bound to fall more heavily on the richer sections of British society, namely the aristocracy. It was a means of financing the war but it was always regarded as a temporary measure!

- Despite the introduction of **income tax** in 1797 (from which the poor were exempt), two-thirds of total tax revenue came from indirect tax on goods (beer, for example). The 'lower orders' in society bore the burden of the continuation of the war effort at a time when they were least able to afford it.

- In 1806, Napoleon, Emperor of France, introduced the Continental System. This was an attempt to starve Britain into submission by preventing other countries trading with it. Britain's response was the Orders in Council in 1807 which restricted a neutral country's ability to trade with France. This was a direct cause of war between Great Britain and the United States of America between 1812 and 1814. This unstable situation caused bankruptcy and unemployment and was made worse by harvest failures of 1809–11.

- As a result of these developments and the demands of fighting a war for over a quarter of a century, Great Britain's national debt – the amount the Government owed – rose from £238 million in 1793 to £902 million in 1816.

What difficulties did the end of war bring for the country?

Coalition: A term used to describe the cooperation of the Great Powers such as Britain, Russia, Prussia and Austria in their common fight against France during the Napoleonic Wars.

In June 1815, Napoleon was defeated at Waterloo, war came to an end and British prestige had never stood higher. Britain was the only European power not to have been defeated by Napoleon Bonaparte, the French ruler since 1799 and its chief military genius. It was British finance that had sustained the **coalition** of powers against France and its navy and goods that had defeated the Continental System. Norman Gash, a leading historian of this period, argues that 'war was an abnormal stimulus to the economy'. Levels of demand for example in those industries associated with the war effort, such as the armaments industry, enjoyed a boom period that lasted only as long as the war did and it was 'almost inevitable that it should be followed by acute depression'. It was the combination of full-blooded industrialisation together with postwar circumstances that made 'peace without plenty' so painful.

In the countryside, crisis conditions had been developing since 1813. Generally, wheat prices fell due to good harvests and the influx of more foreign corn, but the position of farmers had changed during the inflated period of the war. When boom conditions prevailed, they had borrowed heavily to cultivate marginal land. They now had to repay the interest on their loans at a time of falling prices. The farmers eventually received some protection with the passing of the Corn Law in 1815 but even then the positive effects were debatable. Those who survived did so by reducing wages. This made matters worse for the already poor, landless agricultural labourers who were forced to seek poor relief from the Speenhamland system.

Aggregate: A term used to describe something when taken together; in this case all the problems Liverpool's Government faced came at the same time.

In industry, the end of the war and a return to peace meant no substantial improvement either. The Corn Law and the abolition of income tax, in 1816, were used as examples of class legislation. This means that laws were passed to help the landowning class. New changes had to be made by the Government to cope with the reduction in demand for products associated with war (e.g. iron, clothing etc. and the substantial problem of 400,000 demobilised soldiers on an already depressed labour market). The historian Norman Gash, in *Aristocracy and People, Britain 1815–1865* (1987), summarises the problems facing the Government in 1815: 'Any one of these would have caused difficulty for the government of the day. Together they created an **aggregate** of social evils which took 50 years to bring under control.' Perhaps a little exaggerated, but it is certainly worth bearing in mind the sheer scale of the forces undermining society.

1. How severe were the problems facing Lord Liverpool's Government in 1815?

You might highlight the difficulties associated with agriculture, politics, industry and the problems linked to the end of the war.

2.3 How serious was the threat of revolution in the years 1815 to 1822?

It has been alleged that this period was the closest that Britain ever came to an internal revolution in its history, with the possible exception of the civil war in the 17th century. The Tory Government of Lord Liverpool, which had been in office since 1812, faced massive problems that, for the most part, it inherited. The poet Percy Shelley's famous description of the Government at this time as 'Rulers who neither see, nor feel nor know' has been passed down to generations of students as an acceptable opinion. To make matters worse, the period 1815–21 saw an intensification of the Radical movement which went out of its way to try to win over a working class by the use of an extensive radical press and a reliance on open-air mass meetings. Despite the threats the Radical movement posed, the reality was that the Government survived some pretty difficult times relatively unscathed.

How was the Radical threat expressed between 1815 and 1822?

Origins
Those who opposed the policies of the Tory Government in this period had to have an effective platform to voice their opposition. The most persistent and conspicuous opponents of the regime came mostly from outside Parliament. This opposition took many shapes and forms. These Radicals, as they were known, had grown out of a reaction to the American and French Revolutions at the end of the 18th century, where new ideas such as liberty, equality and brotherhood developed. Their demands were:

- A more representative parliamentary system whereby the wishes and opinions of the nation would be better served than in the present situation which represented the narrow interest of the landed aristocracy.

- Annual elections. This would make sure MPs would always act in the interests of their constituents.

- The use of a secret ballot in elections. This would avoid the common practice at election time of intimidation and bribery. For example, a farmer faced the threat of eviction from his land if he did not vote for the landowner or his appointed candidate.

It would be wrong to see Radicalism as the result of economic depression. The historian Walt Rostow's famous 'social tensions chart' identifies political unrest coinciding most sharply with economic hardship. Certainly this is the case, especially in the immediate post-Napoleonic war period after 1815, when wheat prices were at their highest levels for the whole of the century. This opinion, however, tends to take a largely negative view of the ability of the working class to act independently of economic unrest. The historian E.P. Thompson, in his study *The Making of the English Working Class* (1980), argues that working-class political awareness was apparent before these crises occurred. J.R. Dinwiddy, in an article in *The Modern History Review* (November 1990), also maintains that the Radical programme revived after 1815 not only because of economic hardship and the demands of reform, but also because radicals had been deprived of displaying their grievances in a lawful manner during wartime (1793–1815).

What role did the different personalities in the Radical movement play?

The British Radical message was spread in a number of ways during this period.

Major Cartwright's political clubs

Major John Cartwright led a colourful political existence and was prominent in the development of the Radical movement in the 18th century. His major contribution to the movement was to establish over a hundred debating societies known as Hampden Clubs. They held a national convention in London in 1817 and part of their programme was the presentation of their grievances in the form of a petition to Parliament.

The development of a radical press

William Cobbett was the leading Radical journalist of this period. He had spent his formative years studying the American system of government, which left a lasting impression on him. He hoped to make the British system more democratic, like the USA. His famous *Political Register* was published from 1802 to 1835. Unfairly labelled the 'Twopenny trash' by its conservative critics, the paper was important in the development of working-class political education. Other papers, such as Thomas Wooler's *Black Dwarf*, continued in the *Register*'s footsteps and in J.R. Dinwiddy's opinion 'A radical press ... did much to give coherence and unity of purpose to the popular reform movement'.

Henry 'Orator' Hunt's 'platforming' or open-air meetings

Henry 'Orator' Hunt was the most recognisable spokesperson of working-class Radicalism in the postwar years. Yet his background, like that of William Cobbett and John Cartwright, was hardly typical for a radical politician (he owned 3,000 acres of land in the south-west of England). Hunt's claim to radical fame was his ability to stir up protest and feelings among the masses at another key feature of postwar radical development – the open-air meeting.

How effective was the Radical threat between 1811 and 1817?

Luddism 1811–1816

The first major and open display of Radical discontent was machine breaking in the form of the Luddite riots which occurred in the East Midlands and the North of England. The protesters were expressing their hostility towards the increasing use of machines in the textile industry and the resultant unemployment of handloom weavers, shearers and croppers. These difficulties were made worse by a series of bad harvests between 1809 and 1812. Rising prices, unapprenticed and, in most cases, cheap labour together with the refusal of the employers to set a minimum wage, led to the rise of Luddism. There were isolated incidents of open violence, such as the Horsfall incident (where a leading opponent of Luddism was murdered in April 1812), but in reality the movement had peaked by 1812.

Spa Field Riots, December 1816

The emphasis on open-air meetings as a form of protest was first illustrated as a more serious threat to the Government in a series of three meetings at Spa Fields, in London, at the end of 1816. It was organised by a revolutionary political movement known as the Spenceans. Well-known Spenceans included Arthur Thistlewood and the father and son Doctors Watson. At the second such meeting in 1816 a breakaway group attacked a gunsmith and made plans to take over the Bank of England, as well as other leading establishment institutions. Yet as John Plowright contends, in his book *Regency England* (1996), 'strong ale and the prospect of loot, rather than strong words and the prospect of liberty' seem to have influenced those who carried out the disturbances.

The March of the Blanketeers, 10 March 1817

As a direct result of the Seditious Meetings Act of the same month – where

Prince Regent: A prince who is regent of a country, during a minority, or in the absence or disability of the monarch (e.g. title given to George Prince of Wales during the mental incapacity of George III (1811–20)).

Yeomanry : A term used at this time to describe wealthy working farmers below the rank of gentlemen. Whether they were owner-occupiers or tenants was unimportant. The main feature the yeomen had in common was moderate wealth.

large-scale gatherings for political purposes were banned – a small, disorganised band of workers planned a march from Manchester to London to present their grievances to the **Prince Regent** in person. The marchers themselves were predominantly cotton weavers who decided to make their protests more visible by draping themselves in blankets (hence the name). The protest was mainly peaceful and carried out in a legal fashion in defiance of government legislation. The March ended in failure and tragedy when one marcher was killed in a heavyhanded and needless display of brutality by the authorities in Stockport, Cheshire.

Pentrich Rising, 8–9 June 1817
On 8 June 1817, the local **yeomanry** easily suppressed a disturbance in Huddersfield. On the following day, the focal point was to be the East Midlands – always a heartland of postwar Radicalism. Approximately 500 disaffected workers from a variety of occupations set out from villages with the intent of attacking Nottingham Castle as a prelude to a wider national rising moving south towards London. The 'Rising' was a farce and the ease with which the Government suppressed it was in no small part due to the use of government spies, such as the discharged debt collector W.J. Richards (known in radical circles as 'Oliver the spy'). The response of the local authorities was severe and went far beyond the perceived threat. Jeremiah Brandreth, one of the leaders, was executed on 7 November 1817 for his involvement.

Did the Radical threat intensify between 1818 and 1822?

The year 1818 was a relatively quiet time for the Radical movement due primarily to the return of more prosperous conditions and a successful harvest. The Tory Party increased its majority in Parliament as a result of the general election of that year. It seemed that whatever radical 'threat' existed had declined and the 'eye of the radical storm' had passed over Britain with relatively little damage being inflicted. Yet over the next four years the threat to Lord Liverpool's Government was greater than at any time and reached its peak during the Queen Caroline Affair of 1820.

The Peterloo Massacre, 1819
On 16 August 1819, a crowd estimated at around 60,000 gathered at St Peter's Fields in Manchester to support the cause of parliamentary reform. The crowd came to hear the main speaker, Henry Hunt, launch into a determined attack on the corrupt parliamentary system. The Manchester local authorities were alarmed at the prospect of what they saw as an invasion of undesirables on their own doorstep at a time when they lacked the ability to administer peaceful and effective law and order. The Home Secretary, Lord Sidmouth, had urged the authorities to let the protest go ahead, fearing the consequences if it was prohibited. The events of that fateful day have gone down in working-class history as an example of an 'over-the-top' reaction by a repressive government to peaceful and legitimate protest. When the authorities unleashed the local yeomanry (the effective police force of the time) the result was 11 deaths and the injured put at over 400. The response in the country at large was riot in support of what now were working-class martyrs. The Government's reaction was, on the face of it, far more extreme legislation in the shape of the Six Acts or Gagging Acts.

The Cato Street Conspiracy, 1820
The following year arguably the most bold and daring Radical act emerged with the exposure of a plan to assassinate the entire Tory Cabinet. Arthur Thistlewood, a leading Spencean, was believed to be the motive force behind the attempt but the authorities were aware of the plot months in

advance – due again to the spying activities of W.J. Richards. An element of farce underpins the whole episode but the fact that a small but dedicated band of revolutionaries dared the ultimate act of terror is evidence of the contempt that the Government was held in by 1820. Thistlewood and four other conspirators were tried and executed.

The Queen Caroline Affair, 1820–1821
The background to the next threat was the marriage in 1794 of the Prince Regent (later George IV) and a German princess, Caroline of Brunswick. They were two wasteful individuals and the sham marriage was ended in 1796 when Caroline fled abroad, eventually settling in Italy by 1815. The separation was far from friendly and this affected the popularity of the monarchy at the time when the Prince's father, George III, was unfit to govern due to a severe mental illness. The Prince was despised by the public and was regarded as a waster of public money at a time of acute crisis. By 1820, the Prince was fed up with his marital situation and demanded a divorce.

The responsibility was to be handed over to the Prime Minister who attempted to pass a bill through Parliament known as the Bill of Pains and Penalties. The Queen Caroline Affair now took on a more serious turn of events. Caroline was determined to return to Britain and claim what was rightfully hers, namely the title 'Queen of England'. She was also determined that maximum publicity should be given to her case. To a lesser extent, she was used by the Radicals to discredit the Government, and William Cobbett acted as her unofficial adviser. The potential was there for serious embarrassment for both Government and future King. By November 1820, Lord Liverpool came to the conclusion that the Bill of Pains and Penalties would not pass and he abandoned it, thus worsening an already difficult relationship with the Prince.

Rioting and criticism were widespread. Things were made worse by the actions of George IV and Caroline. The whole sorry episode continued into 1821, much to the Government's embarrassment. When it was announced that the King would be crowned in the summer of 1821, the prospect of Caroline appearing at the Coronation was too worrying to contemplate. The crisis was resolved with the offer of a £50,000 settlement, which was accepted. Caroline, however, did not live long enough to spend her newly acquired fortune, dying two months later.

The political consequences for the Government were serious enough to justify the resignation of Lord Sidmouth as Home Secretary, who was blamed for the London mob rioting, and George Canning as President of the Board of Trade amid allegations that he was having an affair with the Queen. Was the crisis worth the resignations of two members of the Cabinet? Definitely not, but they must be seen in the context of the time; namely, that the Government was regarded as being so out of touch with public opinion and from that point of view both ministers were understandable scapegoats.

We now turn to the Government's response to such threats in more detail.

Did the policies of the Tory Party make matters worse between 1815 and 1822?

The Prime Minister of Britain since 1812 had been Robert Banks Jenkinson, Lord Liverpool, whose family had been ennobled as a result of loyal service to George III. Lord Liverpool had served in a variety of important ministerial offices. He had been Foreign Secretary (1801–03) and held office as Secretary for War and Colonies (1809–12). He was also Leader of the House of Lords and a gifted debater. Liverpool was aware of the rising tide of discontent after the war but was hampered by the fact that he was, in many ways, a prisoner of his own party's beliefs and outlook. Most of the Tory Party supporters were aristocrats who felt that their Prime Minister had a duty to protect their interests and save them from the Radical threat outlined above.

The Corn Law, 1815

Laissez-faire: Minimum government intervention in economic matters.

Personally, Lord Liverpool was very much a liberal in economic terms and believed in the philosophy of **laissez-faire**. So it is hard to justify why a law was introduced in 1815 which went against these principles.

The Corn Law guaranteed protection for wheat prices for the agricultural or landowning interest from foreign imports of grain. The concept was not new. A similar law had been introduced in 1804, but to guarantee 80 shillings a quarter (£4 per quarter tonne or £16 per tonne) for producers before foreign grain was permitted to enter the British market seemed to government critics a little excessive. The whole point of the Bill, as far as the government was concerned, was to guarantee landowner profits at a level to which they had become accustomed during the war. Naturally, opponents of the regime – both inside and especially outside Parliament – saw it as a piece of class legislation in that it saved the landowners from cheaper foreign grain, stabilised prices and made it more expensive for the consumer. The consequences for the Government were riots, petitions and demonstrations.

Income Tax Repeal, 1816

Income tax had been introduced at the height of the Napoleonic War, in 1797, by the then Prime Minister William Pitt. It was a tax based on how much you earned and, therefore, bound to fall more heavily on the richer sections of British society, namely the aristocracy. It was a means of financing the war but it was always regarded as a temporary measure, because of its unpopularity with Tory MPs, which would end as soon as the fighting was over. Not surprisingly, an aristocratically dominated Parliament who had taken the brunt of the tax needed no excuse to abolish it. In 1816, they voted by a majority of 37 to repeal or abolish income tax. The problem for the Government was how to fill the gap in revenue left by such a departure. The obvious conclusion they drew was to increase indirect taxation on popular items such as beer, sugar etc. The harm done to the common people by this measure would be greater than the potential damage inflicted by the Corn Law because the lower orders were more likely to suffer as a result of the abolition of income tax as they used these items on a regular basis.

The Game Laws, 1816

These were toughened up in 1816, making poaching against a landowner punishable by up to seven years' imprisonment or transportation, usually to Australia. In a predominantly rural society, where this pastime was considered to be a legitimate way of supplementing income and feeding one's own family at a time of marked economic difficulty, these laws were as unpopular as the two previously mentioned. They were, according to historian E.P. Thompson, 'as much a sign of the continued ascendancy of the landowners as was the protection of the Corn Law itself'.

The suspension of Habeas Corpus, March 1817

Habeas Corpus: This Act protected people from being kept in prison for long periods without being charged.

Following the Spa Fields meetings in December 1816, the Government reacted by suspending **Habeas Corpus**. If this Act was suspended, the Government could hold someone suspected of radical or anti-government behaviour without trial for an indefinite period. The Act's critics saw it as a severe measure introduced at a time of potential revolution and as a denial of basic human rights. Recent historical writing – such as John

This cartoon by George Cruikshank was published in January 1820. It is meant to convey a criticism of the consequences of the Six Acts. Castlereagh is seen tearing up a well-known radical newspaper, the *Twopenny Trash*, while John Bull, representing the public, is imprisoned under the pressure of Lord Liverpool's legislation. The symbol of English liberty, the Magna Carta, has a dagger thrust through it; the musket and cannon show the threat of violence the Government is willing to use to enforce the Act.

1. How useful is the cartoon as evidence of popular feeling towards the Tory regime at this time?

2. What images does Cruikshank use to convey the unpopularity of the Tory regime?

1. How serious was the threat posed by the Radical movement between 1815 and 1821?

2. Did the Government's response make matters worse? Explain your answer with reference to the legislation of the period.

Plowright in *Regency England* (1996) and Eric Evans in *Britain Before the Reform Act* (1989) – however, have been more kind, pointing to its temporary nature during a period when difficult decisions had to be made in the interests of State security. The Act only lasted a year and the small numbers held under its terms were released when it was repealed in 1818. Norman Gash, in *Aristocracy and People* (1987), sums up its impact by claiming it was 'not exactly a reign of terror'. However, the Seditious Meetings Act of March 1817, which forbade the unlawful assembly of more than 50 people and imposed the death penalty for mutiny in the armed forces, must again be seen as temporary. It was used sparingly by the authorities.

The Six Acts, December 1819

'They were a commentary on recent disturbances' as John Plowright claims in *Regency England*, introduced as a response to events in Manchester in 1819. The Six Acts were an attack on any possible threat to the State – ranging from an attempt to restrict the activities of the Radical press, through the speeding up of the judicial process, as well as defining the rights of assembly restricting radical activity by outlawing large-scale protest meetings such as Peterloo. Critics point to the fact that these Acts amounted to the harshest example of the reaction of the Government after 1815. Norman Gash, in *Aristocracy and People*, claims that the 'sinister reputation of the Six Acts is not borne out by the facts'. The measures introduced were a commonsense reaction to a dangerous situation and deserve to be looked at in a more positive light in terms of their supposed severity on the radical threat to the regime.

Source-based questions: The Peterloo Massacre, August 1819

SOURCE A

This meeting was no sooner assembled to 150,000 persons, young and old of both sexes, in the most peaceable and orderly manner, than they were assailed [attacked] by the Manchester yeomanry cavalry who charged the multitude, sword in hand, and without the slightest provocation or resistance on the part of the people, aided by two troops of the Cheshire yeomanry, the 15th Hussars, the 8th Regiment of Foot, and two pieces of flying artillery, sabred, trampled on, and dispersed the offending and unresisting people when 14 persons were killed and upwards of 600 wounded.

A primary source from one of the leaders of the Radical movement, Henry 'Orator' Hunt, who was present at the meeting in St Peter's Fields. It is from *Memoirs of Henry Hunt,* written in 1820 while in Ilchester Jail.

SOURCE B

I saw the main body proceeding towards St Peter's Fields, and never saw a gayer spectacle … The 'marching order' of which so much was said afterwards was what we often see now in the procession of Sunday School children … Our company laughed at the fears of the magistrates and the remark was, that if the men intended mischief they would not have brought their wives, their sisters or their children with them.

A primary source, although published in 1851. It is from *Historical Sketches of Manchester* by A. Prentice who was there at the meeting when the alleged disturbance took place.

SOURCE C

A contemporary drawing of the Peterloo Massacre, published in August 1819. The Captain on the left is saying: 'Down with 'em! Chop 'em down, my brave boys! Give them no quarter. They want to take our Beef and Pudding from us – and remember the more you kill the less poor rates you'll have to pay so go it lads, show your courage and your loyalty!'

SOURCE D

When on 16 August thousands of workers from Manchester and the surrounding cotton districts gathered peacefully in St Peter's Fields to listen to Orator Hunt – their injunctions [demands] were 'cleanliness, sobriety, order and peace', and among their slogans was 'No Corn Laws' – the magistrates, scared of an uprising, employed the local yeomanry to arrest him. When the forces of the yeomanry proved inadequate, they called in regular cavalry to disperse the crowds. A savage struggle followed in which 11 people were killed and over 400 wounded. Within a few days the damaging term 'Peterloo' had been coined.

A secondary source from a modern historian, describing events at Peterloo. It is from *The Age of Improvement 1783–1867* by Asa Briggs, published in 1979.

SOURCE E

Peterloo was a blunder; it was hardly a massacre. Possibly half the deaths, probably even more of the non-fatal injuries, were among those who were trampled underfoot by horses and the crowd in the panic that ensued. The public indignation was a mark both of the strong liberal feeling in the country and of the general restraint normally exercised by the authorities in dealing with large political assemblies. It was because Peterloo was uncharacteristic that it achieved notoriety.

A secondary source from a modern historian who takes a different view of events at Peterloo. It is from *Aristocracy and People, Britain 1815–1865* by Norman Gash, published in 1987.

Source-based questions: The Peterloo Massacre, August 1819

1. Study Source A.

Describe the mood of the meeting at St Peter's Fields in August 1819.

How reliable is Henry Hunt's speech as evidence of popular attitudes at Peterloo?

2. Study Sources C and E.

How do these sources differ in their interpretation of Peterloo?

3. Study Sources C, D and E.

Does Source C agree with either Source D or E in its interpretation of Peterloo?

4. 'Peterloo was a blunder … it was hardly a massacre.' Using the sources and your own knowledge, explain whether you agree or disagree with this statement.

2.4 Why was the Tory government able to survive the problems it faced in the period 1815 to 1822?

So how close was Britain to a French style revolution in this postwar period up to 1821?

The weakness of postwar Radicalism

● The Radical movement was divided between those who advocated a more violent programme of change, such as the Spenceans, and the majority of the Radical movement – those advocating a non-violent response. Hunt, Cartwright and Cobbett all believed in non-violent protest. This division was to weaken the development of a united working-class response. Part of this division is also apparent in the regional differences of the movement's outlook. Hunt tended to represent the northern radicals, while the two other major personalities took a more southern outlook.

● The Radical movement was severely weakened by a lack of weaponry. The success of any revolutionary organisation depends on a successful use of arms to overpower a government. Radicalism lacked the military teeth to make such a possibility realistic.

● It could also be argued that the outbreaks of unrest amounted to nothing more than a local expression of grievances carried out by hopeful protesters and not hardheaded revolutionaries. Luddism was more an expression of dissatisfaction against the new machines themselves rather than part of a serious political threat to the establishment. The March of the Blanketeers and the Pentrich Rising, although claiming to be part of a national uprising, both have elements of comedy. Spa Fields and Peterloo – seen as massive protest meetings at the time – were predominantly peaceful and legal and taken over by a tiny minority of extremists who took the law into their own hands.

How effective were the Tory Party policies in dealing with postwar problems?

In response to these threats, the Tory Government was a major factor in preventing the spread of revolution. There are instances when legislation was not really defensible – for example, the introduction of the Corn Laws in 1815 and the repeal of Income Tax in 1816 are nothing more than pieces

Henry Addington, first Viscount Sidmouth (1757–1844)

An example of the reactionary wing of the Tory Party, Addington had served with distinction as Prime Minister (1801–03) and was appointed Viscount Sidmouth in 1805. During the premiership of Lord Liverpool after 1812, Sidmouth served as Home Secretary and was responsible for the passage of much of the unpopular legislation after 1815; for example, the Gagging or Six Acts of 1819.

of class legislation directed against the working classes. Yet the Government acted firmly and decisively:

1. At a time when the forces of law and order were basic, to say the least, the Government had to rely on the local yeomanry and the armed forces to uphold the law in the areas where the threat was greatest. Twenty-three thousand troops were posted to these areas in the North and East Midlands in an effective show of strength at a time of great difficulty.

2. The use of undercover government agents and spies has been the subject of much criticism especially among those critical of Liverpool's Government. It was alleged that the Government invented plots and exaggerated the threat in order to justify what was regarded as harsh legislation afterwards. The reality was that the use of spies in undermining disorder was a fact of life at this time. In order to understand their use we must appreciate that there were no precedents for this type of potential unrest and that the Government acted as it saw fit to try to stop it. The Spenceans, for example, were a small but dedicated band of revolutionaries.

3. The legislation introduced by the Government in this period has been criticised as an attack on basic civil liberties. They made the Government the most unpopular in living memory, lacking any sensitivity at a difficult period in Britain's historical development. Once again, the condemnation can be dismissed if the legislation is to be understood in its context. The French Revolution hung over the whole period and the Government did not wish to see the **anarchy** of the 1790s being transported across the Channel. The suspension of *Habeas Corpus* and the Seditious Meetings Act were both temporary measures at a time when the radical threat was believed to be at its greatest. Although their sinister reputation suggests a denial of freedom, the Acts were in reality used sparingly and removed once conditions were suitable. The Six Acts, or Gagging Acts as they have become known, represent a commonsense approach by a government firmly in control of the situation.

4. It has also been alleged that the members of the Government were out of touch with proceedings and took a great delight in imposing unpopular decisions. Historians such as John Derry have put forward a more positive image of Lord Liverpool, but the Home Secretary Lord Sidmouth and Castlereagh the Foreign Secretary were seized upon by radical poets, such as Byron and Shelley, as symbolising this reaction. Sidmouth deserves some re-appraisal because as Home Secretary he was at the forefront of the fight against Radicalism. In 1819, for example, before the Peterloo massacre took place, he had urged the Manchester authorities to allow the meeting to go ahead and begged restraint in dealing with it.

At what point was the threat to the Government at its greatest? The Queen Caroline Affair, or 'Carol-loo' as Eric Evans has described it in *Britain Before the Reform Act* (1989), deserves greater attention because at the height of the affair Lord Liverpool lost both Sidmouth and Canning and, perhaps more importantly, the support of the new monarch George IV. The whole episode was neither the creation of difficult postwar circumstances nor a persistent radical threat. Although the Radicals liked to use the scandal for their own gain, they were reacting to, rather than initiating, the political agenda and therefore had little chance of overthrowing the Government.

Anarchy: Situation where nobody seems to pay attention to any rules or laws.

1. What were the main problems facing Lord Liverpool's Government in the years 1815–1821?

2. How successful was Lord Liverpool's Government in dealing with the domestic problems it faced in the years 1815–1821?

3. What do you regard as the most serious threat to the Government in the years 1815–1821? Give reasons to support your answer.

2.5 Historical Interpretation: To what extent did the Cabinet changes of 1821–22 bring about a change in government policy?

The dividing line between a reactionary period before 1821 and a more liberal period after is too convenient for many modern historians to accept. J.E. Cookson was the first to question the term 'Enlightened Tory' in his *Lord Liverpool's Administration, The Crucial Years 1815–1822* (1975). He argued that the term was an invention of modern historians. Norman Gash and Eric Evans continued this theme, pointing to the fact that most of the groundwork for change had been completed before the so-called Liberal or Enlightened Tory administration began. The revisionist or modern explanation is based on four important ideas:

1. The new men were not new in the sense that they had all occupied ministerial office during the so-called reactionary phase before 1821. George Canning, the Foreign Secretary, had a long history of ministerial service that originated during the premiership of Pitt the Younger. He had served as President of the Board of Trade before his resignation in 1820 at the height of the Queen Caroline Affair. Frederick Robinson was known to be a close follower of the supposedly reactionary Viscount Castlereagh and followed in Canning's footsteps at the Board of Trade between 1818 and 1823, before becoming Chancellor of the Exchequer. William Huskisson had served in the rather obscure position of Commissioner for Forests since 1814. He was regarded as an important economic adviser before he became President of the Board of Trade. Finally, Peel had held office in Ireland since 1812 as Chief Secretary and was aware of the difficult situation the Government had to face in the years 1815 to 1821.

These new Enlightened Tories were merely completing work that had been started in the reactionary phase of the administration. But the clear-cut divide that allegedly exists between Castlereagh the Reactionary and Canning as Enlightened or Liberal has been questioned on the grounds that the similarities in policy outweigh the differences. Robinson, according to historian Norman Gash, took the credit for economic prosperity in the 1820s that should have been given to his predecessor at the Treasury, Nicholas Vansittart. It was Vansittart who had taken Britain back to the Gold Standard in 1819, returning the economy to sound money and thereby stabilising the currency. By 1823, Robinson inherited a budget surplus. Huskisson, and to a lesser extent Robinson, owed a great debt to the unsung hero of the move toward free trade: Thomas Wallace, who as Vice President of the Board of Trade in the so-called reactionary period, recommended many of the changes, including the relaxation of the Navigation Laws. Peel was also instrumental in proposing a return to the Gold Standard in 1819, being a member of the influential committee that investigated the matter.

2. A new interpretation of this period questions the view that the period up to 1821 was not as reactionary and repressive as historians would have us believe. The Government's response to a series of unprecedented circumstances in 1815–21 represented a commonsense reaction on the part of a government that was at least trying to survive the difficulties of post-Napoleonic War Britain. The abolition of income tax in 1816 – often seen as an example of reaction that eagerly shifted the burden of taxation from the aristocracy – was opposed by Lord Liverpool, but he was forced to accept it under pressure from influential backbench opinion. There are other examples of so-called

Enlightened laws passed during the reactionary period: for example, the Factory Act 1819 which prevented children under the age of nine from working in the mills and regulated the working hours of other children up to 16. The Truck Act of 1820 attempted to prevent employers from paying wages in goods rather than money and to safeguard the rights of the workers. In addition, a number of important committees were set up to investigate known problems such as the legal system. Why did these policies not come in sooner and assume the more official tone that they seemed to after 1821? The answer lies probably in the circumstances of the time that were not suitable for reform. It is also probably correct to assume that the Government was giving these more liberal proposals serious consideration before the Queen Caroline Affair broke and distracted the attention of Lord Liverpool from the issue of reform.

Social policy: A term used to describe the ways in which the Government tries to deal with issues such as poor housing and prisons and, at the same time, attempt to increase prosperity.

3. There is also some truth in the allegation that the Enlightened Tory legislation passed after 1821 was not as liberal as would first appear. The **social policy** of Peel seems to be the most obvious area of concern. The repeal of the Combination Law in 1824 seems on paper to herald a new relationship between the Government and the trade union movement, but following repeal the country witnessed numerous disputes as workers demanded wage increases. The Government response could hardly be described as 'Enlightened' when, in 1825, they introduced the Amending Act. This allowed trade unions to exist only for the purpose of negotiating wages. The reform of the legal system was not carried out from any humanitarian perspective but from a desire to improve the efficiency of the way in which justice was administered. The motivation behind the Gaols Act was being considered by the so-called reactionary Home Secretary, Lord Sidmouth, before Peel took office. Again, the credit and the groundwork was already well in advance of the Enlightened era.

Why have historians of the Tory Party (1815–27) differed in their explanations of a possible change of policy after 1821?

4. The two most controversial issues of the age were parliamentary reform and the emancipation or equality of Roman Catholics. Lord Liverpool's Government made a conscious effort to avoid both of these potentially divisive issues. Tories avoided the issue of electoral reform, or an extension of those able to vote, because ultimately they felt threatened by the prospect of those they regarded as inferior being allowed to vote and determine their own future. The detailed arguments over this issue are dealt with in Chapter 3. However, if the Government regarded itself as Enlightened then it should have at least attempted to change what was obviously an unfair system. The question of giving political rights to Roman Catholics was another controversial issue. It is dealt with in the next section in relation to the collapse of the Tory Party. Liberals such as Canning favoured emancipation, but **Ultras** such as Wellington and Peel refused even to tolerate it until circumstances forced their hand. Lord Liverpool was in an extremely difficult position because the issue of Roman Catholic rights was potentially explosive. He was determined to avoid this issue at all costs in order to keep the different factions within the Government together. This may be regarded as another commonsense approach by a Prime Minister wanting to avoid potential catastrophe for his party, but it cannot be regarded as the most Liberal of actions.

Ultras: A term used to describe those members of the Tory Party who opposed giving any concessions to dissenters or Roman Catholics. They regarded any concessions as a direct attack on the Church of England.

Continuity seems to be the key in understanding the premiership of Lord Liverpool, both in personnel and policy. As Norman Gash has pointed out in *Aristocracy and People* (1987), 'the mythical transformation of the ministry from reactionary Tory before 1822 to Liberal Tory afterwards was the invention of subsequent historians. Liverpool's objective was not to alter course but to reorganise his crew for a voyage that had already started.' The real changes had begun long before the Cabinet reshuffle took place and the economic situation began to improve, but were only post-poned by the Queen Caroline Affair. Yet it does seem, at first glance, that there was something different about the government attitude in the 1820s that separated it from the dangerous period up to 1821. The real difference lies in the political and economic climate that allowed the government to introduce these changes in the more prosperous 1820s.

The Premiership of Lord Liverpool – arch mediocrity or effective politician?

Arch mediocrity?
Contemporaries of Lord Liverpool were very critical of his policies. They accused him of creating unrest by such measures as the introduction of the Corn Laws and the repeal of income tax. Radical poets such as Byron and Shelley were scathing in their treatment of a government that ignored the wishes of the people, describing them as 'rulers who neither see nor feel nor know'. Personally, Liverpool lacked the intellectual qualities of Peel and the charisma and popular appeal of Canning. He refused to tolerate the major issue of parliamentary reform and even less so Catholic emancipation, which he knew would split the party. This rather negative reputation continued after his death when his fellow Tory, the future Prime Minister Benjamin Disraeli, writing in his political novel *Conningsby* in 1844, described Liverpool as the 'Arch Mediocrity' or someone who lacked the charisma that the author so admired in his public figures. This rather dismissive comment tended to illustrate the career of Robert Banks Jenkinson until recently when an effective defence was put forward.

Effective politician?
Historian John Derry described Lord Liverpool as the 'unobtrusive Prime Minister', meaning that here was a modest and unassuming man carrying out his work with quiet efficiency. There is a lot to be said for modesty in a politician. Lord Liverpool had a talent for moderation and reconciling more hotheaded colleagues, keeping them under the broad umbrella of the Tory Party. This modest efficiency drew great devotion from Cabinet colleagues who were prepared to 'go down with their captain' over issues such as the Queen Caroline Affair, when the King threatened to introduce a Whig ministry.

Lord Liverpool's policies now draw much more applause than they did from contemporaries. Income tax repeal was forced on him by influential backbenchers in the Commons and the Six Acts have been re-assessed as hardly amounting to a reign of terror. Lord Liverpool presided over the prosperity of the 1820s and was a firm and enthusiastic supporter of free trade. You must also remember that it was during Liverpool's ministry that the Napoleonic Wars were finally won. As Prime Minister, he was ulti-mately responsible for all elements of government policy. Also, although there were more able and indeed popular colleagues, it was Liverpool who acted as the continuous link throughout his premiership. As you will note in the next section, his death in 1828 split the Party and ensured a considerable period in the political wilderness.

Robert Banks Jenkinson, second Earl of Liverpool (1770–1828)
Lord Liverpool was Prime Minister between 1812 and 1827. He was the longest single-serving PM of the 19th century. He presided over enormous changes at a time when the Government had little idea how to cope with them. Strangely, he was accused by his critics of an intolerant and unsympathetic attitude towards the plight of the working class, especially before 1821.

Write a brief account of the premiership of Lord Liverpool. Do you think he was an effective politician or an arch mediocrity? Give reasons to support your answer.

2.6 How 'liberal' were the Tory governments between 1821 and 1827?

Following the upheavals of the period 1815–21, the country needed a period of calm and prosperity to recover its economic status and soothe the political situation. The Queen Caroline episode revealed to the Prime Minister, Lord Liverpool, how unpopular the Government had become. It, allegedly, provided the spark for a change of direction in policy. This is the traditional view put forward by a generation of historians, such as W.R. Brock and Derek Beales, who argue that Liverpool's Ministry can be conveniently divided into two parts. The first they claim ran from about 1815 to 1821 and was characterised by an intolerant attitude towards any opposition. It was dominated by harsh legislation such as the Six Acts. The second period was completely different and has been described as 'Enlightened Tory' in outlook. This suggests a far more tolerant and sympathetic government attitude towards economic and political change.

This traditional view has now been challenged by a generation of modern historians, such as Norman Gash, J.E. Cookson and Eric Evans, who reject the idea that the period falls into two convenient divides. Continuity is the idea which they stress, both in personnel and policy.

What does the term 'Enlightened', or 'Liberal', mean?

It can be used to describe a number of different views.

● Freedom of religion
  'Enlightened' or 'Liberal' could mean the ability to worship free from interference from the authorities. Remember that nonconformists – those Protestants that were not members of the official Church of England and Roman Catholics – were denied these freedoms. Most of the Tory Party at this time were committed to maintain this situation and were especially suspicious of Catholicism.

● Political rights
  It could also mean someone committed to a more representative political system. This could mean giving the vote to a wider section of the community and extending their ability to participate in the political process. Remember that, at this time, the landed aristocracy dominated the Tory Party and they did not want an extension of the right to vote.

● The right to free expression
  It could also mean a commitment to the idea that any individual has the right to express their opinions without fear or restraint, even if these views are unpopular with the government of the day. In the period up to 1821, the Tory Government of Lord Liverpool had attempted to prevent this freedom from taking place with the introduction of various laws such as the Gagging Acts (Six Acts).

● Free trade
  This is the idea that there should be no government interference in economic matters and that countries should participate in 'free trade' as a sign of the goodwill that existed between them. Remember that in 1815 the Tories had introduced the Corn Laws to protect the agricultural community, preventing free trade taking place.

What do you understand by the term 'Enlightened or Liberal' as applied to the 1820s?

These characteristics of being Enlightened or Liberal seem to stand in stark contrast to the government record up to 1821. However, the Enlightened Tories will deserve their name if their policies seem to be informed by Liberal ideas and if these ideas seem new to the administration after 1821.

2.7 Liberal Tory reforms

The Cabinet changes that occurred between August 1822 and January 1823 do seem to suggest a change of direction of the Liverpool Government. The new 'so-called Liberal Tories' had a younger and more middle-class outlook than those they replaced. From an examination of their policies, one can detect an attitude that bears a closer resemblance to that definition of an 'Enlightened' or 'Liberal' Tory. The so-called Liberal Tories were:

● George Canning who replaced Viscount Castlereagh as Foreign Secretary between 1822 and 1827.

● Sir Robert Peel who became Home Secretary 1822–27, taking over from Lord Sidmouth.

● Frederick Robinson occupied the vital office of Chancellor of the Exchequer from 1823 to1827, taking over from Nicholas Vansittart.

● William Huskisson who became President of the Board of Trade 1823–27.

Utilitarian: Followers of the political philosopher Jeremy Bentham (1748–1832) argued that government should be efficient and accountable, based on the idea of the 'greatest happiness of the greatest number'. Many of the Whig reforms in the 1830s were based on this concept.

It would be a mistake to assume that these new men were fully Liberal in their outlook, but they shared a desire for greater efficiency in the running of the government. Also, they were all influenced by the **utilitarian** philosopher Jeremy Bentham who believed that the 'greatest happiness of the greatest number' should be the aim of any successful government. The key to this success was the improvement of economic conditions which took away the reasons for criticising government policy.

Economic policy

The main emphasis was on the attempt to improve Britain's trading position with the rest of the world, based on the philosophy of free trade. The Prime Minster, Lord Liverpool, was known to be a supporter of this idea. In a famous speech, in 1820, he argued a need to reduce tariffs or taxes imposed on imports from abroad. Apart from the wishes of the Prime Minister, there were powerful sections among the business community that shared these beliefs in 1820. For example, the merchants of Manchester, Glasgow and London had all petitioned the Government for free trade. They were affected by tariffs which had been imposed to protect the home market from cheaper goods from abroad. Contemporary economists, such as David Ricardo, saw free trade as part of a moral crusade to improve the economic condition of Britain. They followed in the footsteps of the most influential free trade philosopher Adam Smith who argued, in *The Wealth of Nations* (1776), that the fewer restrictions there are on the development of an economy, the more successful it would become. William Huskisson, in his position at the Board of Trade, was especially keen to take up the challenge in the following ways:

1 The Reciprocity of Duties Act 1823
This attempted to change the navigation laws, passed in the 17th century. These were designed to protect British ships from competition from the Dutch at that time by stating that any goods or materials entering Britain or its colonies had to be carried by British ships or the ship of the country of origin of the goods. By the early 19th century, these restrictions were unnecessary and they were doing more harm than good because other countries were responding by excluding British ships from their ports. The Reciprocity Act of 1823 overcame these obstacles by allowing free entry of foreign ships into Britain on the same basis as their British counterparts.

The aim was clear, as far as Huskisson was concerned. It would be seen as a gesture of goodwill abroad, while attempting to reduce the costs of imports to British manufacturers.

2 Relaxing of trade restrictions

The next logical step was to relax the restrictions on trade with Britain's colonies which had previously been subject to strict control. As a result of Huskisson's influence, the colonies could now trade with foreign countries for the first time. He also attempted to retain their support by ensuring that duties were lower on goods trading between Britain and the colonies than non-Imperial trade.

3 The Chancellor's reputation

Frederick Robinson's liberal reputation as Chancellor of the Exchequer was based on his desire to reduce the domestic duties. This tended to complement Huskisson's strategy of promoting free trade. Robinson's main focus was the reduction of import duties on a variety of raw materials and customs and excise duties. For example duties on wool, silk, linen, tea, coffee and rum were reduced to encourage demand and improve economic stability. In addition, in a series of far-sighted Budgets between 1821 and 1827 Robinson managed to reduce indirect taxation on a variety of goods.

Social reform

While improvements in the economy were intended to increase the standard of living, there also had to be an improvement in the living and working conditions as well as an attempt to improve the legal system for the Government to be labelled 'Enlightened Tory'. The minister given the responsibility of supervising these improvements was the Home Secretary, Sir Robert Peel. According to the historian Eric Evans, Peel was suited to the task because of his organisational and administrative skills. His policies can be seen as Liberal or Enlightened in the following ways:

1. Trade unions had been banned in Britain since 1799 because it was felt that they posed a threat to the stability of the state, especially when unity was needed during the middle of the Napoleonic Wars. Trade unions were created to protect the interests of the workers against exploitation by the employer. Every member of the trade union paid a weekly contribution to safeguard them against injury and illness. In order to escape fines and punishment, the unions merely changed their names and became known as 'friendly societies'. Radical MPs such as Joseph Hume and Sir Francis Burdett had campaigned for repeal of the Combination Acts of 1799 and 1800. They argued quite correctly that once workers' rights were reinstated, there would be an improvement in the relationship between employer and employee. Finally, common sense gave way and in 1824 the Combination laws were repealed.

2. The inefficiencies of the English legal system were self evident in an age that liked to see itself as civilised. The **Penal Code** was ripe for reform: over 200 offences carried the death penalty and some were so innocent as to be laughable, such as stealing a loaf of bread. Inter-related to these problems was the condition of prisons. They were filthy and unkempt, and in need of improvement. Peel was determined to improve the system. Although he came under the influence of humanitarian reformers committed to improving the system, such as John Howard and Elizabeth Fry, there is little doubt that matters of efficiency, rather than a genuine concern for the welfare of the criminals and prisoners, dominated Peel's work. As Home Secretary,

---

Frederick Robinson, first Earl of Nocton, Viscount Goderich (1784–1859)
Chancellor of the Exchequer during the Enlightened Tory period after 1823. 'Prosperity Robinson', as he was known, had previously held office as President of the Board of Trade, and was responsible for a series of Budgets that reduced import duties on a variety of goods such as rum and silk.

Penal Code: The list containing punishment for the different crimes.

Peel passed a whole series of reforms, between 1823 and 1830, that transformed the rather outdated system he inherited:

● Between 1825 and 1828, 278 legal reforms were passed which completely changed the practice of justice in England. The Penal Code was improved and the death penalty abolished for over 180 offences. The Juries Regulation Act made the jury aware of its responsibilities during a trial, and the whole system seemed more humane and tolerant.

● In 1823, the Gaols [Jails] Act was passed. It represented an attempt by Peel to streamline the foul conditions inmates had to endure, as well as trying to improve the system that gaolers themselves laboured under. Gaolers were now to be paid and all inmates were to receive a basic education. Policy would, from this point, be conducted on a national basis – as all county and large towns were required by law to possess a gaol or house of correction.

● Peel is perhaps best remembered for the establishment of the Metropolitan Police Force during his second period as Home Secretary, under Wellington in 1829. The creation of a police force to patrol the capital was a unique experiment that was later to be applied to the rest of the country. The 'Bobbies' or 'Peelers', as they were known, attempted to stem the alarming rise in crime that the capital suffered from at this time. The Metropolitan Police Act created 3,000 paid police officers, to be financed by the ratepayers of the city whose livelihoods and interests they were trying to protect. Despite some misgivings that the police were an attack on English liberties, the gradual respect the police enjoyed and a reduction in the crime rate seem to confirm that such a measure was necessary.

1. What changes took place in government policy as a result of the Cabinet reshuffle between 1822 and 1823?

2. Were the changes forced upon the Government or were they a genuine attempt to relieve distress? Give reasons to support your answer.

The differences in government policy outlined above seem to confirm the view that there was a change of direction after 1821. The new men were responsible for a new attitude, if nothing else. This view has come in for criticism recently, and new ideas have emerged.

2.8 Why did the Tory Party collapse between 1827 and 1830?

The death of Lord Liverpool and the disputes over the succession

These events led to party disunity. In February 1827, Lord Liverpool suffered a stroke from which he never recovered. His death the following year robbed the country of one of its most underrated prime ministers. He had held the position since 1812 and had guided the country and his own party through some very difficult times. The quality of his leadership would be demonstrated when, over the next three years, the different factions within the Tory Party argued over policy and major differences appeared between the various personalities contesting the leadership. The succession question was solved temporarily, in the spring of 1827, when George IV appointed George Canning as the new Prime Minister.

Canning was an extremely popular choice in the country at large and he was determined to follow his own agenda. Undoubtedly a brilliant politician with experience of a number of important offices, such as Foreign Secretary, Canning was equally unpopular with large sections of his own party. Wellington and Peel both resigned and refused to serve under him. The major area of dispute between them was Canning's known support for Roman Catholic emancipation, which was completely unacceptable to the

Ultras. There was also the issue of his personality, which was generally considered as being vain and overbearing.

The survival of Canning's ministry depended on an alliance of Enlightened Tories such as Huskisson and Palmerston and members of the other main political party, the Whigs. Unfortunately, the ministry was only to last a few short months until Canning's premature death in the autumn of 1827. The new Prime Minister, Frederick Robinson – created Lord Goderich at the time of the formation of Canning's ministry – was to be one of the worst of the whole century, remaining in office as he did until January 1828. The only realistic alternative as Prime Minister was the Duke of Wellington, the great hero of the Napoleonic Wars but completely unsuited to the position because of his brutal honesty and lack of tact. His appointment split the Party even further. The supporters of Canning – Canningites as they were known – were extremely uneasy at the prospect of a known Ultra at the helm. The ministry of Wellington would finally condemn the Tories to a period in the political wilderness, but in 1828–30 it was policy, as much as personality difference, that would dominate the Party.

Why were there differences within the Tory Party over Catholic emancipation?

Ever since the post-1689 penal laws, passed by William III, Catholics had been treated badly by Britain's Protestant rulers. For a long time, there was a fear of an invasion by foreign Catholic powers, such as France and Spain, and this was used as justification for persecution. By the early 19th century, the only serious threat to the stability of the Protestant dominance came from Irish Catholics. In Ireland, growing conflict threatened the stability of the state. Here, Catholics formed a large majority, yet they were regarded by the British ruling class as second-class subjects. Economically, Ireland was underdeveloped compared with Britain. Agriculture was barely advanced enough to feed a growing population. All land and wealth in Ireland was concentrated in the hands of a small group of Protestants, **absentee landlords**. The wealth and status of the Anglican Church stood in stark contrast to the position of the Catholic Church, which relied on the contribution of its congregation. While Catholics had the vote if they held enough land, they were prohibited from holding any public office – the important offices of state that could change the existing situation. 'Emancipation' would involve the removal of these restrictions and, its supporters claimed, solve all the problems of Ireland.

Violence had been a common feature in Irish politics since the Act of Union of 1800 – when Ireland was made a part of the United Kingdom. The governments of both Pitt and Liverpool had used various measures to contain the situation, but little or nothing had been done to tackle the causes of unrest. There were two major reasons for this:

1. Both George III and his son George IV were hostile to the idea of conceding any ground to the Catholics in Ireland because they were of the belief that Irish Catholics were not loyal subjects.

2. There was a great majority within the Tory Party that shared these ideas. Religious bigotry or hatred was rife and any discussion of the issue threatened the fragile unity of the Party. Under Lord Liverpool, the issue had always been an 'open question', but once he went the disputes between the various factions came out into the open. The ultra-Protestant group, led by Wellington and Peel, were strongly opposed to emancipation; the Canningites were far more open in their support.

William Huskisson (1770–1830)
One of the leading Enlightened Tories after 1822. Huskisson was heavily influenced by George Canning. His appointment as President of the Board of Trade in 1823 ensured that government economic policy became more enlightened – for example, the passage of the Reciprocity of Duties Act 1823. He died after falling under the train making the first run from Liverpool to Manchester – the first railway line built primarily to carry passengers.

Absentee landlords: Those not living on their estates but still taking in the profits at the expense of their poor peasant tenants. They charged high rents and were only interested in profit.

The events of the late 1820s forced the Tories to abandon their open policy and to make some firm commitments. The political situation in Ireland had been changing since 1823 when agitation from Daniel O'Connell's 'Catholic Association' grew, until it was banned in 1825. O'Connell was a brilliant barrister who managed, through non-violent means, to convince the Irish people that emancipation was worth pursuing. His crusade touched a raw nerve with the Whig opposition who sponsored a bill that many Tories such as Canning and Huskisson supported. The bill passed the House of Commons, but was defeated in the Lords. In May 1828, O'Connell saw his opportunity when a by-election was held in County Clare. O'Connell stood against Vesey Fitzgerald, a pro-emancipation Protestant and a popular MP. Fitzgerald was forced to call a by-election because he had become a junior minister in the Government. Here, O'Connell argued, would be an opportunity to test the Government's resolve and to challenge the restrictions against Catholics entering Parliament.

O'Connell was elected with a large majority. Wellington and Peel now realised that unless O'Connell was allowed to occupy his seat, Ireland would be plunged into civil war. In February 1829, both Wellington and his Home Secretary Peel announced their conversion to Catholic emancipation in the interests of law and order. The Ultras were outraged by what they saw as the most humiliating of political U-turns and a denial of one of the most fundamental principles of Tory Party policy. The law was formally proclaimed in April 1829 when Parliament agreed to admit Catholics to its benches and all but a few offices. The 142 Tories who voted against the bill were determined to discredit the ministry up to its conclusion in November 1830. Peel, in particular, never regained his reputation with the Tory Ultras amid accusations of betrayal.

How did the question of parliamentary reform lead to the final collapse of Tory rule in 1830?

The more detailed arguments regarding the issue of reform will be dealt with in Chapter 3. This section will refer mainly to the issue of reform as a factor in the collapse of the Tory Party. Most Tories were staunch supporters of the existing electoral system because it represented their interests as landowners and was a safeguard against revolution on the French model of 1789. Wellington, Peel and the Ultras were firmly against the extension of the franchise (vote) for precisely these reasons. The more Liberal wing of the party – the Canningites – were more enthusiastic. However, George Canning himself was less open about the issue of parliamentary reform than he was about Catholic emancipation. The Whigs, the other main political party, were committed to the idea but had been unable to command a majority in Parliament. The divisions in the Tory Party had been partially exposed in 1828 when an opportunity arose to enfranchise the under-represented cities of Manchester and Leeds. Wellington was opposed to the idea and this led to the resignation of the leading Canningite, Huskisson.

The issue of Catholic emancipation had a knock-on effect on parliamentary reform because peaceful protest had ensured the abolition of what was regarded as one of the fundamental pillars of the Tory Party. Ironically, a small minority of the 142 members who voted against emancipation now became unlikely converts to the idea of electoral reform. They felt a wider franchise would have ensured a rejection of emancipation on the grounds that the people were more trustworthy than Parliament! In a speech on 11 November 1830, Wellington continued his opposition to reform, which forced the Whigs and Canningites into open opposition.

Arthur Wellesley, later Duke of Wellington (1769–1852)
Most famously remembered for his military victories against Napoleon, especially at Waterloo in 1815. Less successful as a politician, he was involved in foreign policy during the 1820s and became Prime Minister 1828–30 after Lord Liverpool's resignation. Known for his anti-Reform and anti-Catholic prejudices, he served briefly as Foreign Secretary and minister without portfolio in Peel's two governments.

1. What do you regard as the most important reason for the collapse of the Tory Party in 1830?

2. Why do you think that the two issues of emancipation and parliamentary reform proved to be such difficult issues for the Tory Government?

The death of George IV in 1830 and the accession of William IV were another blow to those that opposed parliamentary reform. The new king was known to be more tolerant towards the Whig position than his brother had ever been. Economic and political conditions were worsening, high-lighting the need for change. Wellington's Government managed to stutter along until the end of 1830 when it was defeated over an investigation into the Civil List accounts – the annual amount the royal family is awarded by Parliament. The Tories had survived worse crises since 1815, but the Duke of Wellington commanded little loyalty among his own party and was confronted by a resurgent Whig Party led by Earl Grey. The end of Tory rule was now a certainty.

2.9 How successful was Castlereagh as Foreign Secretary?

Robert Stewart, Viscount Castlereagh (1769–1822)
He took the courtesy title Viscount Castlereagh when his father, an Ulster landowner, was made an earl in 1796. Sat in Parliament from 1790 until his death in 1822. As Chief Secretary for Ireland (1797–1801), Castlereagh suppressed the rebellion of 1798 and helped Pitt the Younger secure the union of England, Scotland and Ireland three years later. It was as Secretary for War and the Colonies (1805–06 and 1807–08) that he had to resign after a duel with the Foreign Secretary, George Canning. As Foreign Secretary himself (1812–22), Castlereagh coordinated the European opposition to Napoleon and then represented Britain at the Congress of Vienna (1814–15). At home, he repressed the Reform movement, and popular opinion held him responsible for the 1819 Peterloo massacre.

Contemporaries were highly critical of the policies pursued by the Foreign Secretary between 1812 and 1822 – Robert Stewart, Viscount Castlereagh, who was made the second Marquis of Londonderry in 1821. Ten years at the Foreign Office saw him become the subject of a smear campaign that was without parallel in its severity. The modern historian and American statesman Henry Kissinger stated: 'Castlereagh walked his solitary path as humanly unapproachable as his policy came to be incomprehensible to the majority of his contemporaries.' A more flattering view was put forward by the historian Sir Charles Webster, who argued that the reputation Castlereagh enjoyed was primarily a reaction to his involvement in Irish politics at the turn of the century and his membership of Lord Liverpool's Cabinet during the so-called 'reactionary period' – 1815–21. Modern historians, such as John Derry in the *Modern History Review*, have gone as far as to suggest that 'in his defence of British interests he [Castlereagh] set the course for British foreign policy continued by Canning, Palmerston and Salisbury throughout the next century'.

How far did Castlereagh's early career affect his later policy?

Robert Stewart (Viscount Castlereagh) was born in Dublin, in 1769, of Ulster stock. He spent his early career rejecting the excesses of the French Revolution. Castlereagh's Irish background was important, according to historian John Derry, because 'it gave him an insight which perhaps an Englishman lacked, into the problems of peacemaking or cajoling different communities to co-exist together'. In 1797, Castlereagh was heavily involved in thwarting an intended French invasion of Britain. He used his position as Irish Secretary to warn the authorities of the potential support the invasion would receive in Ireland. His ministerial experience increased when he became President of the Board of Trade in 1802. From 1812, Castlereagh occupied the Foreign Office under the then Prime Minister, Spencer Perceval. Almost immediately, Castlereagh played a vital role in negotiating the Fourth Coalition against Napoleonic France and showed considerable skill in holding it together between 1812 and 1815.

When Britain found itself at war with the United States of America (USA) in 1812, Castlereagh attempted to resolve the disputes over the slave trade and the position of Canada as quickly as possible in order to concentrate on matters in Europe. Although there were still issues to resolve between the two countries, the peace negotiations at Ghent in 1814, which brought the conflict to an end, resulted in an acceptable compromise for all concerned.

The Congress of Vienna (1814–1815)
Having played a major diplomatic role in the defeat of Napoleon,

Castlereagh represented Britain at the European Congress, which concluded peace after almost 25 years of continuous war and revolution. Although virtually all European governments were represented, the proceedings were dominated by the representatives of the five Great Powers. Apart from Castlereagh, Prince Metternich represented Austria, Charles Talleyrand France and Karl Hardenburg Prussia, while Tsar Alexander I led the Russian delegation. Castlereagh's personal attitude to the policy was clear when he stated 'it is not our business to collect trophies, but to try, if we can, to bring the world back to peaceful habits'. How accurate is Castlereagh's statement concerning the Congress of Vienna?

Creation of a European balance of power

At Vienna, Castlereagh broke with the instructions of a cautious government in London and signed a secret treaty in January 1815 with Austria and France. The treaty aimed to prevent Russia and Prussia gaining too much territory at the expense of Poland and Saxony, which could prevent the establishment of a balance of power. In general terms, it must rank as one of Castlereagh's triumphs that a balance of power was created at Vienna which remained largely intact until the outbreak of the First World War.

To ensure that the balance of power would be maintained, Castlereagh was the main force behind Article VI of the Second Treaty of Paris, 1815, which created the Quadruple Alliance between Britain, Russia, Prussia and Austria. It suggested that from time to time the European Great Powers should meet to discuss the affairs of Europe. This treaty and other agreements made in the closing stages of the Napoleonic Wars laid the foundation for the establishment of the Congress System which operated between 1815 and 1823.

The containment of France

In order to prevent France threatening the peace of Europe again it was forced to give up all the territory it had acquired since 1790. In addition, the border areas surrounding France were strengthened. Holland and Belgium were united, with the Great Powers paying for the construction of defensive fortification on the Franco–Belgian frontier. Prussia was given Rhineland/Westphalia, Austria was given Venetia in order to strengthen its hold on north Italy and Piedmont received Genoa.

Legitimacy: A term used to describe the rightful rulers of any given country based on their hereditary rights. In 1815, the restoration of these legitimate rulers was regarded by the peacemakers at Vienna as the best way of maintaining peace and stability in Europe after the upheavals of the Napoleonic Wars.

The principle of legitimacy

In order to offer international support for the restoration of the Bourbon monarchy to France, it was proclaimed at the Congress of Vienna that those monarchs who lost their thrones during the Napoleonic era would regain them. Although there is some evidence to suggest that this was implemented in Germany and France, it did not prevent the Great Powers ignoring the idea when other issues such as the balance of power, the containment of France and their own self-importance were concerned.

Rewarding the victors

All the victorious powers gained extra territory as a result of the Congress:

● Russia gained Finland, the kingdom of Poland and Bessarabia.

● Prussia gained two-fifths of Saxony and Rhineland/Westphalia.

● Austria gained Salzburg and Venetia, though it lost Belgium.

● Territorial acquisitions reinforced Britain's position as the world's premier trading and naval power. Malta, the Ionian Islands and Heligoland provided important naval bases in the Mediterranean and the North Sea. The acquisition of Ceylon (Sri Lanka) and Mauritius gave Britain a major naval presence in the Indian Ocean, while the acquisition of the Cape of Good Hope (purchased from the King of Holland for £6 million) gave Britain strategic control of the seas between the south Atlantic and Indian oceans. The acquistion of Tobago and St Lucia, in the West Indies, increased British control of the sugar trade.

Punishing France

The representatives at Vienna agreed that France should suffer punishment not only for plunging Europe into nearly 25 years of warfare, but also for allowing Napoleon to return for the '100 days' in 1815. France's borders were reduced to those of 1790 and art treasures taken from other states were to be returned. In addition, France had to pay a **war indemnity** and suffer an army of occupation, which was withdrawn in 1818.

War indemnity: A payment made by a defeated side in order to pay the costs incurred by the victors in the war.

What was Castlereagh's policy towards the Congress System 1815–1822?

The first meeting of the Great Powers following Vienna took place at Aix-la-Chapelle (Aachen) in 1818. France was readmitted to the Concert of Europe and the Quadruple Alliance was extended to become the Quintuple Alliance. Although generally regarded as successful, the Congress did witness the beginnings of a future split when Tsar Alexander I proposed an agreement whereby the Great Powers would have the right to intervene in other states. This seemed to be a re-affirmation of the Holy Alliance of 1815 which was also put forward by the Tsar and signed by most European states except Britain, the Vatican (Pope's residences in Rome) and Turkey.

This problem came to a head at the next congress held at Troppau, in Austrian Silesia, in 1820 in the wake of revolutions in Spain and Naples and disturbances in Piedmont-Sardinia. Although Castlereagh agreed that Austria had the right to suppress revolution in Naples (in its capacity as the dominant Great Power in Italy), the British Foreign Secretary opposed intervention in Spain especially if this involved Russian intervention. The Congress's main conclusion was the signing of the Troppau Protocol by the other Great Powers. This accepted the principle that the Great Powers had the right to intervene in any European state where revolution occurred. Castlereagh refused to sign. His counter to this policy had been the State Paper of 5 May 1820. This was a rejection of the idea of intervention, as he told a packed House of Commons:

> 'The [Quadruple] alliance … was never intended as a union for the government of the world … such a scheme was only legitimate where a power or combination of powers were threatening the peace of Europe by threatening to mount aggression against a neighbour.'

From this point on, Britain became less involved in the Congress System. When the Congress at Troppau reconvened, at Laibach early in 1821, Castlereagh did not attend. The cracks that had begun to appear at Troppau widened with the outbreak of the Greek Revolt in 1821 against Turkey. Although Castlereagh sympathised with the Greeks, as did much of educated Britain, he was worried that Russia would intervene on the side of the Greeks who were also Orthodox Christians. Britain's detachment from the other Great Powers of the Congress System seemed to be complete when Castlereagh committed suicide in August 1822.

Europe in 1810

Study the two maps. Explain how the political make-up of Europe changed between 1810 and 1815.

Europe after the Congress of Vienna 1815

How successful was Castlereagh in dealing with the USA?

American historian Bradford Perkins has claimed that Castlereagh was the first British minister to accept American independence and its implications for the conduct of future British foreign policy. Castlereagh, although a strong opponent of the slave trade, realised that it was foolish for the two countries to go on fighting. Following the Peace of Ghent in 1814, Castlereagh attempted to improve relations between the two countries even further. Firstly, in 1818, he accepted that the 49th Parallel should form the basis of the border between Canada and the United States west of the Great Lakes. Although not formally agreed until Palmerston was Foreign Secretary in 1840, this compromise agreement was primarily the result of Castlereagh's cautious diplomacy in this period.

Also in 1818, Castlereagh prevented deterioration in Anglo–American relations following General Jackson's invasion of Spanish Florida and his execution of two British subjects accused of organising Indian raids into US territory. As Castlereagh's biographer Sir Charles Webster notes: 'All that he did was done so unobtrusively and with such little desire to enhance his own reputation that it obtained the obscurity necessary for success.'

In 1819, Britain and the United States concluded the Rush–Bagot Agreement, which aimed at reducing military and naval forces in the Great Lakes area. In addition, potential flash points between the two states over such issues as fishing rights off Newfoundland were resolved amicably, confirming Castlereagh's cautious approach to Anglo–American relations.

Castlereagh's foreign policy: an assessment

The reasons behind Viscount Castlereagh's suicide can be explained partly by a nervous breakdown, and partly by a smear campaign by radical opponents who accused him of homosexuality. Whilst running the Foreign Office in this period, Castlereagh was also leader of the House of Commons and the Government's chief spokesman – bearing in mind that the Prime Minister, Lord Liverpool, sat in the Lords. Castlereagh unfortunately occupied this position at the precise time when the Government's popularity was at an all-time low as a result of its repressive policies.

In addition, Castlereagh felt no need to justify his position to satisfy public opinion. As the historian Muriel Chamberlain states in *'Pax Britannica?' British Foreign Policy 1789–1914* (1988): 'Castlereagh felt no obligation to try and explain his policy to a wider public. International diplomacy he saw as a highly skilled, very technical, entirely confidential profession.' With such an arrogant attitude, Castlereagh became the focus of reaction. Unfortunately for him, those most capable of literary genius were the most critical. Lord Byron's poem 'Don Juan' was written with Castlereagh in mind, as this extract shows:

> States to be curbed, and thought to be confined, Conspiracy or congress to be made – Cobbling at manacles for all mankind – A tinkering slave-maker who mends old chains,With God and man's abhorrence for its gains.

Castlereagh's reputation never fully recovered. During the course of the 19th and early part of the 20th century, he was not regarded as a hero by those Nationalist historians, and his close attachment to Europe alienated those who advocated the policy of splendid isolation. He was, according to Muriel Chamberlain, 'left singularly friendless among historians as well as contemporaries'. Yet Castlereagh's reputation has recently been the subject of re-assessment. Few would now argue that, between 1812 and 1822, he played a main part in the defeat of Napoleon, safeguarded Britain's vital interests in Europe and overseas, created a system of diplomacy that attempted to deal with the contemporary issues, and was associated with a peace treaty at Vienna that lasted at least 25 years after the war ended.

2.10 What problems did Canning face as Foreign Secretary in the years 1822–1827?

George Canning (1770–1827)
Entered Parliament at the age of 23, as a Tory. Served as Foreign Secretary 1807–10. Was forced to resign after a clash with Castlereagh, in which Canning blamed the Secretary of War for two British defeats. The two men fought a duel on Wimbledon Common to settle the matter, during which Canning was wounded in the thigh. Canning was President of the Board of Control 1816–20. On Castlereagh's death in 1822, Canning again became Foreign Secretary. He supported the national movements in Greece and South America. Appointed Prime Minister in 1827 and when Wellington, Peel and other Tories refused to serve under him, Canning formed a coalition with the Whigs. Died after a sudden illness, whilst in office.

Polignac Memorandum: An agreement signed between Britain and France in 1823. France agreed not to intervene in British attempts to reach trading agreements with Spain's former colonies. It was an attempt by George Canning to warn off France from taking advantage of Spain's precarious position in Europe at this time by attempting to intervene in its colonial affairs.

George Canning was one of the most able and brilliant politicians of his day. Like Castlereagh, he had grown up politically under the influence of William Pitt the Younger. He had also occupied a variety of ministerial positions that ranged from Paymaster General in 1800 to a brief occupation of the foreign secretaryship under the Duke of Portland's ministry in 1807. These different positions gave him an insight into the workings of many enemies along the way, especially within his own party. His appointment as Foreign Secretary in 1822, for a second period, appeared to herald a change of direction, from the pro-European stance that Castlereagh adopted to an international policy that paid little attention to cooperation in Europe.

What was Canning's policy towards Spain?

George Canning inherited the problem of a revolution in Spain. At the Congress of Verona in 1822, Wellington, the British observer, was out on a limb in his refusal to support French intervention. Each of the Great Powers argued that legitimacy should be restored, but differed as to who should take the initiative. Tsar Alexander I of Russia wanted a joint European force, but had to agree finally to French intervention in April 1823. The French easily overcame the rebels and the former King Ferdinand VII was restored to the throne in an aggressive display of French power. Canning knew that the danger now lay with the possibility of France intervening in Spain's former South American colonies who had broken away from Spanish control. He was prepared to tolerate what was a diplomatic defeat in Europe, but was determined that French influence should not spread into Spain's former Latin American colonies. In 1823, Canning managed to negotiate the **Polignac Memorandum** with the French ambassador in London forcing France into a position of neutrality over the issue. Canning was determined that Britain's trading rights would be maintained in the area and warned that he was prepared to use force to achieve his objectives.

The whole situation was complicated by the presence of the USA who had enjoyed a frosty relationship with Britain since the war of 1812. The USA had warned of the danger of European intervention and President Monroe had taken the bold step of issuing a doctrine to the same effect in 1823. Britain took the next step and, in 1824, recognised the independence of Columbia, Mexico and La Plata (Argentina). Canning's hostile attitude towards France over the issue of the former Spanish colonies won him much praise from a supportive public. As he told the House of Commons in December 1826: 'I resolved that if France had Spain, it should be not Spain "with the Indies". I called the New World into existence to redress the balance of the old.'

Although the whole affair had been a defeat because he had failed to stop French intervention in Spain, Canning's public anti-French stance hid this fact from most people. The one positive element for Canning was that the crisis had revealed Britain's ability to take successful action independent of other Congress powers. This was an important milestone and ultimately doomed the Congress System to almost inevitable failure.

A new policy towards Portugal?

One of the major successes of Canning's foreign policy occurred in Portugal which had long been an important trading partner as well as enjoying a strong sense of cooperation with the British monarchy. A revolution in 1820 had forced King John VI to accept a liberal constitution, which his son Miguel had attempted to overthrow in 1823. Canning was in a difficult position, initially sympathising with Miguel but realising that there were many similarities with the situation he had squandered in Spain. He was again worried at the prospect of French intervention in what was a traditional British sphere of influence. In the summer of 1823, the Royal Navy was sent to monitor the situation but the counter-revolutionary activity fizzled out and the spirit of liberalism was retained.

This initial success was once again threatened in 1826 when the young Queen Donna Maria Gloria was given the throne. The Portuguese conservatives saw this as an opportunity of restoring Miguel and replacing any liberal sympathies. When Canning found out that Miguel had many Spanish supporters in his entourage, he was again worried at the prospect of a Spanish puppet placed on the Portuguese throne. On 9 December 1826, British troops were sent to protect the young queen and to safeguard the liberal constitution. On the face of it, Canning had intervened to defend constitutional government against conservative reaction. He was again the darling of public opinion fighting the corner of innocence against oppression. Yet Canning was merely doing what he felt to be right, as he told the Commons on 12 December 1826: 'We go to Portugal not to rule, not to dictate, not to prescribe constitutions, but to defend and preserve the independence of an ally.' On this occasion, his policy was a triumph.

The Greek Revolt: a success or failure for Canning's policy?

The decline of the Turkish Empire was viewed with much suspicion in Britain especially as the Russians would be the obvious beneficiary of any such event. British foreign policy strongly advocated maintaining the independence of the Empire and thwarting the many potential forces of **nationalism** in the area. Canning was concerned when the Greeks rose up against the Turks in an attempt to assert their nationalist rights. Russia was particularly concerned at the plight of fellow Orthodox Christians fighting to free themselves from Muslim rule. Initially, Tsar Alexander I had shown much sympathy towards the Greeks but was restrained from intervening by Metternich who argued against supporting nationalist causes.

Canning was in a difficult position as there was much sympathy for the Greek cause in Britain especially among the influential educated élite. The romantic poet Lord Byron was keen to fight and eventually die for the cause. This sympathy increased when the Turks conducted a wholesale massacre of Greek Christians and murdered the Patriarch of Constantinople on Easter Sunday 1821. Canning, having recognised the Greeks as **co-belligerents** in 1823, was now faced with the prospect of Russian intervention in an area of obvious economic and strategic interest. If Canning viewed events from the sidelines, then the Russian influence in the area would increase and threaten these vital interests. The crisis intensified following the Sultan's decision to use his **vassal**, Mehemet Ali of Egypt, to crush the revolt. Between 1826 and 1827, an Egyptian army under Mehemet Ali's son, Ibrahim Pasha, gained the upper hand over the Greek rebels.

The situation took a fresh turn in 1825 when the new Tsar, Nicholas I, openly expressed his desire for direct intervention with or without international cooperation. Wellington was dispatched to St Petersburg to offer

Nationalism: The idea that an individual country had the right to look after its own interests free from influence by a foreign power. The 19th century has been labelled the 'Age of Nationalism' with the unification of Italy and Germany being two of the most significant developments.

Co-belligerents: An attempt to recognise a country's right to defend its interests against aggression. In this instance, Canning realised the rights of the Greeks to take up arms against an unpopular Turkish regime.

Vassal: Someone who holds land as a direct favour from a superior. In this case, Mehemet Ali held land in Egypt directly as a result of a favour from the Turkish Sultan. He was also obliged to help the Sultan if his interests were threatened.

Protocol: An original draft of a diplomatic document agreed to in a conference and signed by all parties.

the new Tsar the possibility of joint mediation to solve the dispute. The outcome was the **Protocol** of St Petersburg of April 1826, by which the British and Russians offered mediation to the Turks as long as Greece retained some form of self-government. The international flavour of the negotiations was confirmed in July 1827: Britain, Russia and France signed the Treaty of London confirming the previous year's arrangements. The difference between the two agreements was that the latter was more strongly worded and implied the use of force if necessary. The rejection of international diplomacy by the Turks led to the sending of a joint British/Russian fleet, which destroyed the Turkish/Egyptian fleet at Navarino Bay on 26 October 1827. The fact that the whole issue was resolved by conflict can be interpreted as a failure on the part of the Great Powers and Canning in particular. Yet by the time the fleet was dispatched, Canning's career had been tragically cut short when he died after a sudden illness, in August 1827.

Wellington as Prime Minister and Aberdeen as Foreign Secretary aimed to reverse many of the policies towards the Turks between 1828 and 1830. Wellington was far more positive in his attitude and understood their importance as a strong presence against Russian influence far more than Canning ever did. Between 1828 and 1829, Russia was at war with Turkey and Wellington felt he was losing the initiative in the area. The Treaty of Adrianople in September 1829 saw Russia make gains on the Black Sea and the Danubian principalities. Greek independence was now a formality, but an acceptable settlement was not reached until November 1830 when Prince Otto of Bavaria became the new king. In 1832, in the Treaty of London, the five Great Powers accepted Greece as an independent kingdom.

How successful was Canning's foreign policy?

George Canning's career as Foreign Secretary in 1822–27 was a mixture of success and failure. His biggest failure was his inability to prevent a French invasion of Spain in 1823, but he had managed to balance these changes in Europe with a more successful strategy in the Americas. His Portuguese policy was a great success and he managed to retain Britain's special relationship with the Portuguese.

Canning's biggest problem was in relation to the Greek Revolt. Working through the Concert of Europe, he devised a policy which would involve cooperation between Britain, France and Russia. However, Canning followed a risky policy that always had the potential of leading to an outbreak of fighting. If Canning had not died prematurely, perhaps his diplomatic skill would have prevented the outbreak of war. As it was, British policy lacked direction after Canning's death in August 1827. This resulted in the battle of Navarino Bay and the outbreak in the following year of the Russo–Turkish War.

Canning's special talent for self-publicity had made British foreign policy more intelligible to the mass of the British public. In addition, he had taken great satisfaction in undermining the Congress System. In the Greek Revolt it was Canning, not Metternich, who acted as the major player in European diplomacy.

1. What do you regard as the most significant development in the conduct of foreign policy under George Canning in this period?

2. Why do you think Canning's foreign policy was so popular with the British public?

Further Reading

Articles

In *Modern History Review*:
'English Radicalism before the Chartists' by J.R. Dinwiddy (November 1990)
' "Liberal" and "High" Tories in the age of Lord Liverpool' by G. Goodlad
    (November 1995)
'The Premiership of Lord Liverpool' by Eric Evans (April 1990)
'Catholic Emancipation' by W. Hindle (April 1995)
'Europe after Napoleon – Castlereagh's Foreign Policy' by John Derry (February
    1993)
Also in *History Review* (formerly *History Sixth*):
'Lord Liverpool – the unobtrusive Prime Minister' by John Derry (20 December
    1994)
'Canning and the Pittite tradition' by J. Derry (March 1996)

Texts designed for AS and A2 level students

Britain before the Reform Act: Politics and Society 1815–1832 by Eric Evans
    (Longman, Seminar Studies series, 1989)
Tories, Conservatives and Unionists 1815–1914 by Duncan Watts (Hodder &
    Stoughton, Access to A Level series, 1994)
Regency England: The Age of Lord Liverpool by John Plowright (Routledge,
    Lancaster Pamphlets, 1996)
Aspects of British Political History 1815–1914 by S.J. Lee (Routledge, 1994)
Peel by Graham Goodlad (Colins Historymakers, 2004)

More advanced reading

Aristocracy and People: Britain 1815–1865 by Norman Gash (Edward Arnold,
    1987)
The Forging of the Modern State: Early Industrial Britain 1783–1867 by Eric Evans
    (Longman, 1983)
Some excellent biographies of the leading political figures:
Castlereagh by J. Derry (Allen Lane, 1976)
Canning by W. Hinde (Punell, 1973)
Lord Palmerston by Muriel Chamberlain (GBC Books, 1987)
'Pax Britannica'? British Foreign Policy 1789–1914 by Muriel Chamberlain
    (Longman, 1988)
Foreign Affairs 1815–1865 by D.R. Ward (Collins, 1972)
The Great Powers and the European System 1815–1914 by F.R. Bridge and R. Bullen
    (Longman, 1980)
Britain and Europe: Pitt to Churchill 1793–1940 by James Joll (A&C Black, 1961)

3 The Great Reform Act of 1832

Key Issues

- Why was parliamentary reform such a controversial issue in 1830–32?

- How serious was the Reform Bill crisis?

- How far did the Reform Act change the British political system?

3.1 How unrepresentative was the electoral system before 1830?

3.2 Why did parliamentary reform become a major issue from 1830?

3.3 What were the main features of the Reform Crisis between 1830 and 1832?

3.4 Historical interpretation: Was Britain on the brink of a revolution in 1830–1832?

3.5 How far did the Reform Act change the electoral system?

Framework of Events

1829–31	Economic distress caused by harvest failure leads to high grain prices and unemployment
1830	January: Formation of Thomas Attwood's political union
	June: Death of George IV; new King William IV
	July: Fall of Charles X in France
	August: Swing Riots take place in southern England
	November: Collapse of Wellington's ministry marks end of Tory rule
	Earl Grey becomes Prime Minister of a Whig ministry
1831	March: First Reform Bill proposed by Lord John Russell; defeated by Tories in committee stage; Earl Grey calls an election
	April: Whigs return to office with an increased majority of 130, committed to reform
	July: Second Reform Bill is introduced
	October: Bill is defeated in Lords by a majority of 31; leads to riots in Nottingham, Derby and Bristol. Prominent members of the Lords attacked, including several bishops
	December: Third Reform Bill is introduced
1832	March: Third Bill passes through the Commons but now faces possibility of defeat in Lords
	May: Grey asks for the creation of 50 new Whig peers to ensure a majority in Lords. William IV refuses to agree and Grey resigns. Wellington tries for six days to form a Tory ministry but is unable to do so. The King asks Grey to return as Prime Minister. New Whig peers not needed as Tory supporters in Lords abstain
	June: Third Bill finally becomes law on 4 June. Separate Reform bills for Ireland and Scotland.

Overview

THE period 1830–32 was dominated by the single issue of parliamentary reform, when events allowed the Whigs to take power under their leader, Earl Grey. The process was not a smooth one and the country seemed on the brink of revolution when the Lords rejected the Second Reform Bill in the autumn of 1831.

The reasons why this situation came about have provoked intense debate among historians. Eric Evans believes that the collapse of Tory rule in 1830 allowed the Whig reformers the chance to introduce reform that would otherwise have been denied to them had the Tories stayed in office. The economic crisis that occurred between 1829 and 1831 heightened the tension, but is not now regarded as the main reason why the crisis emerged.

It must be remembered that the Whig Government, under Earl Grey, was not trying to alter the constitution radically. Instead, it was trying to open the vote to the emerging group in society – the middle classes. Grey was convinced that a moderate measure would satisfy respectable property owners and break the alliance that had grown up between the radicals and the middle class. It would be a mistake to regard Grey as a democrat: he was quite clearly an anti-democrat. He told the House of Lords at the height of the crisis in 1832, 'The principle of my reform is, to prevent the necessity for revolution, there is no one more dedicated against annual parliaments, universal suffrage, and the secret ballot than I am.'

The outcome of the Act has also caused as much debate among historians as it did among contemporaries. Some have claimed that the changes marked the beginning of a new era. Equally, there was bitter disappointment, especially among the working class. They accused the Government of betrayal because of the insistence on a £10 property qualification. This sense of betrayal would fuel further demands for radical change through the Chartist movement.

The Tories found the Reform Act equally unacceptable because they regarded electoral change as a revolutionary measure that would upset the natural influence of prosperity and rank. In addition, the Tories claimed that the House of Commons would be at the mercy of public opinion – as Sir Robert Peel argued: 'when you have established the overpowering influence of the people over this House (i.e. the Commons) what other authority in the State can – nay what other authority ought to – control its will or reject its decisions?'

The crisis over reform and the terms of the 1832 Act also changed the influence of the monarchy over politics through the reduction of patronage. It also made the two political parties, the Tories and the Whigs, establish national organisations in order to contest the votes of the new middle classes. Ultimately, the 1832 Act was the starting point for further electoral change as the century would reveal.

1. Place the reasons in the mind map in order of importance in explaining why the Reform Act was passed.

2. Can you find links between the reasons mentioned in the mind map? For instance, the General Election of 1830 brought the Whigs to power, who were in favour of reform.

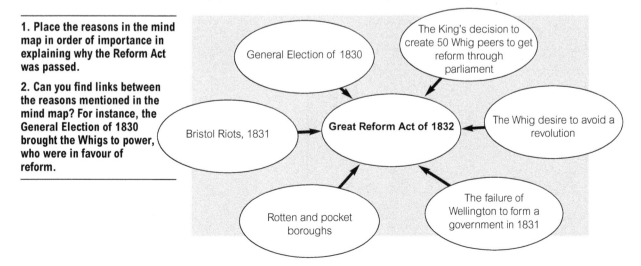

3.1 How unrepresentative was the electoral system before 1830?

The main problem facing those campaigning for parliamentary reform at this time was that the system of electing MPs was rooted in history and had changed little since the middle of the 17th century. There were two basic types of constituency: the counties and the boroughs.

The counties

These, as their name suggests, represented the major counties of England, Scotland, Wales and Ireland. In England and Ireland, each county elected two MPs regardless of its size and population. There were some alarming irregularities in the pre-reform Parliament but, according to its supporters, the system worked because interests were more important than numbers. In Wales and Scotland, only one MP was elected for each county and the charge of serious under-representation cannot be ignored. Qualification for voting in the counties was relatively easy to define but was based primarily on the land you owned. Any man (not woman) who owned land or property worth 40 shillings (£2) a year was eligible to vote. This had been the case since 1430 and the relative decline in the value of property meant that the numbers eligible to vote in elections for county seats had steadily increased.

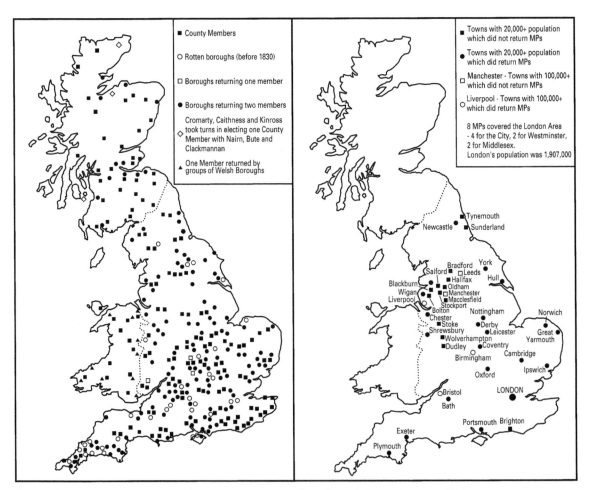

The unreformed electoral system, 1830   The reformed electoral system, 1832

The boroughs

The situation in the borough constituencies was far more confusing. The boroughs were usually the most important towns of each county, as they had been defined in the mid-17th century. Before 1832, most British boroughs had two MPs, whereas in Wales, Scotland and Ireland there was one each. Borough electorates varied enormously: some like Liverpool had over 5,000 members, but some like Old Sarum literally only had a handful.

These latter constituencies were known as '**rotten boroughs**'. They were controlled by wealthy members of society, usually aristocrats. They fulfilled a useful purpose in allowing the election of a promising young MP, but could equally maintain the position of an unpopular member. These rotten boroughs were common: well over 50 English boroughs had fewer than 40 voters, yet each was represented by two MPs. These pre-reform boundaries had been drawn up in the 17th century when Britain was predominantly a rural country, before the industrial revolution had changed the face of the landscape. For example, Birmingham, although a large town, had no MPs because it was not a borough. By 1831, Lancashire with a population of 1.3 million had just 14 MPs, while Cornwall with only 300,000 was represented by 42 MPs.

Rotten boroughs: These were borough constituencies in the pre-reform Parliament, which were very small and used to elect promising young politicians without a contest. The most infamous rotten borough was Old Sarum, which had a population of only 7.

Was there a demand for change?

Britain was a changing society. As a result of the industrial revolution, the middle classes had been growing in economic prosperity. They now possessed economic power and influence, but lacked the political power associated with representation in Parliament and government. This was especially so during the Liverpool Administration when unpopular legislation, such as the Corn Laws and income tax repeal, seemed to weigh heavily against the consumer in favour of the producer. The political system as it existed tended to discriminate against the middle classes, especially in the borough constituencies where many were denied the vote. Their property rights were evidence of a respectable class of men who could be trusted to receive the vote and not abuse it as many Tories feared the working class would. Political philosophers such as Jeremy Bentham, the utilitarian leader, advocated a reform of Parliament as this would satisfy his maxim that any government existed to provide 'the greatest happiness of the greatest number'.

Who had the right to vote before 1832?

Although ownership of property worth over 40 shillings (£2) gave you the vote in county constituencies, the situation was far less clear-cut in the boroughs. A mixture of ancient privileges and eccentricity dictated who could vote in borough elections. In general there were five main types of borough constituency.

● *Freeman boroughs*
  In this type of borough those who could vote were those who had received or had bought the 'freedom' of the borough. This privilege was then passed on to relatives.

● *Burgage boroughs*
  These tended to be very small constituencies, as only those owning certain certain pieces of land or property (burgage plots) were allowed to vote.

● *Scot and Lot boroughs*
  An easy borough to identify as those male householders who paid local rates were entitled to vote. Electorates tended to vary in size here. An example of this type of borough was Preston in Lancashire.

● *Potwalloper boroughs*
This type of borough constituency shows the eccentricity of the pre-reform borough electoral system. Here, incredibly, the vote was given to those who owned a house and fireplace on which to boil a pot. Not surprisingly, the electorates tended to be large in these types of constituency. An example of this type of borough was Taunton in Somerset.

What difficulties would the electorate have in deciding who was entitled to vote in a borough constituency?

● *Corporation boroughs*
Only the corporation or town council were allowed to vote here, so the electorate was very small. Over 90% of this type of borough had fewer than 50 voters.

Critics of this system pointed to the fact that of the 432 borough seats many were prone to electoral corruption. In addition, significant and growing areas of the county had no borough representation at all. As the historian Eric Evans has stated, 'the base of the economy was moving north but none of Manchester, Leeds, Sheffield or Birmingham had a seat in parliament'. Put simply, the North and the Midlands – the centres of the industrial revolution – were heavily under-represented, whilst the South – prominent in the past – was now over-represented in relation to its overall contribution to the wealth of the nation.

Why were elections seen to be unfair?

The modern electoral system takes great care to ensure that every aspect of an election is fair and above accusations of bribery or vote rigging. This was not the case in the early part of the 19th century. The following reasons made the practice of fair elections even more unlikely.

The absence of a secret ballot
Voting in an election today is very much a private affair, conducted in secret by the individual according to his or her conscience. In a 19th-century election, up until 1872, voting was an 'open' affair. Everyone knew the way in which an individual had cast his vote. This, of course, could lead to intimidation because the candidate knew how each person had voted and could bribe or blackmail him to change his mind at the last moment. The tenant, for example, was never free to vote with his conscience because his landlord knew how he voted and might threaten to evict him if he did not follow the landlord's lead.

Bribery and corruption
Any candidate standing in an election at the time knew that in order to ensure victory he would have to spend exorbitant amounts to win unde-cided voters over to his side. This was especially true in constituencies with large electorates: open bribery included cash gifts, free beer and, in some cases, the promise of employment. Usually, the election lasted a fort-night and as the episode drew to a close, the money for the undecided voter increased to unrealistic proportions. In the smaller constituencies, the landlord could nominate his candidate in what was usually a non-event as a contest. These 'pocket boroughs' were used as a tool by their owners to sell to the highest bidder and were usually passed down from father to son.

1. What were the major weaknesses of the unreformed electoral system before 1830?

2. Which weakness do you regard as the most in need of change? Give reasons to support your answer.

3.2 Why did parliamentary reform become a major issue from 1830?

The collapse of the Tory Government in November 1830

The Tories had consistently refused to extend the vote, arguing that owner-ship of property rather than number of voters was the hallmark of Britain's successful political system. Of course, the Tories would be the major losers in any redrawing of the political map. Royal support from both George III and George IV strengthened them. Yet, by the end of the decade, there were bitter internal divisions exposed within the Tory Party over the issue of Roman Catholic emancipation. These produced a climate where the Tory Ultras were even willing to support reform in order to annoy Wellington and Peel and to ensure that a wider franchise would reject issues such as emancipation! Had the Tories not split over the religious issue, then the prospect of introducing reform under a Whig government might not have existed.

The revival of the Whigs

Charles Grey, second Earl Grey (1764–1845)
Grey was one of the leading Whig politicians of the period. A member of an aristocratic Northumbrian family, Grey spent most of his career in opposition, apart from a brief period as Foreign Secretary in 1806–7. Always an advocate of electoral reform, Grey was Prime Minister in 1832 when the first Reform Bill was passed. Following his resignation in 1834, he retired to his Northumbrian estate, where he died in 1845.

Coinciding with the decline of the Tory Party in this period, there was a revival in the fortunes of the Whig Party. The Whigs were far more enthu-siastic about the idea of cautious reform, but could hardly be described as democrats themselves. They believed that any change to the existing polit-ical system had to be done to preserve its key features, rather than destroy it. As a party, the Whigs were far more in tune with the new forces shaping society and, although many Whig MPs were aristocratic by background, it is also true that a significant number were drawn from the rising middle classes – the major beneficiaries of industrialisation. The Whigs had tried to sponsor reform bills previously, but on three occasions – in 1792, 1793 and 1797 – they had failed, all due to the opposition of George III.

The Whig Party had spent the period 1807–30 in opposition, but during the later part of the 1820s had begun to find its political feet. Its leader, Earl Grey, was a known support of moderate reform. He believed that the system had become out of date and the new 'men of property' among the middle classes should be given a say in the running of affairs if the country was to avoid anarchy and chaos. The corruption of the existing political system was arming the radical opponents of the system and detracting from the moderate changes Grey was proposing. The historian John Derry, in an article in *Modern History Review*, claims that Grey 'saw himself as keeping alive the possibility of moderate, practical reform, a safe halfway house between loyalist reaction and radical extremism'.

E.A. Smith goes further by claiming that the motivation behind the Reform Bill was to safeguard the pre-eminence of the aristocracy against the encroachments of royal tyranny. Grey had learnt the lessons of the past when George III had vetoed plans for reform. According to Smith, in an article in *New Perspective*, 'Grey was attempting to restrain the potential violence of a popular uprising and channel moderate opinion into safe-guarding existing constitutional safeguards against royal tyranny'. Grey was fortunate in that he was given the opportunity to implement his ideas when the Tory ranks split in 1830.

The fall of Charles X of France in 1830

The issue of reform was also heightened by events across the Channel in France. The restored Bourbon dynasty that had ruled since 1814 had become increasingly unpopular with the people. This was primarily because its king, Charles X, ruled in a heavy-handed manner and had refused to recognise the results of sweeping election gains for the Liberal opposition in 1829. In desperation, Charles issued the Ordinances of St Cloud, which sparked a revolution in the French capital in July 1830. Critics of the system in Britain argued that if the French monarchy had fallen due to a failure to recognise genuine popular electoral grievances, then surely the potential existed in Britain for the same to happen.

Why did the death of George IV help reform?

The death of the reigning monarch in England, in June 1830, raised reform expectations even higher. George IV had not only been, arguably, the country's most unpopular monarch, but was also a staunch opponent of Roman Catholic emancipation and electoral reform. Under the Tories, he had never had to face the prospect of agreeing to the issue of reform, but was forced to agree to demands for emancipation just before his death. The new king, his brother William IV, although not a reforming enthusiast, was sufficiently realistic to appreciate the need to remedy some of the worst excesses of the existing system. Fortunately for the Whigs, the tide of popular opinion was definitely in their favour and the accession of a new monarch required a new election. Pro-reform candidates did well. The existing Tory Prime Minister was forced out of office and a new Whig ministry, under Earl Grey, was created in November 1830.

The importance of a political alliance between the middle class and working class

A closer relationship was forged between the middle and working classes between 1829 and 1832. The main catalyst for this was Thomas Attwood, a Birmingham banker who formed the General Political Union to agitate for reform. This 'pressure group' organisation was very successful in raising the profile of the reform issue through rallies and petitions. Its success was assured by its emphasis on peaceful protest. The main aim of cautious reformers like Grey was to try to split this alliance and convince the middle-class elements that their future was assured by support for moderate reform.

What do you regard as the most important reason for making parliamentary reform a major political issue between 1830 and 1832? Give reasons to support your answer.

3.3 What were the main features of the Reform Crisis between 1830 and 1832?

When Wellington was forced to resign in November 1830, the Whigs, under Earl Grey, were asked to form a government. The country was in no mood for compromise and reform was to be the key political issue. Grey, given the political and economic climate, felt he had to tackle the reform issue. As he said, 'We did not cause the excitement about reform. We found it in full vigour when we came to office.' Indeed, the Whigs were keen to avoid a worse scenario – namely the breakdown of law and order, and revolution.

The question facing the new government was how to find a balance between preserving the traditional system and securing social peace and public order. Grey's instructions to the four-man committee, whose job it was to frame the Bill, summarised his attitude:

'A reform of such scope and description as to satisfy all reasonable demands and remove at once, and forever, all rational grounds for complaint from the minds of the intelligent and independent portion of the community.'

In March 1831, Lord John Russell introduced the Bill to the House of Commons amid popular excitement in the country at large. It took 15 months before the Bill was finally passed and illustrated the extent of Tory opposition to it, especially in the House of Lords.

Why was the first Reform Bill defeated?

The first Reform Bill, introduced by Russell, aimed to redistribute 100 rotten and pocket boroughs and give seats to the industrial North and Midlands. Generally, the Commons was alarmed at the proposals, which also included a £10 qualification for voting rights in the boroughs. There had been some discussion on the introduction of a secret ballot, but this was dropped after pressure by members of the aristocracy. Thomas Attwood and the political union welcomed the proposals because they would retain the alliance between the middle and working classes. However, some working-class activists had already seen that the property qualification would mean that most of the working class would not receive the vote.

The first Bill managed to pass its second reading in the Commons by one vote, but was defeated in the committee stage. Grey took the initiative and called a general election in April 1831, which became a national **referendum** on the issue of reform. The result was a triumph for Grey. Although the Tories held on to some of the rotten boroughs, the Whigs increased their support in the counties and were returned with a majority of 130. Grey took this as a signal to proceed with his reform plans and a second bill was duly drawn up.

Referendum: A vote in which the people in a country or area are asked to say whether they agree or disagree with a particular policy.

Why did the defeat of the second Reform Bill have serious consequences?

A slightly amended Bill was introduced in the summer of 1831 and by September had passed through the Commons and committee stages relatively unscathed, before reaching the House of Lords. The Lords, at this time, was dominated by Tory peers, who were opposed to the idea of changing the electoral system. They regarded the Bill as the first taste of democracy, equating reform of the lower house (the Commons) as a prelude to changes in the upper house (the Lords). Grey, however, realised that if any Bill was to become law it had to pass successfully through the Lords. As their Lordships possessed an absolute veto on any government bill, however large the majority in the Commons, it was obvious that the second measure was destined for the same fate as its predecessor. In October, the Bill was duly defeated by 41 votes.

The introduction of the third Bill, December 1831

The third measure was presented to Parliament in December 1831. By this time, the Whigs' Commons majority had risen to 162, but more importantly the anti-reformers in the Lords now only had a majority of nine. This could only realistically be overcome if William IV were willing to agree to the creation of Whig peers in the upper house to neutralise the Tory influence. It looked as if the Bill would pass relatively easily through the Commons, but it was surprisingly defeated in the committee stage by a Tory amendment in March 1832.

This had the possibility of weakening the Bill, but Grey pressed on only too aware that the creation of new peers was unavoidable. However, he did so rather reluctantly, claiming at the time 'I wish to God it could be avoided'. The King refused to accept Grey's demands because of the many constitutional implications. Almost immediately, in May 1832, Grey resigned.

How does a Bill become an Act?

In Parliament there are different types of legislation:

A Private Bill: This is a proposal for legislation usually put forward by a private individual or company for a specific purpose. For instance, Acts of Parliament permitting the construction of specific turnpike roads, canals and railways began as private bills.

A Private Member's Bill: This is a proposal for legislation put forward by a Member of Parliament who is not a member of the government. The Merchant Shipping Act, 1875, began life as a private member's bill put forward by the MP for Derby, Samuel Plimsoll.

A Public Bill: This is a proposal for reform put forward by the government.

Private Member's Bills and Public Bills follow the same process. They can be introduced either into the House of Commons or the House of Lords.

First reading: an announcement to the House that a proposal for reform will be considered in the near future.

Second reading: the stage when the principle of the proposal is debated and voted on. If defeated in a vote, the proposal is withdrawn.

The Committee stage: the House appoints a committee of members who study the proposal in detail. Amendments and alterations to the proposal can be made at this stage. Once scrutiny of the proposal has been concluded, the Bill is sent back to the full House. This is the most important stage of the process.

Report Stage: the Bill is then reported back to the House where it can be debated and alterations proposed by the whole House.

Third reading: the amended Bill is then 'read' before being sent to the other House of Parliament where it goes through the same procedure. Up to 1911 the House of Lords had the right to veto (reject) Bills proposed by the House of Commons.

Royal assent: once the bill has passed all its stages in the two Houses of Parliament, the monarch must then sign it before it can become law. Technically, the monarch can veto a Bill by not signing it. The last monarch to do so was Queen Anne in 1703 with the Scottish Militia Bill.

Why was the 'May Days' crisis of 1832 important?

The country was once again plunged into the depths of potential catastrophe. The King had no alternative but to approach the Duke of Wellington to try to form a Tory ministry. The Duke's opinions on reform were well known and if any reform was passed the public knew it would be severely diluted. The public outcry reached revolutionary intensity once again. Mass demonstrations were organised in Birmingham by the National Union, under Thomas Attwood. In London, Francis Place's political union

Run on the banks: Francis Place encouraged people to close down their bank accounts. As banks keep only a fraction of deposits in the form of cash, such a policy could cause banks to collapse through an inability to meet their debts.

Why do you think it was so difficult to pass the Reform Act of 1832?

---

urged a **run on the banks**, refusal to pay taxes and a proposed takeover of local government. 'To stop the Duke, go for gold' was the rallying cry as strikes and demonstrations gripped the country once again.

In the event, Wellington's attempts to form a government proved useless. William IV was now prepared to agree to the creation of the new peers to solve a major constitutional crisis. Accordingly, the King asked Grey to form a ministry four days later. Under the most severe public pressure, the anti-reform stance collapsed completely and the threat of the creation of the new peers was enough to convince the Lords they had to give way. Most Tory peers abstained and the Bill was passed on its third reading, by 106 to 22. On 7 June 1832, the Bill received royal approval.

3.4 Was Britain on the brink of revolution in 1830–1832?
A CASE STUDY IN HISTORICAL INTERPRETATION

It is usually the case that revolutions occur when political change fails to respond to economic distress. Criticism of any unpopular regime usually has an economic motive, and this was certainly the case in Britain in 1830. The mounting pressure to change an unrepresentative electoral system was given further impetus by a sharp deterioration in the economy.

The crisis was caused by harvest failure, high prices and unemployment that fell most heavily on the agricultural sector and was restricted geographically to the south of the country. The rural unrest started in the summer of 1830, and has been described by the historian Asa Briggs as the 'village labourers' revolt'. The unrest took on many different forms, such as the destruction of threshing machines and the burning of corn. It also had a political slant, expressed in hatred towards tithes and the administration of the **Poor Law**. Gaining momentum through the made-up name of 'Captain Swing', these so-called 'swing riots' lasted for over a year and alarmed the landowners who had always regarded the south-east of England as the most loyal part of the country.

Poor Law: This related to the support of paupers in the community, especially when there was no concept of a welfare state as we have today. Before 1834, each parish was responsible for its own poor. However, after the 1834 Poor Law Amendment Act the system became much harsher.

Magistrates: Officials who act as judges in law courts which deal with less serious crimes or disputes. They decide whether cases are important enough to be passed on to higher courts.

The Whig Government was in no mood to compromise, and dealt with the unrest swiftly and decisively. Lord Melbourne, the Home Secretary, urged **magistrates** to take a hard line: special courts were established to deal with the rioters and, in September 1830, nine labourers were hanged and many more transported abroad. These disturbances were not an attempt to incite a national revolution and many issues were localised and dealt with effectively by the authorities. They were, however, a sharp reminder to those in charge at Westminster that the country could not tolerate any more delay over the main political issues of the day.

The case for

Was this situation the most serious threat a government has had to face in Britain in peacetime? The political crisis over electoral reform created an almost revolutionary climate in Britain in 1830–32. The defeat of the Second Reform Bill by the Lords, in October 1831, caused widespread unrest. The historian E.P. Thompson claims that 'Britain came within an ace of revolution between 1830 and 1832'. There is no doubt that, in the autumn of 1831, this comment may well have been most applicable. Eric Evans suggests that 'Britain was never as close to revolution as in the autumn of 1831'. The public's high expectations had been badly let down by the Lords who were regarded as being completely out of touch with the people's wishes. This defiant gesture by a small grouping provoked an immediate outburst all over the country.

As well as pressure from the Birmingham Political Union, Francis Place made London the centre of opposition to the Lords but not the Whig Government. Elsewhere, there were violent protests throughout the country. Many members of the Lords who identified with anti-reform, such as the Duke of Wellington and the Duke of Cumberland, were attacked as mob rule threatened to overrun the country. Furthermore, some Anglican bishops came under attack for their decision to vote against the Bill. Riots spread from the capital and large-scale incidents occurred in Derby and Nottingham. The most serious rioting occurred in Bristol on 29 October, when a violent mob attacked the city centre in what can only be described as a serious breach of public order. The only thing that prevented full-scale revolution at this stage was the Government's desire to proceed with reform. The Whig Government decided not to resign at this very tense time but to carry on with their reform proposals and attempt to direct violent protest into 'safe and legitimate reform'.

The May Days crisis of 1832 again saw the public anger for reform reach the intensity of the previous autumn. Demonstrations in London and Birmingham were especially critical of Wellington's refusal to entertain the idea of reform, but thankfully the Lords gave way and the tension diffused itself.

The case against

The Whig determination to proceed with reform regardless of the public opposition of the Tories and the King must be regarded as the most important reason. Earl Grey was enough of a politician to realise that the defeat of the first two Bills and the public disturbances that followed would increase the desire to proceed with reform. Public opinion was something that he was acutely aware of, but as always his intention was 'reforming to preserve' rather than letting the floodgates open to democracy.

The decision in May 1832 to allow the Third Bill through the Lords was a momentous one. The upper house had been a constant brake on any change but their decision to absent themselves deserves some praise, even though they only agreed to the measure because they feared for their own position within the constitution if the disturbances had continued. Moderate reform was more of a safeguard of their position than violent revolution.

The violence of the period also proved too much for the fragile alliance between the middle and working classes. Once the terms of the Act became clear, the artisans under Attwood signified their disapproval of the more radical elements of the working classes. This split in the reform movement made the potential for armed revolution much easier to control. The disappointment of the radicals would be much more acute when the terms were finally approved in the summer of 1832.

1. Using the evidence, choose two reasons for and against the view that Britain was on the brink of revolution between 1830 and 1832.

2. Using material from both this and previous chapters, why do you think the period 1830–1832 was such a difficult situation for the Whig Government?

3.5 How far did the Reform Act change the electoral system?

The main changes brought about by the 1832 Reform Act can be summarised as follows:

- The same number of seats was retained, at 658.

- 56 boroughs of fewer than 2,000 votes in England were totally disenfranchised.

- 31 small boroughs lost one of their two MPs.

- 22 new two-member constituencies were created (for example, Manchester, Leeds and Birmingham).

- In addition, 20 new single-member constituencies were created.
- Representation of the counties was increased by 61 members to a total of 253.
- Uniform property qualification of £10 in boroughs.
- Scottish electorate increased substantially to 65,000, while Ireland had three times the population of Scotland but less than twice the representation.
- New electorate totalling approximately 813,000 out of a population of 24 million (less than 500,000 before 1832). Electorate increased substantially but still only a small percentage of the population. Now about one in seven males could vote.
- All voters to enlist to qualify for the vote.
- No secret ballot. Landlord intimidation could still occur.

What were Whig motives in passing the reform?

Grey was speaking the truth when he talked of the Bill as an aristocratic measure that was designed primarily to safeguard the country against revolution. As the historian E.A. Smith claims, 'Grey presented reform as a means to restore the old constitution, not to create a new democratic one'. Although the Whigs had on the face of it changed the political map forever, their achievement was limited and would be in need of severe modification at a later date, notably in 1867 and 1884.

How did the electoral changes affect the middle class?

One of the major changes was the enfranchisement of the 'respectable classes' (i.e. those that qualified for the uniform £10 householder franchise). These included small-scale businessmen, shopkeepers and some skilled craftsmen. This had the desired effect of splitting the alliance between the middle classes and the working class.

Contemporary middle-class newspapers such as the *Leeds Mercury* and the *Manchester Guardian* received the news of reform with 'strong emotions of joy and hope'. Yet there was no immediate influx of middle-class MPs into Parliament, as local politics were seen to be far more rewarding than the laborious tasks of central government.

Moreover, most middle-class gentlemen simply could not afford the cost of being a Member of Parliament. There was no salary, and with Parliament sitting for most of the year it was seen as a full-time job. The composition of Parliament, therefore, remained largely unaltered from what it had been before 1832. The aristocracy continued to exert an enormous influence on events at Westminster long after the Act was passed.

Why did the working class feel betrayed by the terms of the Act?

The *Poor Man's Guardian*, a mouthpiece of radicalism, was correct when it claimed in 1832, 'the millions will not stop at shadows but proceed onwards to realities'. The working-class sense of betrayal was deepened by the terms of the 1832 Reform Act. The Whigs made no attempt to deny that the £10 test was designed to exclude the lower classes from the vote. As the National Union of the Working Classes claimed, 'the Bill is a mere trick to strengthen the towering exclusiveness of our blessed constitution'. This sense of disappointment could only lead to demands for further reform and, towards the end of the decade, the Chartist movement was born from the ashes of the Reform Act.

How did reform affect the House of Commons and the Lords?

The profile of the House of Commons, the representative element in the constitution, was strengthened as a result of reform. The crisis revealed the power a determined government possessed, especially when armed with a majority in the Commons and backed by public opinion, to overcome the opposition of nobility and monarchy. As far as the House of Lords was concerned, the abolition of the nomination boroughs (pocket boroughs) reduced the scope for exercising their patronage in choosing representatives in the Commons.

Even so, this over-estimates the impact of the Act on Parliament. The aristocracy and landowning classes continued to have a strong and influential role in affairs. For example, up until 1858 county members had to possess a landed estate of £600. As Robert Stewart claims, in *Party and Politics 1830–52* (1989), 'politics was a money-spending, not a money-making, occupation'. It has been calculated that only 52.5% of elections were actually contested between 1832 and 1867, and the opportunities for corruption may even have increased. Grey's refusal to entertain the idea of a secret ballot meant intimidation still occurred at elections – whole estates being coerced into voting for their landlord.

Why did the Crown's influence decline as a result of the Act?

The Act severely restricted the power the Crown had in influencing events at Westminster. Rotten and pocket boroughs had been a powerful source of royal patronage in the Commons. In addition, the crisis revealed the failure of the monarchy to deliver a majority in Parliament at a time of crisis – William IV was forced to rely on Grey after Wellington's failure to form a ministry in May 1832. Put simply, a ministry could now survive without the support of the Crown and Lords but not without the support of the Commons.

How did the Act promote more effective party organisation?

The reform crisis and the terms of the Act increased the possibility of a two-party system. The Act made provisions for the registration of voters who had to enrol to qualify for, and satisfy, the £10 property qualification. The result was that both Whigs and Tories had to organise themselves on a national basis and be acutely aware of public opinion by way of local party managers. The establishment of the Tory Carlton Club (1832) and the Whig Reform Club (1836) was a further impetus to this trend. Scotland, Wales and Ireland increased their representation, and any contested election in these countries tended to be won by the Whigs, who gradually built up their influence outside the southern counties. Even so, the influence of independent MPs continued to be considerable and in many constituencies local, rather than national, issues tended to dominate.

Why did the 1832 Reform Act lead to demand for future changes?

1. What do you regard as the most important consequence of the 1832 Reform Act?

2. Which groups were most pleased and most disappointed by these changes? Give reasons to support your answer.

Perhaps the most important consequence of the 1832 Reform Act was that it prepared the way for further political, social and economic change. It was the first and most important assault on the 18th-century constitution and the starting point on the road to democracy, even though that was not the intention of those who sponsored the Act. The Whigs had regarded it as a final settlement but the trickle of electoral reform eventually became a flood in 1867 and 1884. As historian John Derry claims, 'Earl Grey's Reform was conservative in the best sense of the word as it prepared the way for a century of peaceful political evolution.'

Source-based questions: Great Reform Act 1832

SOURCE A

Such, generally speaking, as the House of Commons is now, such it has been for a long succession of years: it is the most complete representation of the interests of the people, which was ever assembled in any age or any country. It is the only constituent body that ever existed, which comprehends within itself those who can urge the wants and defend the claims of the landed, the commercial, the professional classes of the country: those who are bound to uphold the interests of the lower classes, the rights and liberties of the whole people. It is the very absence of symmetry* in our elective franchises which admits of the introduction to this House of classes so various.

* symmetry = common rights to vote

From a speech by Sir Robert Inglis to the House of Commons, March 1831. Sir Robert Inglis was a strong opponent of reform.

SOURCE B

A criticism of the Pre-Reform Parliament by Cruikshank, 1831. Cruikshank was a leading cartoonist and savage critic of the existing system. The date is important bearing in mind how close it was to the passage of the Reform Act in 1832. 'St Stephens' refers to the House of Commons and the people around the trough are the recipients of the money and corruption from the closed or rotten boroughs (listed on the waterwheel). The whole system is propped up by muskets which suggest it can only be defended forcibly. Sleeping below 'St Stephens' are people unaware of the situation, preferring to sleep through rather than challenge obvious corruption and waste of public money.

SOURCE C

The end of government is the happiness of the people; and I do not conceive that, in a country like this, the happiness of the people can be promoted by a form of government in which the middle classes place no confidence, and which exists only because the middle classes have no organ by which to make their sentiments known.

A speech in the House of Commons, March 1831, by T.B. McCauley, a Whig MP who supported the idea of limited reform.

SOURCE D

27 Feb.   Anything which amounts to the formation of a new Constitution I oppose …

2 March   We are quite appalled. There is not the remotest chance of such a Bill being passed by this or any House of Commons … This really is a revolution ? … It is unquestionably a new constitution. The general sentiment is that the measure goes a good deal too far. It is applauded by the Radicals and by some Whigs, but it is very distasteful to a great part of the Whig Party.

3 March   The general belief is that the Bill must be thrown out on the second reading. I expect Ministers will then resign and anarchy begin … I feel inclined as a choice of evils to support and even speak out in favour of the Bill.

5 March   The measure takes very much with the country.

8 March   I still consider the Bill dangerously violent, but apprehend less danger from passing it than rejecting it.

27 March The chance of the Bill being carried by the present Parliament is the certainty that it would be carried by the new parliament.

From the diary of John Campbell, 1831. Campbell was a moderate Whig; he was unaware that some modification of the system was needed.

Source-based questions: Great Reform Act 1832

1. Study Source D.

What is meant by 'second reading' in the passage of the 1832 Reform Act?

2. Study Source C.

How reliable is this source as evidence of support for the reform of Parliament?

3. Study Sources B and D.

How far do these sources agree on the weaknesses of Parliament before the passage of the 1832 Reform Act?

4. Study Sources C and D.

How, by use of language and style, do both authors suggest that the reform of Parliament was needed?

5. 'The pressures for the reform of Parliament were both widespread and inevitable.' Using the sources and the rest of this chapter, how far do you agree with this statement?

Further Reading

Articles

'The Great Reform Act Reconsidered' by Eric Evans, *History Sixth* No. 3 (1988)
'An Aristocrat fights the old political order: Political changes probable' by E.A. Smith, *New Perspective* (1995)

Texts designed for AS and A2 level students

The Great Reform Act by Eric Evans (Routledge, Lancaster Pamphlet, 2nd edition 1994)
Britain before the Reform Act: Politics and society 1815–32 by Eric Evans (Longman, Seminar Studies series, 1989)
Democracy and Reform 1815–83 by D.G. Wright (Longman, Seminar Studies series, 1989)
Government and Reform 1815–1918 by Robert Pearce and Roger Stearn (Hodder & Stoughton, Access to A Level series, 1994)
Whigs, Radicals and Liberals by D. Watts (Hodder & Stoughton, Access to A Level series, 1995)

More advanced reading

Aristocracy and People – Britain 1815–65 by Norman Gash (Edward Arnold, 1987)
The Age of Improvement 1763–1867 by Asa Briggs (Longman, 1969)
The Great Reform Act by M. Brock (Oxford University Press, 1973)
Reform or Revolution? A Diary of Reform 1830–1832 by E.A. Smith (Sutton, 1992)
Party and Politics 1830–1852 by Robert Stewart (Macmillan, 1989)
England in the 1830s: A Decade of Reform by G. Finlayson (Edward Arnold, 1969)

4 Chartism

Key Issues

- Why did a working-class protest movement emerge in the 1830s and 1840s?

- How serious was the Chartists' threat to the political system?

- Why did Chartism fail?

Framework of Events

1832	Reform Act fails to satisfy the working classes who are denied the vote
1834	Poor Law Amendment Act produces a hostile reaction, especially in North of England
1836	London Working Men's Association (LWMA) founded
1837	January: LWMA draws up the six points of the Charter
	May: Birmingham Political Union revived by Thomas Attwood
	November: *Northern Star* first published in Leeds
1838	People's Charter first published
1839	February: General Convention meets in London
	May: Convention moves to Birmingham
	June: First Petition presented to Parliament
	July: Petition rejected by 235 votes to 46
	November: Newport Rising. Severe economic crisis begins
1840	July: National Charter Association (NCA) founded in Manchester
1841	August: Feargus O'Connor released from jail
1842	January: Complete Suffrage Union (CSU) founded in Birmingham
	May: Second Chartist Petition presented to Parliament and rejected by 287 votes to 49
	August: Strikes break out in 23 English counties. Plug Riots. Trade begins to revive
1843	William Lovett abandons the movement
1845	April: Chartist Land Cooperative founded
1846	June: Act passed to repeal the Corn Laws
1848	Third Petition presented to Parliament
1851	National Land Cooperation wound up
1855	Death of Feargus O'Connor.

Overview

THE Chartist Movement had its origins in the radical tradition that flourished in Britain during the 18th century. It aimed to change the existing post-1832 political settlement to create a fairer system that would meet the political wishes of the working class, as well as the middle class. It was certainly the largest

William Lovett (1800–1877)

and most important assault by the lower orders on the political establishment during the 19th century and tended to provoke a very hostile reaction, especially in Parliament. The reasons why Chartism developed can be explained partly by the failure of the 1832 Reform Act to satisfy the expectations of those denied the vote, as well as other more immediate causes, such as the introduction of the new Poor Law in 1834. Its impact also fluctuated depending on the economic health of the nation: Chartism was more popular when the dark shadow of unemployment and high prices affected the lives of ordinary working people. Economic slumps in 1837–42 and 1847–48 coincided with large-scale unrest.

There is no doubt that, at its height, Chartism did attract the mass support the 3 million signatures of the Second Petition of 1842 suggest. Yet it still was not able to penetrate the minds of the majority of MPs who rejected several petitions point blank. During the 1840s, it also attempted to widen its appeal through a potential alliance with the other major protest movement of the period, the Anti-Corn Law League. The fact that this alliance collapsed suggests a fundamental difference between those Chartists who looked for a peaceful or '**moral force**' solution and the more extreme '**physical force**' part of the movement. The last major expression of Chartism was in 1846–50, but after the rejection of the Third Petition and a return of prosperity in the 1850s, it seemed that the Chartist message had failed.

The movement produced many celebrated figures, such as William Lovett and Feargus O'Connor, who attempted to expand Chartist activity into a Land Plan and a more comprehensive education programme for the working classes. This broadened the appeal of the movement, but in the short term Chartism failed to achieve its objectives due primarily to the strength of Peel's Government. To simply dismiss Chartism as a failure would not do justice to the vital lessons working people learnt in organising themselves against what they regarded as an abuse of basic human rights. Over a period of time, all but one of the six points of the Charter were implemented, which may suggest that it was not the complete failure some historians would have us believe.

'Moral force' Chartism: This was the idea that Chartism could achieve its aims through non-violent, peaceful protest and make closer links with the moderate elements of the middle class. William Lovett was the leading spokesman for this view.

'Physical force' Chartism: These Chartists believed that the only way to change the existing political system was through violence when all other forms of protest had failed. 'Physical force' Chartists were especially prominent in the Newport rising of 1839.

1. Place the reasons mentioned in the mind map in order of importance in explaining why Chartism failed.

2. Which of these reasons for failure were self-inflicted by the Chartists themselves?

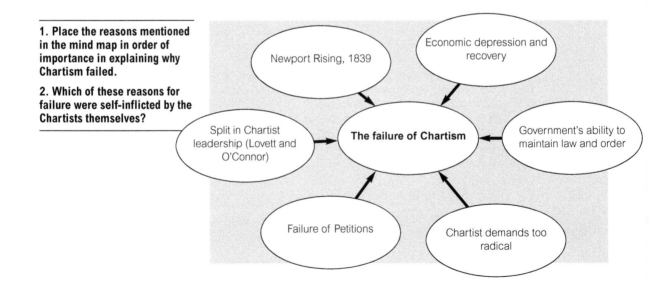

4.1 What were the causes of Chartism?

Chartism was the world's first working-class movement. It aimed to change the existing political situation in Britain by widening the electoral laws. Historians find it a difficult movement to categorise, primarily because of the fact that it had such varied components and interests. However, in identifying what produced the movement in the 1830s and 1840s a number of factors are now considered vitally important.

1 The disappointment of the 1832 Reform Act

The passage of the 1832 Reform Act was heralded by its supporters as the final settlement of a difficult constitutional issue and one which had averted a potential revolution in Britain. The major beneficiaries were the middle classes who were now given a say in the election of MPs to Parliament. The Act, however, was viewed in a completely different manner by the working classes, who saw the Bill as treachery of the highest order. Many working-class boroughs, such as Middlesex, had been disenfranchised, as well as those with burgage tenants and Scot and Lot taxpayers (see page 63). The working class, without the property qualification that was required to vote, still felt alienated from the political system that was being used as they saw it to undermine their interests. As the historian S.J. Lee claims, in *Aspects of British Political History 1815–1914* (1994) 'the Chartists aimed at removing the cut off point each social class seemed bent on applying against the class immediately below itself'.

2 The continuing tradition of radical politics

Since the 18th century, there had always been a strong radical tradition in British politics despite the attempts of Lord Liverpool's Government to crush it between 1815 and 1821. Key figures such as Henry Hunt, William Cobbett and Major Cartwright continued to press their demands for political and economic change. Even the deaths of Hunt and Cobbett in 1835 failed to stop the spread of the radical message, as new leaders such as Feargus O'Connor filled their shoes. The continuity of working-class protest against the inequalities of the political system is a key point to understand in assessing Chartism.

3 The unstamped press

Part of this strong radical tradition had always been an emphasis on the written word via a strong, radical press. William Cobbett's *Twopenny Trash* and Thomas Wooler's *Black Dwarf* had been instrumental in creating a climate for educated discussion in the coffee houses of the major industrial centres. The Six Acts of 1819 had attempted to stifle the press by introducing a 'stamp duty'. This pushed up prices and made it very difficult for the radical press, as it existed, to survive. Yet, between 1830 and 1834, hundreds of small political papers were established, such as Hetherington's *Poor Man's Guardian* which was deliberately published 'contrary to the law', failing to carry a stamp or sell at a minimum legal price of 7d (3p). The paper continued to be published despite 'the so-called taxes on knowledge'. This gave the emerging Chartist Movement, through its influential newspapers *Northern Star* and *The Poor Man's Guardian*, a wider audience for their ideas. A network of local agents was already well in place by the time the Chartist message began to widen, and one of Chartism's key subsidiary organisations – the London Working Men's Association – had strong connections with the printing industry.

4 Opposition to Whig social legislation

Working-class discontent was increasing because of the effects of the factory system and the operation of the New Poor Law of 1834. In the factories, the long working hours were the subject of numerous campaigns, notably the '10 Hours Movement' which attempted to reduce the workday to ten hours and to keep children out of the factories. Reaction to the New Poor Law was even more marked. The abolition of existing forms of poor relief and their availability only in the dreaded workhouse created the idea that poverty was due to laziness. Ending the current system, it was argued, would force people to look for work, but the Act had completely underestimated the causes of poverty in England and helped fuel the flames of working-class discontent.

The movement against the Poor Law was especially strong in the North of England where depression had hit the textile industry in 1837–38, while technological change had led to the erosion of jobs, wages and the social position of the handloom weavers (an influential group supporting Chartism). It has been estimated that with the rise of mechanised textile factories about 400,000 handloom weavers faced economic ruin. As a result of these pressures, there were inevitable violent incidents, such as in Huddersfield and Bradford where the Poor Law Guardians had to be protected by the local cavalry, and at Todmorden where police constables were attacked and troops called in to restore law and order. By 1837, Feargus O'Connor had established the *Northern Star* in Leeds to campaign for an end to the Poor Law. The movement, although failing to influence the Government, did have an important bearing on future Chartist strategy.

5 Economic origins

To many historians, Chartism was a 'knife and fork question' – that is, it was most closely associated with periods of economic hardship and with the transformation of the British economy through the process of industrialisation. Chartism reached its height during periods of economic depression: the late 1830s, 1842 and 1837–48. This seems to suggest that the appeal of the Charter came from a desire to alter the political system in order to gain economic change. The process of industrialisation also meant that certain trades faced decline with the onset of mechanisation. The most significantly affected group were the handloom weavers. Numbering approximately 400,000 in the early 1840s, this section of the work force faced the prospect of declining wages as new machines were introduced into the textile industry.

As a result, Chartism tended to be strongest in areas undergoing change through industrialisation such as Stockport in Cheshire and the West Riding of Yorkshire.

1. What were the major reasons why Chartism developed as a movement by 1839?

2. Did the movement owe its origins to the circumstances of the 1830s or were there longer-term reasons for its growth?

4.2 What was so appealing about the Charter?

The appeal of the People's Charter

The publication of the Charter, in the spring of 1839, was made by the London Working Men's Association. The six points of the Charter need individual explanation.

- *The vote for all males over 21*
  This had obvious appeal as it stated that all men, regardless of the property they owned, were worthy of a vote in the election of MPs and therefore should have a say in the political affairs of the nation. This was finally introduced in 1918.

- *Secret ballot*
  Many voters had been intimidated by their landlords or employers to vote not according to their conscience but under the threat of eviction. A secret ballot, it was claimed, would take away this pressure. Finally introduced in 1872.

- *Equality of constituency size*
  This was demanded so that each constituency would be the same size. The idea behind it was that regional variations would disappear and each town and city would have equal representation in Parliament. Even the strongest Chartist supporters, however, were aware of the problems that an increased number of Irish MPs would bring at Westminster. Finally introduced in 1885.

- *No property qualifications for MPs*
  Radicals claimed that the need for a property qualification to enter Parliament prevented many from standing for office. Feargus O'Connor, for example, was disqualified from his seat in 1835 for that precise reason. This was abolished in 1858.

- *Annual Parliaments*
  Originally passed in 1716, the Septennial Act ordered that elections need only take place every seven years but the reform crisis had revealed the system to be outdated as three were held between 1830 and 1832. Annual general elections would be genuinely democratic and give a fairer representation of the people's views because MPs had to face re-election each year. This has never been implemented.

- *Payment of MPs*
  Since all these changes would alter the social composition of MPs at Westminster it was demanded that MPs should be paid and not be reliant on private income, as they had been previously. This was finally passed in 1911.

1. Which of the six points of the Charter do you find the most appealing?

2. Why would the People's Charter have aroused such criticism from a Tory aristocrat?

Give reasons to support your answers.

4.3 What were the main features of the Chartist movement between 1839 and 1850?

Thomas Attwood (1783–1856)

The failure of the Three Petitions

The First Petition, 1839

The unrest and hatred towards the Whig Government of the 1830s obviously had to have some visible form of protest. The London Working Men's Association, formed in 1836, and the revival of Thomas Attwood's Birmingham Political Union in 1837 were at the forefront of the protests. In 1838, Attwood drew up a petition based on the ideas put forward by the People's Charter. During the course of the year, a number of high-profile mass meetings were held that were especially well attended in the North of England. The idea of a petition was not new, but the question emerged of what to do if Parliament rejected it? A national convention was called in London, in 1839, to discuss strategy and to develop the idea of a 'national holiday' or general strike. O'Connor advocated using the threat of physical force, but the more moderate members of the leadership, under Lovett, maintained that peaceful methods were more likely to succeed. By May 1839, 1.2 million signatures had been gathered. However, Parliament was in recess as a result of Melbourne's resignation over the Jamaican constitution, so the convention moved to Birmingham where there was continued talk of violence and armed struggle.

For a while it seemed as if popular pressure would force Parliament to make changes as it had in 1832. Yet Parliament showed a greater resolve in rejecting the petition by 235 votes to 46. Disappointed by this outcome, the idea of 'a sacred month' of strikes was put forward but the whole episode revealed inherent weaknesses such as a division in the leadership over strategy and a lack of support in Parliament.

Cartoon from *Punch* published in 1848.

NOT SO *VERY* UNREASONABLE !!! EH?

1. Study the cartoon. How are the Chartists portrayed?

2. Do you think the cartoonist is in favour of, or against, the Chartists' message? Give reasons to support your answer.

The Second Petition, 1842

Despite the failures of 1839, a hard core of Chartists still believed in the vision of a new society based on the six points of the Charter. Although morale was low and many of the leading personalities had been imprisoned, the hard core was determined to continue the fight for what they regarded as 'natural justice'. Economic recession, which had always been a stimulus to political unrest in this period, re-emerged with increasing vigour in 1841–42. Unemployment, low wages and despair were to be the raw materials for a more violent outburst of Chartist activity in 1842. This coincided with the establishment of the second Chartist convention, which met in London in April 1842. It presented Parliament with a new petition containing 3.3 million signatures the following month. The petition was again rejected by 287 votes to 49, despite the lawful, peaceful protest. Once again, the political establishment had held firm and resisted pressure to change the political system.

The Third Petition, 1848

The usual cocktail of ingredients reappeared towards the end of the 1840s to bring the Chartist message to the fore once again. A depression had hit all the major industrial areas and unemployment had risen dramatically. This provoked O'Connor into action once again. In 1847, he was elected as MP for Nottingham and drew up plans for the relaunch of a National Convention and the presentation of a new petition to Parliament. On this occasion, his plans seemed to be more ambitious, as there was talk of a new Republican constitution with O'Connor as President. In addition, the Chartist message was given a sharper focus by the news of a revolution in France, in February 1848, that overthrew the unpopular government of Louis Philippe. By April 1848, plans were made for a huge open-air rally on Kennington Common, London, which would coincide with a march to present the Third Petition to Parliament.

The whole atmosphere was very tense, but the response of Russell's Government ensured that the whole protest fizzled out. The march on Parliament was banned and only a handful of Chartists were allowed to accompany O'Connor to present the Petition, which was found to contain a disappointing 2 million signatures. Also, the Government had put the defence of the capital in the hands of the ageing Duke of Wellington and created thousands of special constables, including the future Napoleon III of France. Not surprisingly, Parliament rejected the petition by a huge majority. This proved to be the last great upsurge in Chartist support. The circulation of the *Northern Star*, a useful indicator of Chartist support, dropped dramatically and O'Connor was declared insane before he died in 1855.

The use of violence

The Newport Rising, 1839

The failure of the National Convention and the rejection of the First Petition were two of the many reasons why the South Wales valleys rose in revolt at the end of 1839. The area had been a hothouse of industrialisation, especially in the iron and coal industries, but living and working conditions remained appalling, spawning a rich radical and trade unionist tradition.

On 3–4 November 1839, a demonstration was held in Newport, centred on the Westgate Hotel. It degenerated into violence, and soldiers fired on the conspirators. Modern historians such as D.J.V. Jones now accept that the Newport insurrection was not part of a national strategy and was merely part of a local expression of unrest. However, the event did have national consequences. John Frost and Zephania Williams, two of the

Feargus O'Connor (1794–1855)

The most well-known spokesman of the Chartist movement, O'Connor was MP for Cork 1832–35. He was at the forefront of the anti-poor law campaign and this led to his involvement with the Chartist protest. Initially through the *Northern Star* but gradually through his powerful public speaking, O'Connor advocated the 'physical force' element of Chartism and was associated with the failed Land Plan of the 1840s. In 1847, he was elected MP for Nottingham. Always controversial, his career was tragically cut short when he was declared insane in 1852 and died three years later.

Plug Riots at Preston,
Lancashire, August 1842

leading conspirators, were transported abroad for life whilst other leading Chartists, such as Lovett and O'Connor, were arrested and imprisoned. The first period of Chartist activity had been a resounding victory for the authorities.

The Plug Riots, 1842

The revival of the Chartist message coincided with a serious outbreak of Chartist unrest in 1842. There were violent protests during the summer months in Staffordshire, Lancashire, Cheshire and Yorkshire, as well as in many other counties in England. Part of this was the so-called Plug Plot (a sabotage campaign to remove the plugs from factory boilers), especially in the North and Midlands. The extent to which Chartists were involved in these activities remains uncertain but the desire to implement the six points of the Charter was a convenient excuse used by many across the country.

The New Charter Association general council meeting in August 1842 was unwittingly forced to approve a general strike to take place on 14 August. Yet many Chartists had reservations and Peel's Government was able to turn the issue on its head by accusing the Chartist leadership of organising a general strike. The violence of 1842 was far worse than 1839, but the authorities had again won the day and ensured that imprisonment and transportation were standard punishment for industrial unrest. By the end of the year, misery, hopelessness and hunger were forcing people back to work and in such a desperate situation support for Chartism levelled off.

Political organisations

Chartism created a number of important political organisations in this period. The most significant of these was the New Charter Association (NCA), founded in Manchester in July 1840. This organisation provided the central organisation that the Chartist movement had previously lacked. According to historian Edward Royle, 'The New Charter Association became the backbone of Chartism for the next 12 years'. The national structure ensured that 'localities' were well represented: by April 1842, there were 401 such organisations with a membership of around 50,000. Increasingly, the NCA began to make tentative links with other campaigning groups, such as the Anti-Corn Law League. The League was predominantly a middle-class organisation and gradually became uneasy about the presence of O'Connor and other 'physical force' Chartists. Indeed, further links were made and the 'moral force' element of the movement increased by the establishment of the Complete Suffrage Union (CSU) in 1842. The CSU had grown out of the Birmingham Political Union and was moderate enough to recognise that cooperation between itself, the NCA and the Anti-Corn Law League was the way forward. Lovett and Lowery were leading members, together with Joseph Sturge and Edward Miall.

Other areas of Chartist activity

Chartism was far more than just a political movement and a number of leading Chartists attempted to widen the appeal of the movement in a number of important areas.

Education
William Lovett, for example, had always been keen to stress the link between Chartism and education. For him, the two were important concepts: political change could not come about without an educated public. Lovett had always been attracted by the non-violent appeal of the movement and had never denied the attraction of closer cooperation with the Anti-Corn Law League. To men like Feargus O'Connor, this was unacceptable and by 1843 personal dislike, as well as division over future policy, had forced Lovett out of the movement.

Christian Chartism and local government
Chartist activity was also prominent in religious circles. In Scotland, the idea of 'Christian Chartism' developed, stressing the link between God and the democratic freedom Chartists demanded. Individuals, such as Joshua Hobson in Leeds and Isaac Ironside in Sheffield, were also prominent in local government affairs.

The Land Plan
Feargus O'Connor was credited with the idea of developing a Chartist Land Plan in this period. The idea was to ease the unemployment situation as well as giving the settlers freedom and self-respect. The establishment of the Chartist Cooperative Land Society in 1845 was based on the following ideas:

- each family was given a 4-acre plot and cottage, paying an annual rent of £1.5s an acre

- Chartists bought shares for £1.6s each.

The whole experiment was a costly failure as the settlers were unused to farming methods and there was talk of financial irregularities. By 1851, the whole land experiment had been wound up in complete failure. However, some of the Chartist land settlements survived, such as Charterville (near Witney, Oxfordshire).

1. What kind of splits became apparent in the Chartist movement between 1839 and 1846?

2. Between 1839 and 1846 Chartist activists pursued their political interests in a variety of ways. How might this have

(a) strengthened the movement

(b) weakened it?

3. At what point during this period do you think the movement had the greatest chance of success?

Source-based questions: Feargus O'Connor

SOURCE A

I regard Feargus O'Connor as the chief marplot [troublemaker] of our movement … a man who, by his personal conduct joined to his malignant [destructive] influence in the Northern Star, has been the blight of democracy from the first moments he opened his mouth as its professional advocate [spokesman] … By his great professions, by trickery and deceit, he got the aid of the working classes to establish an organ to promulgate [make known] their principles, which he soon converted into an instrument for destroying everything intellectual and moral in our movement … the *Star*, a mere reflex of the nature of its master … By his constant appeals to the selfishness, vanity, and mere animal propensities [feelings] of man, he succeeded in calling up a spirit of hate, intolerance and brute feeling, previously unknown among Reformers.

From *The Life and Struggles of William Lovett* by William Lovett, published in 1876. Lovett rejected O'Connor's 'physical force' Chartism, preferring peaceful methods. The two men were great rivals.

SOURCE B

Of the importance of Feargus O'Connor as a national leader, there can be no question … O'Connor has been seen as the evil genius of the movement. In fact, so far from being the exploiter and distorter of the movement, O'Connor was so much the centre of it that, had the name Chartism not been coined, the radical movement between 1838 and 1848 must surely have been called O'Connorite Radicalism. Remove him and his newspaper and the movement fragments, localises and loses its continuity.

From *The Chartists* by Dorothy Thompson, 1984. The author takes a more sympathetic view of O'Connor's ability and writes from a left-wing standpoint.

SOURCE C

If ever men deserved to be classed among cowards and poltroons [spineless cowards], and to meet with the scorn and derision of mankind, it must be frankly confessed by all readers of Irish history that the kings of Ireland were entitled to that distinction, and none more so than the ancestors of O'Connor.

He showed himself to be either cowardly or treacherous towards those whom he styled his friends. A love of popularity was the besetting [most obvious] sin of the latter [O'Connor]. To win and retain that popularity, with O'Connor all means were justifiable.

From *History of the Chartist Movement 1837–1854* by R.G. Gammage, 1854. This was the first history of Chartism and was heavily biased against O'Connor. However, it is a useful source, drawn from contemporary observations of the leading members of the movement.

SOURCE D

A Punch cartoon from the 1840s. It compares O'Connor to Titus Annius Milo, a political radical in Rome during the 1st century BC. Like O'Connor, Milo was regarded with great suspicion by the authorities and attempted to use popular protest to change the system. In the cartoon, O'Connor is shown shaking the foundations of Peace and Order (shown by the tree) due to his emphasis on universal suffrage and vote by ballot. The lion symbolises the anger of the British public, whilst Peel and Wellington hide in the tree.

SOURCE E

No one matched O'Connor in the qualities demanded of a national leader. He was a superb platform speaker with a splendid presence, wonderfully racy and vivid in his language, and wildly funny both on the platform and in his writings. Many historians have seen only his braggadocio [boasting], the ... expressions of prophecies and claims that could never be fulfilled. But much more important was the confidence that [he] generated among the poor and downtrodden. It was this crucial belief in the righteousness of the cause, and his ability to communicate it in unequalled terms, that allowed O'Connor to tower above his fellow Chartists.

From *1884* by John Saville, 1987. This secondary source analyses the effectiveness of forces of law during the last revival of the movement.

1. Study Source A.

What is the 'Northern Star' mentioned in the source?

2. How, by his use of language and style, does William Lovett criticise Feargus O'Connor's influence on the Chartist movement?

3. Study Sources A, C and D.

How far are the sources in agreement over their criticism of Feargus O'Connor?

4. Study Source B.

How reliable is this source as evidence of O'Connor's character?

5. 'Feargus O'Connor was vital to the success of the Chartist movement.' Using the information in this chapter and the sources above, how far do you agree with this statement?

4.4 Chartism – political or economic movement?
A CASE STUDY IN HISTORICAL INTERPRETATION

Case for the 'political view'

The view that Chartism represented a politically aware working class figures strongly in the writings of historians Dorothy Thompson and James Epstein. Both argue that the movement had a coherence and organisation that allowed it to withstand the many criticisms of the working classes as incapable of being trusted with the vote. Thompson is especially keen to see the movement as 'the response of a literate and sophisticated working class' who tended to act independently of any economic conditions. This view has recently been supported by John Belchem, who dismisses the view that Chartism was merely a 'knife and fork' question. He argues that:

● the movement was political and not economic;

● based around the six points of the Charter, the movement organised its ideas on an identifiable political grievance, namely the campaign for parliamentary reform;

● this history of political protest can be traced back to the end of the Napoleonic Wars when a prominent radical tradition developed;

● Chartism itself grew out of this tradition and directed itself against anti-working-class political legislation that had been drawn up by the Whigs, such as the new Poor Law of 1834;

● ultimately, 'Chartism cannot be understood by the changes in the trade cycle, by the study of economic statistics and charts of social tension'.

Case for the 'economic view'

The economic motives in the development of the Chartist movement are also plain to see. The historian Edward Royle takes this view, claiming that 'Chartism was fired by economic discontent, not the demand for political rights'. Quite simply, economic depression and unrest helped to create the climate where political change could take place.

There is no question that Chartism grew in strength at precisely the time when the economy was undergoing recession. W.W. Rostow's social tensions theory claims that in times of 'high' tension – 1838–39, 1841–42 and 1847–48 when bread prices were high – Chartist activity was strongest. Yet, in 1843 to 1846, when Peel's ministry was at its most effective, 'low' social tension as a result of cheap bread prices weakened the strength of the Chartist message.

Chartism was strongest in areas where domestic industry was in decline, such as the West Country, and made little progress where the railway boom had soaked up the excess unemployment. This view is supported by Mark Howell who agrees that Chartism was a movement created by the 'impatience engendered by breakfastless tables and fireless grates', whilst Elie Halévy claims that Chartism represented 'the blind revolt of hunger'. It is certainly true that Chartism was more popular when jobs were scarce and bread prices high.

Ultimately, interpretation depends entirely on whether you see Chartism as 'a knife and fork question' or as a defined political movement. Recent research has tended to see both political and economic components as being interrelated. The historian P. Gregg claims that 'Chartism was a political movement based on economic grievances'. This modern interpretation seems to do most justice to the complexities of this fascinating academic debate.

> **To what extent was Chartism a movement for political rather than economic change?**

4.5 Why did the Chartists fail to achieve their aims?

The attitude of Parliament

After the passage of the 1832 Reform Act, Radicals had always hoped for an extension of the vote and the implementation of the six points of the Charter. The common feeling was that popular pressure had forced the Government into change in 1830–32, so why should similar pressure not succeed a number of years later? Yet in spite of these hopes, the parliamentary élite refused on three occasions – in 1839, 1842 and 1848 – to approve the demands of the Charter.

Why did this occur? The establishment felt it had already changed the constitution once and was not prepared to do so again. The organisation of government was small and compact and the same people who ran Parliament controlled both the Church and the Army. In 1834, the Prime Minister, Earl Grey, warned against 'a constant and active pressure from without to the adoption of any measures the strict necessity of which has not been fully proved, and which are not strictly regulated by a careful attention to the settled institutions of the country'. Faced with such an attitude, it was no surprise that the Chartist message failed to influence the majority of those in Parliament and among the nation's establishment.

Divisions among the leadership

Chartism was such a large umbrella organisation that it was bound to arouse different views and ideas regarding its purpose. Initially, the divisions in the movement were kept hidden, but during the 1840s two completely different attitudes emerged.

● 'Moral force' Chartism placed strong emphasis on non-violent protest, educating the working classes and, if necessary, cooperating with middle-class pressure groups such as the Anti-Corn Law League. The leaders of this tradition were William Lovett and Francis Place. The former left the movement in 1843.

● An alternative tradition was 'physical force' Chartism, which supported the idea that an armed struggle was likely and, in some cases, welcome. The Newport Rising of November 1839 and the Plug Riots of the summer of 1842 represent the high point of this tradition.

A third aspect of Chartism was illustrated by the career of Feargus O'Connor who used the threat of violence but who remained within the law during his political career. Through his powerful platform speeches and the messages carried in his *Northern Star* newspaper, he managed to convince the majority of Chartists to follow his lead. It was almost impossible for one movement to contain these alternative traditions.

A personality clash between Lovett and O'Connor added to the divisions and exposed the contradiction of a movement demanding constitutional change having to resort to violence to bring it about.

Regional differences

Chartism was strongest in the North, but weakest in the South. This is a generalisation, but successful revolutions such as the French Revolution of 1789 have shown that control of, and the support of, the capital is vital for success. As S.J. Lee claims, in *Aspects of British Political History*, 'London was merely the stage on which Chartism acted out its major role'. The Chartist movement tended to act in isolation and there were few examples of a coordinated national strategy to undermine the Government. Different areas interpreted Chartism in their own way. The North, under the control of O'Connor, was strongly in favour of physical force, whilst Birmingham was heavily influenced by the Complete Suffrage Union with its close links to 'moral force' Chartism and the Anti-Corn Law League. In Scotland, the Chartist message was spread by the idea of 'Christian Chartism'. Thus, each region had a different agenda and the government was able to divide and rule successfully. In *Chartist Studies* (1963), historian Asa Briggs highlights these regional differences.

Strength of the British State

Both the Whig Government of Melbourne and the Conservative ministry of Peel had few problems in resisting the potential threat of Chartism. Following the 1832 Reform Act, the political system was relatively stable and both the Army and Police were loyal to the Government. The passage of the Rural Police Act in 1839 ensured that a nationwide police force was able to monitor and deal with any outbreak of discontent. In 1848, for example, Russell's Government was highly organised in dealing with the Kennington Common demonstration. It ensured that the capital was well secured by 7,000 soldiers, 4,000 police and 85,000 special constables, with bridges and railway stations guarded. In addition, both Whig and Conservative governments acted swiftly to arrest known troublemakers and to transport them abroad if necessary. The new railway network was also used to transport troops to meet any threat where it existed and telegraph communication could warn authorities of any danger in advance. As Robert Stewart claims, in *Party and Politics*

1830–1852 (1989), 'Chartism's fatal weakness was that it had neither parliamentary strength nor the means of gaining it. It had to develop into a revolutionary movement or collapse.'

Lack of middle-class support

The physical force element of Chartism ensured that the majority of the middle classes refused to support Chartism. Despite the efforts of Lovett, the close cooperation that had existed in 1831–32 was conspicuously absent in this period. The middle class now had an organisation of their own, the Anti-Corn Law League, that was prepared to campaign on an issue closer to their hearts than anything Chartism could promote. The League was successful in gaining middle-class support on a single issue. In addition, the middle classes were content with the gains they had made in 1832 and did not want their property subject to the violence of O'Connor and his mob.

The success of Peel's reforms

> 1. What do you regard as the most important reasons why Chartism failed?
>
> 2. Was its failure due more to its own internal problems or the strength of the authorities?

The popularity of Chartism usually coincided with an economic crisis. The factors that helped the Chartist message to spread were countered in a series of far-sighted laws, such as the Mines Act of 1842 and Repeal of the Corn Law in 1846. The mid-Victorian boom had been created and was to continue well into the future. This prosperity was reflected in rising wages and increased food consumption. As living standards improved support for the Chartists declined.

Summary

> 1. What do you regard as the most significant developments in the Chartist movement between 1839 and 1850? Give reasons to support your answer.
>
> 2. Using the information in this chapter, do you think the Charter posed a threat to the existing order or was it merely an attempt to redress obvious weaknesses in the system?

All these reasons stated would seem to suggest that, in the short term, Chartism achieved little. However, is this a fair evaluation of such a complex movement? It is fairer to say that Chartism did achieve a great deal in the long term. All but one of the six points of the Charter had been put into effect by 1918. The establishment of 'annual parliaments' was the only point of the Charter that failed to pass the test of time. Time has proved, however, that any successful government needs at least five years to promote successful legislation and to transform the society it inherits. The lessons learnt from the Chartist struggle were to be of vital importance when the question of the extension of the franchise appeared once again in 1867 and 1884. The rise of the Labour Party has many of its origins and experiences with the Chartist movement. Rather than dismiss the movement, E. Hopkins, in *A Social History of the English Working Classes, 1815–1945* (1979), claims that the Chartists represented 'the most striking and widespread working-class movement for political reform in the 19th century'.

Further Reading

Articles

'The Nature of Chartism' by H. Cunningham in *Modern History Review* (April 1990)

'Taking Chartism seriously' by C. Behagg in *Modern History Review* (April 1994)

'The Origins and Nature of Chartism' by E. Royle in *History Review* (issue 13, 1992)

Texts designed for AS and A2 level students

Chartism by E. Royle (Longman, Seminar Studies series, 1996)
Labour and Reform, Working Class Movements 1815–1914 by C. Behagg (Hodder & Stoughton, Access to A Level series, 1995)
Chartism (Access to History in Depth) by Harry Browne (Hodder, 1999)
Chartism (Longman History in Depth) by Chris Culpin and Eric Evans (Longman 2000)
Chartism (Cambridge Perspectives in History) by Richard Brown (CUP, 1998)
Chartism (Lancaster Pamphlets) by John Walton (Routledge, 1999)

More advanced reading

The Chartist Experience: Studies in Working-class Radicalism and Culture, 1830–60 edited by James Epstein and Dorothy Thompson (Palgrave Macmillan, 1982)
The Chartists by Dorothy Thompson (Temple Smith, 1984)
Chartism and Society edited by F.C. Mather (Batsford, 1980)
The Last Rising: The Newport insurrection of 1839 (Oxford University Press, 1985)
The Lion of Freedom: Feargus O'Connor and the Chartist Movement, 1832–42 by James Epstein (Routledge, 1982)

5 Electoral reform in Britain, 1850–1885

Key Issues

- How important were electoral reforms in moving Britain towards democracy in the period 1850 to 1885?

- How did the Reform Acts of 1867 and 1884 affect the electoral system?

- What impact did developments in the electoral system have on the Whig/ Liberal and Tory/Conservative parties?

5.1 Why was there a demand for further parliamentary reform in the period 1850 to 1865?

5.2 Why was a second reform Bill proposed in 1865, and why was it defeated?

5.3 How and why was a Second Reform Act passed by 1867?

5.4 How significant were the electoral reforms made by Gladstone's ministries in the period 1868 to 1885?

5.5 Historical Interpretation: How significant was the impact of electoral reform on the development of British political parties?

Framework of Events

1858	Abolition of property qualification for MPs (one of the six demands made by the Chartists)
	Followers of the Jewish faith allowed to become MPs
1859	Failure of 'Fancy Franchises' Bill
1865	Lord Palmerston dies
	Lord John Russell becomes Liberal Prime Minister
1866	Defeat of the Liberal reform Bill
	Hyde Park Riots
1867	Lord Derby forms a minority Conservative government
	Conservatives introduce their reform Bill
	Representation of the People Act passed
1872	Ballot Act passed
1883	Corrupt and Illegal Practices Act passed
1884	Third Reform Act passed
1885	Redistribution of Seats Act passed

Overview

John Russell, first Earl Russell (1792–1878)
Russell was Leader of the Commons 1852–55, Foreign Secretary 1859–65, and Prime Minister 1846–52 and 1865–68.

In 1832 the Great Reform Act became law. One of its leading supporters was the Whig politician, Lord John Russell. The Act, which was passed to prevent revolution, was claimed to be the final change in the electoral system. However, in the years after 1832 the demand for further electoral reform did not go away. From the mid-1830s the main supporters for further reform were the Chartists. This movement went into decline, however, and by 1850 demand for reform had decreased. Even so, in the late 1850s the property qualification for

John Henry Temple, third Viscount Palmerston (1784–1865)

John Henry Temple succeeded to his Irish peerage at the age of 18. As a Tory he became an MP in 1807, and was Secretary at War (1809–28). Palmerston broke with the Tories in 1830 and sat in the Whig Cabinets of 1830–34, 1835–41, and 1846–51 as Foreign Secretary. His foreign policy was marked by distrust of France and Russia. He was Home Secretary in the coalition government of 1852, before becoming Prime Minister for two spells: in 1855–58, he put right Aberdeen's mismanagement of the Crimean War, suppressed the Indian Mutiny and carried through the Second Opium War; in 1859–65, he was involved in the American Civil War on the side of the South. Although he was popular with the people and made good use of the press, his high-handed attitude annoyed Queen Victoria and other ministers.

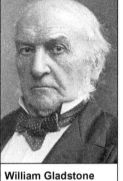

William Gladstone (1809–1898)
Gladstone became a Tory MP in 1832. He was Conservative Minister from 1841 to 1846; Chancellor of the Exchequer 1852–55 and 1859–66; Leader of the Liberal Party from 1867 and Prime Minister 1868–74, 1880–85, 1886 and 1892–94.

Skilled workers: Working people who had acquired a skilled trade, such as carpenters, plumbers, boilermakers, bricklayers.

Home Rule: Desire for Ireland to receive its own parliament.

Identify the three most important electoral reforms between 1850 and 1885.

Explain why you think these were important.

MPs was abolished and members of the Jewish faith were allowed to enter the House of Commons.

In the early 1860s demands for further reform began to rise again. The main source of pressure came from outside parliament – from organisations such as the Reform Union and the Reform League. However, a major obstacle to reform was Lord Palmerston (Prime Minister 1855–58 and 1859–65). Following his death, the ruling Liberal Party did attempt to extend the right to vote. This proposal split the Liberal Party, and it was forced from office. In 1867 a minority Conservative Government passed a reform act which extended the right to vote to **skilled workers**.

However, the Liberal Party was also central to electoral reform in the period 1868 to 1885. Under the leadership of Gladstone, the Liberals passed the Ballot Act of 1872. This introduced the secret ballot, a major Chartist demand.

During Gladstone's second ministry (1880–85) three important acts were passed which laid the foundations of modern parliamentary democracy. In 1883 the Corrupt and Illegal Practices Acts introduced heavy penalties, including imprisonment, for persons who attempted to bribe or intimidate voters. In 1884 the Third Reform Act extended the right to vote to most adult males over 21. In the following year the Redistribution of Seats Act abolished multi-member constituencies and created single-member seats – the basis of the current system of parliamentary election.

The increase of the electorate from 1850 to 1885 had a big influence on the way political parties operated and developed. In the 1860s and 1870s the Conservatives completely reorganised their national organisation to meet the new challenges created by the 1867 Reform Act. In the 1870s and 1880s the Liberals followed the Conservative example and created their own nationwide party organisation. The Ballot Act of 1872 had a major influence on the growth of the Irish **Home Rule** Party. By 1885 the Home Rule Party won eighty-six seats and held the balance of power between Conservatives and Liberals.

The 1850 to 1885 period, therefore, saw fundamental changes in electoral law which helped transform the British political system.

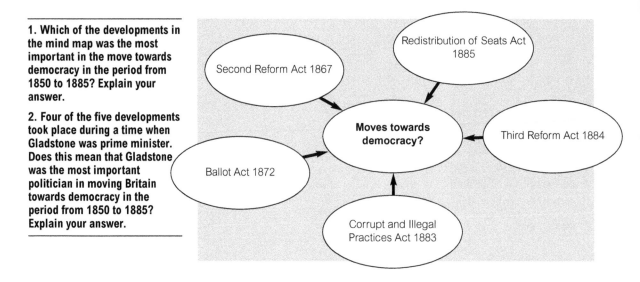

1. Which of the developments in the mind map was the most important in the move towards democracy in the period from 1850 to 1885? Explain your answer.

2. Four of the five developments took place during a time when Gladstone was prime minister. Does this mean that Gladstone was the most important politician in moving Britain towards democracy in the period from 1850 to 1885? Explain your answer.

5.1   Why was there a demand for further parliamentary reform in the period 1850 to 1865?

In 1850 the possibility of further electoral reform in Britain seemed to be a distant hope. From the mid-1830s to 1850 the Chartist movement had attempted to persuade and intimidate parliament into accepting the People's Charter. However, all its attempts ended in failure. In 1850 many of its leaders – such as Ernest Jones – were in prison or had been transported to Australia.

The decline of the Chartist Movement has been a subject of debate among historians. Those historians who have highlighted the economic causes of Chartism can point to the development of the 'mid-Victorian economic boom' (1850–73) as the main cause for decline. Other historians have mentioned the importance of other developments, such as the rise of **New Model Unions** amongst skilled workers. An important factor which tends to be overlooked is the strength of the Victorian state. The Whig, Conservative and Whig/Liberal governments from the mid-1830s to 1850 were able to deal very effectively with Chartist agitation. This was shown in the **Newport Rising** of 1839 or the use of special constables in London in 1848 when the final Chartist petition was presented to Parliament.

New Model Unions: Trade unions of skilled workers.

Newport Rising: Chartist uprising in South Wales, 1839.

The Conservatives and parliamentary reform, 1858–59

In 1830–32 the main political party in support of parliamentary reform was the Whigs. But in the late 1850s the party that was interested in reform was the Conservatives. Following the repeal of the Corn Laws in 1846 the Conservative Party of Sir Robert Peel split in two. One group, the Peelites, eventually joined the Whigs and Liberals from 1852. The other group retained the name 'Conservative'. From 1846 to 1874 the Conservative Party did not win a general election. Instead it formed three minority governments, 1851–52, 1958–59 and 1867–68.

However, between 1858 and 1859 the Conservatives were responsible for supporting further parliamentary reform. In 1858 they made two changes to electoral law. The discrimination against members of the Jewish faith was lifted. A major supporter of the move was Benjamin Disraeli. Although racially a Jew, he was a member of the Church of England. Also

Sir Robert Peel (1788–1850)
Tory/Conservative leader from 1832. Conservative Prime Minister 1834–35 and 1841–46. He modernised the Tory Party. In 1835 in the Tamworth Manifesto he accepted the changes made by the 1832 Reform Act. In his ministry of 1841–46 he introduced major social and economic reforms. His decision to repeal the Corn Laws in 1846, as a way to aid the Irish Famine, split the Conservative Party.

in the same year one of the Chartist six demands was introduced – the abolition of the property qualification for MPs. This was a major obstacle for the less wealthy trying to enter parliament. However, MPs still did not get paid. (This wasn't introduced until 1911.) As a result, MPs still had to have a private income.

The major attempt at reform was the Parliamentary Reform Bill of February 1859. It was introduced by the Deputy Leader of the Conservatives, Benjamin Disraeli. The Bill attempted to increase those parts of the electorate that were likely to vote Conservative. These included those who owned houses in towns worth £10 or more. It also tried to include a wide variety of occupations, such as the **Anglican clergy**, doctors, schoolteachers, university graduates, government pension holders and those who possessed at least £60 in a savings bank. As a result, the Bill became known for its 'fancy franchises'.

The Bill was seen by Whigs and Liberals as a party political attempt to gain electoral advantage. As the Conservatives were in a minority in parliament the Bill was defeated. However, a more significant reason for the defeat was the lack of interest in further parliamentary reform in the country as a whole. All this was to change in the early 1860s.

The increasing demand for further parliamentary reform in the early 1860s

i) The impact of the American Civil War, 1861–65
The American Civil War helped increase public interest in further reform. Although Britain did not intervene in the war, the conflict had a profound effect. From 1862 the Union Government in America aimed to abolish slavery if they won the war. This created considerable support in Britain for the North side of the conflict, which seemed to be waging a moral crusade. In Britain, the war was seen as a conflict between the democratic North and the slave-owning South.

The war had a major economic effect on north west England. The North blockaded the South in the war, which prevented cotton from the South reaching the textile mills around Manchester. It resulted in a 'cotton famine' in 1863 and thousands of textile workers were made unemployed. The unemployed did not riot – they helped each other to get through the difficult times. This convinced senior Liberal politicians, like Gladstone, that working-class people were mature enough to receive the right to vote.

ii) The visit of Garibaldi, 1864
An event which caused considerable public excitement was the visit of Italian nationalist Guiseppe Garibaldi. He had helped unite Italy into one state in the years 1859–60 and was one of Europe's greatest supporters of parliamentary government. Tens of thousands went to see him arrive in London.

iii) The formation of the Reform Union and the Reform League, 1864–65
In Manchester, in April 1864 the Reform Union was created. It was a mainly middle-class organisation which supported the secret ballot, three-year parliaments, and the redistribution of seats to reflect changes in population. Its most radical aim was to extend the right to vote to most adult males.

In February 1865 the Reform League was created. This was a mainly working-class organisation which wanted universal manhood **suffrage** – the right to vote for every adult male. In other words, it supported democracy.

iv) The death of Palmerston, 1865
Lord Palmerston dominated British politics from 1855 to 1865. He was Prime Minister from 1855 to 1858 and again from 1859 to 1865. He

Benjamin Disraeli (1804–1881)
Disraeli was a Tory MP from 1837. He became Conservative Leader of the Commons in 1851; was Chancellor of the Exchequer 1852, 1858–59; and became Prime Minister in 1867.

Anglican clergy: Vicars and curates of the Church of England.

Giuseppe Garibaldi (1807–1882)
Son of a fisherman from Nice (Nizza), part of the kingdom of Piedmont-Sardinia. At 15, he ran away to sea and joined Mazzini's 'Young Italy' movement. Garibaldi was sentenced to death for taking part in Mazzini's planned invasion of Piedmont-Sardinia in 1833, but escaped to South America where he spent many years of exile. He fought in the civil wars in Argentina and gained a reputation as a guerrilla leader. He returned home in 1848 and devoted himself to the nationalist cause.

Suffrage: The right to vote.

1. List three reasons why the demand for parliamentary reform reappeared after 1858.

2. How did the American Civil War influence the demand for parliamentary reform?

opposed further parliamentary reform. When he died in 1865, a major obstacle to reform was removed. The new Liberal Prime Minister, Lord John Russell, facing pressure from the Reform Union and the Reform League was willing to introduce further reform.

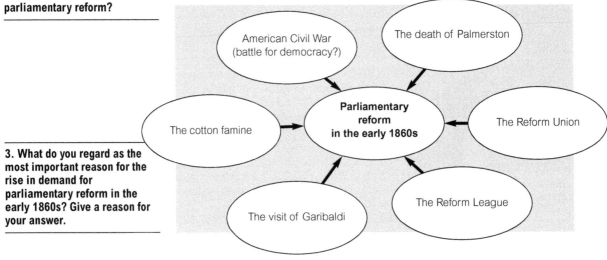

3. What do you regard as the most important reason for the rise in demand for parliamentary reform in the early 1860s? Give a reason for your answer.

5.2 Why was a second reform Bill proposed in 1865, and why was it defeated?

The death of Palmerston and growing public demand for further parliamentary reform led to a Liberal reform proposal. It was an attempt to extend the right to vote but not to introduce universal manhood suffrage.

The Bill proposed to:

Borough: A parliamentary seat in a town.

- reduce from £10 to £7 the property qualification to vote in **borough** seats;

- give the vote in borough seats to lodgers who paid at least £10 a year rent;

- reduce from £50 to £14 the property qualification to vote in county seats.

These changes were a deliberate attempt to extend the right to vote to most middle-class voters. It was also an attempt to ensure that the working class was excluded. As a result, the Bill was a compromise. It was an attempt to find a mid-way between conservative opponents of reform and the supporters of the Reform Union and Reform League.

Adullamites: A reference to the Bible and a group of Israelites who were always discontented.

In the House of Commons debate, the Conservative Party opposed the Bill. It was also opposed by right-wing Liberals, led by Robert Lowe. Lowe feared the Bill would lead eventually to democracy, which he opposed. Following his lead, thirty right-wing Liberals joined the Conservatives to defeat the Bill. This group were called **Adullamites** by their Liberal opponents, in particular John Bright.

1. Produce a timeline of the events which led to the failure of the Liberal reform proposal.

2. What do you regard as the main reason for the failure of the Liberal proposal? Explain your answer.

The result of the defeat was the resignation of Lord John Russell's Liberal government. It was replaced by a minority Conservative government, led by Lord Derby, with Disraeli as the Conservative leader in the House of Commons.

5.3 How and why was a Second Reform Act passed by 1867?

Although they had opposed the Liberal Bill, by 1867 the Conservatives had passed their own Parliamentary Reform Act. This was more radical than the Liberal proposal of 1865–66. Why and how did this happen?

A period of crisis, 1865–67

Not only was Britain faced by growing demands for parliamentary reform. A combination of other issues made this period one of considerable excitement and crisis:

i) The Fenian movement
From 1865 to 1867 attempts were made by an Irish secret society to create, by violent means, an independent Irish Republic. Attacks were made in Britain, Ireland and Canada.

ii) The Jamaica Rebellion, 1865
An uprising by the black population of Jamaica was crushed with great severity by the British Governor, Eyre. This caused outrage among Liberals in Britain.

iii) The financial crisis of May 1866
A major London bank, Overend & Gurney, collapsed, causing a major financial panic. Friday 11 May (Black Friday) saw a major fall in share prices on the London Stock Exchange.

iv) The Austro-Prussian War of 1866
In central Europe a major conflict took place between Austria and Prussia. It lasted seven weeks in June/July and resulted in significant political change in the region.

v) The Hyde Park riots, July 1866
Within weeks of taking office, the Conservatives were faced with a political riot in central London. A meeting by the Reform League ended in a major riot when the police attempted to prevent the meeting taking place. The event caused great alarm, many fearing a return to the revolutionary activity associated with the Great Reform Bill crisis of 1830–32.

Opportunism or political principle?

Considerable historical debate has surrounded the decision by the Conservatives to introduce their own reform after opposing the Liberal proposal of 1865–6. Was it just opportunism or was it based on political principle?

i) Bowing to popular pressure?
With growing political support across the country, linked to the Reform League and the Reform Union, it could be argued that the Conservatives were merely bowing to popular pressure. If a reform Bill had not been introduced at this time there was a danger of growing political unrest.

ii) 'Dishing the Whigs'
Were the Conservatives merely trying to gain political advantage over their Whig/Liberal opponents? The Liberals had split over their own reform proposal. The Conservatives were just exploiting this split in order to stay in power. For Disraeli, this was the most important reason for reform.

iii) A time for change
Since the Conservative split of 1846, the party had not won a general election. It seemed that the electoral system was stacked against the Conservatives winning an absolute majority of seats. Without a further

extension of the right to vote this situation might never change. Even Lord Derby, the Conservative leader, had come round to the idea that electoral reform was required.

The Conservative reform proposal, March 1867

- In borough seats, anyone paying the local tax (rates) would get the vote.

- In county seats, householders with houses worth £12 rent a year would get the vote.

These two changes would add approximately 750,000 to the electorate.

- 'Fancy franchises' would give the vote to Anglican clergy, university graduates, those who paid £1 a year in direct taxes, and those who held a bank account in excess of £50.

This change would add a further 300,000 to the electorate.

The Bill was introduced as a compromise proposal, after three Conservative ministers had resigned, including Robert Peel (Secretary for War) and Cranborne (Secretary for India).

How did the Conservative Bill pass?

i) Disraeli's ability to compromise and outwit the Liberals
The Liberals, led by Gladstone, attempted to defeat the Conservative Bill and force them out of office. The Liberals objected to the 'fancy franchises' proposal, and Disraeli dropped it. Disraeli also used the press, especially *The Times*, to win support for his proposals.

ii) Liberal divisions
The split between the Liberals which had led to the defeat of their own proposal the year before persisted into 1867. When Gladstone attempted to defeat the Bill, at its second reading, forty-five Liberals supported the Conservatives and a further twenty-eight **abstained** from voting.

Abstain: Decide not to vote.

iii) The Hodgkinson amendment
At the committee stage of the Bill, a Liberal introduced an amendment which simplified the property qualification to vote in borough seats. It added 500,000 to the electorate. Disraeli had to work hard to persuade his Cabinet colleagues to accept these changes, in order to save the Bill from defeat.

iv) Conservative control of the House of Lords
A major reason why the 1832 Reform Act had taken so long to pass was opposition in the House of Lords. The Conservatives had a large majority in that house, and Lord Derby used his influence to get the Lords to agree to the Bill. It was passed in the Lords on 6 August 1867.

What impact did the Second Reform Bill have on the electoral system?

The Second Reform Act – the Representation of the People Act, to give it its official title – transformed the electoral system. Taken with the Ballot Act, 1872 the Second Reform Act laid the foundation of the modern electoral system.

- The passage of the Act was a personal achievement for Disraeli. Despite being a member of a minority Conservative government he was able to pass a Bill against both Conservative and Liberal opposition. Lord Cranborne (the future Lord Salisbury) called it a 'surrender'. Thomas Carlyle, the Victorian historian called it 'shooting Niagara'. Robert Lowe, the leader of the Adullamites believed that it was time 'to educate our masters'. He was referring to the new voters. It is more than coincidence that the Act was followed by the first national education act, Forster's Act of 1870.

- The Act had a profound effect on party organisation outside parliament. Both the Conservative and Liberal parties transformed their party organisation in the decade after the Act.

- The most significant change was the rise in the electorate from 717,224 (after the 1832 Act) to 2,225,692 in 1869. The majority of the new voters came from towns and represented members of the skilled working class.

- It continued the work begun by the Reform Act of 1832 with regard to **rotten boroughs**. Under the Act, fifty-two seats were redistributed. Seven towns lost their seat because of electoral corruption. A further forty-five seats were lost to towns with populations under 10,000. twenty-five of these seats went to the counties and twenty went to new borough seats. London University received a seat.

- The total number of seats in the House of Commons was 658. Ireland still had 105. However, Scotland's number went up from 53 to 60. This reflected the rise in population. In England, the number of seats fell from 471 to 464.

Unfortunately, for Disraeli, the immediate effect of the Act was to aid his opponents, the Liberals. In the 1868 general election the Liberals, under Gladstone, won a resounding victory.

Rotten boroughs: Borough seats with very small electorates.

Changes in the size of the electorate 1830–1886

Electorate	England & Wales	Scotland
1831 (est.) (Before the Great Reform Act of 1832)	435,391	4,579
1833 (After the Great Reform Act of 1832)	652,777	64,447
1869 (After the Second Reform Act of 1867)	1,995,086	230,606
1886 (After the Third Reform Act of 1884)	4,376,624	560,580

Proportion of adults who had the vote

	England & Wales	Scotland
1833	1 in 5	1 in 8
1869	1 in 3	1 in 3
1886	2 in 3	3 in 5

(Source: Adapted from J.K. Walton, *The Second Reform Act*, 1987, Routledge)

1. Why was the period 1865 to 1867 described as a period of crisis?

2. How important was Disraeli to the passage of the Conservative reform proposal?

3. List three important changes made by the 1867 Reform Act. Which changes do you regard as the most important? Give a reason for your answer.

Source-based questions: The Second Reform Act of 1867

SOURCE A

5 March 1867 … The state of the Reform Question and of the ministry is now more critical than it had been at any former time. There is not, as far as I can judge, much excitement or violence of feeling amongst the people, but a great deal of interest, and on the part of the educated classes, some not inconsiderable apprehension of possible results. The radical newspapers are of course screaming their loudest. *The Times* disapproves of the recent resolutions … but is anxious for a Bill of some sort to pass, and not averse to it being done by the present government.

From Journals and Memoirs by Lord Derby

SOURCE B

Commentators have praised Disraeli's brilliant opportunist tactics and, above all, his flexibility. Having formed a temporary alliance with the right wing (Adullamite) Liberals in 1866, to unseat the Liberal Government, he now made common cause with the left-wing, radical element of the Party. He was willing to see borough representation radically reformed rather than allow the bill to be lost. Unlike Lowe, he did not fear the urban masses, and he was unwilling to accept a much larger working-class borough electorate.

From Government and Reform by Robert Pearce, published in 1994.

SOURCE C

I think the danger would be less, that the feeling of the larger numbers would be more national, than by giving the vote to a sort of class set aside, looking with suspicion on their superiors, and with disdain on those beneath them. I think you would have a better chance of touching the popular heart, of evoking the national sentiment, by bringing in the great body of these men who occupy houses and fulfil the duties of citizenship by the payment of rates.

Disraeli in the House of Commons, July 1867

SOURCE D

I had to prepare the mind of the country, and to educate – if it be not too arrogant to use such a phrase – to educate our Party. It is a large party and requires its attention to be called to questions of this kind with some pressure. I had to prepare the mind of Parliament and the Country on this question of reform … when you try to settle any great question, there are two considerations which statesmen ought not to forget. First of all, let your plan be founded upon some principle … and let is also be a principle that is in harmony with the manners and customs you are attempting to legislate for.

Disraeli in a speech in autumn 1867, after the Reform Act became law.

---

1. Study Sources B and D.

Explain the meaning, in the context of the 1867 Reform Act, of the following phrases:

(a) 'the right-wing (Adullamite) Liberals'

(b) 'to educate our Party'

2. Study Source C.

What arguments in favour of reform is Disraeli putting forward?

3. Study Sources A and D.

How valuable would these sources be to a historian studying the 1867 Reform Act?

4. Using all the sources and the information in this chapter, explain why the Conservative Government passed a Reform Act in 1867 when it had opposed a milder one in 1866.

5.4 How significant were the electoral reforms made by Gladstone's ministries in the period 1868 to 1885?

Gladstone and Disraeli were the two great political rivals of the mid-nineteenth century. Both were instrumental in bringing significant electoral reform.

Disraeli's contribution had been the end of discrimination against Jews entering Parliament, passed in 1858, and the Second Reform Act of 1867.

Gladstone's greatest triumph came with the Ballot Act of 1872 and the great electoral reforms of 1883 to 1885.

The Ballot Act 1872

The use of the secret ballot at elections was one of the Chartist demands in the 1830s and 1840s. Before the Ballot Act, elections were noted for considerable bribery and corruption. Voters had to register their vote in public and many borough seats had very small electorates, some as low at 3,000. As a result, voters were often intimidated, bribed with money or offered free drink to vote in a particular way. Tenants could face eviction if they voted against the views of the person who owned their home. The 1852 general election, in particular, was notably corrupt.

The Ballot Act, therefore, aimed to prevent large-scale intimidation and bribery.

The Corrupt and Illegal Practices Act 1883

The Ballot Act of 1872 went a long way to ending bribery and intimidation, but it did not eradicate it completely. The Corrupt and Illegal Practices Act set rigid rules for the conduct of elections and, for the first time, it set a limit on how much candidates could spend. It also set heavy penalties on those guilty of corruption.

The Third Reform Act 1884

The most important electoral reform between 1867 and 1918 was the Third Reform Act. The aim of extending the right to vote to most adult males was a major demand by Radical members of the Liberal Party.

The right to vote was still based on a property qualification. But now all occupiers of houses got the vote, as well as lodgers who paid £10 rent per year. This change had a dramatic effect on the size of the electorate. The 1832 Act had added approximately 500,000 to the electorate. In 1867 a further 1 million were added. The 1884 Act doubled the size of the electorate again, to 2 million.

Unlike the 1832 and 1867 reforms (which had separate Acts for England, Scotland and Ireland) the 1884 Act applied to the whole United Kingdom. However, not all adult males received the right to vote. Approx. 40 per cent of adult males could still not vote, for a variety of reasons. They included bachelors living with their parents, soldiers living in barracks and domestic servants living with their employers.

Universal manhood suffrage, another Chartist aim, did not become law until 1918.

The Redistribution of Seats Act 1885

A major problem facing the passage of both the 1832 and 1867 Reform Acts was the attitude of the House of Lords. Until 1911 the House of Lords had an absolute veto on all legislation. In 1832 it took the intervention of the King to persuade the Lords to accept electoral reform. In 1867, the clever persuasion of Derby and Disraeli gained the Lords' support.

In 1884 the Conservative-dominated House of Lords was prepared to accept the Third Reform Act, as long as it was accompanied by a major redistribution of seats. This was achieved with the Redistribution of Seats Act in 1885. It was passed in May 1885, a month before the fall of Gladstone's second ministry. Multi-member seats were abolished. It also established the important principle of equal electoral districts, where the number of electors was roughly equal in each constituency – yet another Chartist demand that was achieved.

1. In what ways were the Reform Act of 1884 and the Redistribution of Seats Act 1885 linked?

2. How did Gladstone's reform change the electoral system?

5.5 Historical Interpretation: How significant was the impact of electoral reform on the development of British political parties?

The increase in the electorate from under 500,000 in 1831 to over 4.5 million in 1886 had a profound effect on the British political system – especially the party system.

Before the 1832 Reform Act the two major political parties were the Whigs and the Tories. Both these parties were made up of members of the landowning class. The main difference between the parties had been their attitude towards the role of the monarchy in politics. The Tories were in favour of an important role for the monarch, and from 1760 to 1830 they dominated parliament.

However, from 1827 onwards the Tory dominance of parliament began to disintegrate, following the retirement of Lord Liverpool as Prime Minister. His successor reopened an important political controversy, Catholic emancipation, an issue which split the Tory Party. In 1829, in the Catholic Relief Act, Catholics were allowed to become MPs. In 1828 non-conformists had been given the same right. Finally, in November 1830, the Tory government of the Duke of Wellington lost the general election.

Impact of the 1832 Reform Act

The 1832 Reform Act increased the electorate from under 500,000 to 650,000. Those who had the right the vote now included members of the upper middle class, such as factory owners and businessmen. From 1832 the Whig Party in parliament was joined increasingly by 'liberal'-minded businessmen who wanted further reform. By 1846 the political party was known as the 'Whig-Liberal Party'. Finally, in 1859, a new political party was created, the Liberal Party. The Liberal Party contained Whigs, Liberals and Radicals, and it dominated British politics from 1859 to 1886.

The Tory Party also changed after 1832. Under its new leader, Sir Robert Peel, it changed its name, in January 1835 to the Conservative Party. In his **manifesto** to the electors of Tamworth, Peel declared that his party had abandoned all opposition to further reform. If reform could be proved to be justified, the Conservatives would support it. From 1835 to 1846 the Conservative Party comprised both landowners and businessmen. In 1846 the party split, over the abolition of the Corn Laws. The business element of the party followed Peel as 'Peelites'. They eventually joined the Liberal Party in 1859. The remainder of the party kept the title 'Conservative'. They would not win another general election until 1874.

Manifesto: List of policy commitments made at an election.

Changes in Conservative organisation

The 1832 Reform Act not only changed the composition and policies of the two major parties, it also changed their organisation. Under the 1832 Act voters could be registered. As a result Peel created a national party organisation to register known Conservatives. He also appointed a national agent, R. F. Bomford, to coordinate the activity. This helps explain why the Conservatives won the 1841 general election.

The 1867 Reform Act had an even more radical effect on political parties. From 1867 the Conservative Party completely reorganised itself, creating first a national organisation of Conservative Associations. In 1870 the Conservative Central Office was established as party headquarters. Under the national agent J.E. Gorst, the party had a party organisation in all English seats by 1874. Today's party organisation had its origins at this time.

In 1883 the Primrose League was formed – the first major political organisation in Britain which was aimed at involving women. Also in the

1880s the Conservatives created Workingmen's Clubs, which provided alcoholic drink and social events. Finally, in 1884, the new national agent, Capt. Middleton, helped mould all these different groups into an effective national organisation.

Changes in Liberal organisation

The Liberals were also keen to attract as many new voters as possible. In Birmingham, the Liberal politician Joseph Chamberlain created a 'caucus'.

This was a local political organisation designed to get as many Liberals to vote. Between 1867 and 1877 local Liberal groups formed their own caucuses.

In 1877, under the guidance of national agent Francis Schnadhorst, the National Liberal Federation was created. It was intended to set the political aims of the national political party.

Gladstone and Liberal policy

The national Liberal leader, W.E. Gladstone, was aware of the need to win as many votes as possible, and he came up with an electoral slogan at each general election as a way to gain votes. In 1868 it was 'Justice for Ireland'. In 1874 it was about the abolition of income tax. In 1880, it was about opposition to Disraeli's foreign and imperial policy. In 1886, and again in 1892, it was 'Home rule for Ireland'.

1. Identify three ways in which electoral reform helped change the organisation of the two main political parties.

2. In what ways did the Tory/Conservative Party react to changes in the increase in the size of the electorate between 1832 and 1885?

3. Write down the main changes to party policy and party organisation following the 1832 Reform Act.

4. Write down the main changes to party policy and organisation following the Second Reform Act of 1867.

5. Which party made the greater changes in organisation between 1832 and 1885, the Tory/Conservative Party or the Whig/Liberal Party? Explain your answer.

Disraeli and Tory democracy

Disraeli, the Conservative leader, also began to change party policy in order to win votes. His policy of 'Tory Democracy' has caused a debate among historians. Some see it as a genuine response by the Conservatives to the newly enlarged electorate after 1867. It suggested that the Conservatives were in favour of social, economic and political reform. Other historians see it as yet another part of Disraeli's opportunism. It was seen as an election slogan not a genuine move in favour of reform. Of more importance were Disraeli's two policy speeches of 1872, in Manchester and at the Crystal palace in London. In both speeches, Disraeli declared that the Conservatives would defend the British Empire, defend the monarchy and support social reform.

Ireland and electoral reform

Electoral reform also had a profound effect on other political parties. The 1872 Ballot Act greatly helped the development of the Irish Home Rule Party. By 1874 it had replaced the Liberal Party as the main opposition to the Conservatives in Ireland. Following the 1884 Reform Act, the Irish Home Rule Party gained 85 of the 105 Irish seats, transforming the political landscape of Ireland.

Further Reading

The Second Reform Act by J.K. Walton (Routledge, 1987)
Parliamentary Reform 1785–1928, Questions and Answers by Sean Lang (Routledge, 1998)
Parliamentary Reform c.1770–1918 by Eric Evans (Longman Seminar Studies, 1999)
Growth of Democracy in Britain by Annette Mayer (Access to History series, Hodder, 1999)

6 Poverty, public health and the growth of government, 1830–1875

Key Issues

- How did attitudes to the poor change, 1830–1875?

- In what ways did State provision for the poor change, 1830–1875?

- Why did reform take place so slowly?

6.1 Why was there opposition to the unreformed Poor Law?
6.2 What did the 1832 Poor Law Commission recommend?
6.3 What were the results of the Poor Law Amendment Act?
6.4 How did policy change in the 19th century?
6.5 Why was effective factory reform so difficult to achieve?
6.6 What efforts were made to improve public health?
6.7 How did housing policy change, 1866–1875?

Framework of Events

1802	Health and Morals of Apprentices Act
1832	Poor Law Commission
1833	Althorp's Act
	First Government Grant to Education
1834	Poor Law Amendment Act
1835	Municipal Corporations Act
1837	Compulsory registration of births introduced
1842	Mines and Collieries Act
	Chadwick's Report on sanitary conditions of labouring population of Great Britain
1844	Factory Act
1847	Poor Law Act; Second Factory Act
1848	Public Health Act
1850	Another Factory Act
1858	Disappearance of General Board of Health
1862	Revised Code introduced by Robert Lowe
1866	Sanitary Act
1868	Torrens Act
1870	Forster's Education Reform Bill
1875	Public Health Act; Artisans' Dwellings Act

Overview

Collectivist: Opposite to *laissez faire*; describes the belief that government intervention in social and economic affairs can be of benefit to society.

DID governments steadily respond, in a humanitarian way, to the exposure of appalling conditions, as argued by historians such as Oliver MacDonagh? Public opinion, it is said, forced a remarkable change in making the State face its responsibilities to protect the poor. The State made a **collectivist** response by stepping in to help the weakest members of society.

On the other hand, was the growing trend towards collectivism restrained by *laissez-faire* values? The historian Dicey argues that it was these values which emphasised the activities of the free, competitive market at the expense of those who required state protection. In this model, state intervention was held back by a prevailing attitude to 'let things alone'.

In a sense, the study of social reform during the 19th century was the result of the stresses between these sets of forces: *laissez faire* and collectivism. Often, it was a case of two steps forward, and one pace back – both at a local and national level.

Much depended on individuals and radical pressure groups. There was not only a reluctance to spend ratepayers' money, but also doubts about the capacity of administrative structures to support change.

1. Of the factors in the mind map, which do you regard as the most important in increasing government involvement in social affairs in the period from 1834 to 1875? Explain your answer.

2. Which do you regard as the more important social reform – the Poor Law Amendment Act 1834 or the Public Health Act 1848? Explain your answer.

3. To what extent was Edwin Chadwick the most important person in the development of social reform in the period from 1834 to 1875?

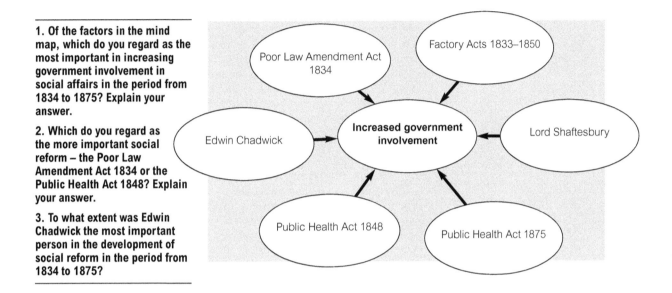

6.1 Why was there opposition to the unreformed Poor Law?

The 'old' Poor Law which existed at the beginning of the 19th century was based on the Elizabethan Poor Law Acts of 1597–98 and 1601. These Acts had made each parish responsible for its poor by collecting a poor rate. The belief persisted that poverty was the result of laziness and that a proper living could only be made through hard work. Beggars and vagrants were to be severely punished. It was acknowledged that the sick and aged could not look after themselves, hence poor-houses were built for them. In addition, outdoor relief (sometimes money, but often food) was provided for individuals who could not work through no fault of their own.

Levels of poverty continued to rise and the system for supporting the poor was disorganised and out of date. Action was clearly needed in the 1790s when distress and disturbances resulted from poor harvests and increases in prices because of the war with revolutionary France. The most famous response to this alarming situation was from the magistrates of Speenhamland in Berkshire, in 1795. Relief from the rates was added to wages according to a sliding scale depending on the size of a labourer's family and the price of bread. At least this system avoided the worst examples of starvation; and it suited the employers who were spared social disruption and who managed to keep a pool of cheap labour.

However, the 1830s saw the case being made for a complete overhaul of the way industrial society dealt with their poor. By then the 'Swing' riots of

Why did the Poor Law need reforming by the early 1830s?

1830–31 revealed rural discontent. Speenhamland and its local variations had 'tied' farm labourers to their parishes. Population movement to urban areas, where there was demand for workers, was suppressed. The rural poor had become dependent on their form of poor relief, which was seen as heavy-handed and paternalistic. It was reliant on handouts and charity, which sapped dignity and initiative. Inevitably, employers kept wages low as the heavy financial burden was passed to the rates. Twenty per cent of national expenditure was spent on the poor. In 1832, it amounted to £7 million when it had only been £1½ million in 1776.

6.2 What did the 1832 Poor Law Commission recommend?

In 1832, the 26 members of the Poor Law Commission set out to investigate the operation of the Poor Law system. Among its members were those such as Edwin Chadwick who adopted the views of Jeremy Bentham, that everything had to be subjected to the test of utilitarianism. Did the Poor Law, as it existed, provide 'the greatest good of the greatest number' (Bentham), or could it be more efficient? Were the poor actively seeking work (which in turn would lead to prosperity and the happiness of many), or were they being demoralised by relying on public charity?

There was also an acceptance that the complete abolition of outdoor relief was impossible, although that aim was strongly canvassed. The young, the sick, the old and the disabled would have to be supported. This was the beginning of that 'collectivist' view which would become more apparent as the 20th century approached. It was a collectivism that acknowledged that society and the State would need to intervene to defend those who could not support themselves.

When the report was published in 1834, its moral tone was clear. Employers were helping to keep wages artificially low so that they would be made up from the rates. The free labour market was being upset and the labouring poor were becoming sluggish.

The 'Principles of 1834' were set out by the Commission, and they became the Poor Law Amendment Act.

- 'Less eligibility' applied to those workhouses that had to be built for the able-bodied who could not find employment. Conditions had to be worse in the workhouse than for the poorest workers outside it. In other words, they were less eligible for decent conditions. Here was Bentham's influence – encouraging workers back to work at the first opportunity.

- The 'Workhouse Test' was to test if a pauper was sufficiently in need by seeing if the individual would accept a place in a workhouse. Hence outdoor relief was forbidden (except for the old and sick) and the only place to receive it was in a workhouse. Refuse the offer of relief and the pauper would fail the test.

- Finally, parishes were to be grouped into unions to build workhouses. A Board of Guardians would be elected by ratepayers to control a workhouse. In an effort to ensure the uniform application of the system, to replace the inefficiency and corruption that preceded it, a national administration would be created. There would be three Poor Law Commissioners in London, with Chadwick as Secretary. Twelve Assistant Commissioners would inspect the operation of what was the Poor Law Amendment Act. It set forward the intention of a centralised, national system with the Commissioners independently trying to ensure the uniform application of the rules.

What were the main differences between the old Poor Law and the recommendations of the Poor Law Report?

6.3 What were the results of the Poor Law Amendment Act?

On the face of it, the Poor Law Commissioners could take some satisfaction from the savings made and the reduction of corruption. Outdoor relief appeared more limited as the poor rate which cost over £6 million in 1833–4 fell by over £1 million over the next ten years.

In other aspects, the Poor Law Amendment Act failed to achieve its aims. Even Chadwick had to admit that some of his hopes had been dashed. Separate workhouses – for the young, aged and sick – were never built. 'General' workhouses were constructed, often overcrowded and disease ridden. A variety of standards was applied to the provision of relief from locality to locality, much against the intentions of the 1832 Commissioners.

The belief that the moral lot of paupers would improve if they found work, was never likely to amount to much. The poor of industrial districts hated the workhouse. Their full horror became apparent during the 1837 Great Depression and the 'Hungry 40s'. **Trade cycles** created conditions in northern towns over which no one had much control. It was here where anti-Poor Law agitation erupted into violence against the guardians. There were attacks on workhouses. Poverty occurred through no fault of the individual. If there was no work to be had, the workhouse deterrent meant nothing. Crucially, the provision of out-relief had to continue to the able-bodied. In Sheffield, this accounted for much of the increase in Poor Law costs, from £12,000 in 1837 to £55,000 in 1843. The harshness of the Act attracted fierce comment, and condemnation. Workhouses were characterised as 'Bastilles', where inmates were exposed to harsh discipline, poor standards of diet, and dangerous or pointless tasks such as oakum picking and bone crushing. Families were separated, and meals were taken in silence. Charles Dickens' portrayal of conditions in *Oliver Twist* stands alongside the Scandal of the Andover Workhouse, where inmates were forced to chew animal bones to relieve their starvation. Although the Guardians had mismanaged affairs, they had kept to the spirit of the Act.

Trade cycles: The changes in economic condition from boom, through recession to depression (slump), recovery and then a return to boom.

Poor Law Hospital

Why was there opposition to the Poor Law Amendment Act across Britain, but especially in the North of England?

The 1847 Poor Law Act replaced the Commissioners with a Minister who was responsible to the Government and Parliament. However, little changed.

The Poor Law continued to be applied, although it is clear that many of its original principles had been undermined in practice. Workers, meanwhile, turned to Chartism for an improvement in their conditions of life.

6.4 How did policy change in the 19th century?

Democracy: A system of running organisations, businesses, government etc. in which each member is entitled to vote and participate in management decisions.

From the 1860s, new attitudes to social welfare slowly began to accompany the growth of **democracy** and the acceptance that the State had a broader responsibility for the individual. Progress was slow and difficult. Old habits and attitudes persisted even when the inadequacy of the old Poor Law had been demonstrated. Concessions to the sick and aged amounted to little, and were often given grudgingly. They went alongside the acceptance of a more 'collectivist' outlook, which underpinned the setting up of the Local Government Board in 1871. The two decades that followed witnessed the introduction of compulsory elementary education, the spread of a public health service, royal commissions on housing, changes in the franchise and the rise of mass trade unionism.

After 1867, a change of heart about the treatment of the sick came with plans to start building pauper hospitals. However, alongside it came a campaign to reduce the numbers claiming outdoor relief, in the hope that private charity might fill the gap. Despite the 1870 Depression, the numbers of people receiving out-relief fell by one-third. People wanted to avoid the workhouse at all costs.

Meanwhile, the public was being made aware of the extent of poverty in the midst of plenty. Reports from Charles Booth and Seebohm Rowntree, and books such as Sims' *Horrible London* and Mearn's *The Bitter Cry of Outcast London*, shocked the public and exposed the gaps in provision. It may have been true that workhouse conditions were improving – in 1892, men were provided with tobacco and, in 1894, women were allowed tea to mash themselves. This was tinkering with the discredited principles of 'less eligibility'. In 1909, the Poor Law Commission reported that 'the great principle of 1834 is not adequate to the new position'.

Why did attitudes towards poverty change between 1834 and 1875?

6.5 Why was effective factory reform so difficult to achieve?

Despite the bleak realities of life in pre-industrial England, it seems that agricultural and cottage workers were extremely dissatisfied with the working conditions in the new factories. If the domestic system had brought long working hours and poor living conditions, factories brought a loss of control over their lives and an integration with the pace of machines. The way of life in a factory was alien to working people and it was necessary for owners to enforce factory discipline on a labour force unwilling to conform. Initially, the family might impose discipline where it was able to work together. However, owners were not inclined to consider conditions of employment when concentrating on the growth of their enterprise. There was pressure to take children too young and to sub-contract the imposition of discipline to foremen and managers, rather than family groups. Technical advances were mainly responsible for this collapsing kinship system. Richard Robert's automatic mules meant that an adult spinner needed nine young assistants, not a family working together.

Workers were losing control of their lives. The worst expression of this

The Main Factory Acts

The 1833 Factory Act (Althorp's Act)

- Children aged 9–13 could work up to 9 hours a day and only 48 hours per week.
- Children aged 14–18 could work up to 12 hours a day and 65 hours per week.
- No child could be employed under the age of 9 and children aged 9–11 were to be given 2 hours schooling a day.
- The crucial aspect was the appointment of 4 inspectors, clearly not enough, but the first step towards enforcement.

1837: The compulsory registration of birth

- This was essential if children of working age were to be regulated.

1842: Mines and Collieries Act

Following two reports into mining conditions:

- no women and girls could work underground
- no boys under 10 could work underground
- inspectors were to be appointed in 1843.

1844: Factory Act

- The minimum age for children to start work was lowered to 8.
- Children under 13 could only work 6½ hours a day.
- Women and the young between 13 and 18 could only work a maximum 12-hour day.
- Dangerous machinery was to be fenced.
- The 'Ten Hours Movement' regarded the Act as unsatisfactory. Men like Oastler, Fielden, Stephens (the Chartist leader) and Tory Lord Ashley had campaigned for a Ten Hours Bill ever since the first one failed in 1831. Fielden tried again in 1847.

The 1847 Factory Act

- Restricted the hours of woman and young people to 10 hours a day.
- Nothing so far had limited the hours of men. It had been hoped that, as children's hours fell then it would be necessary to limit the running of machines so that men's hours would fall too. Not so. Owners got round this by using teams of children in relays. Hence the 1850 Act was passed.

The 1850 Factory Act

- Established a uniform working day.
- Woman and the young were to work between 6 a.m. and 6 p.m. or between 7 a.m. and 7 p.m.
- There would be 1½ hours for meals.
- Work on Saturday would cease at 2 p.m.

was the cruelty and exploitation suffered by children. Reformers were at work, both in the 1802 Health and Morals of Apprentices Act and in 1819, to limit child labour. Little was achieved, as there was no proper system of inspection or enforcement.

Nevertheless, there were forward-looking groups who pushed on. Progress was slow as supporters of reform were diverse and therefore disorganised. There were pioneering owners, such as Robert Owen and John Fielden. Benthamite Edwin Chadwick was soon involved, as well as representatives of both agricultural and industrial interests in sections of the Whig and Tory Parties. Both parties were divided among themselves on the issue of factory reform. Men such Richard Oastler, the steward of a landed estate, joined with northern clergymen to attack the savage treatment of young children and employers who took no paternalistic interest in their workers.

Moral concerns often outweighed humanitarian ones. Evangelical reformers were keen to root out the evils and corruption of industrial society. Select committees and royal commissions again set out to gather evidence as the ground work to legislation. Famously, the Mines Commissioners were shocked to find, in 1842, evidence of half-naked females and males working closely underground. They published, in the Blue Books, what they had intended to find out anyway.

Apostles of *laissez faire* defended the *status quo* and individual liberty, as well as raising the spectre of economic failure if workers' hours were lessened and pay improved. The free-market economists emphasised that individuals should enter into their own contractual arrangements and work to their own best interests. Owners were obsessed by the idea of fixed capital. They had invested in machinery, and output and profit varied according to how long they worked. Employers were in a position of strength given the size of the labour force and the fact that so many women and children were seeking employment. Nor were owners impressed by the argument that good treatment of workers would improve output, despite the example of employers like Robert Owen.

This was all very well for owners. Reformers pointed out that women and children were in no position to determine the nature of the 'free market' contract. By the 1840s, when the worst abuses were publicised, particularly in spinning, there was an acceptance that concessions might be necessary to head off excessive interference in their businesses.

Hence the debate centred on the extent to which the State would step in to protect workers. (The major Acts passed before 1850 are described on the previous page.)

What remained to be done after 1850?

There was a rearguard action against further reforms. However, on balance, there was more to be done than had been achieved by 1850.

Textile factories were covered, but conditions in mines remained poor. Workshops were not covered and further Acts were needed to extend protection to the metal trades, printing, bleaching and dyeing, blast furnaces and all small workshops. Dangerous occupations, such as match making, remained unprotected and it was not until 1866 that sanitary regulations were enforced in factories.

The gang system of itinerant women as agricultural labourers was not regulated until 1867, while the shocking use of chimney boys was not outlawed until 1875.

The Act of 1878 codified over 100 different Acts, applying standards to all factories and workshops.

● No children could be employed under 10.

1. What were the main obstacles to the introduction of factory reform?

2. What do you regard as the most important factory reform passed between 1819 and 1878? Give reasons for your answer.

● Women's hours were a maximum of 56½ in textiles and 60 hours in other factories.

Men continued to be neglected, and nothing had been done to regulate the 'sweated trades'. Even by the end of the century, most workers remained unprotected, exploited and in danger.

6.6 What efforts were made to improve public health?

The pace of urbanisation was startling. In 1800, only 25% of the population lived in towns. By the end of the century, the figure was 75%. Between 1801 and 1851, when death rates were at their highest, the population doubled from 10.5 million to 20.8 million.

Houses were built at enormous speed. They were unplanned and insanitary, with no thought of the health of occupants. An unregulated free-market economy produced housing, which had a catastrophic effect on the lifespan of their inhabitants. In 1842, labourers in Manchester had an average age of death of only 17 years of age. This was unsurprising in overcrowded, insanitary back-to-backs where there was neither clean water nor the means of disposing of sewage. Regular visitations of cholera – in 1831, 1848, 1853 and 1866 – highlighted the dreadful mortality rates, especially since the disease visited all classes, not just slum dwellers. Lack of knowledge about disease was only part of the problem. True, doctors had little success in curing people. Medical science had not yet discovered that germs cause disease (not until 1864). What was more significant was the lack of interventionist responsibility. *Laissez-faire* attitudes left landlords to do as they wished with their properties. Social prejudice dictated that the poor were weak, feeble and lazy. There was no will to make inroads into public health problems. Henriques refers to apathy and 'the collapse of communal responsibility'. Collectivism had not taken hold and

Gustav Doré's 'Over London by Rail' – a view of London in the 19th century

local government was in chaos. Four hundred local improvement acts, passed up to 1845, made hardly any impact.

Who would pay for better drains and improved water supply on the scale required? Certainly not ratepayers. They had no intention of paying for it. Before 1835, there was no single 'system' of local government. The local Boards of Health that had been set up to deal with the cholera epidemic of 1831 were closed down as soon as it was over. In 1835, Parliament set up 178 councils in towns or boroughs with charters, through the Municipal Corporations Act. Male householders could now elect the council to take over from 'Improvement Commissioners' who carried out street cleaning, paving, lighting and water supply. But 13 years later, a third of English towns still had no drainage or street cleaning. Places like Sheffield and Glasgow, which only gained charters to become towns in the 1840s, had to be included in the Act later. It was possible to bring some order out of the confusion of local government, but progress was slow.

The late 1830s and early 1840s saw attempts to capture the public's attention with the scale of the squalor in Britain's slums. The historian S.E. Finer acknowledges that England 'appeared for the first time to get a sense of sight and smell and realise that they were living on a dungheap'. Having a system of local government did not necessarily lead to reform. The new ratepayers – local members of the middle classes – were committed to individualism, the free market and limited expenditure of their own money. A major shift in such values would be slow in coming, despite the accumulation of evidence about the state of public health. For example, in 1838, Dr Southwood Smith investigated Whitechapel in London. He found 1,400 cases of poverty linked to cases of fever.

Edwin Chadwick, as Secretary to the Poor Law Commissioners from 1834, was very aware of the cost of disease and the consequent wasteful burden on the rates. If the wage-earner fell ill, the family would have to claim poor relief. Chadwick's 'Report on the Sanitary Conditions of the Labouring Population of Great Britain' (1842) brought together evidence from doctors all over the country. It was a bestseller. Significantly, the report was printed under Chadwick's name instead of under the name of the Poor Law Commission. The Commission had recognised that the Report contained findings that could upset ratepayers. Chadwick's obsession with clean water supplies, better drainage and good ventilation (as he blamed disease on harmful smells) would certainly carry a high cost. He wanted a system of small earthenware pipes with water flowing through, to flush out the sewage. However, the confused system of local administration and the inefficiency of the water companies, who could not guarantee supplies, meant that 'sanitary engineering' was unlikely to succeed in the short term. It relied on water pipes being connected to every house and more than two or three hours of supply a day.

It mattered little to the 'Dirty Party' – that groups of MPs who most strongly supported *laissez-faire* principles – that money could actually be saved on Poor Law expenditure if something was done to moderate the spiral of poverty and disease, by cleaning up towns.

Peel set up the royal commissions on 'large towns and populous districts', which published their reports in 1844 and 1845. They showed that little seemed to have been done since the cholera outbreaks of 1831 and 1832. It would take another disastrous outbreak of cholera, in 1848, before anything was done.

The 1848 Public Health Act set up a General Board of Health, in London. It could create local Boards of Health if 10% of the local ratepayers asked for one or where the death rate was above 23 per 1,000 of the population. Local Boards of Health had a wide role to control water supplies, cemeteries, sewage, the paving of streets and their drainage.

However, the reform was only grudgingly passed, almost as a favour rather than as a right. There was widespread suspicion of centralised control because local ratepayers might lose control over their expenditure. The whole principle of the authority of central government to interfere locally was not accepted. Tories could sense the imposition of taxes on rural areas to solve the problems of towns. Here was a national problem to which there was no national consensus about its solution.

The 1848 Act was undermined from the start by opponents. The General Board of Health could not force local action. The local boards could only advise – their powers were entirely permissive. Medical Officers of Health could be appointed, but there was no compulsion. Manchester did not have one until 1868. By 1854, only one-sixth of the population was covered by local Boards of Health. Chadwick, who had sat on the General Board of Health, resigned in the same year. His constant interfering and tactless manner meant that his resignation was greeted with delight. The General Board of Health itself had disappeared by 1858. The strong local forces against centralised reform had won, but only for the time being.

On the one hand, reformers were disappointed at national developments. There is a clear case that really improving public health would remain beyond the Victorians. Mortality rates were slightly higher in the early 1870s than they were in the 1840s. Cholera struck again in 1865 and 1866, and claimed 20,000 lives. Medical officers were frustrated by the fact that different authorities looked after burial grounds, urban sanitation and water supplies. Tuberculosis (TB) thrived in the slums and smallpox still managed to kill 44,000 people in the 1870s.

On the other hand, certain principles had been established for later action. In 1853, the compulsory vaccination of babies against smallpox was introduced. Sanitary engineering had evolved technically and John Simon (Medical Officer of Health in London 1848–55) proved that piped water and effective sewers could make an impact on mortality rates.

A Sanitary Act of 1866 forced local authorities to appoint sanitary inspectors. Parliament was in a position to insist on the removal of 'nuisances' and on the provision of sewers and good water supplies.

In 1868, a Royal Sanitary Commission into the health of towns eventually led to the formation of a Local Government Board in 1871 to oversee local provision. The 1875 Public Health Act was a major step forward and laid the foundations for reduced mortality rates at the turn of the century.

The Public Health Act, 1875

A mass of regulations, introduced over a period of 30 years, were brought into one Act. It contained little that was new but it laid foundations that would last well into the 20th century.

1. Every area had to have a Medical Officer of Health and sanitary inspectors.

2. Councils were given powers to build sewers, drains, public toilets and reservoirs.

3. Councils were to ensure that refuse was collected and to control the supply of pure water.

4. Local authorities had the power to disinfect houses where people had caught infectious diseases.

1. To what extent was the 1875 Act a 'turning point' in development of public health legislation?

2. Why was there so much opposition to reform, despite the obvious evidence of need?

The Government was trying to prevent disease at last. After 1874, doctors also had to sign death certificates showing each cause of death. Eventually, they had to give notification of infectious diseases.

6.7 How did housing policy change, 1866–1875?

The same set of values that held back factory and public health legislation also hindered attempts at improving housing. Not all landlords were obstructive, but many were. Since land lay at the heart of their beliefs, the problem of dealing with slums, which still had a commercial value despite their condition, would be doubly difficult to solve. Compensation would be needed if slums were to be cleared or improved. Who would pay? How much compulsion was required? How far would the private interests of the slum landlord be compromised in the interests of public health, public order and public morality? The need for action was all the more urgent as demand for houses far exceeded supply.

Private charities and individuals such as George Peabody and Octavia Hill did what they could. Hill bought and repaired slum properties, letting them out at profitable rents to families who would take a pride in them. A few employers tried to lead the way, such as George Cadbury at Bournville and William Hesketh Lever at Port Sunlight. Such shining examples of model villages made little impact on Britain's gloomy and overcrowded slums. Central government proved as ineffective as ever. In all, 27 housing Acts were passed in the second half of the 19th century. Once again, local ratepayers could delay reform. The lack of proper administrative bodies at local level further slowed down progress.

- In 1866, the Treasury made loans available if local authorities wanted to build houses. Only Liverpool applied.

- In 1868, The Housing (Torrens) Act said that landlords had to keep property in good repair. If repairs were not carried out, the local authority could use their powers and make sure that houses were made good.

- In 1875, the Artisans' Dwellings Act – the work of Disraeli's Home Secretary Richard Cross – gave local authorities even more power. They could clear whole areas of poor housing and re-house people nearby. Landlords were to be paid compensation if their property was pulled down. The Act also laid down the thickness of walls, the size of rooms, the spaces between buildings and standards of sanitation.

However, the Acts may well have shown the State as willing to interfere in property matters, but the powers were hardly used by local authorities. In the 10 years following the 1875 Act, only 11 councils gained permission to pull down slums and only four bothered to replace houses they demolished. Clearly, this made overcrowding worse. Only Birmingham, under Joseph Chamberlain's leadership, made spectacular improvements, but it was the only town of any size to take action.

Futher Reading

Texts designed for AS and A2 level students

Laissez-faire and State Intervention in the Nineteenth Century by A.J.P. Taylor (Macmillan, 1972)

The Poor Law in Nineteenth-Century England and Wales by A. Digby (Historical Association, 1982)

Endangered Lives. Public Health in Victorian Britain by A. Wohl (Dent, 1983)

Before the Welfare State by U. Henriques (Longman, 1979)

The Coming of the Welfare State by M. Bruce (Batsford, 1968)
Education for the Nation by R. Aldrich (Cassell, 1996)
Education in the Twentieth Century by P. Gosden (Methuen, 1976)
State and Society: A Social and Political History of Britain, 1870–1997 by Martin
   Pugh (Arnold, 1999)
British Society since 1945 by A. Marwick (Penguin, 1996)

More advanced reading

Modern Britain: an Economic and Social History by S. Glynn and A. Booth
   (Routledge, 1996)
Social Conditions in Britain 1918–39 by S. Constantine (Routledge, 1984)
Class and Cultures. England 1918–51 by R. McKibbin (Oxford University Press,
   2000)

7 Gladstone, 1868–1894

Key Issues

- Why was the Liberal Party affected by internal disunity?

- How successful was Gladstone as party leader and Prime Minister?

- How far did the Liberal Party bring social and political change to Britain?

7.1 What was Gladstonian Liberalism?
7.2 How successful was Gladstone's First Ministry in bringing social and political change?
7.3 Why did the Liberal Party lose the 1874 general election?
7.4 Historical interpretation: Gladstone and Chamberlain
7.5 'A Ministry of Troubles': Gladstone's Second Ministry, 1880–1885
7.6 What impact did Gladstone have on late Victorian politics?

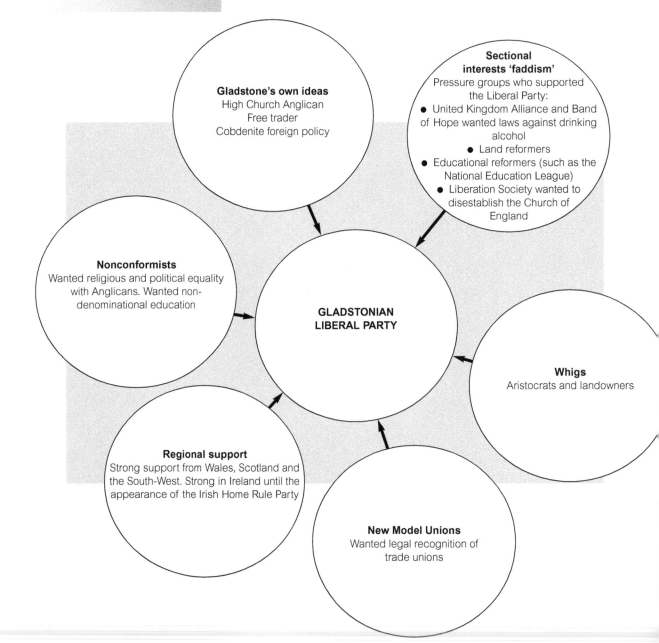

Gladstone's own ideas
High Church Anglican
Free trader
Cobdenite foreign policy

Sectional interests 'faddism'
Pressure groups who supported the Liberal Party:
- United Kingdom Alliance and Band of Hope wanted laws against drinking alcohol
- Land reformers
- Educational reformers (such as the National Education League)
- Liberation Society wanted to disestablish the Church of England

Nonconformists
Wanted religious and political equality with Anglicans. Wanted non-denominational education

GLADSTONIAN LIBERAL PARTY

Whigs
Aristocrats and landowners

Regional support
Strong support from Wales, Scotland and the South-West. Strong in Ireland until the appearance of the Irish Home Rule Party

New Model Unions
Wanted legal recognition of trade unions

Overview

T HE Liberal Party was the dominant political party for most of the period 1868–94. In 1868, 1880, 1886 and 1892 the Liberal Party formed the government, although on the last two occasions with the support of the Irish Home Rule Party.

As the Liberal Party dominated in British politics, so William Ewart Gladstone was the dominant force within the Liberal Party. Indeed, to many of his fellow Liberals Gladstone 'was' the Liberal Party. Gladstone's remarkable political career began in 1832 when he was elected as a right-wing Tory MP. As a minister in Peel's governments of 1835 and 1841–46, he was one of the rising stars of the 'Peelite' Conservative Party. Following the party split on the Corn Laws in 1846, Gladstone became a leading figure in the Peelite faction of the House of Commons. As Chancellor of the Exchequer in the Whig–Peelite coalition of 1852–55, he developed a national reputation for cutting taxes and placing Britain on the road to free trade. In 1859, as a supporter of Italian unification, he joined Palmerston's Liberal Government, thus completing his political journey from right-wing Tory to Liberal.

Gladstone was, undoubtedly, the leading Liberal politician of his era. He supported free trade and, under his leadership, his governments passed many significant reforms which abolished privilege and moved Britain towards a **meritocracy**.

Meritocracy: The idea that the appointment of individuals to positions of authority should be based on ability and qualifications, not upbringing.

He did not, however, always represent the views of his Liberal supporters. As a **High Churchman** and a supporter of the right of the aristocracy to govern, Gladstone led a party where many opposed the privileged position of both the Church of England and the aristocracy. One of the main themes of this period is the potential disunity of the Liberal Party. In 1873–74, and again in 1880–86, the Liberal Party was affected by division within its ranks. Eventually the Party did split, over the issue of Irish Home Rule, into two factions: the Gladstonian Liberals and the Liberal Unionists.

High Churchman: A member of the Church of England who supported the Oxford Movement's view that Anglican church services should be similar to the Catholic Church but without recognising the Pope as head of the Christian Church.

Politics was changing rapidly during this period. In 1867, the franchise had been widened to include the skilled workers in urban areas. In 1872, the secret ballot was introduced and, in 1884, the right to vote was extended to most adult males. Both major parties, the Liberals and Conservatives, developed nationwide party organisations in reaction to the changing circumstances. In the general election campaigns of 1880 and 1885, politicians such as William Gladstone and Joseph Chamberlain campaigned across the country on national issues. The years 1868 to 1894, therefore, represent the foundation of the modern party political system.

Gladstone led the Liberal Party during a period of considerable political change. But he was also a politician of an older generation compared with his major rivals within the Liberal Party: Gladstone was 59 when he became Prime Minister for the first time in 1868. When he retired as Prime Minister, in 1894, he had reached the advanced age of 85. He was often out of step with younger politicians. His main rival for much of this period, Joseph Chamberlain, was a **nonconformist** from Birmingham who possessed a radically different view of which policies the Liberal Party should follow. The disunity within the Liberal Party and the split of 1886 had much to do with the rivalry between Gladstone and Chamberlain.

Nonconformist: A Protestant who is not a member of the Church of England. Examples are Methodists, Quakers and Baptists.

7.1 What was Gladstonian Liberalism?

Gladstone led a political party that was itself the product of the changing social and economic conditions taking place in Britain during the 19th century.

In Parliament

The party in Parliament was a mixture of Whigs, Peelites, Liberals and Radicals who had all come together in the period following the split within the Conservative Party in 1846.

- The **Whigs** were members of the British aristocracy who had opposed too much monarchic influence in politics and had passed the Great Reform Bill of 1832. Among active Whigs were some of the largest landowners in the country, such as Lord Hartington (later the 8th Duke of Devonshire). The leading Whigs were members of the House of Lords. However, junior members of the Whig families sat as MPs.

- The Peelites were the former followers of Sir Robert Peel who supported free trade. Predominantly from industrial and commercial backgrounds, they included Gladstone among their number.

- **Liberals** were also from industrial and commercial backgrounds, having joined forces with the Whigs in the 1830s and 1840s to support free trade, the freedom of the press and freedom of religion.

- **Radicals** was a term used to describe a wide variety of MPs who wished to see radical change in certain aspects of British society. Some were nonconformists who opposed the privileged position of the Church of England as the **State Church**. Others advocated reform in areas such as education, the laws governing alcohol and land reform.

State Church: The Church of England was recognised as the official religion of England, receiving financial support from the Government.

The issue that finally brought this rather disparate group of politicians together was their combined support for Italian unification and their desire to remove a minority Conservative government under the Earl of Derby. At Willis' tea rooms, on 5 June 1859, the Liberal Party was formally launched as a distinct parliamentary party.

Outside Parliament

The Party received support from a variety of social and economic groups. In his book *The Formation of the Liberal Party 1857 to 1868*, John Vincent identifies three forces which helped to create the party as a nationwide institution.

- First, the rise of political nonconformity and its desire to receive equality of treatment with the Church of England. The Liberation Society, a pressure group led by Edward Miall, called for the removal of the privileged position of the Church of England as the State Church and the preferential treatment enjoyed by Anglicans in institutions such as Oxford and Cambridge universities. Backing from this group explains why the Liberal Party received strong support from areas such as Wales, Scotland and the West Country, where nonconformists were numerous. In addition, until 1868 the Liberal Party received considerable support in Ireland. Thereafter, following the formation of the Home Rule Party, the Liberal Party there went into terminal decline.

New Model Unions: Trade unions that represented skilled workers such as engineers and boilermakers.

- Second, the Party received support from **New Model Unions** which represented the interests of skilled workers such as engineers, carpenters

Friendly Societies: Independent, non-profit-making organisations providing financial support for members during illness or in death, in return for weekly/monthly subscriptions (e.g. Hearts of Oak Friendly Society).

---

1. Who were the main supporters of the Gladstonian Liberal Party? Give reasons to support your answer.

2. 'The Gladstonian Liberal Party was made up of a mixture of competing interests.'

Using the information in this section, explain what this statement meant and why it proved to be a major problem for the Liberal Party under Gladstone.

Beaconsfieldism: The name given to Disraeli's foreign and imperial policies, which were seen as costly and aggressive.

Retrenchment: The policy of keeping government expenditure to a minimum.

and boilermakers. This social group largely received the vote with the passing of the Second Reform Act of 1867. They were also faced with the problem of lack of legal recognition for their trade unions. Many had operated as friendly societies, under the **Friendly Societies** Act of 1855. This meant they could offer their members financial support in the event of sickness or death. However, they could not bargain for wage rises nor strike. In the court case Hornby *versus* Close, 1867, these unions found that their funds were not protected from theft. They, therefore, supported the Liberal Party in the hope that legislation would be introduced to grant them legal protection.

● Finally, Vincent refers to the importance of the rise of provincial newspapers as a means for spreading support for the Liberal Party. With the development of railways and the removal of taxes on newspapers in 1861, the newspaper industry outside London grew rapidly. Newspapers such as the *Manchester Guardian* and the *Leeds Mercury* supported Liberal causes.

These three developments all took place during the mid-Victorian economic boom of 1850–73, when there was a major increase in the size and wealth of the industrial and commercial classes in relation to the aristocracy which owed its wealth and status to agriculture. As a result, the Liberal Party received strong support from urban areas, such as the growing industrial cities of Birmingham, Manchester and Leeds.

Gladstone's views

On top of this background of a political party made up of many different, often competing factions, there are Gladstone's own political views. These were sometimes in tune with the views of the majority of Liberal supporters but, at other times, were at odds with them.

A central key to understanding Gladstone's views is to realise that he was a deeply religious man who believed that his involvement in politics was related directly to his religious beliefs. Much of his stature as a politician was based on his ability to think of political problems as moral issues. His opposition to the Bulgarian Horrors, his opposition to **Beaconsfieldism** in 1879–80, and his campaigns on Irish issues all seemed like religious crusades. Gladstone's moral stance on political issues annoyed many of his political foes. For example, one complained about Gladstone always having the ace of trumps up his sleeve and, particularly, the fact that Gladstone always claimed that God had put it there.

In practical terms, Gladstone was a firm supporter of free trade for the whole of his political life. Alongside this was his dislike of government interference in the lives of its citizens. As a result, Gladstone supported **retrenchment**, thereby lowering taxation. This was combined with a constant drive to improve the efficiency of government and other national institutions.

The basis of Gladstone's view of the 'minimalist' state was the importance of the individual. Gladstone did not see society as a set of competing economic classes, but of individuals where each should have the opportunity to fulfil their potential. As he stated, 'I will always back the masses against the classes.' This did not mean that Gladstone was a democrat. He was, even by the norms of the time, a social conservative. In 1878, he said to the art critic, John Ruskin, 'I am an out-and-out inequalitarian.' He believed in rule by those individuals in society who had a tradition of service to the State and possessed sufficient wealth to be above the charge of possible corruption. He was, therefore, a supporter of the traditional roles of monarchy and aristocracy.

An overall assessment of the Gladstonian Liberal Party

It is clear that the Gladstonian Liberal Party was a complex political phenomenon. Gladstone himself did not reflect the views of many Liberals. Inside Parliament, a rift grew between Whigs and Radicals that led to the split of 1886. Outside Parliament, the Party comprised a wide variety of competing groups, each in pursuit of its own political aims.

Historians such as D.A. Hamer, in *Liberal Politics in the Age of Gladstone and Rosebery* (1974), and Martin Pugh, in *The Making of Modern British Politics* (1982), have referred to 'faddism' within the Liberal Party: meaning that the Party was susceptible to splits. Even before Gladstone had become Liberal leader, the Party had split over the issue of parliamentary reform when Robert Lowe led the 'Adullamite' faction against Gladstone's electoral bill in 1866.

This problem was to affect the Gladstonian Party throughout the period. When Gladstone retired as Prime Minister, in 1894, the Party had been split into two distinct factions for eight years.

Punch cartoon, December 1879, entitled 'The Colossus of Words'.

THE COLOSSUS OF WORDS.

1. Using information contained within the chapter, explain the meaning of 'retrenchment' (bottom left-hand corner of the cartoon).

2. Do you think this cartoon is in support of Gladstone? Give reasons to support your answer.

Source-based questions: The social backgrounds of Liberal Party MPs

TABLE A

Background of Liberal MPs (as a percentage)

Interest	1859–74	1892	1914
Land	49.2	8.1	6.0
Business and finance	30.1	44.2	40.0
Law	16.7	24.8	22.0

Table B

Backgrounds of Conservative and Liberal MPs in 1892 (as a percentage)

Interest	Liberal	Conservative
Land	8.1	28.5
Business and finance	44.2	25.9
Law	24.8	24.1

1. Study Table A.

In what ways did the backgrounds of Liberal MPs change between 1859 and 1914?

Explain why the changes took place.

2. Study Table B.

How different were the social backgrounds of Liberal and Conservative MPs in 1892?

Explain why these differences existed.

7.2 How successful was Gladstone's First Ministry in bringing social and political change?

Introduction

Gladstone became Prime Minister for the first time in December 1868, when the Liberal Party ousted a minority Conservative government under Benjamin Disraeli, winning a majority of 106 seats over their rivals (Liberals 382; Conservatives 276).

Gladstone's first Cabinet reflected the diverse composition of the Liberal Party. It contained three former Peelites (Gladstone, Cardwell and De Grey), with three Liberals (Childers, Goschen and Bruce) and two Radicals (Lowe and Bright). However, the largest group within the Cabinet was the Whigs, who held seven posts including Foreign Secretary, Irish Secretary and Colonial Secretary. All the Cabinet members belonged to the Church of England, except John Bright who, as a Quaker, was the first nonconformist to hold Cabinet rank.

The government over which Gladstone presided has been described by Michael Bentley, in *The Climax of Liberal Politics* (1987), as 'one of the most energetic and prolific administrations of the 19th century'. In *Gladstone* (1975), E.J. Feuchtwanger stated that 'Gladstonian Liberalism can be defined largely in terms of the reforms accomplished in this period'.

The main principles of Gladstonian Liberalism were clearly present in the reforms passed. Support for free trade, administrative efficiency in government, retrenchment and individual self-expression are all apparent in many of the reforms. Many contemporaries saw the ministry as one that was engaged in an attack on privilege to create a meritocracy.

However, many of the reforms were also aimed at satisfying the political demands of pressure groups associated with the Liberal Party. Education reform (National Education League), trade union reform (New Model Unions), and licensing reform of the liquor trade (United Kingdom Alliance and the Band of Hope Union) highlight a key feature of the Liberal Party: its diversity of support.

We need to ask two questions when assessing the reform programme of Gladstone's First Ministry:

● How far did the reforms bring social and political change?

● Did the reforms satisfy the aspirations of the various pressure groups which supported the Liberal Party?

Irish reform

These reforms and Gladstone's policy towards Ireland are dealt with at length in Chapter 10. However, Gladstone did use the slogan 'Justice for Ireland' as his major rallying cry during the 1868 general election to unify the disparate elements of the Liberal Party.

The disestablishment of the Church of Ireland Act in 1869 did possess major features to please Liberal supporters. The Liberation Society, which wished to disestablish the Church of England, saw Irish disestablishment as a first step towards their ultimate goal. Liberals, in general, also saw the Act as removing an obvious Irish grievance. However, many Whigs viewed this attack on the Irish 'Establishment' with deep suspicion. The later Irish Land Act was seen as an attack on the rights of property and helped push the Whigs towards the Conservative Party, where most were to end up after 1886.

The most controversial aspect of Gladstone's Irish policy was his Universities Bill of 1873. This had the uncanny knack of upsetting both conservative Whigs and left-of-centre Radicals. The Government's defeat on the Bill by three votes, in March 1873, forced Gladstone to resign temporarily from office. However, Disraeli's refusal to form another minority Conservative administration forced Gladstone to continue in office for another ten months.

Education reform

The Liberal Ministry's involvement in educational matters covered a wide spectrum.

● In December 1868, it passed the Public Schools Act, which revised the governing bodies of the 'Clarendon' schools such as Eton, Harrow and Winchester. This was followed, in 1869, by the Endowed Schools Act, which aimed to improve secondary education by appointing three commissioners to revise the trust deeds of schools such as Manchester Grammar School. Any further proposals for reorganisation had to be submitted to the Education Department.

● Of greater significance was the University Tests Act, 1871, which dealt with a major nonconformist grievance in higher education. The Act allowed non-Anglicans to take up teaching posts at the universities of Oxford, Cambridge and Durham. It also allowed non-Anglicans to qualify for scholarships and fellowships at these universities.

● By far the most important educational reform, and one that stands out as a milestone in English educational reform, was the Forster Elementary Education Act, 1870. This Act laid the foundations of the English elementary education system. Until 1870, elementary education (children from 5 to 11 years) was carried out in church schools administered by either the Church of England through the

National Society, nonconformists through the British and Foreign School Society or by the Roman Catholic Church. Since 1833, these schools had received some financial assistance from the State. From 1839, a government department supervised expenditure.

Demands for reform came from those, such as industrialists, who feared that Britain's competitive edge in world trade and industry was being damaged by the lack of an effective education system. They pointed to both the USA and Prussia, Britain's two major economic rivals, as states that, by 1870, had introduced free, compulsory, state-funded education at elementary level. It would be an exaggeration to state that the spectacular military successes of the Prussian army in 1866 and 1870 were the prime cause for reform. However, Gladstone stated, in an article in the *Edinburgh Review* in 1870: 'Undoubtedly, the conduct of the campaign, on the German side, has given a marked triumph to the cause of systematic popular education.'

To support a campaign for change along these lines Joseph Chamberlain, a Birmingham industrialist, launched the National Education League in 1869. This pressure group campaigned for free, compulsory, **non-denominational** elementary education. They were opposed by the National Education Union, which wanted to retain education under direct Church control.

Non-denominational: Christian education without a bias towards one type, e.g. Anglican or Catholic. Usually based on Bible reading.

The Act that was eventually passed was a compromise between these two positions. It created what became known as the 'Dual System', whereby elementary education was provided either by Church schools or locally administered State schools, known as Board schools. W.E. Forster, the Vice-President of the Education Department of the Privy Council, who was responsible for the passage of the Bill, declared that he wished to 'complete the voluntary system and fill up the gaps' and 'to cover the country with good schools'.

School Boards were created, elected by ratepayers with the task of creating schools where Church schools did not exist. London was to make up one School Board. These School Boards were given the power to levy local rates to meet part of the cost of Board schools but not Church schools. The rest of the money was provided by central government.

Within Church schools, denominational religious teaching continued. In Board schools, only Bible teaching was permitted. However, if a parent wished to have denominational religious teaching for their child, under the Cowper-Temple clause of the Act, they had the power to remove their children from a Board school to attend religious teaching of their choosing. As a result, religious classes were always timetabled at the end of the school day to allow this practice to take place. Fees were to be paid by parents to Board schools but School Boards could, under Clause 25 of the Act, establish free schools in poor districts. This could mean 'voluntary' or Church schools. The National Education League (NEL) was outraged by this, because they were against any financial support for these schools.

Although the Act had considerable long-term consequences, it fell far short of the aspirations of the National Education League. The League took the unprecedented step of running its own candidates against the Liberals in the 1874 general election. Further legislation in 1876, 1880 and 1891 went a long way to meeting the NEL's aims but to this day the 'Dual System' has survived.

Army reform

The reforms in the Army, made under the direction of Edward Cardwell, Minister of War, contained many of the principles underpinning

Gladstonian Liberalism: the improvement of efficiency, an attack on privilege and the enhancement of individual self-expression.

The demand for reform came from many quarters. First, there was the memory of British military incompetence during the Crimean War (1854–56). More recently, the experience of the American Civil War and the successes of the Prussian army in wars against Denmark and Austria during the 1860s meant that the British Army was in dire need of modernisation.

To meet these challenges, Cardwell made the Commander-in-Chief of the Army subordinate to the Minister of War. This was meant to ensure the political control of the Army. Queen Victoria, however, insisted on her son, the Duke of Cambridge, retaining the position of Commander-in-Chief until the 1890s, even though he lacked the qualifications for the post.

● The War Office Act, 1870, divided the War Office into three departments: the Commander-in-Chief, Surveyor-General and Financial Secretary. This was in a bid to improve efficiency.

● Improved efficiency was also the purpose behind two further acts. The Army Enlistment Act, 1870, permitted a three-year enlistment in the army in addition to the normal 12 years. The Army Regulation Act, 1871, increased the size of the Army from 200,000 to 497,000. The country was divided into military districts, usually a county, each with a central barracks, to encourage recruitment. Authority for the militia was transferred from the Lord Lieutenant of a county to the War Office.

● To bring the British Army into line with other modern forces such as France, Prussia and the USA, a new breech-loading infantry rifle – the Martini-Henry – was introduced to replace the muzzle-loading Enfield rifle musket.

● In an attack on privilege, the most controversial aspect of Cardwell's reforms was the abolition of the purchase of commissions. In future, promotion within the officer class was to be based on merit only. This proposal met such fierce opposition in the House of Lords that it was introduced by royal warrant, not Act of Parliament, in July 1871.

Another area of controversy was the decision to withdraw British troops from the self-governing colonies, in particular Canada and New Zealand. Gladstone believed that these colonies would only be truly self-governing if they looked after their own defence. This decision created considerable opposition in Canada, which feared US invasion and had experienced the Red River Revolt in 1867, and from New Zealand, where the Maori Wars were in progress. Benjamin Disraeli, the Conservative leader, even went so far as to claim that this proposal was part of a Gladstonian plot to dismember the British Empire.

Civil Service reform

As another aspect of the promotion of a meritocracy, in June 1870 the Government, by Order-in-Council, made all public posts within the Home Civil Service open to competition through public examination. This completed work begun by the Northcote-Trevelyan reforms of 1854. However, the Diplomatic and Foreign Civil Service were exempt.

Licensing reform

Under pressure from the United Kingdom Alliance and the Band of Hope Union, the Home Secretary H.A. Bruce introduced the Licensing Act of

1872. This gave Justices of the Peace (JPs) the right to grant licences to publicans, to fix opening and closing hours and to check on the adulteration of beer. The Act disappointed the two Liberal pressure groups who felt it was too lenient. However, the Act did upset the brewing interests and the 'drinking masses'. As the historian R.C.K. Ensor states, the Act saw 'a positive and permanent shift of the publicans and brewers to the Tory Party'.

Electoral reform

In 1872, the Government implemented one of the Chartists' six points with the passage of the Ballot Act. The reform was introduced by W.E. Forster. It declared that voting in elections should be by secret ballot and that candidates should no longer be nominated at the **hustings**. Although this enhanced the right of voters to cast their votes without intimidation, it did not end electoral malpractice. In 1883, the second Gladstone Administration had to pass the Corrupt and Illegal Practices Act.

Hustings: Political activities such as speeches that take place in the period just before an election.

Trade union reform

An important pressure group, which supported the Liberal Party in the 1868 election, had been the New Model Unions. They were keen to gain legal recognition following the Hornby *versus* Close case of 1867. The Trade Union Act, 1871, gave trade unions the legal protection they wanted.

Gladstone also wanted 'to prevent violence and, in all economic matters, for the law to take no part'. The Liberal Government therefore passed the Criminal Law Amendment Act, also in 1871, which aimed to prevent violence in strikes by making intimidation illegal. However, in the Gas Stokers' Case of December 1872, the judge, Justice Brett, declared that trade unionists could be charged for intimidation under the law of conspiracy, while JPs interpreted the term 'intimidation' very widely to include such actions as dirty looks at strikebreakers.

This legislation and its interpretation in the courts caused great resentment among trade unionists. By November 1873, the Liberal Cabinet had come to the conclusion that a reform of the law was required. It agreed to a proposal similar to that eventually passed by the Conservative Government as the Conspiracy and Protection of Property Act, 1875.

The Supreme Court of Judicature Act, 1873

This legislation was the work of the Lord Chancellor, Lord Selborne. It established one Supreme Court, divided into the High Court and the Court of Appeal. The courts of Queen's Bench, Common Pleas, Exchequer, Chancery, Admiralty, Probate (Wills), and Divorce, which had all been independent of each other, were to become three divisions of the High Court (Queen's Bench, Chancery and Admiralty, Probate and Divorce [wills, wives and wrecks]).

This Act was part of Gladstone's attempt to streamline institutions and to introduce administrative efficiency. However, Selborne's attempt to abolish double appeals was not successful and in 1876 appeals were allowed to the House of Lords.

Local government reform

One of Disraeli's last acts as Prime Minister, in 1868, was to set up a royal commission on sanitary matters. It reported in 1871 and recommended 'that the present fragmentary and confused Sanitary Law should be made uniform'. As a result, the Government passed the Local Government Act in

1871, which reorganised health administration under a Minister for Local Government.

In 1872, another act – the Public Health Act – established the Urban and Rural Sanitary Authorities responsible for public health in local areas. These were the forerunners of Urban and Rural District Councils.

Summary

Gladstone's First Administration was certainly responsible for wide-ranging reforms. Legislation such as the Local Government Act, the Supreme Court of Judicature Act, the Forster Elementary Education Act and Cardwell's Army reforms were all significant in improving the efficiency of the nation's institutions.

The Ballot Act went a considerable way to ensuring freedom of choice at elections. The Trade Union Act allowed trade unions to operate legally, while the Criminal Law Amendment Act attempted to allow those who still wished to work during an industrial dispute to go to work unmolested. Much of the legislation also bore the mark of pressure group demands for reform, such as the Universities Test Act, the Licensing Act, the Forster Education Act and the Trade Union Act.

However, the ministry is regarded as a landmark in the attack on privilege and the promotion of a meritocracy. The Irish Church Act, the abolition of purchase of army commissions, the Universities Test Act and the open competition for Home Civil Service posts all contributed to making Gladstone's First Administration a great reforming ministry. As E.J. Feuchtwanger states, in *Gladstone 1874 to 1898* (1995): 'In terms of legislative achievement the Government was to become one of the greatest of the 19th century and by far the most important of the four governments of which he was head.'

1. Use the information on pages 119–124 to list those reforms which helped to move Britain towards a meritocracy. Then list those reforms aimed at pleasing a pressure group associated with the Liberal Party.

2. On balance, do you think the Gladstone Ministry was more concerned with creating a meritocracy than supporting the demands of Liberal pressure groups?

Give reasons to support your answer.

1. Place the reforms passed by Gladstone's ministry in order of their importance.

2. Do you think this mind map contains all the important reforms passed by Gladstone's first ministry? If not, can you identify any other reforms?

3. Why, in spite of so many reforms, did Gladstone lose the general election of 1874?

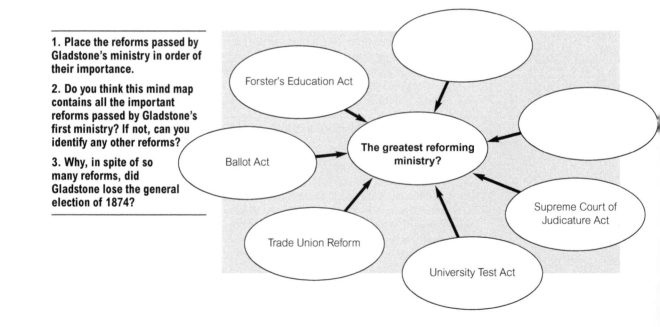

7.3 Why did the Liberal Party lose the 1874 general election?

Given E.J. Feuchtwanger's verdict of Gladstone's First Ministry, why did the Liberals lose the 1874 general election so convincingly, winning only 242 seats to 352 for the Conservatives?

Disraeli's leadership of the Conservative Party

At the time, many Liberals believed the pattern of politics of the previous 25 years would re-occur, with Liberal governments followed by a minority Conservative government for a short period. Disraeli signalled his unwillingness to follow this path when he declined office, in March 1873, after Gladstone had resigned over the Irish Universities Bill.

Tactically, Disraeli's refusal to take office allowed the Liberal Government to disintegrate between March 1873 and February 1874. By the time Gladstone resigned over a Cabinet disagreement on reducing military expenditure, the Liberals were fighting as much among themselves as against the Conservatives.

In addition, the Conservative Party had undergone considerable reorganisation since 1867. A National Union of Conservative Associations and a Central Office had been created under the guidance of Principal Agent J.E. Gorst. As a result, by 1874 the Conservatives had a highly effective electoral machine. Conservative chances were also enhanced by Disraeli's policy programme outlined in 1872 at Manchester and the Crystal Palace.

Alienation of important groups within the Liberal Party

Although the Administration was successful in passing many reforms, it also upset a considerable number of its own supporters. The National Education League was disappointed with the Forster Education Act and put up candidates against official Liberal candidates in the 1874 general election. In the election, 200 out of the 425 Liberal candidates were pledged to repeal Forster's Act. The United Kingdom Alliance was disappointed with the Licensing Act and the New Model Unions were campaigning against a repeal of the Criminal Law Amendment Act.

Unlike 1868, when Gladstone was able to rally the Liberals with the slogan 'Justice for Ireland', his campaign slogan for 1874 – 'the abolition of income tax' – did not have the same effect.

Alienation of important sections of the electorate

The reforms passed by the Liberals had also upset important groups who could influence the outcome of the election. Landowners were suspicious of the possible impact of the Irish Land Act on property rights. They were able to persuade their tenants to vote Conservative. The Church of England was dismayed by the Irish Church Act and Universities Test Act, and the officer class and landowners by the attacks on privilege, in particular the abolition of the purchase of commissions.

According to Gladstone, the brewing interest also had an influence on the election. Having been forced into second place in a two-member constituency at Greenwich by a Conservative distiller called Boord, he exclaimed that 'we have been borne down in a torrent of gin and beer'. The brewing interest clearly had an influence on the Greenwich election, but its influence nationwide has been exaggerated.

Unpopularity of some policies

One important area of electoral discontent was Gladstone's imperial and foreign policy, which was decidedly unpopular. Disraeli exploited disquiet over the 'Alabama' affair and imperial issues to some effect in the election. There were also fears about indirect taxation. In 1871, Robert Lowe, the Chancellor of the Exchequer, unsuccessfully attempted to place an indirect tax of ½d on a packet of matches.

The ministry was also plagued by a number of scandals, including the controversial appointment of Sir Robert Collier to the Privy Council and a Cambridge graduate to the parish of Ewelme, Oxfordshire (a parish reserved for Oxford graduates). However, the most important scandal involved irregularities at the Post Office in the summer of 1873. The scandal led to the dismissal of the Postmaster-General and a Cabinet reshuffle.

The most significant problem was the Irish Universities Bill of 1873, which created such an outcry that it led, temporarily, to Gladstone's removal from office. The ministry never really recovered from this crisis.

The rise of the Home Rule Party in Ireland

Following its formation as the Home Government Association in 1870, the party grew rapidly capturing 58 seats in the 1874 election, mainly at the expense of Irish Liberals.

Summary

Gladstone lost the 1974 general election primarily because of problems within the Liberal Party itself and the alienation of large sections of the electorate. However, Disraeli and the Conservatives exploited Liberal difficulties very effectively.

---

1. Which of the reasons for Liberal defeat in 1874 mentioned above were outside Gladstone's immediate control?

2. 'The Liberal Party lost the 1874 general election because it upset sections of the electorate.' Using the evidence contained in this section, do you agree with this statement? Give reasons to support your answer.

Source-based questions: The general election of February 1874

SOURCE A

The signs of weakness multiply, and for some time have multiplied, upon the government, in the loss of control over the legislative action of the House of Lords, the diminution of the majority of the House of Commons without its natural compensation in increase of unity and discipline, and the almost unbroken series of defeats in [by]elections in the country.

From a letter from Gladstone to Lord Granville,
the Foreign Secretary, 8 January 1874.

SOURCE B

As I sat opposite the Treasury Bench the Ministers reminded me of one of those marine landscapes not very uncommon on the coasts of south America. You behold a range of exhausted volcanoes. Not a flame flickers on a single pallid crest.

From a speech by Disraeli in April 1872 describing
the Liberal Cabinet.

SOURCE C

When we look at the poll in the City of London, in Westminster, in Middlesex, in Surrey, in Liverpool, Manchester, Leeds and Sheffield, in the metropolitan boroughs and in the home counties, in all centres of middle-class industry, wealth and cultivation, we see one unmistakable fact, that the trading class, and the comfortable middle class has grown distinctly Conservative. The inference is unmistakable. The effective force of the middle class has grown for a season Conservative. The Conservative Party has become as much the middle-class party as the Liberals used to be.

This, then, appears to us the great lesson of the elections of 1874 that the middle classes have gone over to the enemy bag and baggage.

From 'The Conservative Reaction', published in
The Fortnightly Review after the election of 1874.

Source-based questions: The general election of February 1874

SOURCE D

The underlying cause of the Liberal defeat was the simultaneous loss of working and middle-class voters. The working classes were disappointed because Liberal reform, for all its achievements, had not really changed their lot. The middle classes were alarmed not merely by what the Liberal Party had done, but by events such as the Paris Commune, which seemed to portend threats to all property and security in the future. The alienation of particular groups of Liberal activists meant that the Liberal Party could probably not realise its full voting potential.

From *Democracy and Empire: British History 1865 to 1914*
by E.J. Feuchtwanger (1985).

1. Study Source A.

How reliable is this source as an explanation for Liberal defeat in the general election of 1874?

2. Study Source B.

How, by his use of language and style, does Disraeli explain how the Liberal Government had 'run out of steam'?

3. Study Sources C and D.

How far do the sources agree on the reason for Liberal defeat in the 1874 election?

4. Use all the sources and your own knowledge to answer the following question:

'Do these sources provide a full explanation for the Liberal defeat in the 1874 general election?'

Give reasons to support your answer.

7.4 Gladstone and Chamberlain
A CASE STUDY IN HISTORICAL INTERPRETATION

In the history of the Liberal Party between 1868 and 1894 one of the dominant themes was the conflict between William Gladstone and Joseph Chamberlain over who should lead and direct the Party and what role the Government should play in the lives of its citizens. The conflict between the two politicians was a major factor behind the split in the Party over Irish Home Rule in 1886.

Radical Joe?

Gladstone and Chamberlain came from two very different social and political backgrounds. Gladstone was a High Churchman, born in 1809 into a rich Liverpool commercial family. He attended Eton and Oxford. Chamberlain was born in London in 1836. He was a nonconformist (a Unitarian) and did not attend university. Chamberlain made his commercial and political reputation in the West Midlands, centred on Birmingham. He represented a new kind of politician for mid-Victorian politics. Unlike Gladstone, he made his political reputation outside Parliament. Beginning with the Birmingham Liberal **Caucus**, he then founded and led the National Education League. From 1873 to 1876, he was Lord Mayor of Birmingham and was responsible for the complete urban renewal of the city. His use of the power of local city government to transform the water, lighting and housing of Birmingham made him a fervent supporter of the positive benefits of elected local government. In 1884, he put forward his Central Board Scheme, which he believed would solve the 'Irish problem': elected local government was what Ireland required, not Home Rule.

To ensure that the Liberal Party should follow this path, Chamberlain was the driving force behind the creation of the National Liberal

Caucus: A local party organisation made up of active, committed members.

Federation of 1877. The aim of this body was to supply effective party organisation throughout the country. More importantly, it would decide Liberal Party policy, thus allowing radicals like Chamberlain to have a major influence on party affairs.

By 1877, it would seem that Chamberlain had laid the foundations for the success of his version of Liberalism. The Liberal organisation in the country was falling into the hands of radical Liberals like himself. After Gladstone's decision to resign the leadership of the Liberal Party in 1875, the Party was led by a Whig aristocrat, Lord Hartington. However, Gladstone's return from political retirement in 1876 to lead the Bulgarian Agitation against Disraeli's Near Eastern policies allowed Gladstone to wrestle back control of the Party. The historian R.T. Shannon, in *Gladstone and the Bulgarian Agitation* (1963), described Gladstone's return from retirement as 'the ruin of radicalism'. It may not have ruined radicalism as such but it did thwart Chamberlain's chances of capturing the Liberal Party.

Although a member of Gladstone's Government from 1880 to 1885, as President of the Board of Trade, Chamberlain spent virtually the entire ministry at odds with the Prime Minister. Gladstone refused to consider Chamberlain's plans for elected county local government. Chamberlain was frustrated at Gladstone's preoccupation with Irish affairs and with what he saw as Gladstone's over-reliance on the Whigs.

In June 1885, in an unprecedented move, Chamberlain published his Radical or 'Unauthorised' Programme in which he stated his own version of radicalism. This included free schools, payment for MPs, **manhood suffrage**, compulsory land purchase to provide farm labourers with small-holdings and allotments, graduated property tax, reform of the House of Lords, triennial parliaments (elected every three years) and the end of the Church of England's role as the State Church. The aim of the programme was nothing less than an attempt to capture the policy-making platform of the Party. As Chamberlain wrote on 7 October 1885 in a letter to a Liberal minister, A.J. Mundella, 'we shall sweep the country with free education and allotments and the Tories will be smashed and the Whigs extinguished'.

While Chamberlain differed from Gladstone on the role of government in society, he also differed markedly on the importance of the British Empire. Chamberlain had been greatly influenced on this subject by a series of lectures in 1882 and 1883 by John Seeley, a noted Cambridge historian, entitled 'The Expansion of England'. Seeley claimed that the main theme of British history since the Norman Conquest had not been the gradual erosion of the power of the monarchy and the creation of parliamentary government. Instead, he said that the main theme of British history had been the creation of the world's largest empire. Seeley also contended that unless the British Empire was strengthened it was likely to lose its world power status to rising states such as the USA and the Russian Empire in the early 20th century. To Chamberlain, Irish Home Rule threatened to split the mother country of the Empire apart. As a result, he was honour bound to oppose it.

Chamberlain was, therefore, both a radical and an imperialist. He was a social imperialist, a politician who advocated widespread social reform at home, in order to strengthen the 'mother country' and support imperial expansion abroad.

'The People's William'?

To many contemporaries, Chamberlain seemed like a politician in a hurry to implement change. Gladstone, on the other hand, was thought to be

Manhood suffrage: The right of all adult males over 21 years to vote in elections.

approaching the end of his political career. Unfortunately for them, many politicians incorrectly predicted Gladstone's retirement. This is not surprising. In 1874, Gladstone was 65 years old. Very few people at that time would have thought Gladstone would still be Prime Minister 20 years later!

Gladstone's retirement from public life seemed to have happened in 1875, when he resigned as Liberal leader. However, he did not resign his seat at Greenwich. What frustrated many of his colleagues was Gladstone's insistence, on a number of occasions, that his involvement in politics was associated with one issue. From 1876 to 1880, it was hostility to Disraeli's foreign and imperial policies. During his Second Ministry, it was Ireland. After 1886, it was Irish Home Rule. Even after he had retired as an MP, Gladstone returned in 1896, at the age of 87, to lead a campaign against Turkish atrocities in Armenia!

To the end of his political career, Gladstone maintained his support for the fundamental principles that had underpinned his commitment to Liberalism since the 1850s: free trade, administrative efficiency, the minimalist state and a peaceful foreign policy ('Peace, Retrenchment and Reform'). Indeed, he resigned as Prime Minister in 1894 in opposition to increases in naval expenditure. Was Gladstone therefore 'the ruin of radicalism', as suggested by R.T. Shannon? Was he the politician who split the Liberal Party over Irish Home Rule in 1886; or did he help unite the Liberal Party and lead it to victory in 1868, 1880, 1886 and 1892?

As a politician who had been involved in the formative stages of the Liberal Party, Gladstone possessed considerable support within the party. In addition to the middle-class supporters of liberalism within the electorate, Gladstone's name was directly linked to the achievement of free trade and the economic boom with which it was associated. From the mid-1860s, he also became associated with the extension of the right to vote to skilled workers. By the time he became Prime Minister, he had already gained a national reputation as a statesman and politician: the 'People's William'. Therefore, whenever Gladstone supported a particular policy his standing in the Party and the country was sufficient to gain mass support.

Gladstone realised, perhaps more than any other politician, the diverse nature of the Liberal Party and its capacity to split into competing groups. Between 1859 and 1895, each Liberal Administration had fallen from power because of internal divisions. To hold the different aspects of the Liberal Party together, Gladstone believed that a single issue, which contained clearly defined Liberal principles, should be used to force unity on the party at election times. In 1868, Gladstone used the rallying cry of 'Justice for Ireland', in 1874 'Abolition of Income Tax', in 1880 'Anti-Beaconsfieldism' (opposition to Conservative foreign policy) and in 1886 and 1892 'Irish Home Rule'. It is true that Gladstone did lead the Party to stunning victories in 1868 and 1880. Yet, in 1886, his decision to support Irish Home Rule split the Liberal Party in two. Although Round Table Conferences took place between the two factions (Gladstonians and Liberal Unionists) in 1887, unity was never restored. After 1895, the Conservatives and Liberal Unionists 'fused' to become the Unionist Party.

Gladstone, Chamberlain and the split of 1886

Which of these differences help to explain why Chamberlain crossed the floor of the House of Commons during the Home Rule debate in 1886 to join 92 of his Liberal colleagues as the Liberal Unionist faction supporting the Conservatives? Chamberlain's decision seems somewhat odd in the sense that most of the Liberal Unionists were the Whigs he had been attacking over the previous decade. Secondly, by crossing the

'Political trinity at loggerheads' – a cartoon illustrating Liberal divisions, from the Conservative journal, *St. Stephen's Review*, published at the time of the 1885 General Election. Gladstone scatters copies of the Liberal Party Manifesto, while Lord Hartington struggles to prevent Joseph Chamberlain from throwing traditional institutions overboard.

floor he helped split his own radical supporters. Those radicals who became Liberal Unionists were mainly from the West Midlands (Chamberlain's own power base).

Since 1886, historians have produced several explanations for Chamberlain's action. Many cite his personal dislike of Gladstone and his frustration with the Liberal leader over issues such as elected county local government. With the formation of his Third Ministry in 1886, Gladstone had attempted to reduce the ministerial salary of Jesse Collings (Chamberlain's closest political supporter) from £1,500 to £1,200. Others point to Chamberlain's ambition to reach the top in politics by whatever method. With Gladstone coming to an end of his political career, a split in the Liberal Party could speed up this development with Chamberlain eventually taking over as leader of a reunified party.

However, Chamberlain's main reason lay with his belief that Irish Home Rule would split the United Kingdom and damage the Empire at a particularly turbulent period of world history. Chamberlain, in the final analysis, was an imperialist first. His radicalism was as much to do with his fear of the rise of socialism as with a genuine attempt to improve the material wellbeing of the poor. As G. R. Searle notes, in *The Liberal Party, 1886 to 1929* (1992), the formation of the Social Democratic Federation in 1883 as Britain's first Marxist party alarmed Chamberlain as to the prospect of a British party similar to the German SPD threatening the Liberal Party's position. In this sense, he did foresee the threat of a labour party replacing the Liberals.

On the other hand, historians such as A.B. Cooke and J. Vincent, in *The Governing Passion* (1974), see the split on Home Rule as part of a deliberate act by Gladstone to reassert his control of the Liberal Party. By 'ditching' Chamberlain and his immediate following, Gladstone was able to regain control. Although disagreeing with the timing and precise purpose of Gladstone's Irish policy, T.A. Jenkins – in *Gladstone, Whiggism and the Liberal Party* (1988) – believes the Liberal leader's actions are explained by his desire to lead the Party effectively.

1. In what ways did Gladstone and Chamberlain represent different types of Liberal?

2. Using the evidence contained in this section, who do you think was more responsible for causing the split in the Liberal Party in 1886, Gladstone or Chamberlain?

Give reasons to support your answer.

7.5 'A Ministry of Troubles': Gladstone's Second Ministry, 1880–1885

While Gladstone's First Ministry is associated with widespread reform, his Second Ministry is linked with crisis and conflict. Why?

Ireland

When Gladstone came to power, Ireland was in a state of considerable unrest. The Land War between peasants and landlords was in full swing. In Parliament, the Irish Home Rule Party led a campaign of obstruction that disrupted the working of the House of Commons so effectively that the Speaker, Henry Brand, introduced major reforms of procedure, which included the Closure and the Guillotine to bring debate to a vote. From 1880 to 1885, Ireland was in a state of almost permanent crisis.

Imperial and foreign affairs

Between 1880 and 1885, the Government faced serious crises in the Transvaal (1881), Egypt (1882), southern Africa (1884–85), the Sudan (1885) and a major crisis with Russia over Afghanistan, known as the Penjdeh incident (also in 1885).

Gladstone's leadership

When Gladstone became Prime Minister in 1880, he claimed that his main aim was to reverse the costly and aggressive foreign and imperial policies associated with Disraeli's Conservative Government – what he termed 'Beaconsfieldism'. (Disraeli had been made Lord Beaconsfield in 1876.) As R.T. Shannon stated, in *The Crisis of Imperialism* (1976): 'Gladstone looked upon his return to office as a temporary expedient, a duty imposed on him to restore the natural and legitimate pre-1874 order but not obliging him to stay on after this had been achieved.'

Gladstone had no clear view of what he wanted to achieve as Prime Minister beyond this limited aim. Many Liberals thought he might take the opportunity of the 50th anniversary of his entry into Parliament, 1882, as a suitable time to retire. Instead, he continued as Prime Minister. As a result, the Government lacked firm leadership and direction, allowing divisions within the Liberal Party to surface. This worked to Gladstone's advantage. As H. Matthew notes, in *Gladstone* (1995), by suggesting that he intended to retire in the near future, Gladstone could always delay consideration of any major problem which required a long-term solution.

The conflict between Whig and Radical

The division between aristocratic Whig and Radical came to a head during the ministry. Gladstone upset the Radicals by filling his Cabinet with Whigs. There were nine Whigs compared with three Radicals (Bright, Chamberlain and Dilke). Whig representation in the Cabinet far outweighed their numerical support within the Party. Gladstone believed he was balancing the various factions of liberalism. Instead, he helped cause resentment among the Radical faction.

For most of the period, it seemed as though civil war had broken out between these two groups. Whigs favoured repression in Ireland, while the Radicals wanted reconciliation. When Gladstone introduced his Compensation for Disturbance Bill, in 1880, 60 Whig peers voted with the opposition. In imperial affairs, the Whigs were generally in favour of expansion of the Empire while the Radicals were against, although Chamberlain did support the acquisition of territory in southern Africa in 1885.

The crisis came to a head following Chamberlain's publication of the Radical Programme in 1885. So, by the time Gladstone announced his support for Irish Home Rule in 1886, it was not surprising that a large number of Whigs were willing to desert Gladstone to form the Liberal Unionist faction.

The Bradlaugh Case

Charles Bradlaugh, an avowed atheist, was elected as Liberal MP for Northampton in 1880. He refused to take the religious oath which was necessary if he wished to sit in the House of Commons. The Evidence Amendment Acts of 1869 and 1870 and the Parliamentary Oaths Act, 1866, gave Bradlaugh the right to refuse. However, this right was refused by the Speaker after consultation with the Clerk of the House, Erskine May. A select committee was established. It rejected Bradlaugh's claim by the casting vote of the chairman. Bradlaugh stood for Parliament for Northampton on two further occasions, was re-elected and then refused entry to the Commons. Finally, in 1885, he was allowed to take his seat.

The reason this relatively minor issue caused so many problems for the Gladstone Administration was that it was used by a small group within the Conservative Party to launch attacks on the Conservative leadership in the House of Commons. Since the death of Disraeli, the Conservative Party had been led by Lord Salisbury in the Lords and Sir Stafford Northcote in the Commons. A group of young Conservative MPs, known as the 'Fourth Party' (The Liberals, Conservatives and Irish were the other three), comprising Randolph Churchill, Drummond Wolff, John Gorst and Arthur Balfour (Salisbury's nephew), were dissatisfied with Northcote's inability to exploit the ministry's problems for the benefit of the Conservatives. Although their opposition was not directed at Gladstone, their activities did disrupt Commons proceedings whenever Bradlaugh's case was discussed.

What were the achievements of Gladstone's Second Ministry?

● Dealing with the Agricultural Depression

When Gladstone came to power, the country was in the grip of a major agricultural depression that had begun in the mid-1870s. Pressure groups such as the Farmers' Alliance had hoped the Liberals would provide some security for tenant farmers against eviction.

The Liberals did pass a number of reforms to aid tenant farmers. The Abolition of the Malt Tax, 1880, repealed the malt tax and replaced it with a tax on beer. This eased the tax burden on farmers who had to pay a tax on malted barley. The Ground Game Act, 1880, allowed tenant farmers to shoot hares and rabbits as a supplement to their diet. In 1883, the Agricultural Holdings Act made Disraeli's permissive legislation of 1875 compulsory. This gave tenant farmers extra security of tenure.

● Irish reform

The Administration passed the Land Act of 1881, which gave tenant farmers the three 'Fs' of free sale, fair rent and fixity of tenure. However, the most successful aspect of government policy was coercion from 1880–83, which helped to bring the Land War to an end.

● Parliamentary reform

A major aim of radicals within the Party was the extension of the right to vote. Between 1883 and 1885, the Liberal Government passed three Acts making significant changes to the electoral system. These stand, along with the 1832 and 1867 Reform Bills, as milestones on the road towards parliamentary democracy.

In 1880, in spite of the Ballot Act of 1872, serious electoral corruption was uncovered which led the Government to pass the Corrupt and Illegal Practices Act in 1883. It laid down rigid rules for the conduct of parliamentary elections, including a strict limit on expenses by candidates and heavy penalties for bribery and intimidation of voters.

The most significant Act was the Representation of the People Act, 1884, which extended the right to vote. Approximately 2.6 million new voters were added to the electoral roll, increasing it from 3.1 million in 1883 to 5.7 million in 1885. The Act also applied to the entire United Kingdom, unlike in 1832 and 1867 when three separate reform bills had to be passed for England, Ireland and Scotland. In specific terms, it still defined the right to vote on property qualification but this was made the same for both borough (town) and county constituencies. However, there still remained seven ways of qualifying for the vote.

It would be an exaggeration to say that the Act gave the vote to all adult males. As the historian Neal Blewett points out, in *Peers, Parties and the People* (1972), about 40% of the adult male population remained without the vote until 1918. However, the Act did have a big impact on Ireland where the electorate grew from 220,000 to 740,000, helping the Irish Home Rule Party to gain over 75% of the Irish seats in the 1885 election (85 out of 103).

The proposals also caused considerable unease among Conservatives who believed the electoral changes would benefit the Liberals. As a result, Lord Salisbury opposed the Bill unless a separate bill to redistribute constituencies accompanied it.

A Redistribution of Seats Act followed, and was passed in May 1885, a month before the fall of the Government. Multi-member constituencies, like Gladstone's old seat at Greenwich, were phased out and the principle of constituencies with equal numbers of voters was introduced. This meant constituencies were much smaller, covering areas with either distinctly working-class electors (West Ham North or Woolwich) or areas with middle-class voters (Ealing, Kingston and Wandsworth). Boundary Commissioners were appointed to maintain equality between seats and to redistribute seats when the movement of population occurred.

These three acts were a considerable change to the electoral system. As H.J. Hanham states, in *The Reformed Electoral System in Great Britain, 1832 to 1914* (1968): 'The whole system of election had to be created afresh. The parties had to create new divisional associations and divisional office, to find new candidates, to help get new registers ready and generally to begin things anew.'

1. What were the main problems facing Gladstone in domestic affairs during his Second Ministry?

2. Which reform passed by Gladstone's Second Ministry do you regard as the most important?

For both questions, give reasons to support your answer.

Other reforms

The Liberals were also active in other areas. The Burials Act, 1880, was designed to please nonconformists who were now allowed to bury their dead in parish churchyards without any religious service. The Mundella Education Act, 1880, made elementary education compulsory and created the position of truancy officer to enforce attendance.

The Employers' Liability Act, 1880, was the first act to provide financial compensation of workers injured at work. In 1882, the Women's Property Act gave married women legal protection for their property. Before that date, on marrying, the husband gained legal possession of all his wife's property.

1. What do you regard as the most important development in Gladstone's second ministry?

2. Which parts of the mind map do you regard as a success and which do you regard as a failure? On balance, was Gladstone successful as prime minister in the period from 1880 to 1885?

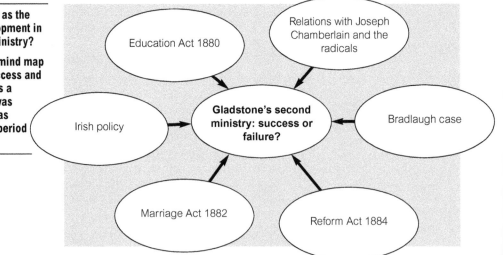

7.6 What impact did Gladstone have on late Victorian politics?

Protectionism: Policy of placing taxes on imported goods.

In *Gladstone 1874–1898* (1995), H. Matthew states that 'It is not difficult to see the latter part of Gladstone's public life as a failure: religion on the wane, the free-trade order giving way to militarism and **protectionism**, Britain bloated by imperial expansions, Home Rule unachieved, the Liberal Party divided.'

This September 1891 cartoon from *St Stephen's Review* unkindly suggests that Gladstone subsituted the force of his own rhetoric for concrete policy proposals.

Is this an accurate assessment of Gladstone's career after 1868? It does seem to be rather harsh. Gladstone had been Prime Minister on four occasions. During his time in power, he had led governments that had done much to destroy the Anglican/landowning monopoly of political power. He passed a large number of reforms during his First Ministry, which attacked privilege and helped to establish a meritocracy. His Cabinets were the first to contain nonconformists (Bright in 1868 and Chamberlain in 1880) and a Catholic (Lord Ripon in 1886). In 1883 to 1886, he passed electoral reform which moved Britain closer towards manhood suffrage. Just at the time when he left office, in 1894, the Liberal Government passed the Parish Councils Act which extended elected local government down to village level in the counties.

On the other hand, Gladstone's decision to support Irish Home Rule split the Liberal Party in two and led to 20 years of Conservative domination of British politics.

Yet, as T.A. Jenkins suggests in *Gladstone, Whiggism and the Liberal Party* (1988), Gladstone's leadership may have split the Party in 1886 but it was also a major factor in holding the diverse elements of liberalism together in the years 1868 to 1886. As a politician who appealed to Radicals and Whigs alike, Gladstone had the unique ability of holding the Party together, winning power in 1868 and 1880. Gladstone deliberately balanced Whiggism and Radicalism, as shown in his choice of Cabinet Ministers in 1880. It could be said that without Gladstone the Liberal Party would not have stayed united for so long! Following his resignation as party leader in 1894, the Party was led, in turn, by Lord Rosebery (1894–96), William Harcourt (1896–98) and Sir Henry Campbell-Bannerman (1898–1908). None of them had the ability to lead and unify the Party as Gladstone had done before 1886.

As for Gladstone's ideas, free trade remained the central feature of economic policy until the First World War. It was the main reason for the Liberals' landslide success of 1906. Gladstone's support for the minimalist state survived until the rise of New Liberalism after 1908. However, Liberal support for Irish Home Rule remained a difficult and unpopular policy to defend.

The historian E.J. Feuchtwanger wrote in 1975: 'Gladstone was a towering figure in the Victorian age. The shape and the content of politics would have been quite different without him. Towards the end of his long public life there was a sense in which he had outlived himself, but the values he championed with such fervour have perennial validity.'

Further Reading

Articles

In *Modern History Review*:
'Gladstone and Liberalism' by Paul Adelman (Vol. 2 No. 3)
'The Man who refused to be Prime Minister' [on Lord Hartington] by Patrick Jackson (Vol. 3 No. 1)
'John the Baptist of Gladstonian Liberalism' [on John Bright] by John Vincent (Vol. 3 No. 2)
'Parliamentary Reform in the 1880s' by M. Pugh (Vol. 4 No. 1)
'Juggler Joe: Radical and Unionist' by D. Watts (Vol. 5 No. 1)
In *History Review* (formerly *History Sixth*):
'Whigs in the Gladstonian Liberal Party' by E.J. Feuchtwanger, No. 7 (Sept. 1990)
'Joseph Chamberlain and the Liberal Unionist Party' by D. Dutton, No. 18 (March 1994)

Texts designed for AS and A2 level students

Gladstone, Disraeli and Later Victorian Politics by P. Adelman (Longman, Seminar Studies series, 2nd edn, 1987)
Joseph Chamberlain, Radical and Imperialist by H. Browne (Longman, Seminar Studies series, 1974)
Joseph Chamberlain and the Challenge of Radicalism by Duncan Watts (Hodder & Stoughton, 1992)
Whigs, Radicals and Liberals 1815 to 1914 by Duncan Watts (Hodder & Stoughton, Access to History series, 1995)
Gladstone and the Liberal Party by M. Winstanley (Routledge, Lancaster Pamphlets, 1990)
Government and Reform 1815 to 1918 by Robert Pearce and Roger Stearn (Hodder & Stoughton, 1994)
Gladstone by Graham Goodlad (Collins Historymakers, 2004)

More advanced reading

Gladstone 1809 to 1874 by H. Matthew (Oxford University Press, 1988)
Gladstone 1874 to 1898 by H. Matthew (Oxford University Press, 1995)
Democracy and Empire: British History 1865 to 1914 by E.J. Feuchtwanger (Arnold, 1985)
The Making of Modern British Politics 1867 to 1939 by Martin Pugh (Blackwell, 1982)

8 The Conservative Party of Disraeli and Salisbury, 1868–1895

Key Issues

- What contribution did Disraeli make to the development of the Conservative Party?

- To what extent did the Conservatives bring social and political change to Britain?

- Why were the Conservatives the dominant political party after 1886?

8.1 Was Disraeli the founder of the modern Conservative Party?

8.2 To what extent did Disraeli's Second Ministry, 1874–1880, bring social and political change to Britain?

8.3 Why did the Conservatives lose the 1880 election?

8.4 Historical interpretation: Gladstone and Disraeli compared

8.5 How successful was Salisbury in domestic affairs between 1885 and 1892?

8.6 What impact did Disraeli and Salisbury have on late Victorian politics?

Framework of Events

1867	Formation of National Union of Conservative and Constitutional Associations
1868	February: Disraeli succeeds 14th Earl of Derby as Conservative leader and Prime Minister after 29 years as MP
1870	Formation of Conservative Central Office
1872	January/February: Conservative meetings at Burghley House in a bid to replace Disraeli with 15th Earl of Derby
	3 April: Speech at the Free Trade Hall, Manchester
	24 June: Speech at the Crystal Palace, London. These speeches outline the main principles of Disraelian Conservatism.
1873	March: Disraeli refuses to form minority Conservative government following fall of the Gladstone Government over the Irish Universities Bill
1874	First Conservative leader to win a general election since Peel in 1841
	Factory Act, Public Worship Regulation Act
1875	Public Health Act, Artisans Dwellings Act, Sale of Food and Drugs Act
	Conspiracy and Protection of Property Act, Employers and Workmen Act
	July: Beginning of Near Eastern Crisis
	November: Disraeli purchases shares in Suez Canal Company
1876	Merchant Shipping Act, Education Act, Enclosure Act
	August: Disraeli becomes the Earl of Beaconsfield
1877	Outbreak of Russo-Turkish War
	Start of agricultural depression
1878	Carnarvon and Derby resign from Cabinet over British policy in the Near Eastern Crisis
	Factory and Workshops Act, Epping Forest Act
	July: Treaty of Berlin
	Gorst resigns as Principal Agent – replaced by W.B. Skene
	Great Depression worsens with rise in unemployment
1879	Start of Land War in Ireland
	Crises in Zululand (southern Africa) and Afghanistan
	Gladstone's first Midlothian campaign

1880	March: Disraeli loses general election
1881	19 April: Disraeli dies. Leadership of Party assumed by Salisbury and Northcote
1882–84	Fourth Party attacks on Northcote's leadership
1883	Primrose League is formed
1884	Capt. Middleton becomes Principal Agent, coordinates Conservative organisation
1885	Salisbury forms First Ministry after June general election
1886	Crisis over Home Rule, Liberal Party splits and Salisbury wins general election to form his Second Ministry
1887	Randolph Churchill resigns as Chancellor of the Exchequer, thereby removing a major challenger to Salisbury's leadership
1888	County Councils Act
1892	Liberals form government with Irish Home Rule Party support
1895	Conservatives win election and Salisbury forms Third Ministry.

Overview

THE history of the Conservative Party between 1868 and 1895 is one of a major political institution adapting to change. This change took many forms. In the period 1850–73, there was considerable economic growth, in particular in manufacturing and commerce, but from 1873 to 1896 economic growth began to slow down with contemporaries calling the period the Great Depression.

There was also considerable social change. The population grew from 28.9 million in 1861 to 37.7 million in 1891. This was accompanied by a major shift in population from the countryside to towns. Between 1861 and 1901, the number of towns in England and Wales with populations over 50,000 rose from 37 to 75, and the proportion of the population living in urban areas rose from 36% to 45%.

After the passage of the 1867 Reform Act, the electorate increased by 1 million, with the vote being extended to skilled workers in urban areas. In 1884, the right to vote was extended further, by approximately 2 million, to include a majority of adult males.

All these changes affected the Conservative Party. Firstly, the Party had been seen, in particular after 1846, as the party of landowners. With the widening of the franchise and the social and economic transformation of Britain, the political, social and economic position of landowners came under threat.

Secondly, if the Conservative Party wished to remain a major political force it needed to widen its political appeal beyond the landowning classes who, after 1867 and 1884, were making up a smaller proportion of the electorate. Although the largest party in Britain from 1846 to 1859, the Conservatives had always been outvoted by a combination of Whigs, Liberals and Radicals. Between 1846 and 1868, although the Party had formed the government on three occasions (1851–52, 1858–59 and 1866–68), it had been in a minority.

Between 1868 and 1902, the Party was led by two very different personalities. Benjamin Disraeli was party leader from February 1868 until his death in 1881. Disraeli stands out as a unique character in 19th-century politics. He did not attend a public school or go to university. He was from a Jewish background, although he was a member of the Church of England. His wealth came from writing popular novels and from having married a rich widow. Unlike Robert Peel, who represented the factory-owning class, or Lord Salisbury, who represented the landowning class, Disraeli's position within the Party was based on his own talents as a parliamentary debater and orator. He was the classic outsider at a time when **anti-Semitism**, both in the Party and the country, was high.

Anti-Semitism: Against Jews or the Jewish religion (Judaism).

Lord Salisbury led the Party from Disraeli's death (initially with Sir Stafford Northcote, 1881–85) until his own retirement in 1902. Although not as flamboyant as Disraeli, he can be regarded as the most successful leading politician of the century. A member of the Cecil family, who had been Elizabeth I's chief ministers, he strongly reflected the right of the aristocracy to rule, and was the last Prime Minister to govern from the House of Lords. He won four of the six general elections he fought – in 1885, 1886, 1895 and 1900. In 1885, he was only out of office for seven months.

By 1895, the Conservative Party, under these two leaders, had transformed its party organisation and broadened its electoral support to include important sections of the middle class (Villa Toryism). It had also changed from being a party that had formed brief minority governments into the dominant political party in Britain.

1. From the list of points in the mind map, what do you regard as Disraeli's greatest success? Explain your answer.

2. Place the list of points in order of significance.

3. Which benefited more from Disraeli's leadership – the country or the Conservative Party? Explain your answer.

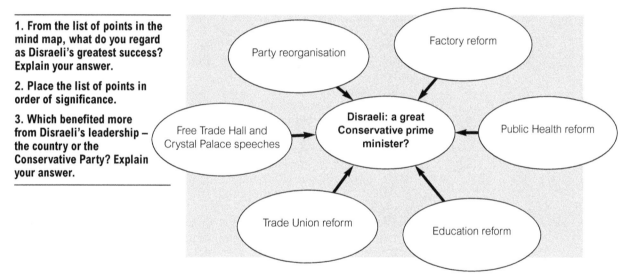

8.1 Was Disraeli the founder of the modern Conservative Party?

Of all the leaders of the 19th-century Conservative Party, Disraeli is the only one still regularly quoted by senior Conservative politicians. As John Walton wrote in his article in *History Review* 'Disraeli: Myth and Reality', 'no other politician has such an enduring popular aura; no other statesman can be relied on to influence the attitudes of voters a century or more beyond the grave'.

So, to what extent can Disraeli be regarded as the founder of the modern Conservative Party?

The case for

Party organisation
If a modern Conservative returned to the 1870s, he or she would recognise much of the party organisation and structure that had been established during Disraeli's leadership. The Party established organisations in

response to the need to win votes from the new electorate following the passage of the 1867 Reform Act. A 'National Union of Conservative and Constitutional Associations' was founded in November 1867. Lord Blake, a leading historian of the Conservative Party, has called this 'the first centralised mass organisation to be formed by a British political party'. In 1870, J.E. Gorst was appointed the Party's Principal Agent and started to organise working men's associations and clubs, and registration societies. In the same year, Conservative Central Office was created, under the guidance of C.J. Keith-Falconer who worked closely with Gorst. From 1872 onwards, Central Office and the National Union were closely linked through a common headquarters and Gorst's position as agent and honorary secretary of the National Union.

This new organisation was an important factor behind the Conservatives' general election success in 1874 – its first since 1841. Sixty-five of the 74 Conservative gains in England and Wales occurred under the direction of active local associations.

Policy

In the period before Disraeli's leadership, the Conservative Party was known as a 'Little England' party, because of its opposition to furthering British interests abroad. After the famous policy speeches at Manchester and Crystal Palace in 1872, Disraeli firmly associated the Conservative Party with defence of the British Empire and British interests around the world. Since then, the Conservatives have been identified as the patriotic party.

More controversially, Disraeli is associated with the idea of 'One Nation' Conservatism, whereby the Party is thought to represent the interests of all the electorate rather than just one section of it. Some historians, such as P.R. Ghosh, claim a direct link between Disraeli's policies in government and the social comments on the idea of two nations – rich and poor – which he made in his novels of the 1840s, most notably *Sybil*. Other historians, however, such as Paul Smith, believe that Disraeli's policy of 'elevating the condition of the people' which he made in his 1872 speeches was of a more recent origin.

The idea of 'One Nation' Conservatism is closely linked to the belief that Disraeli was a supporter of 'Tory Democracy' – the idea that the Party was committed to aiding the poor and underprivileged of society. The social reforms of Disraeli's Second Ministry that dealt with a wide range of issues, such as factory reform, housing, public health and trade union reform, all seem to support this view.

This view of Disraeli, and his role in the Party's history, was first put forward forcibly by Lord Randolph Churchill during the mid-1880s and was supported by the Primrose League founded in Disraeli's memory. This important Conservative organisation was established in November 1883 and named after Disraeli's favourite flower. With slogans such as 'True Union of the Classes', its members regarded Disraeli as their inspiration. By 1891 the League's membership exceeded 1 million.

The case against

Disraeli's own views

Disraeli did not believe that the policy and organisational changes made under his leadership meant he was creating a new party. In 1880, he wrote to Lord Lytton stating 'they [the Tory Party] have existed for more than a century and a half as an organised political connection and having survived the loss of the American colonies, the first Napoleon and Lord Grey's Reform Act, they must not be snuffed out'.

Throughout his political life, Disraeli believed he was maintaining a long political tradition, not changing it. He always believed that he should defend the aristocratic and monarchic traditions of the country. In this respect, his support for a parliamentary reform act in 1867 and of social reforms were more to do with winning support for a party that defended this principle than anything new.

The views of historians

Although P.R. Ghosh argues, in *Style and Substance in Disraelian Social Reform* (1987), that Disraeli's Second Ministry (1874–80) marked the real beginning of a lasting Conservative willingness to pursue policies of social reform through legislation, most historians tend to play down Disraeli's commitment to social and economic change. Bruce Coleman, in *Conservatism and the Conservative Party in Nineteenth-Century Britain* (1988), states that 'Disraeli, like other Conservatives, had seized the plentiful opportunities offered by Gladstone's First Ministry, but he did little to reshape Conservatism significantly in either thought or policy. In so many respects it is the continuity and traditionalism of Disraeli's ministry that stands out, not any new departure.'

The Conservative Party was simply adjusting naturally to the post-Palmerstonian situation and reasserting its traditional commitment to stability and security both at home and abroad, in contrast to what the Liberals seemed to offer. This view is echoed by John Walton who regards Disraeli's skills in presentation, through speeches and style, as a greater contribution to the development of the Party than his changes in policy. In this sense, Disraeli is more like a modern politician than a politician associated with a particular set of policies. He was prepared to adopt the policies necessary in order to win power so that he could preserve the privileged position of the monarchy, the aristocracy and the Church of England.

As John Vincent noted in his short biography of Disraeli, in *Modern History Review*, in 1975: 'He left the Tory Party very much as he found it. Below the surface, changes were taking place that were to turn the Tories from the "country party" of the squires into the Party of business, the residential suburbs and the genteel south-east.'

> **1. In what ways did the organisation and policies of the Conservative Party change after 1868?**
>
> **2. Which of the two cases mentioned above – 'for' and 'against' – do you find most convincing? Give reasons to support your answer.**

8.2 To what extent did Disraeli's Second Ministry, 1874–1880, bring social and political change to Britain?

Introduction

Disraeli's First Ministry had lasted from February to November 1868. He had succeeded the 14th Earl of Derby as party leader. During that ministry, the parliamentary reform acts for Ireland and Scotland and a Corrupt Practices Act were passed. Public executions were also abolished, mainly because of loss of life among the crowd at the execution of a **Fenian**, and a royal commission into sanitary laws was set up.

Although he had arrived 'at the top of the greasy pole' of politics late in life, at 64, Disraeli was not safe from challenge as party leader. In 1872, at Burghley House, a group of leading Conservatives attempted to replace him with the 15th Earl of Derby. It was only because of Derby's reluctance that this challenge was not successful.

Disraeli's Cabinet on the formation of his Government in 1974 was the smallest between 1832 and 1916, with only 12 members. It was dominated by members of the aristocracy, with Lord Derby at the Foreign Office, Lord

Fenian: A member of an Irish revolutionary movement formed among Irish immigrants in the USA in 1858 by James Stephens. The movement spread to Ireland in 1865. The name was derived from the *Fianna*, the legendary Irish heroes. The Fenians were largely responsible for awakening Gladstone to the urgency of the Irish problem.

Carnarvon at the Colonial Office and Lord Salisbury at the India Office. In terms of domestic reform, the most important members were Richard Cross, the Home Secretary, George Sclater-Booth, President of the Local Government Board and Lord Sandon as Vice-President of the Privy Council.

According to Cross, the Home Secretary, Disraeli had no clear legislative programme on coming to office. E.J. Feuchtwanger, in *Democracy and Empire: British History 1865 to 1914* (1985) states: 'Not only was Disraeli disinclined and ill-equipped to hatch such a design, he knew that his victory owed much to a desire in the country for a quiet life.' Indeed, Disraeli had written to Cross: 'We came in on the principle of not harassing the country.'

How significant were Disraeli's domestic reforms?

Factory reform
In the 1874 general election, many Conservative candidates, particularly in Lancashire and Yorkshire, had openly supported the Nine Hours Movement pressure group. The 1874 Factory Act failed to meet the full demands of the Nine Hours Movement, although it did reduce the hours workers were forced to do in a day to 10 hours, allowing for a half-day on Saturday. This had a major impact on the development of team sports, such as football and rugby. Cross also set up a royal commission into factories. This led to the 1878 Factory and Workshops Act, which brought both factories and workshops under general government inspection.

Housing reform
The Artisans' Dwelling Act, 1875, was regarded as one of the most important Acts of the administration. It allowed local authorities to impose the compulsory purchase of slums deemed unhealthy and to oversee their replacement with planned housing. This was to be financed with government loans at low interest, but the houses were built by private enterprise. Disraeli referred to it as 'our chief measure'.

However, the Torrens Act of 1868, passed by the Liberals, would have covered similar ground if it had not been blocked by the House of Lords. The 1875 Act was also heavily influenced by pressure from the Charity Organisation Society and was supported by the Liberal Party. In addition, the Act was so hedged around with restrictions and so expensive to implement that it was little used. In 1879, Cross had to introduce an amending act to deal with the burden of excessive compensation costs, and even then the legislation proved largely ineffective. Apart from the celebrated case of Joseph Chamberlain in Birmingham, by 1881 only 10 out of 87 English and Welsh towns had taken any action under the Act.

Public health reform
George Sclater-Booth, whose exclusion from the Cabinet may suggest the low priority Disraeli gave to public health reforms, was responsible for the passage of the Public Health Act, 1875. This brought all previous legislation dealing with the subject under one Act. It also established a system of powers and checks on sewage and draining, public lavatories and cellar dwellings. The Sale of Food and Drugs Act, 1875, emerged from a report by a select committee of the House of Commons and laid down regulations about the adulteration of food. Its impact was reduced by the failure to compel local authorities to appoint analysts to assess adulteration. Similarly, the Rivers Pollution Act, 1875, failed to offer an adequate definition of pollution or ways of punishing polluters once these were identified.

Trade union reform

The Criminal Law Amendment Act, 1871, had aroused considerable opposition from the New Model Unions. The Liberals had already decided to change this legislation before they lost office. On coming to power the Conservatives passed the Conspiracy and Protection of Property Act, 1875, which allowed peaceful picketing.

The Conservatives also planned to introduce a Master and Servant Act, but this gave way to the Employers and Workmen Act, 1875. This Act recognised the relationship of employer and employee in a mature capitalist economy. It was the result of a royal commission set up by Richard Cross. The Act accepted that breaches of contract by employers and workmen should be treated as offences under civil law. Prior to the Act, employers could be tried under civil law and if found guilty were liable to a fine, whereas workmen could be tried under the Criminal Law, where, if found guilty, they could face both a fine and imprisonment.

As a result of this legislation, Disraeli declared that he had 'satisfactorily settled the position of labour for a generation'. Alexander MacDonald, a trade unionist, Liberal MP and member of the 1875 Royal Commission, was moved to declare that 'the Conservatives had done more for the working classes in six years than the Liberals had done in 50'. However, the historian Bruce Coleman believes that 'the considerations which persuaded Cross and Disraeli to take a major step in the reform of labour law seem to have been largely ones of electoral expediency'.

Education reform

Lord Sandon's Education Act, 1876, increased pressure on working-class parents to send their children to school by setting up School Attendance Committees. The motivation for such reform came from the Church of England whose schools, particularly in rural areas, were short of both pupils and income due to the competition from Board Schools, set up under the Forster Act of 1870.

Economic reforms

In 1874, the Chancellor of the Exchequer, Sir Stafford Northcote, reduced income tax, abolished duties on sugar and extended grants in aid for local authority expenditure on police and asylums. The following year, he established a Sinking Fund to reduce the National Debt. However, income tax was raised later in the ministry to meet the expense of the agricultural depression and colonial wars in South Africa.

In 1875, the Government passed the Friendly Societies Act, based on the findings of a royal commission set up by the Liberals. The Act attempted to establish the registration of societies and to improve their financial stability without involving any responsibility for the Government.

In the following year, the Merchant Shipping Act was passed, also based, in part, on the findings of a royal commission that had been set up by the Liberals in 1873. The driving force behind this legislation was the Liberal MP for Derby, Samuel Plimsoll. Intense pressure from shipping interests made the Conservatives reluctant legislators. Their Unseaworthy Ships Act, 1875, failed to produce any real change. Even the use of maximum load lines set out in the Merchant Shipping Act was not made compulsory.

Agricultural reforms

From 1875, British agriculture entered a period of depression. However, with the Conservative Party heavily influenced by the landlord interest, limited assistance was made to the rural community.

The Agricultural Holdings Act, 1875, was a measure supported enthusiastically by Disraeli. It was intended to extend to farmers in England something of the protection given to their Irish counterparts by the 1870

Land Act ensuring compensation for improvements. However, the Act was permissive, with landlords' rights preserved.

The Enclosures Act, 1876, helped to protect the remaining areas of common land, while an act of 1878 saved Epping Forest (north-east of London) from destruction.

In Ireland, by 1879, the agricultural depression had resulted in the outbreak of the Land War. Unlike Gladstone, Disraeli made no effort to solve Irish economic problems. However, in 1878, an Intermediate Education Act was passed giving schools the right to receive surplus funds created by the Irish Church Act, 1869. In the same year, the Irish Secretary, Lord Lowther, passed an Act creating the Royal University of Ireland.

By 1880, much of Great Britain and Ireland were suffering the adverse effects of a succession of wet summers and falling prices for agricultural goods. Yet the Disraeli Government did virtually nothing to alleviate the problem.

Licensing reform

In response to the opposition from brewers and distillers to the Bruce Licensing Act, 1872, the Conservatives passed the Intoxicating Liquors Act, 1874. However, in some areas, the Act curtailed licensing hours even further and, in the end, pleased nobody.

Religious matters

Perhaps the most controversial legislation by the Conservative ministry was the Public Worship Regulation Act, 1874. Even before Disraeli took office, the Archbishop of Canterbury, Archibald Tait, was planning a campaign against 'ritualism' in the Church of England. This was the practice of adopting Roman Catholic forms of worship associated with the rise of '**Anglo-Catholicism**' within the Anglican Church. It was introduced by Tait in the House of Lords as a Private Member's bill, but received government backing. Although supported by the Queen, it outraged Anglo-Catholics in the Cabinet such as Hardy, Carnarvon and, above all, Salisbury. It helped to deepen the splits within the Anglican Church.

Anglo-Catholicism: This was a movement within the Church of England which began at the University of Oxford in the 1830s and 1840s. Led by John Henry Newman, the 'Oxford Movement' – while denying the Pope's authority over the Church of England – wished to adopt Roman Catholic religious practices.

Summary

The reforms of Disraeli's Second Ministry have received a 'mixed press' from historians. Some historians, such as P.R. Ghosh, believe the changes to be very significant; others, such as Paul Smith and Bruce Coleman, take a more sceptical position. Overall, a number of features emerge.

- Firstly, many of the reforms were continuations of work begun by the preceding Liberal Government. Alterations to the laws on picketing, the law on friendly societies and merchant shipping law were all set in train by the Liberals. In addition, many other Acts, such as the Artisans' Dwellings Act, received Liberal support.

- Secondly, the Government introduced legislation to aid its supporters, such as the Education Act and Public Worship Act to defend the Church of England. Although the country was facing the effects of an agricultural depression after 1875, little was done to aid the farming community at the expense of the aristocracy.

- Finally, much of the legislation was permissive in character. Without compulsion, statutes such as the Agricultural Holdings Act, the Artisans' Dwellings Act and the Merchant Shipping Act, had a very limited impact. As historians P. Norton and A. Aughey, in *Conservatives and Conservatism* (1981), state, 'the reforms gave "self-help" an institutionalised push offering no opposition to established orthodoxies about the sanctity of property and the role of the state in the economy'.

1. Which of the reforms passed by Disraeli's Second Ministry do you regard as the most successful in bringing either political or social change to Britain?

Give reasons to support your answer.

2. 'On balance, Disraeli's ministry cannot be regarded as a reforming administration.'

Using the information in this section, how far do you agree with this statement?

Source-based questions: The Conservative Party

SOURCE A

'Gentlemen, I have referred to what I look upon as the first object of the Tory Party – namely, to maintain the institutions of the country, and reviewing what has occurred, and referring to the present temper of the times upon these subjects, I think the Tory Party, or, as I will venture to call it, the National Party, has everything to encourage it.

Gentlemen, there is another and second great object of the Tory Party. If the first is to maintain the institutions of the country, the second is, in my opinion, to uphold the Empire of England. Gentlemen, another great object of the Tory Party, and one not inferior to the maintenance of the Empire, or the upholding of our institutions, is the elevation of the condition of the people.

From Disraeli's speech at the Crystal Palace, 24 June 1872.

SOURCE B

If the Tory Party is to continue to exist as a power in the State, it must become a popular party. The days are past when an exclusive class, however great its ability, wealth and energy, can command a majority of the electorate. The liberties and interests of the people at large are the only things which it is now possible to conserve: the rights of property, the Established Church, the House of Lords, and the Crown itself must be defended on the grounds that they are institutions necessary to the preservation of civil and religious liberties and securities for personal freedom. Unfortunately for Conservatism, its leaders belong solely to one class; they are a clique composed of members of the aristocracy.

From 'Conservative disorganisation', published in
The Fortnightly Review, 1882

SOURCE C

In 1865 the Conservatives' strength lay in England where 221 of their 294 MPs held seats, particularly in counties and small boroughs. Their representation even in counties was threatened by urban expansion. Yet their perilously narrow electoral base was to be modified in three ways. First, the Liberal hold on Scotland strengthened slightly, and on Wales greatly, while in Ireland the Home Rulers mopped up 80% of the seats after 1874. In this way the Conservative position as the English party was considerably accentuated. Second, the Liberals extended their base in the counties following the 1884 franchise reform. Thus, whereas in 1868 Conservatives had won 115 out of 154 English county seats, in 1885 they held only 105 out of 239; counties had become a key element in an overall Liberal majority. Conservatives were saved only by their growing support in large boroughs and suburban seats, which reached a climax in 1900 when they took 177 English boroughs as against 162 English counties.

From *The Making of Modern British Politics 1867 to 1939*
by Martin Pugh, published in 1982.

---

1. Study Sources A and B.

With reference to both sources, and to information contained within this chapter, explain the meaning of the two highlighted terms as they applied to Britain in the third quarter of the 19th century.

(a) 'the elevation of the condition of the people' (Source A)

(b) 'the Established Church' (Source B).

2. Study Source B.

How useful is this source to a historian writing about the Conservative Party in the 1870s?

3. Study Sources A and B.

How far are the authors of these sources in agreement on the aims of the Conservative Party?

4. Study all three sources and use information contained in this chapter.

To what extent had the Conservative Party become the 'National Party', as mentioned by Disraeli in Source A, in the years 1868 to 1895?

8.3 Why did the Conservatives lose the 1880 election?

In 1880, the Conservatives lost most of the seats newly won in 1874. Losses occurred in all types of constituency in all parts of the United Kingdom. Even Lancashire, where the Conservatives had made major gains in 1874, saw a swing to the Liberals. In all, the Conservative Party lost 100 seats. With a total of only 238 in the new House of Commons, the performance was worse than 1868 and the Conservatives were even in a minority in English seats. So why had the Party performed so badly?

The timing of the general election

A.B. Forwood, the leader of the Liverpool Conservatives, had advised Disraeli to call a general election immediately after the foreign policy triumph of the Treaty of Berlin, in 1878. Instead, Disraeli continued in power, choosing to call the election in March 1880 after some favourable by-election results. These results proved to be misleading. In Liverpool, the Conservatives held a seat that the Liberals thought they might win. However, the Liberal share of the vote increased. In Southwark, London, the Conservatives won because the Liberal vote was split between a radical and a moderate.

Party organisation

The Liberal Party organisation had improved greatly since 1874. In 1877, Joseph Chamberlain had helped to establish the National Liberal Federation (NLF), giving the Party a national organisation for the first time. By the time of the 1880 general election, over 100 local Liberal organisations were affiliated to the NLF. Under the secretaryship of Francis Schnadhorst, the Liberal Party was able to fight an effective campaign.

In contrast, the Conservative Party organisation had deteriorated. Gorst had resigned as Principal Agent in March 1878. He was replaced by W.B. Skene, who proved to be entirely unsuitable for the post. During the campaign, he was criticised for his incompetence and he resigned shortly after the defeat.

Disraeli's election campaign

Like the party organisation, Disraeli's election campaign was far from effective. Due to ill-health he had been elevated to the peerage, as the Earl of Beaconsfield, in 1876.

As a peer, he followed the custom that peers should not campaign in elections. His only involvement in the campaign was an attempt to make the problems in Ireland an election issue. In his place, the Leader of the Conservatives in the Commons, Sir Stafford Northcote, proved no match for the Liberal front bench team in electioneering.

Little was said on either side about future legislation. The Liberals suggested they might change land property law, which would attract the farming vote. The Farmers' Alliance, a pressure group of tenant farmers linked to the Liberal Party, was active in many rural constituencies and received pledges of support for almost 60 candidates, all of them Liberals.

The agricultural depression

From 1877 onwards, the country suffered a major agricultural depression. The import of cheap North American grain had led to a fall in corn prices, while a partial potato famine had caused major problems in Ireland.

The Conservatives lost 25 English county seats, reflecting the effects of the depression. Disraeli noted, 'Hard times, as far as I can recollect, has been our foe and certainly it is the cause of our downfall.'

The effects of the depression led to the formation of the Farmers' Alliance, in 1879, which campaigned against the Conservatives and was a major reason for the loss of at least 19 seats.

The 'Great Depression'

From 1873, like most other European economies, the rate of growth in the British economy slowed down – what contemporaries referred to as the 'Great Depression'. In Britain, the depression led to a fall in real wages. Real wages fell by 5% between 1873 and 1879. The average level of unemployment rose from 1%–2% in 1871–74 to 6%–8% in 1878 and 11.4% in 1879. Although the Great Depression was not the result of Conservative policies, the Government suffered adversely at the polls because of its impact.

Imperial issues

In his two Midlothian campaigns of 1879 and 1880, Gladstone concentrated his attack on the Conservatives by criticising Disraeli's imperial policy. He attacked 'Beaconsfieldism', which he regarded as an aggressive and expensive foreign and imperial policy that was not in Britain's interest. Gladstone criticised the terms of the Treaty of Berlin because Disraeli had committed Britain to the defence of Turkey's Asiatic territory. He also attacked the foreign wars in Afghanistan and southern Africa, which he called pointless and barbarous.

Rise in taxation

1. Of the reasons mentioned above which one can be regarded as a political reason and which one can be regarded as economic?

2. Which of the reasons mentioned above do you think was the most important in causing the Conservative defeat at the 1880 general election? Give reasons to support your answer.

Although Northcote had been able to reduce income tax in 1874, the wars in Afghanistan and southern Africa had led to a rise in expenditure. This forced the Government to increase income tax from 2 pence in the pound (£) in 1874 to 5 pence in the pound in 1880.

The absence of 'sectionalism' in the Liberal Party

Unlike the period 1873–74, the Liberal Party had overcome the problem of internal disunity by 1880. Nonconformists, who had deserted the Party over educational issues in 1874, supported Gladstone's attack on Beaconsfieldism. Trade unionists who had disliked the Criminal Law Amendment Act, 1871, were now satisfied with the Conservative trade union laws and, rather ironically, returned to support the Liberals.

8.4 Gladstone and Disraeli compared
A CASE STUDY IN HISTORICAL INTERPRETATION

Introduction

In British parliamentary history it would be difficult to find a more intense rivalry than that which developed between Disraeli and Gladstone. Disraeli referred to Gladstone as 'AV' (arch villain).

They first became opponents during the debate on the repeal of the Corn Laws, in 1845–46, when Gladstone supported Peel and Disraeli agricultural protection.

Following the Conservative split, Gladstone became a Peelite and Disraeli became the leading protectionist spokesman in the Commons. During the short-lived Conservative Ministry of 1851–52, it was

> **Benjamin Disraeli (1804–1881)**
> Disraeli was a Tory MP from 1837. He became Conservative Leader of the Commons in 1851; was Chancellor of the Exchequer 1852, 1858–59; and became Prime Minister in 1867.

Gladstone's attack on Disraeli's budget that led to the fall of the government. Following the fall of the Whig–Peelite coalition in 1855, the Earl of Derby approached Gladstone with the offer of the post of Chancellor of the Exchequer in a Conservative government. Gladstone declined the job because he refused to serve in any government containing Disraeli. The rivalry intensified during the reform debates of 1866–67 and during the Liberal Ministry of 1868–74. Perhaps the height of their rivalry came over foreign and imperial policy, between 1876 and 1880, with the Gladstone-led Bulgarian Agitation and his Midlothian campaigns.

Did Gladstone and Disraeli differ on policy or were they merely rivals for power?

	Gladstone	Disraeli
The role of the State	Gladstone believed the idea of the 'minimalist' state, keeping government intervention to a minimum. His support for 'laissez-faire' policies covered trade, taxation and the role of government in society. Forster's Education Act, 1870, the Local Government Act, 1871, and the Licensing Act, 1872, all emphasise the importance of local decision making.	In a study of the domestic legislation of 1874–80 it is clear that Disraeli also supported a *laissez-faire* attitude to government regulation. Much of the legislation passed was permissive in character (e.g. the Artisans' Dwellings Act, 1875). The idea that Disraeli championed the cause of social improvement, in direct contrast to Gladstone, is difficult to support.
Taxation	Throughout his career, Gladstone tried to reduce taxation, cut public spending (retrenchment) and restrict defence spending. During his periods as Chancellor of the Exchequer, 1852–55 and 1859–65, there was a major reduction in taxes, in particular indirect taxes such as customs duties, paving the way for Britain to become a free trade nation. In the 1874 general election, he campaigned for the abolition of income tax.	Disraeli was Chancellor of the Exchequer in 1851–52 and again in 1858–59. He lacked Gladstone's expertise in finance but did believe in the importance of low taxation. His appointment, in 1874, of Sir Stafford Northcote to the Treasury and the retrenchment-minded G. Gathorne-Hardy to the War Office reinforce this view. Although his Second Ministry is noted for imperial expansion in southern Africa and Afghanistan, Disraeli was against both wars and abhorred the costs. His refusal to provide relief to those suffering distress during the agricultural depression after 1877 was due, in part, to his fear of raising taxation.
Trade	Throughout his political life – from his role as President of the Board of Trade in 1841–45 until his death – Gladstone was an advocate of free trade. His period at the Treasury in the 1850s and 1860s was a major factor in making Britain a free trade nation by 1865.	Disraeli rose to political prominence during the Corn Law debates of 1845–46 as a major defender of agricultural protection. However, following the defeat of his 1852 budget Disraeli, like the rest of the Conservative Party, abandoned protection and adopted free trade. Yet, during the agricultural depression in 1877, Disraeli did toy with the idea of re-imposing import taxes on grain.

	Gladstone	Disraeli
The Church of England	Although the leader of a party with a strong nonconformist element, Gladstone was a devout Anglican. He supported the branch of the Church of England known as Anglo-Catholicism, which supported the use of Roman Catholic style services. Religion was a central feature of Gladstone's life. He began his political career believing that the foundation stone of society should be the close link between the State and the Church of England, as stated in his 1838 book, *The State and its Relations with the Church*. In his later political life, however, he moved away from the idea of a State-supported Church. He was responsible for the passage of the Irish Church Disestablishment Act, 1869, and other legislation which helped remove the Anglican Church's privileged position in society.	In his speeches in 1872 at Manchester and the Crystal Palace, Disraeli emphasised his support for the Church of England. He opposed the Irish Church Disestablishment Act, 1869, and the University Tests Act, 1871, on religious grounds. During his Second Ministry, Sandon's Education Act, 1876, was designed specifically to aid the Church of England. However, Disraeli supported Archbishop Archibald Tait's attacks on ritualism (the name given to Anglo-Catholic religious practices) which was the aim behind the Public Worship Regulation Act of 1874. Also, unlike Gladstone, Disraeli always supported the position of the Church of England as the State Church.

Punch cartoon, August 1878, entitled 'A Bad Example'. Dr Punch (headmaster) is saying: 'What's all this? You, the two head boys of the school, throwing mud! You ought to be ashamed of yourselves!'

A BAD EXAMPLE.

Dr. Punch. "WHAT'S ALL THIS? YOU, THE TWO HEAD BOYS OF THE SCHOOL, THROWING MUD YOU OUGHT TO BE ASHAMED OF YOURSELVES!"

1. How are Gladstone and Disraeli portrayed in this cartoon?

2. How reliable is this cartoon in its depiction of Gladstone and Disraeli?

	Gladstone	Disraeli
The role of the aristocracy	Although head of a radical party, Gladstone believed in the natural governing right of the aristocracy. In his Cabinets of 1868–74 and 1880–85, he chose Whig aristocrats in numbers which far outweighed their numerical importance in the Party as a whole. However, towards the end of his plitical life, in 1893–94 Gladstone began campaigning for a reduction in the political power of the House of Lords.	In his 1872 speeches, Disraeli defended the position of the House of Lords and the role of the aristocracy in politics. In the 1867 Reform Act, Disraeli attempted to protect the power of Tory squires in rural constituencies with the maintenance of the 1832 freeholder franchise and the over-representation of county compared to borough seats. During his Second Ministry, although many social reforms were passed, none of them threatened the political or economic position of property or landed wealth.
Ireland	For most of his political career after 1868, Gladstone was associated with this issue. There has been much controversy about Gladstone's motives in Irish policy, but it is clear he spent considerable time on the issue and passed several significant reforms.	In contrast, Disraeli never visited Ireland and avoided the issue for much of his political career. In 1844, he referred to Ireland as having 'the worst executive in the world' but did nothing to alter it when he was in power in 1851–52, 1858–59 and 1866–68. During his First Ministry, in 1868, he was involved in subduing the Fenian movement and during Gladstone's First Ministry he defended the Anglican Church in Ireland and Irish landowners. In his own Second Ministry, the position of Irish Secretary was not given Cabinet rank, but Sir Michael Hicks-Beach and Lord Lowther, the Irish Secretaries, did pass some minor reforms even though they did not deal with the land issue. Although he made an attempt to make Ireland an issue in the 1880 election, Disraeli had little positive involvement in Irish affairs. During the 1880 election, he described Home Rule as 'scarcely less disastrous than pestilence and famine'.
Foreign policy	There are considerable differences between Gladstone and Disraeli on foreign policy. Gladstone believed in using the Concert of Europe to maintain European peace. He supported the arbitration of international disputes such as the 'Alabama' Award and the Penjdeh incident. He also opposed an aggressive foreign policy, which was likely to increase government spending.	Disraeli strongly criticised Gladstone's foreign policy in 1872 and, according to the historian Richard Shannon, 'took up the mantle of **neo-Palmerstonianism**'. During his Second Ministry, he followed an active foreign policy during the Near Eastern Crisis of 1875–78.

Neo-Palmerstonianism: Following an aggressive foreign policy to defend Britain's interest, in the manner of Lord Palmerston.

	Gladstone	**Disraeli**
Imperial policy	During his First Ministry, Gladstone, and his Colonial Secretary to 1870, Lord Granville, were accused of trying to dismantle the British Empire. The withdrawal of British troops from New Zealand in 1869, the granting of self-government to Cape Colony in 1871 and the attempted sale of Gambia to France were all seen as part of this process. During his Second Ministry, however, Gladstone's Government invaded and occupied Egypt in 1882 and participated in the partition of west and southern Africa. These policies seem contradictory. Gladstone believed in 'freedom and voluntaryism' in imperial relations. Throughout his career he tried to create an association of self-governing nations held together by a common allegiance to the monarchy and a common language, history and tradition. This was to be limited to colonies that were governed by whites, such as Canada, the Austirlian colonies, New Zealand and Cape Colony. Gladstone's most important statement on the Empire came in September 1878, in 'England's Mission', an article in the periodical *Nineteenth Century*. Gladstone stated that Britain had a civilising mission to spread the benefits of English civilisation throughout the world. In this respect, British rule in India and Africa was for the benefits of the native inhabitants because Britain provided sound administration and enlightened government. He was, supposedly, opposed to aggressive, expansionist policies to enlarge the Empire. Hence his opposition to Beaconsfieldism in 1876 to 1880.	There has been debate about Disraeli's sincerity in imperial matters. However, since S.R. Stembridge's 'Disraeli and the Millstones' in the *Journal of British Studies* (1965) and F. Harcourt's 'Disraeli's Imperialism' in the *Historical Journal* (1981), it has now become accepted that he had consistent views about the importance of the Empire throughout his career. Although he showed little interest in Canada, the Australian colonies and New Zealand, the Empire, to Disraeli, was the commercial and military basis of Britain's claim to be a world power. At the centre of the Empire was India. He used troops from the British Indian Army in Abyssinia in 1867–68 and in Malta in 1878, during the Near Eastern Crisis. In contrast to Gladstone, Disraeli saw the Empire as a military machine. This helps explain why the Near Eastern Crisis was so important to Disraeli because of its impact on the sea route to India through the Suez Canal. Although in favour of a powerful Empire, Disraeli was not always in favour of imperial expansion. He opposed the war with the Zulus in 1879 and the conflict in Afghanistan. The fact that aggressive policies occurred during his Ministry was due to personal weakness by Disraeli not design.

1. Using the information contained above, write down those areas of policy where Gladstone and Disraeli were in general agreement.

2. Then write down where you think they disagreed.

3. Then explain how far you think this is an accurate assessment of Gladstone and Disraeli.

Punch cartoon, 1880, entitled 'The Choice of Hercules'.

THE CHOICE OF HERCULES.

1. In what ways does this portrayal of Gladstone and Disraeli differ from the *Punch* cartoon of 1878 (see page 149)?

2. Hercules represents the British electorate in the general election campaign of 1880.

What choice does he face when choosing between Gladstone and Disraeli in the election?

Explain your answer.

8.5 How successful was Salisbury in domestic affairs between 1885 and 1892?

Following Disraeli's death, the leadership of the Conservative Party passed to Lord Salisbury in the Lords and Sir Stafford Northcote in the Commons. Throughout Gladstone's Second Ministry, Northcote's leadership was criticised heavily by the group of Conservative backbench MPs known as the Fourth Party. By the time of the general election of 1885, Salisbury was regarded as leader.

During Salisbury's period as Conservative leader, the Party became the dominant force in British politics and passed many significant reforms. Why?

The Liberal split of 1886

The Home Rule crisis brought the Liberal dominance of mid-Victorian politics, which had lasted from 1859 to 1886, to an end. The crisis led to the creation of the Liberal Unionist Party, which supported the Conservatives throughout the period 1886–95. Led by Lord Hartington, this party contained a large number of Whigs and a group of radicals closely associated with Joseph Chamberlain.

Villa Toryism

There was a marked increase in middle-class support for the Conservative Party. The commercial classes, who had formed one of the pillars of Gladstonian Liberalism, were becoming disillusioned with many of the radical causes put forward by pressure groups associated with the Liberal Party, such as nonconformists and land reformers.

As middle-class suburbs developed around Victorian cities, the Conservatives began to win seats in urban areas. This trend was enhanced by the redistribution of seats in 1885, which created single-member constituencies.

Conservative Party organisation

The formation and popularity of the Primrose League after 1883 and the development of Conservative working men's clubs helped spread the electoral support for the Party. With the appointment of Captain Middleton as Principal Party Agent and his coordination of Conservative organisation after 1884, the Party gained an effective electioneering machine.

Imperialism

The Conservatives became associated with the main issues of the day, most notably imperial expansion. Although there was an influential group within the Liberal Party called the Liberal Imperialists, the Liberals were generally against the growth of the Empire.

'Angels in Marble': working-class Toryism

Although trade unionists supported the Liberal Party, the newly enfranchised voters of 1867 and 1884 had a significant pro-Conservative element. These groups were prominent in areas with large Irish Catholic minorities, such as northern Ireland, Lancashire and central Scotland. The anti-Catholic elements in these areas tended to vote Conservative. Towns with a large military and naval presence, such as Portsmouth, were attracted by the Party's policy on defence spending, while the Liberal Party's attachment to licensing reform meant a large proportion of the 'drinking masses' voted Conservative.

Finally, although the secret ballot had been introduced in 1872, the politics of deference (voting on the advice of your social superiors) continued to exist. Tenants on large estates and those in domestic service were most affected by this.

Domestic reforms, 1885–1892

● Ireland

Under the guidance of the Irish Secretary, A.J. Balfour, a policy of land purchase and coercion helped bring order to the Irish countryside through a policy termed 'Constructive Unionism' or 'Killing Home Rule through Kindness'.

● Labour reform

Against the background of the agricultural depression and high unemployment, which led to the Trafalgar Square Riots of 1887, the

Salisbury Government passed a number of reforms. The Working Class Dwellings Act, 1885, extended the power of local authorities to remove slums. This was extended by the Housing of the Working Classes Act, 1890. The Labourers' Allotment Act, 1887, allowed labourers to achieve 'manly independence' by allowing local authorities to provide land for allotments. This was extended with the Small Holdings Act, 1892, where small plots of land were made available for agricultural labourers. The Mines Regulation Act, 1887, extended government regulation of the coalmining industry.

- **Education reform**

  The 1891 Education Act abolished school fees and was mainly due to the work of Joseph Chamberlain.

- **Local government reform**

  The most significant Act passed in this period was the County Councils Act, 1888. This extended the householder franchise from the towns to the countryside, creating 62 county councils directly elected by the ratepayers. Although a significant piece of legislation, its main aim was to pre-empt the Liberals introducing a more radical measure in the future. Considerable power was still left in the hands of JPs.

Summary

1. In what ways did Salisbury's Administration bring about social and political change?

2. Using the information in this section, how far was Salisbury's success as Prime Minister due to the split in the Liberal Party?

Although the legislative record for the period 1886–94 is slight compared with its immediate Liberal and Conservative predecessors, the changes brought about were not inconsiderable. Most benefited the farming community, not surprising as the Conservatives were the traditional party of the landowner. However, several reforms also benefited the farm labourer. To emphasise the priority given to farming matters a Board of Agriculture was established, in 1889, with a minister at its head.

8.6 What impact did Disraeli and Salisbury have on late Victorian politics?

Perhaps the biggest change in British politics in the period 1868 to 1895 was the revival in the fortunes of the Conservative Party. Much credit for this development has been given to Disraeli. Although historians such as Bruce Coleman believe Disraeli's contribution to this process has been exaggerated, Disraeli did play a major role. His policy speeches of 1872 laid the foundation for Conservative policy for the rest of the century. Perhaps more important was the myth of Disraeli, put forward by Randolph Churchill and the Primrose League, as the supporter of 'One Nation' Conservatism. It would seem that Disraeli's impact on the Conservative Party was greater after his death than during his lifetime.

Lord Salisbury, in terms of winning elections and length of time as Conservative leader, was more successful than Disraeli. However, his long-term impact on the Conservative Party was not as great as Disraeli's. According to Salisbury's biographer, Robert Taylor, 'it was Irish Home Rule that made Salisbury'. The split in the Liberal Party enabled Salisbury to occupy the centre ground in British politics. He became 'the safe pair of hands' on the ship of state which helped attract a large number of middle-class voters. By the time of his retirement from politics, in 1902, the Conservatives had become the party of the majority of the middle class.

Salisbury was also a very capable politician. Robert Taylor states that 'Far more than Disraeli, and even Gladstone, Salisbury was a shrewd, though unwilling, practitioner of the arts of party management'.

Under Salisbury's leadership party organisation was used effectively to win new middle-class supporters through the Primrose League and working-class supporters through Conservative working men's clubs.

To become undisputed Conservative leader, Salisbury had to first overcome Sir Stafford Northcote. This he had achieved, partly through the actions of the 'Fourth Party', by 1885. Salisbury was fortunate to see the removal of the potential rivalry of the Party's rising star, Lord Randolph Churchill, in 1887, when the latter resigned from the post of Chancellor of the Exchequer on a minor matter. From 1887 to 1902, Salisbury was able to lead the Party without a clear rival.

1. Who do you regard as the more successful as Conservative leader, Disraeli or Salisbury?

Give reasons to support your answer.

Further Reading

Articles

In *Modern History Review*:
'Disraeli: Political Outsider' by Robert Blake (Vol. 1 No. 2)
'Perspectives: Tory Democracy' by Paul Smith and Bruce Coleman (Vol. 1 No. 4)
'Concepts: Conservatism' by Bruce Coleman (Vol. 6 No. 3)
'Lord Salisbury and Late Victorian Conservatism' by Graham Goodlad (Vol. 2 No. 3)
In *History Review* (formerly *History Sixth*):
'Disraeli: Myth and Reality, Policy and Presentation' by John Walton (No. 14, December 1992)

Texts designed for AS and A2 level students

Gladstone, Disraeli and Later Victorian Politics by P. Adelman (Longman, Seminar Studies series, 2nd edn, 1987)
Tories, Conservatives and Unionists 1815 to 1914 by Duncan Watts (Hodder & Stoughton Access to History series, 1994)
Disraeli by John Walton (Routledge, Lancaster Pamphlets, 1990)
Aspects of British Political History 1815–1914 by Stephen Lee (Routledge, 1994)
Disraeli by Mary Dicken (Collins Historymakers, 2004)

More advanced reading

Disraeli by Ian Machin (Longman, Profiles in Power, 1995)
Lord Salisbury by Robert Taylor (Allen Lane, 1975)
Democracy and Empire: British History 1865 to 1914 by E.J. Feuchtwanger (Arnold, 1985)
The Conservative Leadership 1832 to 1932 edited by D. Southgate (Macmillan, 1974)
Conservatism and the Conservative Party in the Nineteenth Century by Bruce Coleman (Arnold, 1988)
The Conservative Party from Peel to Thatcher by Robert Blake (Fontana, 1985)
The Making of Modern British Politics 1867 to 1939 by Martin Pugh (Blackwell, 1982)

9 British foreign and imperial policy, 1856–1895

Key Issues

- What were the aims of British foreign and imperial policy?

- How far did Britain's foreign and imperial policy change between 1856 and 1895?

- How successful was Britain's foreign and imperial policy?

9.1 What principles governed British foreign policy between 1856 and 1895?

9.2 What British issues were involved in the 'Eastern Question'?

9.3 What were the results of the Crimean War?

9.4 What were the main problems in British foreign and imperial policy, 1856–1868?

9.5 How successful was Gladstone's foreign and imperial policy, 1868–74?

9.6 What impact did Disraeli make on foreign and imperial policy?

9.7 Historical Interpretation: Why did Britain take part in the partition of Africa?

9.8 What were the foreign and imperial problems facing Gladstone's second ministry, 1880–1885?

9.9 To what extent was Britain in a state of 'splendid isolation' by 1895?

Framework of Events

1856	Treaty of Paris ends Crimean War
1857	Indian Mutiny
1857–1860	Chinese Wars
1867–68	The Abyssinian Campaign
1870	Franco-Prussian War breaks out
	Revocation of Black Sea Clauses of Treaty of Paris by Russia
1872	'Alabama' Award
	Speeches at Manchester and Crystal Palace: Disraeli puts forward policy of defending the Empire
1873	Ashanti War begins
1874	Annexation of Fiji
1875	Purchase of Suez Canal Shares
	July: Revolt breaks out in Bosnia and Hercegovina against Turkish rule
	December: Andrassy Note
1876	Royal Titles Act
	Lord Lytton becomes Viceroy of India
	April: Bulgarians rebel against Turkish rule
	May: Berlin Memorandum rejected by Britain and Turkey
	July: Reports reach England of Bulgarian horrors
	Reichstadt Agreement
	November: Serbia defeated
	December: Constantinople conference
1877	Transvaal joins British Empire
	April: Russia declares war on Turkey
	May: British warnings to Russia
	July: Siege of Plevna
1878	Second Afghan War
	Zulu War

	January: Russians reach outskirts of Constantinople
	February: British fleets reaches Constantinople
	March: Treaty of San Stefano
	April: Britain mobilises for war. Indian troops sent to Malta
	May–June: British agreements with Austria-Hungary, Russia and Turkey
	July: Congress of Berlin
1879	Third Afghan War
1880	Britain withdraws from Afghanistan
	First Boer War
1881	Treaty of Pretoria with the Transvaal
1882	Invasion of Egypt
1883	Failure of Ilbert Bill in India
1884	Treaty of London with the Transvaal
1885	Creation of Bechuanaland Protectorate
	General Gordon in the Sudan
1885–87	Bulgarian Crisis
1887	Mediterranean Agreements
1889	Naval Defence Act
1890	Heligoland–Zanzibar Agreement with Germany
1893	Franco–Russian Alliance.

Overview

I N 1856 Britain was a world power. Britain had been the first country to undergo an industrial revolution and by 1856 it was seen as 'the workshop of the world'. Over three-quarters of all cotton textiles produced worldwide came from the Manchester area. In addition, Britain was the financial capital of the world. In London the Stock Exchange was the centre for investment, the Baltic Exchange was the centre for shipping, and Lloyd's was the world's major insurer.

Britain also possessed the world's greatest navy. Since the Battle of Trafalgar, in 1805, British seapower was unchallenged. In 1889 Britain passed the Naval Defence Act. This created the 'two-power standard' whereby the Royal Navy was to be as large as the next two largest world navies combined.

Perhaps, the greatest claim to world power status was the British Empire. Centred on India – 'the jewel in the crown' – this was the largest empire in the world.

By 1895 Britain's position in the world had changed dramatically. In economic and commercial terms Britain now faced strong rivalry from Germany and the United States. But in terms of imperial possessions Britain had also acquired a vast empire in Africa. By the time of Queen Victoria's Diamond Jubilee in 1897 – she had reigned for 60 years – the British Empire covered one quarter of the globe and contained one third of the world's population.

The period begins with victory over Russia in the Crimean War (1854–56). On two further occasions Britain faced another war with Russia. Between 1875 and 1878 and again in 1885 Anglo-Russian relations were very tense.

Britain also fought a number of colonial wars. The most serious was the Indian Mutiny of 1857. British rule was seriously threatened but the mutiny was crushed. Britain also fought wars against the Chinese in 1858–60; in West Africa in 1874; and in South Africa – against the Zulus in 1878–79 and against the Boers in 1880–81. Finally, Britain fought two brief campaigns in Egypt in 1882 and the Sudan in 1885.

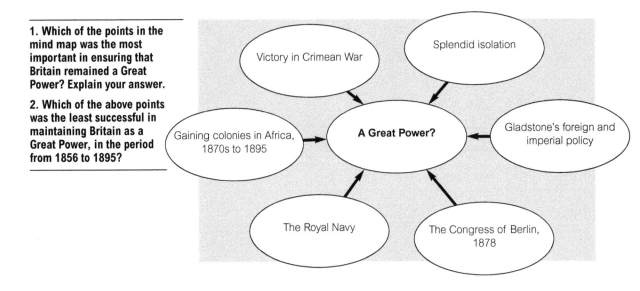

1. Which of the points in the mind map was the most important in ensuring that Britain remained a Great Power? Explain your answer.

2. Which of the above points was the least successful in maintaining Britain as a Great Power, in the period from 1856 to 1895?

9.1 What principles governed British foreign policy between 1856 and 1895?

The balance of power

At the end of the Napoleonic War, in 1815, a balance of power was created at the Treaty of Vienna. The aim was to prevent future wars where one country would try to dominate Europe. The peacemakers at Vienna divided territory in Europe in order to prevent such a development. As a result, five countries had enough significant military power to be described as 'Great Powers'. These were Britain, France, Prussia, Russia and Austria. In 1871 an enlarged Prussia became the German Empire.

Throughout the period 1815 to 1914, Britain supported the balance of power. Whenever there was a threat to the balance of power, Britain intervened in European affairs. The most serious example during this period was the Crimean war. In 1854 Britain believed Russia was attempting to destroy the balance of power. Allied with France, Turkey and, eventually, Piedmont-Sardinia, Britain waged war against Russia, in the Crimea between 1854 and 1856. The Treaty of Paris of 1856 re-established the balance of power.

When, in 1877–78, Britain felt the balance was under threat again – by Russia – Britain again threatened war. In 1914 Britain went to war with Germany to preserve the balance of power. The only time when Britain did not intervene in Europe when the balance of power was changed was in the Franco-Prussian War of 1870–71.

Expanding trade and the empire

A major British aim was to ensure that it could trade with the rest of the world. Throughout the nineteenth century Britain attempted to establish free trade agreements with other countries. The wars with China were part of a plan to open up that empire to British trade.

For much of the period 1815–1880, Britain established an 'informal empire', in which it dominated the trade with certain areas without formally governing them. This involved much of West Africa and countries such as Uruguay and Argentina in South America.

However, from 1880 onwards Britain took part in the partition of Africa where European powers such as Germany and France – along with Britain – began to establish formal control.

The fear of Russia

A common theme throughout the period 1856 to 1895 was fear of Russia.

Russia threatened British interests in a number of areas. First, Russia attempted to force the Ottoman Empire (Turkey) to allow Russian warships to enter the Mediterranean Sea via the Straits. In order to stop this development Britain had gone to war with Russia between 1854 and 1856 and again threatened war in 1877–78.

Russia was also seen as the European power most likely to 'unbalance' the balance of power. This centred on Russia's desire to gain territory in the Balkans. This desire was most apparent in 1877–78 , particularly in the 1878 Treaty of San Stefano.

A greater threat for Britain came with Russian expansion into Central Asia from 1855 to the 1880s. Russia conquered the area which now comprises Kazakhstan, Turkmenistan, Uzbekistan and Tadzikistan. This brought Russia uncomfortably close to the border of British India – where, it was feared, Russia might foment unrest. As a result, both Russia and Britain attempted to gain influence over Afghanistan.

Support for constitutional states

Lord Palmerston dominated British foreign policy between 1830 and his death in 1865. One of his aims was to 'export' the British Constitution. As a result, Britain supported liberal regimes in other states. These included the former Spanish and Portuguese colonies of Latin America. It also meant support for liberals in Spain and Portugal. The greatest example of this support came with British support for Italian unification. The creation of the Liberal Party in 1859 took place against the background of such support.

1. What do you regard as the most important issue in British foreign and imperial policy between 1856 and 1895? Give reasons for your answer.

2. In what ways did Britain's fear of Russia change between 1856 and 1895?

3. Can you find any links or connections between the main principles which governed foreign and imperial policy? Draw a mind map linking the above principles.

9.2 What British issues were involved in the 'Eastern Question'?

An important issue in British foreign policy from the 1850s was the 'Eastern Question' – the international problem created by the rapid decline of the Ottoman Empire (Turkey). From the sixteenth century to the eighteenth, the Ottoman Empire dominated North Africa, the Middle East and south-east Europe. However, from the 1770s onwards the Ottoman Empire went into a period of decline. It was led by corrupt officials and it failed to modernise its government and armed forces. In a series of wars against Russia in 1768–74, 1806–12 and 1828–29, the Ottoman Empire was defeated. Over the period 1768 to 1854 the Ottoman Empire lost large tracts of territory in North Africa and south-east Europe. From the 1830s to the First World War, Britain saw one of its main aims as preserving the Ottoman Empire. For Britain, the collapse of the Ottoman Empire would have a number of adverse effects. Lost of territory to Russia would affect the balance of power. The ability of the Russians to send warships into the Mediterranean Sea would affect British influence in that area. The increase of Russian influence in the Middle East would threaten the overland route to India. And, from 1869 it would also threaten the Suez Canal.

1. What was the 'Eastern Question'?

2. How would the collapse of the Ottoman Empire affect Britain and its empire?

9.3 What were the results of the Crimean War?

When Britain declared war on Russia in 1854, its main concerns were the maintenance of the European balance of power and the need to prevent the Russian navy entering the Mediterranean Sea.

Following the Russian evacuation of Moldavia and Wallachia, the British and French decided to capture the Russian naval base on the Black Sea, Sebastopol. Although this was a sound military objective, the Anglo–French campaign was poorly organised. The campaign did not begin until September 1854, allowing the Russians to fortify the city. The British and French were forced to spend the winter of 1854–55 besieging Sebastopol. This campaign exposed how badly the British Army was organised and supplied. Battles at Balaklava, in October 1854, and Inkerman, in November, showed both the bravery of British troops and the poor quality of their generals.

The Times correspondent William Howard Russell wrote damning newspaper articles about living conditions and bad organisation, which helped to defeat Lord Aberdeen's Government in 1855.

Aberdeen was replaced by Palmerston. Military organisation was improved and Austria, Sweden and Piedmont-Sardinia joined the side of Britain and France. In 1855, Sebastopol fell, mainly to an assault by French troops. In Paris the following year, the peace treaty between Russia and the Allies was signed.

The Crimean War brought about many changes. The war had the first 'on the spot' war correspondent in W.H. Russell. It was also the war that saw Florence Nightingale make her reputation as a nurse, laying the foundations of modern British nursing, at the British military hospital at Scutari, near Constantinople.

Europe in 1871

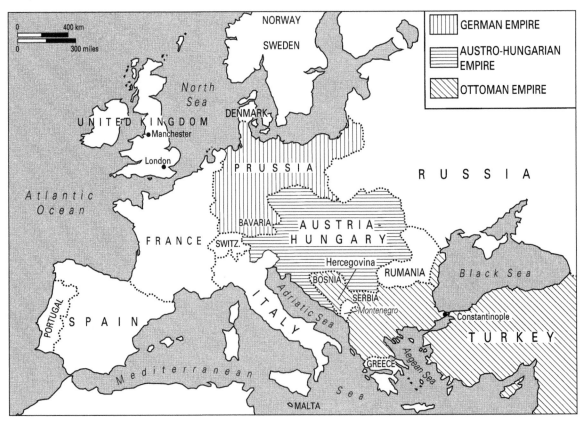

In international terms, Britain achieved its major objectives. The European balance of power was maintained. Neither Russia nor Turkey was allowed a fleet in the Black Sea, thereby removing any potential naval threat to Britain in the Mediterranean. The Turks promised to improve the treatment of Christians within their Empire. In addition, Moldavia and Wallachia were given independence but were not allowed to unite. Russia lost southern Bessarabia.

However, the war had other far-reaching consequences. Austria's decision to side with Britain and France against Russia split the Holy Alliance. In the years after 1856, the lack of Russian involvement in European affairs was an important reason behind the Austrian defeat in Italy by France in 1859 and by Prussia in the Seven Weeks' War of 1866. It would be true to say that the split in the Holy Alliance helped to reshape central Europe.

1. What changes were made by Britain's involvement in the Crimean War?

2. Do you regard Britain's involvement in the Crimean War as having been successful? Give reasons to support your answer.

Although Britain was successful, many of its gains proved short-lived. Moldavia and Wallachia united in 1858 and became the kingdom of Romania in 1861. The Sultan's promise to improve the treatment of his Christian subjects was not implemented. Most important of all, the demilitarisation of the Black Sea came to an end in 1870, when at the height of the Franco–Prussian War, Russia declared that it was no longer bound by the Treaty of Paris of 1856. The Crimean War brought a lull in the Eastern Question. The issue again brought Europe into crisis and war in the 1875–78 period.

9.4 What were the main problems and issues in foreign and imperial policy in 1868?

As one of the European Great Powers, Britain supported the balance of power that had been created at the Treaty of Vienna in 1815. The only time Britain went to war with another European Great Power between 1815 and 1914 was against Russia in the Crimean War of 1854–56, in order to preserve the balance of power. In 1868, Britain's main commitment in European affairs was to uphold the terms of the Treaty of Paris of 1856, which ended that war. The most important provision of that treaty was that neither the Turkish Empire nor Russia were allowed to keep warships in the Black Sea.

Between 1859 and 1871, however, there was a major transformation in European international relations. Italy became a unified country between 1859 and 1861. More importantly, in 1866, Prussia defeated Austria, and became the dominant German-speaking state. In 1870–71, Prussia then defeated Europe's major military power, France, and created the German Empire. By 1871, the old balance of power of 1814–15 had been altered: Germany was now the continent's main Great Power. Under the influence of the important European statesman of the time, Otto von Bismarck, Chancellor of Germany, an alliance system centred on Germany was created, with the aim of isolating France.

Major changes also took place within the British Empire. In 1867, the British North America Act gave Canada internal self-government. In the course of the second half of the 19th century, other 'white dominions', such as New Zealand, the Australian colonies and Cape Colony, also received self-government.

In 1865, the report of a select committee of the House of Commons recommended a withdrawal from the west African colonies, which were deemed unprofitable. This started a major debate on how the British Empire should develop.

Perhaps the greatest threat to the British Empire came from Russia. Between 1856 and 1870, the Russians conquered the central Asian states of Khiva, Bokhara and Samarkhand. These conquests provided Russia with a border very close to the British Indian Empire. For the rest of the century, Britain attempted to protect India's north-west frontier against possible Russian incursion. This involved both states in trying to gain influence in Afghanistan.

As the historian C.C. Eldridge has stated, Britain 'was both a European state threatened by the menace of continental politics and an imperial power with distant obligations'. Britain's main military force for defending the mother country from invasion, and for protecting the Empire overseas, was the Royal Navy. Since the Battle of Trafalgar in 1805, Britain had been the world's greatest naval power. In the period after 1868, however, British naval power was in decline.

Which of the issues and problems, mentioned above, do you regard as the most important facing Britain in the years 1868 and 1895? Explain your answer.

9.5 How successful was Gladstone's foreign and imperial policy 1868–1874?

Gladstone's views

Gladstone derived his views on foreign and imperial affairs from a number of sources.

● Firstly, he believed in the 'Concert of Europe'. This was the idea that the European Great Powers should act together (in concert) to preserve peace by upholding the balance of power.

● Secondly, he believed war to be both expensive and damaging to trade. He therefore favoured the arbitration of international disputes.

● Thirdly, he believed that British rule over the Empire was a duty and responsibility. Britain had the task of providing efficient administration to the subjects of the Empire. However, when internal self-government was given to colonies Gladstone was of the opinion that they should not have to rely on British military assistance for their internal security.

During his First Ministry, Gladstone, and his Foreign Secretary (after 1870) Lord Granville were heavily criticised by their political opponents for following a foreign and imperial policy, which was against Britain's interests.

The Franco–Prussian War, 1870–71

Prussia's victory over France transformed the balance of power in Europe. However, Gladstone's Government did not intervene directly in the war. The Government received very little criticism for its actions. The main criticism was that Britain did not do enough to stop France declaring war in July 1870.

Once the war had begun, Gladstone's only intervention was to get an agreement from both sides not to invade Belgium, in August 1870. Once the war was over, Lord Granville did intervene to get the war indemnity France had to pay Prussia under the terms of the Treaty of Frankfurt reduced to 5,000 million francs.

The revocation of the Black Sea clauses of the Treaty of Paris

At the height of the Franco–Prussian War, Russia took the opportunity to renounce the section of the Treaty of Paris of 1856 forbidding the Russians to have a fleet in the Black Sea. To Britain, this had been the most important part of the treaty and one of the main reasons why it had fought the Crimean War.

In line with Gladstone's belief in the Concert of Europe, Lord Granville organised an international conference in London, in March 1871, in which all the Great Powers took part. Russia was invited to ask the conference to revoke the Black Sea clauses, and accepted.

The 'Alabama' Award, 1872

This episode was an example of Gladstone's faith in international arbitration. The USA had demanded £9 million in compensation for the damage inflicted on the Union merchant fleet during the American Civil War of 1861–65 by a number of Confederate raiders, the most notable being the 'Alabama'. Britain was accused of breaching its neutrality because many of these raiders had been built at Birkenhead, in Cheshire. In the Treaty of Washington (May 1871), both Britain and the USA agreed to international arbitration in Geneva, Switzerland, to settle the dispute.

In September 1872, the arbitrators awarded the USA damages of £3.25 million (one-third of the original claim).

Although the award ended a long-standing dispute between Britain and the USA, it was deeply unpopular at home. Many believed Britain had not broken its neutrality in the war. In addition, the fact that Britain dropped any claim for damages for the Fenian raid from the USA on Canada in 1866 and gave the USA the right to fish off the coast of Canada, made the award seem like a diplomatic defeat for Britain.

Imperial issues

Disraeli severely criticised Gladstone's Government on imperial matters, claiming that the Liberal leader wanted to dismantle the British Empire. A number of matters seemed to support Disraeli's claim:

- The decision to withdraw British troops from Canada and New Zealand when these colonies faced internal revolts.

- The decision to offer the Canadian Prime Minister, Alexander Galt, a knighthood, even though Galt was in favour of Canadian independence.

- The announcement, in June 1870, that Britain planned to abandon Gambia in west Africa to France.

1. Disraeli heavily criticised Gladstone's handling of foreign and imperial policy.

Write down the areas of policy where you think Disraeli's criticism was valid.

Then write down where you think Gladstone was successful.

2. On balance, was Gladstone a failure in foreign and imperial affairs? Give reasons to support your answer.

Gladstone, on the other hand, believed that white-controlled colonies that had received self-government, such as Canada and New Zealand, should be responsible for their own internal security. He also believed that the British Empire should develop into a group of white self-governing colonies. As part of this plan, Cape Colony was given self-government in 1872.

Also, the Liberals were willing to defend the Empire when problems arose. For instance, in 1873 King Coffee Calcalli of the Ashanti threatened the British West African colony of Gold Coast (now Ghana). The British Government sent a military expedition, which defeated King Coffee in the Ashanti War of 1873–74 and extended British colonial control to include the Ashanti nation.

9.6 What impact did Disraeli have on foreign and imperial policy?

In contrast to Gladstone, Disraeli has been seen as a great defender of the British Empire and British interests abroad. However, the sincerity of Disraeli as an imperialist has been questioned. The Canadian historian, John Morison, stated that Disraeli had no real understanding of the Empire, while R. Koebner and H. Schmidt in their study *Imperialism: The Story and Significance of a Political Word* believed that Disraeli's interest in the Empire was merely a piece of self-advertisement.

This view has been challenged by a number of historians. The most notable was S.R. Stembridge in an article 'Disraeli and the Millstones' (published in 1965) where he pointed to a long-standing interest in Empire throughout Disraeli's career.

Yet Disraeli's foreign and imperial policy has an element of self-advertisement about it. Disraeli, like Palmerston, was able to use foreign and imperial policy to boost his popularity at home. A good example of this was in 1867–68 when he sent 12,000 troops to free some British hostages in Abyssinia. It can also be seen in his handling of the Near Eastern Crisis of 1875–78.

Imperial issues

Contrary to what many contemporaries believed, there was a high degree of continuity between the imperial policies of Gladstone and Disraeli. In his study 'The Imperial Frontier in the Tropics' (1967), W.D. McIntyre noted that in Fiji, the Malay States and west Africa the Conservatives merely carried on policies begun by the Liberals.

The historian C.C. Eldridge goes further by claiming that 'Conservative policy was often the result of a series of uncoordinated developments which did not always meet with Disraeli's personal approval. Disraeli was interested in ideas. He could never be bothered with details. Disraeli never wished to dictate colonial policy. This was left to the Colonial Secretary, Lord Carnarvon.'

As a result, many of the decisions affecting the Empire were made by ministers or officials overseas (men on the spot). In October 1874, Commodore Goodenough annexed Fiji, against the wishes of Lord Carnarvon. In 1874, the Governor of Singapore, Sir Andrew Clarke, was chiefly responsible for establishing British 'residents' in each Malay state. In west Africa, the Conservatives concluded the Ashanti War begun by the Liberals.

The purchase of the Khedive of Egypt's Suez Canal shares, 1875
One area where Disraeli did show initiative was his decision, without gaining Cabinet approval, to buy the Khedive (ruler) of Egypt's shareholding in the Suez Canal Company. Using £4 million acquired from the Rothschild family, Disraeli purchased a 44% share in the operation of the Suez Canal, which had become one of the world's major sea routes since its opening in 1869.

The Royal Titles Act, 1876
On the suggestion of the Queen, Disraeli created the title of Empress of India. The British Indian Empire had been in existence since 1858 and the new title helped to strengthen links with India.

The Confederation of South Africa, 1877
The main influence on this policy was the Colonial Secretary, Lord Carnarvon. Carnarvon planned to **confederate** the three British colonies of Cape Colony, Natal and Griqualand West with the two Dutch Boer Republics of the Orange Free State and Transvaal. The intention was to

Confederate: To bring a number of states together in a political union.

strengthen Britain's hold on southern Africa. In 1877, Transvaal agreed to confederate with the British colonies, mainly because of fear of Zulu attacks on its eastern territory.

The Zulu War, 1878

After Carnarvon's departure from the Colonial Office in 1878, the new minister, Sir Michael Hicks-Beach, had no experience of colonial matters and left British policy in southern Africa in the hands of Sir Bartle Frere, the British High Commissioner. It was Frere who decided on a policy of confrontation with the Zulu kingdom, north of Natal. In 1878, this policy led to war, where the British suffered a humiliating defeat at Isandlwana before eventually defeating the Zulus at Ulundi. Disraeli was furious when war broke, but it was too late to prevent it.

The Afghan Wars of 1878 and 1879

Annex: To seize another country, usually by force, and take control of it.

British policy in India was in the hands of the India Secretary, Lord Cranbrook, and the Indian Viceroy, Lord Lytton. They believed the best way to preserve British control in the face of the Russian threat was to **annex** states on the north-west frontier of India. In 1876, Baluchistan was annexed, and in 1878 the decision was taken to install a pro-British ruler in Afghanistan. This led to a British invasion in November 1878. Following the murder of the British agent, Sir Louis Cavagnari, in September 1879, a further British military expedition was made. It was this policy that was criticised heavily by Gladstone in his Midlothian campaigns of 1879 and 1880.

However, as C.C. Eldridge noted, 'once again it had been his [Disraeli's] own weakness as Prime Minister and the blundering of his Secretary of State for India, Lord Cranbrook, that were responsible for the mess. Disraeli's contribution to these events was purely negative: a failure to oversee Cabinet ministers and to control the men on the spot.'

The Near Eastern Crisis, 1875–1878

Eastern Question: The international problem created by the belief that the Turkish (Ottoman) Empire was in a state of imminent collapse.

The crisis which developed in south-eastern Europe (the Balkans) in the mid-1870s was another episode in the **Eastern Question** and proved to be the most serious foreign policy problem faced by the Disraeli Government.

For the first two years, 1875–76, the crisis was limited to a clash between the Turkish Empire and the Christian peoples of the Balkans, most notably the Serbs, Croats and Bulgarians. During this period, the Great Powers attempted to localise the conflict and prevent it turning into a major European war. The Concert of Europe no longer acted as the main diplomatic force in European affairs. In its place was the *Dreikaiserbund* ('Three Emperors' League') of Germany, Russia and Austria-Hungary, established by Bismarck in 1873. From 1875 to 1877, the *Dreikaiserbund* attempted to find a diplomatic solution through discussion, suggestion and advice. It was not until 1877 that Russia decided upon direct action and declared war on Turkey.

The limitations of British policy

During the period 1875 to 1878, British policy towards the crisis was hampered by a number of factors.

● Firstly, there were major disagreements within the Cabinet between Disraeli, who wanted decisive action, and the Foreign Secretary, Lord Derby. Ever since Lord John Russell's humiliation over the Schleswig-Holstein crisis of 1863–64, Derby had been highly reluctant to take an active role in foreign affairs. As Foreign Secretary (then known as Lord Stanley) in the Conservative Government of 1866–68 he had refused to intervene in the Austro-Prussian War of 1866. Likewise, in the early years of the Near Eastern Crisis, Derby did not want to become involved.

- Secondly, Disraeli's main aim, in the early years of the crisis, was to disrupt the *Dreikaiserbund*. Ever since its creation, Disraeli had been suspicious that this league would work against British interests in Europe. Like his mid-century predecessor, Lord Palmerston, Disraeli believed Britain's interests were best served by the preservation of the Turkish Empire and the minimising of Russian influence in the Balkans. In particular, Disraeli followed a traditional policy of trying to prevent Russian warships entering the Mediterranean through the Straits.

- Finally, Disraeli's support for the Turkish government was compromised by the 'Bulgarian Horrors' of 1876, when Turkish troops massacred Bulgarian civilians. This resulted in the anti-Turkish Bulgarian Agitation of 1876, led by Gladstone. With an important section of British public opinion opposed to aiding the Turks, Disraeli's Government found it difficult to intervene on the Turkish side.

The development of British policy, 1875–1876

Following the outbreak of a revolt against Turkish rule in the provinces of Bosnia and Hercegovina, the first major diplomatic attempt to end the crisis came from the Austro-Hungarian Foreign Minister, Count Gyula Andrassy. In the so-called 'Andrassy Note' to the Turkish government, reforms in religion, taxation and landholding were proposed to end the revolt, with a mixed Muslim/Christian commission to supervise the changes.

Disraeli accepted the 'Note' mainly because the Turkish government, Italy and France had accepted it. But he did so with some reluctance. Disraeli believed that he could not let the *Dreikaiserbund* be seen to take the initiative in the crisis. As he stated: 'unless we go out of our way to act with the Northern Powers [*Dreikaiserbund*], they can act without us, which is not agreeable for a state like England'.

Unfortunately, by early 1876 it was clear that the Turks had no intention of implementing the terms of the Andrassy Note. So, on 13 May 1876, the *Dreikaiserbund* produced the Berlin Memorandum, which attempted to arrange a ceasefire in Bosnia and Hercegovina together with the reforms suggested in the Andrassy Note. Disraeli's Government rejected the memorandum, which had the effect of wrecking it. Disraeli made the rejection for several reasons. Firstly, the memorandum was submitted to Britain, for immediate approval, at a weekend. Disraeli believed Britain was being treated 'as if she were Montenegro or Bosnia'. Secondly, Derby was naturally reluctant to follow any fixed policy. However, most importantly, Disraeli wished to prevent the *Dreikaiserbund* from taking the diplomatic initiative. Instead, Britain took an independent line by sending the Royal Navy to Besika Bay. This move infuriated Bismarck and the *Dreikaiserbund* powers, and gave the Turks the hope that they could rely on British support. As a result, the Turkish government rejected the memorandum.

During the first two years of the crisis, Disraeli's attempt to prevent the *Dreikaiserbund* from taking the initiative had prevented a settlement. By the summer of 1876, the Bulgarian Horrors had taken place and the crisis had worsened with the intervention of Serbia and Montenegro on the side of the rebels. This led to a rise of **Panslav** feeling in Russia which the Tsar found it difficult to control. In July 1876, in the Reichstadt Agreement, Austria-Hungary and Russia agreed, in general terms, to divide the Balkans between them. In November, the Russians mobilised 160,000 troops along their Balkan frontier.

Panslav: Movement for the unity of all Slav peoples, under the guidance of Russia.

The Constantinople Conference, 1876–1877

At the end of 1876, Disraeli had become concerned about the deteriorating situation and took the initiative by proposing a conference of Great Powers at Constantinople, the capital of Turkey. Initially, the Conference was successful. All the Great Powers attended and the British representative, Lord Salisbury, worked closely with his Russian counterpart, Count Ignatiev. The Conference agreed on the union of Bosnia and Hercegovina under nominal Turkish rule, an increase in the size of Serbia and Montenegro at Turkey's expense, and self-government for Bulgaria, with the latter divided into two regions.

Unfortunately, the Conference ended prematurely on 20 January 1877 when the Turkish Sultan refused to accept its suggestions. This was due to the military success of Turkey in its war with Serbia and Montenegro. The Russian representative made a last-ditch diplomatic move with the London Protocol of 9 April. When this was rejected by the Sultan, the Russians declared war on Turkey on 24 April. Britain decided to stay neutral but warned the Russians, on 6 May, not to send warships through the Straits.

Using the information contained in the map, explain the differences between the changes made by the Treaty of San Stefano of March 1878 and the Treaty of Berlin, July 1878.

The Treaties of San Stefano and Berlin, 1878

In 1878, Britain came close to war with Russia. This was due mainly to the Russian military success in the war. Although delayed for several months in besieging Plevna, the Russian army reached Constantinople in January

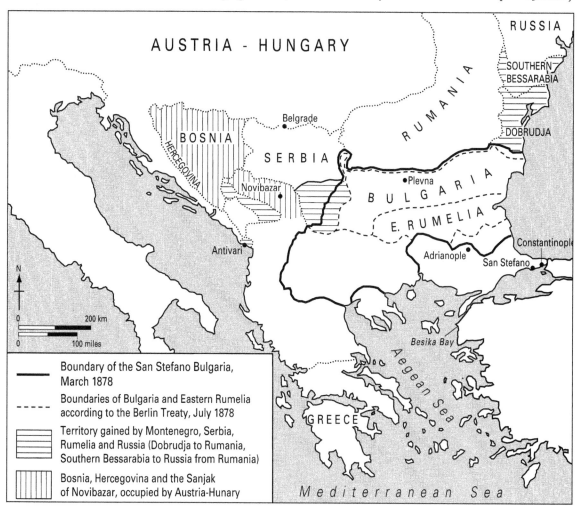

Boundary of the San Stefano Bulgaria, March 1878

Boundaries of Bulgaria and Eastern Rumelia according to the Berlin Treaty, July 1878

Territory gained by Montenegro, Serbia, Rumelia and Russia (Dobrudja to Rumania, Southern Bessarabia to Russia from Rumania)

Bosnia, Hercegovina and the Sanjak of Novibazar, occupied by Austria-Hunary

1878. The Royal Navy was sent to the Sea of Marmora on 23 January and Constantinople itself on 19 February, to prevent a possible Russian attack on the Turkish capital. This British action helped to produce a ceasefire in the war. However, the policy had its cost. Both Derby and Carnarvon resigned from the Cabinet.

The most serious threat of war with Russia came in March, following the publication of the Treaty of San Stefano (see map on previous page). This treaty was negotiated for Russia by Ignatiev. As soon as the terms were published, it stirred up opposition throughout Europe – even in Russia itself. Count Shuvalov, the Russian minister, described it as 'the greatest act of stupidity we could have committed'. Britain opposed it for three major reasons. It raised the possibility of allowing Russian warships into the Mediterranean, it disrupted the European balance of power, and it threatened the continued existence of the Turkish Empire.

No sooner had the treaty been published than the Russians, under German pressure, offered to renegotiate it at an international congress in Berlin. Before the congress met, Disraeli made secret agreements with Russia, Austria-Hungary and Turkey to protect British interests. On 30 May, the Russians agreed that the new Bulgarian state should be reduced in size. On 4 June, the Turks agreed to give Cyprus to Britain. In return, Britain offered to protect Turkish Armenia in Asia Minor. On 6 June, the Austro-Hungarians accepted a reduction in the size of Bulgaria in return for their occupation of Bosnia and Hercegovina.

Disraeli and Salisbury were able to achieve many of Britain's aims at the Congress of Berlin. The new state of Bulgaria was reduced in size and Turkey survived as a European power. However, British policy towards the Straits changed. Instead of insisting that they remain closed to warships, Britain accepted that they were an open waterway.

Summary of Disraeli's policy towards the Near Eastern Crisis

The case against
Disraeli's policy of disrupting the *Dreikaiserbund*, in 1875 and 1876, helped to prolong and deepen the crisis. It was also unpopular in Britain. Once the Russo–Turkish War began, public opinion changed. However, Disraeli's policy of threatening the Russians split the Cabinet and led to the resignation of two ministers. Disraeli brought Britain to the brink of war with Russia without the support of an ally with a large army, and with an obsolete Royal Navy. In the Treaty of Berlin, he had offered to protect Turkey's Asian frontier with Russia without having the military means to achieve it. This was criticised by Gladstone in his Midlothian campaigns.

The case for
Disraeli, at the Congress of Berlin, had re-established Britain's international reputation. His diplomacy had saved the Turkish Empire and preserved the European balance of power. He acquired Cyprus for the Empire. He had achieved these mainly through bluff and the threat of force.

1. Using the information contained in this section, write down those parts of Disraeli's foreign policy that you regard as a success. Then write down those parts of his policy you regard as unsuccessful.

2. On balance, do you regard Disraeli as successful? Give reasons to support your answer.

Source-based questions: The Near Eastern Crisis of 1876

SOURCE A

We are always treated as if we had some peculiar alliance with the Turkish Government, as if we were their peculiar friends. We are, it is true, the Allies of the Sultan of Turkey; so is Russia, so is Austria, so is France, and so are others.

What our duty is at this crucial moment is to maintain the Empire of England. Nor will we ever agree to any step, though it may obtain for a moment comparative quiet and a false prosperity, that hazards the existence of the Empire.

From a speech by Disraeli in the House of Commons, 11 August 1876.

SOURCE B

We wished to maintain Turkey as an independent political state. It is very easy to talk of the Ottoman power being at the point of extinction. But when you come practically to examine the question there is no living statesman who has ever offered any practical solution of the difficulties which would occur if the Ottoman Empire were to fall to pieces. One result would be a long and general war, and that alone, I think, is a sufficient reason for endeavouring to maintain the Ottoman Empire.

From a speech by the Earl of Beaconsfield (Disraeli) in the House of Lords, 16 May 1879.

SOURCE C

It can be said that Disraeli achieved all his major aims at Berlin. He had preserved some Balkan territory for Turkey, and so Turkey could be expected to act as a barrier to Russian expansion. Certainly Russia was kept out of Constantinople. He had also gained prestige for Britain (and for himself), together with a new possession, Cyprus, which was of strategic value in the eastern Mediterranean. He had avoided war, using only the threat of war to achieve his aims, and had thus forged a successful middle course between hawks and doves in the country.

From Britain and the European Powers 1865 to 1914 by Robert Pearce, published in 1996. A view on Disraeli's role at the Congress of Berlin, 1878.

SOURCE D

" HUMPTY-DUMPTY"!

" HUMPTY-DUMPTY SAT ON A WALL;
HUMPTY-DUMPTY HAD A GREAT FALL.
DIZZY, WITH CYPRUS, AND ALL THE QUEEN'S MEN,
HOPES TO SET HUMPTY-DUMPTY UP AGAIN."

Punch cartoon, 20 July 1878, entitled 'Humpty-Dumpty'. An accompanying verse reads: 'Humpty-Dumpty sat on a wall; Humpty-Dumpty had a great fall; Dizzy with Cyprus, and all the Queen's men, Hopes to set 'Humpty-Dumpty up again.'

1. Study Source A.

What, according to Disraeli, was the basis of British policy towards the Turkish Empire in 1876?

2. Study Sources B and C.

How far is the view of Disraeli in Source B supported by Robert Pearce's assessment in Source C?

3. Study Sources C and D.

Does this cartoon support or oppose the view of Disraeli's performance at the Congress of Berlin put forward in Source C?

4. Use all the sources and information contained in this chapter.

Do the sources printed above provide an adequate explanation of British policy towards Turkey in the years 1875 to 1878?

Give reasons to support your answer.

9.7 Why did Britain take part in the partition of Africa?
A CASE STUDY IN HISTORICAL INTERPRETATION

Even though Europeans had traded with Africa for centuries, it was not until 1880 that the rapid expansion of European control known as the 'Scramble for Africa' took place. There has been intense debate ever since on why this development took place.

This expansion, and similar colonial expansion in Asia and the Pacific, took Britain by surprise. Gladstone was extremely reluctant to take part. Lord Salisbury, who more than any other British statesman was responsible for colonial enlargement, stated in 1885, 'I do not know exactly the cause of this sudden revolution. But there it is.'

So why did Britain take part?

Investment overseas?

An early explanation came from the British liberal, Joshua Hobson, who produced a book in 1902 called *Imperialism: A Study*. Hobson believed Britain had acquired territory as a base for investment, due to the inequality of incomes between rich and poor in Britain. This created underconsumption of goods and surplus capital to invest and was seen as a malfunction of the capitalist economic system.

Hobson's views were taken a stage further by the founder of Russian communism, Vladimir Lenin, who in 1916 produced *Imperialism: The Highest Stage of Capitalism*. Lenin believed that it was inevitable for capitalist economies to acquire colonies as a guarantee of raw materials and markets for goods.

Neither Hobson nor Lenin, however, had attempted to provide an explanation for the whole partition of Africa. Hobson was trying to explain why Britain became involved in the Second Boer War, while Lenin was trying to explain why the First World War began.

Great Power rivalry

From 1920 to 1961, the main view put forward to explain the partition of Africa was rivalry between the Great Powers. Following the unification of Germany, European states had little opportunity to expand within Europe so they acquired colonies overseas. This was due to several reasons:

● The need to gain prestige was an important factor in French imperialism.

● The belief that Europeans were superior to other races and, therefore, had the right to acquire territory, was called **Social Darwinism**.

● Once the partition began, powers feared missing out on acquiring territory and, therefore, were forced to participate.

The official mind

Social Darwinism: The belief that human society is based on conflict between racial groups in which certain groups are believed to be superior to others. The superior races were seen to have the right to rule so-called 'inferior' races. Charles Darwin (1809–82) developed the theory of the origin of the human species.

In 1961, the most important book on the partition appeared. *Africa and the Victorians* by R. Robinson and J. Gallagher put forward the view that the partition was started by the British invasion of Egypt in 1882. This took place for strategic reasons, to protect the Suez Canal and with it the sea route to India. Robinson and Gallagher saw the protection of the sea routes to India, via the Suez Canal and the Cape of Good Hope, as the prime aim for Britain. They stated, 'without the occupation of Egypt there is no reason to suppose that any international scrambles for Africa either east or west would have begun when they did'.

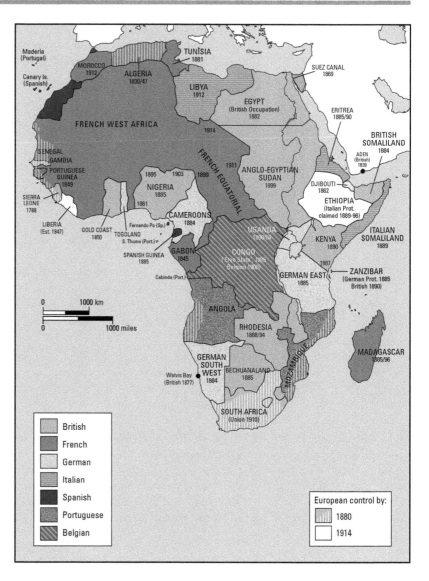

Study the map of the European partition of Africa.

Using information contained in the 'A Case Study in Historical Interpretation' section, give reasons why Britain acquired territory in Africa after 1880 (as marked on the map).

In 1962, Robinson and Gallagher took their theory a stage further in their contribution to Volume XI of the *New Cambridge Modern History* entitled 'The Partition of Africa'. They stated that Britain had been forced reluctantly to take over African territory because of African resistance to British trade and influence. Britain therefore annexed Egypt and the Sudan, territory in the Gold Coast and Nigeria in west Africa and territory in southern Africa.

The main criticism of Robinson and Gallagher's view was that it failed to take into consideration other reasons for British involvement, such as missionary work and, in particular, economic reasons.

Trade

Several historians of the partition of west Africa, such as John Hargreaves, Colin Newbury and D.K. Fieldhouse, have mentioned the importance of protecting trade as a motive for annexation. The Great Depression in the European economy after 1873 forced states to acquire colonies in order to guarantee raw materials and markets for their goods. Once this process began, other states had to take similar action. Britain had been the major

European trading nation in Africa in the 19th century. Faced with French and German colonial expansion, Britain was forced to turn its informal control of an area into a formal colony. Robinson and Gallagher had argued, as far back as 1953, that Britain preferred to have economic rather than political control of an area. This 'informal empire' existed before 1880. Therefore, Britain was forced reluctantly to take part in the partition. Even then, Britain tried to do so 'on the cheap' by declaring protectorates rather than full colonial control. This took place in Nigeria in the 1880s and in Bechuanaland in 1885.

Other theories

1. Using the information contained in this section and the map, which territories did Britain acquire in the years 1880 to 1895?

2. Using the information contained in this section and the map, which explanation for Britain's involvement in the partition of Africa do you find most convincing? Give reasons to support your answer.

Britain's involvement in the partition of East Africa and the occupation of Nyasaland had much to do with helping to abolish the slave trade and with missionary work by David Livingstone. The acquisition of Rhodesia (1886–89) had much to do with Cecil Rhodes' desire to create his own area of colonial control.

However, in *The Theory of Capitalist Imperialism* (1967), D.K. Fieldhouse puts forward the view that 'the historian should begin by studying as fully as possible the general forces operating within Europe and in other parts of the world, and then study each particular case of annexation as a special problem, and, finally, come to some conclusion about why colonisation took place in each case'.

Britain's involvement in the partition of north Africa, with the acquisition of Egypt and the Sudan, had different causes than Britain's involvement in the partition of east, west and southern Africa.

9.8 What were the foreign and imperial problems facing Gladstone's Second Ministry, 1880–1885?

Gladstone returned to power in 1880 to reverse what he saw as the aggressive and costly foreign and imperial policies of Disraeli. In the Midlothian campaigns of 1879–80, he virtually committed himself to restoring the independence of the Transvaal and withdrawing from Cyprus, Asia Minor and Afghanistan. Yet, during his ministry, Britain invaded and occupied Egypt and acquired extensive territories in west and southern Africa.

Also, during his Second Ministry, the Liberal Cabinet split on the issue of foreign and imperial policy. Broadly speaking, moderate Liberals stood for the consolidation of Empire. The Whigs, on the other hand, desired expansion. Issues such as the Transvaal and Egypt saw radicals and moderates opposing Whigs. However, over southern Africa, the Whigs received support from two Radicals, Joseph Chamberlain and Sir Charles Dilke, who had heavily criticised the Whigs over Ireland and domestic issues.

The Transvaal and the First Boer War

On achieving office, Gladstone decided to keep Sir Bartle Frere as High Commissioner in South Africa and to continue British rule of the Transvaal because he wished to pursue Carnarvon's policy of confederation. In December 1880, however, the Transvaalers rose in armed revolt and a general Boer rebellion across southern Africa seemed likely. The issue split the Cabinet between Whig and Radical. In February 1881, at Majuba Hill in Natal, the Boers defeated British forces under the Governor of Natal, Sir George Colley.

At the Convention of Pretoria in August 1881, Transvaal was granted internal self-government but Britain retained control over Transvaal foreign policy, known as 'suzerainty'. This meant that Britain had no direct control of the Transvaal but was still responsible for it. In 1884, in the Treaty of London, Anglo-Transvaal relations were placed on a formal footing. However, suzerainty was not mentioned. After 1884 Britain still believed it controlled Transvaal foreign policy while the Transvaal believed it was completely independent. This confusion helped create the conflict which led to the Second Boer War in 1899.

Afghanistan

In 1880, Gladstone intended withdrawing from Afghanistan. However, the new Indian Viceroy, Lord Ripon, believed withdrawal could lead to a breakdown in law and order, and possible Russian intervention. A compromise was reached whereby Britain accepted responsibility for Afghanistan's defence: another example of responsibility without control.

In 1884, the Russians annexed Merv in northern Afghanistan. In March 1885, Russian and Afghan troops clashed at Pendjeh and the Gladstone Government was called upon to meet its guarantee of Afghan independence. Gladstone diffused the situation by submitting the matter to international arbitration.

The Turkish Empire

Gladstone succeeded in dropping the Conservative plan of defending Turkey's Asian border with Russia. British 'military' consuls were withdrawn to be replaced by civilian ones.

After a brief demonstration of force by the Royal Navy off the eastern Balkans, a conference of ambassadors met in London in 1880, which persuaded Turkey to hand over the province of Thessaly to Greece. This was the only example of Gladstone's use of the Concert of Europe during his ministry.

Egypt, 1882–1885

Britain had vital interests in Egypt, both in investments and in the Suez Canal. In 1876, the Khedive of Egypt was declared bankrupt and a Public Debt Commission was created to look after the interests of foreign investors. However, when this arrangement failed, in 1878, two ministers – one British and one French – were appointed to run the financial side of the Egyptian government.

Under the Law of Liquidation of July 1880, the six major European powers were given 66% of Egypt's revenue to pay off its foreign debt. This, not surprisingly, sparked off a nationalist reaction which led to a revolt led by an army officer, Arabi Pasha, at the end of 1881.

Gladstone had hoped for joint action by Britain and France to suppress the revolt, but the plans failed for a number of reasons. The French government went through a period of instability in 1881 and 1882. At first, Prime Minister Léon Gambetta wanted joint action with Britain, but he fell from power on 27 January 1882. In May 1882, a joint naval demonstration at Alexandria was planned, but the French failure to involve Turkey meant that it was ineffective and only sparked off anti-western riots in the city on 11 and 12 June. On 11 July, Admiral Seymour, in charge of the British naval force, misinterpreted his instructions and bombarded Alexandria.

The British now faced a complete breakdown of law and order in Egypt, so on 20 July Gladstone reluctantly agreed to send a military expedition to restore order, thereby protecting British investments and the Suez Canal.

Gladstone had hoped for a 'rescue and retire' expedition. However, once the British had entered Egypt they found it almost impossible to leave without sparking off another breakdown in law and order.

Under Lord Dufferin, the British decided to put Egypt on a sound financial footing. In December 1884, Britain attempted to negotiate an international loan. However, at the London Conference of March 1885, the European powers failed to agree and Britain was forced to remain in control of Egypt – a situation which lasted until 1922.

The Sudan, 1883–1885

The Sudan was a possession of Egypt. In 1881, Mohammed Ahmad (the Mahdi) started a fundamentalist Muslim *jihad* ('holy war') against the Egyptians and westerners. In November 1883, he destroyed an Anglo-Egyptian army and threatened the Egyptian presence in the Sudan. Instead of withdrawing, the Cabinet sent General Gordon to the Sudanese capital, Khartoum.

This proved to be a disastrous choice. Gordon was unwilling to withdraw, yet the Liberal Government was unwilling to send him military aid. Finally, at the end of December 1884, the Government sent a relief force which arrived at Khartoum on 23 February 1885, two days after Gordon had been killed by Mahdist troops who had taken the city. Gordon's death caused uproar in Britain and the episode proved an electoral liability in the June 1885 general election.

The Berlin West Africa Conference and the Scramble for Africa, 1884–1885

For most of the century, Britain had informal control over much of west Africa. In the 1880s, however, France and then Germany began to take formal control of west African territory. In 1884, representatives of 15 nations gathered in Berlin at Bismarck's invitation to decide on who should control west Africa. Gladstone was forced to abandon British informal control in areas such as Cameroon, Togoland and the Congo basin in favour of Germany, France and King Leopold II of Belgium.

Elsewhere in Africa, Britain was on the defensive. In 1884, the Germans claimed control over south-west Africa and the east coast of Africa near Zanzibar. In 1885, the Government took control of the Bechuanaland Protectorate in order to prevent a common border between the Transvaal and German-controlled south-west Africa.

India

On his return to office, Gladstone replaced Lord Lytton with Lord Ripon as Viceroy of India. Instead of trying to protect British rule in India through acquiring territory on the north-west frontier, Ripon attempted to win support from the western-educated Indian élite. In 1883, he put forward the Ilbert Bill which planned to allow Indian magistrates the right to sit in judgement on whites. This sparked off widespread white opposition and resulted in the Bill being withdrawn. The result was that Ripon upset both whites and educated Indians. One consequence was the creation of the Indian National Congress in 1885 by educated Indians to fight for Indian rights.

An assessment of Gladstone's foreign and imperial policy

In 1880, Gladstone hoped to use the Concert of Europe and friendship with France to ensure European peace and to further British interests. Unfortunately, he completely underestimated the impact of Bismarck's

1. Using the information contained within this section, write down those aspects of Gladstone's foreign and imperial policy you regard as successful. Then write down those aspects of his policy that you regard as a failure.

2. On balance, was Gladstone successful in foreign and imperial affairs during his Second Administration? Give reasons to support your answer.

3. During his Second Ministry Gladstone has been described as a 'reluctant imperialist'.

Using the information contained above, how far do you agree with this view?

diplomatic revolution. The Dual Alliance with Austria-Hungary (1879), the renewal of the *Dreikaiserbund* (1881) and the Triple Alliance (1882) had led to the isolation of France and the end of the Concert of Europe.

The invasion of Egypt in 1882 soured Anglo–French relations for a generation and upset Turkey and Italy. Gladstone's commitment to Afghanistan led to direct confrontation with Russia in 1885. In Africa, Gladstone proved to be a reluctant imperialist, reacting to events rather than controlling them.

Gladstone was ill-served by his Foreign Secretary, Lord Granville, whose illness and financial problems affected his performance. Foreign and imperial affairs also helped widen the gap between Whig and Radical within the Liberal Party.

9.9 To what extent was Britain in a state of 'splendid isolation' between 1885 and 1895?

On 26 February 1896, the First Lord of the Admiralty, George Goschen, stated: 'Our isolation, if isolation it be, was self-imposed. It arose out of our unwillingness to take part in Bismarck's system. Why are we isolated? We are isolated because we will not promise things which possibly we might be unwilling to perform.'

Ever since that time, politicians and historians have referred to Britain's international position in the late 19th century as one of 'splendid isolation'. How far is this description accurate? Isolation in the context mentioned by Goschen refers to Britain's decision not to be involved in the European alliance system of the late 19th century. In 1879, Germany signed a formal defensive alliance with Austria-Hungary (the Dual Alliance). This was expanded to include Italy in 1882 (the Triple Alliance, or Triplice). Between 1892 and 1894, France and Russia signed a formal defensive alliance (the Franco-Russian Alliance). By 1895, therefore, Britain was the only European Great Power not involved in a formal alliance.

However, in the 1880s, Britain's fear of Russian naval ambitions towards the Mediterranean had led to the signing of the Mediterranean agreements of May and December 1887 with Austria-Hungary and Italy. Although negotiated by Lord Salisbury, they were not followed by Gladstone (Prime Minister 1892–94) or Lord Rosebery (Prime Minister 1894–95). When Salisbury returned to office in 1895, he did not revive the agreements. In 1889, Bismarck tried to persuade Salisbury to make Britain an associate member of the Triple Alliance, but Salisbury refused.

Of the two alliance systems in existence by 1895, the one that seemed to be the greater threat to Britain was the Franco–Russian Alliance. Diplomatic relations between Britain and France had been strained since Britain's invasion of Egypt in 1882. These relations were made worse by Anglo–French colonial rivalry in west Africa. Russia was also seen as a threat to Britain's international position. This threat was seen at the Straits, in Central Asia, in Afghanistan and, by 1895, in the Far East and in

Naval Defence Act, 1889: This Act set the limit on the size of the Royal Navy. From 1889, the Navy was to be at least as large as the next two largest navies in the world combined.

northern China. When Britain passed the **Naval Defence Act** in 1889, the Government had France and Russia in mind.

Several contemporaries were pleased Britain had not become involved in formal defensive alliances in Europe. They regarded Britain's isolation as 'splendid' because they felt Britain was above involvement in European politics. It was also based on the belief that Britain was sufficiently powerful not to require permanent allies. Perhaps the main reason was the fact that Britain's foreign policy interests were outside Europe. Therefore, on occasion, Britain did sign treaties with European states to protect the British Empire. In 1885, the Gladstone Government signed the West Africa Act, in Berlin, with France, Germany and other European powers over colonial boundaries in west Africa. In 1890, in the Heligoland–Zanzibar Agreement, Britain settled colonial claims with Germany over east Africa.

Conclusion

1. What does the historical term 'splendid isolation' mean when applied to Britain?

2. Explain why Britain was described as being in a state of 'splendid isolation' in foreign affairs.

During the period 1868–95, Britain's international position came under increasing threat. In India, Britain was threatened by the expansion of Russia into Central Asia. In Africa, Britain's informal empire was threatened by the colonial claims of countries such as France and Germany. This development helped to provoke the European Partition of Africa. By 1895, however, Britain still possessed the largest colonial empire in the world while the Royal Navy was still seen as 'ruling the waves'. Although a major European war almost took place over the Eastern Question, in 1878, the period was generally one of stability. This was due in large measure to Bismarck's skilful diplomacy.

Further Reading

Articles

A particularly good article in *New Perspectives*:
'The Eastern Question' by A.L. Macfie (September 1996)
In *Modern History Review*:
'Pax Britannica' by Muriel Chamberlain (September 1996)
'European Imperialism in the late 19th Century' by Andrew Porter (Vol. 2 No. 4)
'Conflict in the Balkans 1876–1878' by John Morison (Vol. 3 No. 1)
'British Idea of Empire' by Kathryn Tidrick (Vol. 4 No. 1)

Texts designed for AS and A2 level students

Foreign Affairs by D.R. Ward (Collins, 1982)
The British Empire 1815 to 1914 by F. McDonough (Hodder & Stoughton, Access to History series, 1994)
Britain and the European Power 1865 to 1914 by Robert Pearce (Hodder & Stoughton, Access to History series, 1996)
The Scramble for Africa by Muriel Chamberlain (Longman, Seminar Studies series, 1974)
The Eastern Question, 1774–1923 by A.L. Macfie (Longman, Seminar Studies series, 1989)
The Partition of Africa by J. MacKenzie (Routledge, Lancaster Pamphlets 1983)
Disraeli by J. Walton (Routledge, Lancaster Pamphlets, 1990)

Advanced reading

Palmerston by J. Ridley (Constable, 1970)

Palmerston by Muriel Chamberlain (GBC Books, 1987)

The Foreign Policy of Victorian England by K. Bourne (Longman, 1970)

Britain and the Eastern Question by G. Clayton (University of London Press, 1971)

'Pax Britannica'?: British Foreign Policy 1789–1914 by Muriel Chamberlain (Longman, 1988)

Victorian Imperialism by C.C. Eldridge (Hodder & Stoughton, 1978)

Democracy and Empire by E.J. Feuchtwanger (Arnold, 1985)

Crisis of Imperialism by R. Shannon (Paladin, 1976)

10 Ireland, 1798 to 1922

The 'Irish Question'

THE 'Irish Question' is the name given to the set of issues which affected British–Irish relations. It involved political, economic, religious and strategic issues.

Irish issues caused the resignation of British Prime Ministers on several occasions. In 1801, William Pitt the Younger resigned because of King George III's opposition to Catholic emancipation. Robert Peel fell from power, in 1846, over the repeal of the Corn Laws. William Gladstone split the Liberal Party, in 1886, with his conversion to Irish Home Rule. The Liberal Government from 1912 to 1914 faced a serious crisis over Ulster, which was brought to a temporary conclusion by the outbreak of the First World War. Finally, David Lloyd George's fall from office, in 1922, was due in part to his handling of the Irish Question in 1921.

Therefore, as a theme, the 'Irish Question' must be regarded as an important – if not the most important – aspect of British domestic history.

1. Which of the points in the mind map best explains the reason why Ireland was an important issue in British politics from 1798 to 1922? Explain your answer.

2. Which of the points were general reasons for causing problems between Britain and Ireland and which were specific developments in British–Irish relations?

3. What do you regard as the most important factor in British–Irish relations between 1798 and 1922? Give reasons for your choice.

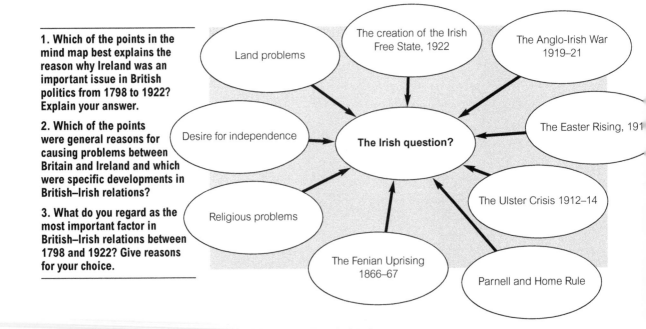

10.1 Theme 1: Who opposed the Union?

Key Issues

■ Why did opposition to the Union develop in the 19th century?

■ What form did opposition to the Union take?

■ What were the reasons for the initial failure, and final success, of the Irish nationalists?

10.1.1 What was the situation in Ireland in 1798?

10.1.2 Why was the Act of Union passed in 1800? Why did opposition to the Union start almost immediately?

10.1.3 What were the next stages of opposition to the Union?

10.1.4 Why did opposition to Union grow after 1900 and culminate in war and final independence?

Framework of Events

1798	Wolfe Tone or United Irish Rebellion
1800	Act of Union
1824	Formation of Catholic Association
1828	County Clare Election
1845–49	Great Famine
1848	Young Ireland Rising
1858	Irish Republican Brotherhood (Fenians) founded in USA
1866–67	Fenian outrages in Britain, Ireland and Canada
1870	Butt forms Irish Home Government Association
1871	Obstruction process starts in House of Commons
1879	Formation of Irish Land League
1880	Parnell leads Irish Nationalist Party
1882	The Phoenix Park Murders
1885	Irish Home Rule Party hold balance of power in Commons following June 1885 general elections
1886	Gladstone converts to Irish Home Rule
1888	Parnell falsely accused of involvement with Phoenix Park Murders of 1882
1890	Parnell falls from leadership of Irish Home Rule Party; Party splits into pro- and anti-Parnell factions
1891	Parnell dies
1900	Irish Home Rule Party re-united under John Redmond
1905	Creation of United Ulster Unionist Council
1912	Passage of Third Home Rule Bill starts Ulster Crisis. Creation of Ulster Volunteer Force
1913	Irish Volunteers is formed
1916	The Easter Rising
1917	de Valera is elected leader of Sinn Fein
1917–18	Meeting of Irish Convention
1918	Sinn Fein wins majority of Irish seats in UK general election
1919–21	The Anglo-Irish War
1920	Government of Ireland Act gives Home Rule to Northern Ireland; rejected in southern Ireland
1920	Bloody Sunday in Dublin
1921	Anglo-Irish Treaty creates Irish Free State with dominion status within British Empire Anglo-Irish Treaty accepted by Dail.
1922	Civil war in Irish Free State over the Treaty.

10.1.1 What was the situation in Ireland in 1798?

The majority of the Irish population viewed the English as alien colonisers there to exploit them. There were profound differences between the mass of the population and the ruling minority. The mass (about 6 million) tended to be Roman Catholic, illiterate, landless and usually extremely poor. The ruling minority was Protestant, wealthy and landed. They controlled the political system and owned more than 95% of the land and much of the limited industrial wealth.

The history of Ireland in the 18th century is marked by:

● poor social conditions

● frequent food shortages

● a rising population

● very limited economic progress

● a growing sense of anger against trade restrictions, which seemed to benefit English manufacturers.

Tithes: A tax payable to the Church based on one-tenth of your property; usually paid in kind with animals from the land. This was a very unpopular system.

The official 'State' religion was the Protestant Church of Ireland, yet the vast majority of the population was Roman Catholic. They were forced to pay **tithes** to support a Protestant church they hated. Roman Catholics were discriminated against by law, and not allowed to hold official positions, or to become Members of Parliament. However, the Roman Catholic religion was officially tolerated and was growing in influence over the majority of the population. Protestant nonconformists, who were not members of the Church of Ireland, were another important religious minority. These included Quakers and Presbyterians. Most lived in north-east Ireland.

Agrarian violence: Trouble in rural areas, usually caused by problems relating to agriculture.

Agrarian violence was a regular feature of Irish history in the 18th century, particularly between 1760 and 1780. A group known as the Whiteboys made some particularly savage attacks against landlords. The Government in London reacted with a series of Acts of Parliament, which ordered the death penalty for most forms of protest.

However, the British Government – perhaps frightened that their Irish colony might go the same way as the American colonies, towards independence – began to relax some of the stronger restrictions. Some Roman Catholics were allowed to vote, for example, and it became easier for Roman Catholics to purchase land by the end of the 18th century. It is worth remembering that the bulk of the population were Roman Catholic and that they might feel resentful of being 'allowed' by the English to vote and purchase land in Ireland – their own land.

Why did a serious rebellion break out in 1798?

The concessions made by London over voting and land purchase were inadequate for many Irishmen. The French Revolution, which had broken out in 1789, inspired many Irish to seek their freedom. The ideals of the French Revolution – liberty and equality – inspired many Irishmen. Hatred of rule by aliens, with a strong flavour of Roman Catholic versus Protestant and the poor Irish against the rich English, led to open rebellion in 1798. The leader of the revolt was Wolfe Tone (1763–98), a Protestant Irish lawyer inspired by the examples of both the American and the French Revolution. He took advantage of the simmering hatred between many Irish people and their English rulers to try to get the French to invade Ireland as part of their war against England.

The French fleet failed to land troops and weapons, mainly due to bad weather and poor seamanship, and the armed rising largely died out, after a brief skirmish in 1798 known as the 'battle' of Vinegar Hill. The British Government passed laws that allowed imprisonment without trial. Tone was captured, but he committed suicide before he could be executed. Many English people felt that the Irish had behaved treasonably in helping the French. They failed to realise that they, the English, were seen as an 'enemy' by the Irish people – in the same way that the English viewed the French as an enemy. In fact, many Irishmen saw the French as potential liberators, just as the Germans were to be seen in 1916.

10.1.2 Why was the Act of Union passed in 1800? Why did opposition to the Union start almost immediately?

One reaction by the British Government in London to the revolt of 1798 was strong coercive (repressive) measures. Although these were measures designed to punish and deter, it was not the only reaction. The Prime Minister, William Pitt the Younger, adopted a more positive and proactive role. His suggestion, backed by Lord Castlereagh, the Minister responsible for Ireland, was the Act of Union.

This Act would end the Parliament in Dublin (Protestant dominated and with limited powers), and replace it with a system whereby MPs and peers were elected or chosen in Ireland and then represented Ireland in the UK Parliament in London. These MPs would have the same power and status as 'normal' UK MPs. A number of Irish peers were allowed to sit in the House of Lords. Other Irish peers had to seek election to the House of Commons. Lord Palmerston was an example.

This was designed to end all Irish problems, as the Irish would have the same rights as any other UK citizen. Pitt and Castlereagh felt that this would end opposition to English rule. They hoped it would make the Irish feel and react in the same way as any other UK citizen. Union would lead to peace and integration.

Castlereagh, sometimes using corrupt methods, persuaded the Irish Parliament to vote itself out of existence. The Act of Union was passed in 1800. The first Irish MPs and peers arrived in the UK Parliament in London in that year.

However, there were major flaws in the Act of Union. The first was that Pitt and Castlereagh indicated that Catholic emancipation would follow the Act of Union, and implied it in the negotiations. It did not follow. Some historians argue that this was because the King, George III, refused to sign the Bill as it might break his coronation oath. Others suggest that Pitt and Castlereagh never intended it to happen. It was unlikely that the House of Lords in London would ever pass an Act giving Roman Catholics a seat in Parliament.

The Union of Britain and Ireland therefore got off to a bad start. Many Catholics felt betrayed and conned into a deal. Only 20% of all the MPs in London were Irish, and anger was felt at Irish problems now being looked at from a 'London' perspective. In addition, Roman Catholics were now a minority in the whole of the UK.

However, Ireland remained reasonably quiet and loyal for the rest of the Napoleonic Wars, so England benefited from not having to worry about potential treason coming from the West.

The end of the Napoleonic Wars, in 1815, brought major economic problems to the whole of the UK, but they were felt particularly keenly in Ireland. There was no welfare system at all in Ireland, so poverty was more extreme. Roman Catholics still had to pay the hated tithe to support what they felt was an alien religion based in London. Irish local government was dominated by Protestant (and frequently absent) British landlords and was corrupt and inefficient. It was still felt that 'London' deprived Ireland of its fair share of wealth and trade.

The overwhelming feeling in Ireland, by 1820, was that the Union had been an elaborate trick to keep Ireland quiet. It was solely to benefit the United Kingdom.

How was emancipation for Roman Catholics gained?

The first signs of protest against London's 'rule', and its methods, started in 1804 with the formation of the Catholic Committee. This was designed to protect and advance Irish interests in general, and to gain full citizenship rights for Catholics in particular. The Government repressed this in 1811, but the idea of united action by both Catholic and Protestant Irishmen against 'British' rule was born again.

In 1823, a more powerful pressure group was created. This was the Catholic Association. Its objective was to end all discrimination against Roman Catholics. Its leader was Daniel O'Connell. He was one of the first Roman Catholics to be allowed to practise law in Ireland, after the Catholic Relief Acts of the 1790s. What was different about the Catholic Association was that not only did it have O'Connell's charismatic leadership, but also the Roman Catholic Church enthusiastically supported it. In addition, its membership was not just middle-class merchants and lawyers, but by being cheap to join it attracted a mass membership among the working class. The Catholic Association became remarkable in that it was probably the first truly national mass-membership pressure group in modern British history. It was also successful. Although the British Government tried to suppress it in 1825, it re-formed and still attained its objective. Emancipation cleared the House of Commons in 1825, but failed in a House of Lords dominated by Tories and members of the Church of England.

In a by-election in 1828, Daniel O'Connell stood as a candidate for Parliament. Technically speaking, this was impossible, as he was a Roman Catholic. He was duly elected, but was unable to take his seat, until Peel and Wellington (the Tory leaders in London), frightened of a possible uprising in Ireland, passed Roman Catholic emancipation. This allowed Roman Catholics to become MPs in the House of Commons.

What was the impact of emancipation and the Catholic Association?

Emancipation made O'Connell into a national hero in Ireland. It also gave Ireland a leader, which it had not really possessed before. This enabled O'Connell to get the London Government to focus on further reforms, such as reforming Irish local government and ending the tithes paid to the Church of Ireland. O'Connell was also anxious to increase the number of those entitled to vote. He raised the political consciousness of Catholics and Irishman, particularly among the poorer sections of society. Pressure politics had clearly worked, mass protest had attained difficult objectives, and that lesson was not forgotten. O'Connell fanned Irish nationalism and set the issue of an independent Ireland very much on the agenda of Ireland, if not England. He wanted a separate Irish parliament to deal with Irish issues. Another product of his success was that he raised huge fears among the Protestant population of the North of Ireland, and they started to organise to defend their ideas and values.

Daniel O'Connell (1775–1847)
O'Connell was a Catholic lawyer and landowner. He led the campaign for Catholic emancipation in the 1820s and was elected MP for County Clare in 1828. O'Connell established the Irish Party at Westminster, which successfully campaigned for tariff reform and brought down Peel's Government in 1835 after the Lichfield House Compact. He was extremely important in maintaining the Whigs in power after 1835. O'Connell also led the campaign for the Repeal of the Act of Union in the 1840s. This resulted in his arrest in 1844, which was quashed on appeal to the House of Lords.

10.1.3 What were the next stages of opposition to the Union?

By 1840, O'Connell had founded the Repeal Association. This was openly committed to ending the Act of Union and setting up a separate Irish parliament. He organised huge mass meetings, some with over 100,000 present. With the Roman Catholic Church supportive of his movement, O'Connell looked like making as much progress towards independence as he had towards Catholic emancipation. However, Sir Robert Peel (Prime Minister 1841–46) refused to consider such a proposal. The attitude of both the Conservative Government and the Liberal Opposition was that much had been done for Ireland in recent decades, and that the Act of Union was of considerable benefit to Ireland. This huge misunderstanding, that Union had in some ways been a favour to Ireland, was to be a key reason for the growth of an Irish 'problem' in the coming decades.

Peel's reaction to the agitation of O'Connell was twofold. O'Connell was imprisoned in 1844. On the other hand, Peel put forward reforms in an attempt to pacify the growing Irish Catholic middle class. These reforms were in areas such as landlord–tenant relations, Catholic education and the education of Roman Catholic priests. Peel was not totally successful, as the Young Ireland movement was to demonstrate.

Young Ireland was a radical group of nationalists, founded in 1842. They were less inclined to accept the moderate separation looked for by O'Connell. They founded a paper called the *Nation*. They achieved little as the movement was split between those who wished to work with O'Connell and those who did not, and those who were prepared to use violence to attain separation and those who were not. An armed rebellion failed in 1848, when the famine and strong coercion brought to an end most protest. Internal division was often a reason why Irish opposition to 'English' rule could be unsuccessful.

What was the impact of famine on the opposition to the Union?

In many ways the Great Famine of 1845–49 was a turning point in the history of opposition to the Union. It accelerated the move towards Home Rule for an independent Ireland. O'Connell had helped to create modern

O'Connell addressing a Repeal meeting in September 1843

Irish politics, a political machine capable of taking the issue forwards, with a strong sense of a national identity.

The Great Famine created a sense of anger and injustice. It also raised social tensions to a much higher level. Many died and more emigrated. It was easy to blame the richest country in the world, with its huge resources, for the human, social and economic devastation of Ireland in the late 1840s.

Most Irish people felt bitterly they had been betrayed and abandoned by the English. There was huge anger at the perceived treatment of the Irish masses by an incompetent and uncaring 'English' Government.

The general election of 1852 led to at least 40 of the Irish MPs backing major social and economic change. This group formed the Independent Irish Party, from 1850 to 1859. As often happened with such Irish MPs, they were divided between those who were prepared to work under British rule to improve things and those who were not. This became apparent with two Irish MPs, Keogh and Sadlier, who joined the Whig–Peelite Coalition of 1852–55 as junior ministers. However, unity among opponents grew when the Irish Tenant League, founded by Charles Gavan Duffy in 1850, determined to gain for Irish tenants in the (Catholic) South the same sort of tenure rights that England and the North (Protestant) of Ireland got. The Catholic Defence Association, founded in 1851, allied with it to form another powerful anti-Union pressure group. It was this linking of different pressure groups that gave anti-Union sentiment such force.

With Ireland devastated by famine, and politically divided, opposition could attain little in the 1850s. It was clear that the peaceful methods inherited from O'Connell had failed, and Young Ireland had been too badly organised to succeed.

In 1858, a more radical group – the Irish Republican Brotherhood (IRB), nicknamed the 'Fenians' – was formed in the USA. Many of the key figures in the IRB had been involved in the Young Ireland Rising of 1848. The key figure was James Stephens (1824–1901), and it aimed to overthrow English rule, by violence if necessary. It had no social or economic programme, its members just wished to create an Irish Republic free from English rule.

The IRB embarked on a programme of violence, in Ireland, Britain and Canada. This led to persecution and executions of Fenian leaders. The movement began to decline by 1867. Many opponents of the Union were bitterly divided over both the objectives and the methods of attaining them.

Why did opposition to the Union grow in intensity after 1870?

Several factors combined to start a process, which led finally to Home Rule. Economic conditions in the South of Ireland grew particularly bad after 1870. This led to social distress. This naturally encouraged support for a break from England, which was seen as the cause of their economic distress. There was growing hatred of the system of land tenure in the South of Ireland, which gave the landlords (frequently Protestant, English and absent) much greater control of their tenants than was the case elsewhere.

Again a powerful social and economic pressure group, the Land League, fanned by hunger and poverty, joined forces with another pressure group, the Home Rulers, who were led by a highly charismatic and able leader, Charles Parnell.

Although Gladstone's legislation had removed some of the worst grievances of the Irish between 1868 and 1874, the feeling in Ireland was that this was totally insufficient. While official opinion in England felt that by

Charles Stewart Parnell (1846–1891)
Parnell was elected MP for Meath in 1875. He supported a policy of obstruction and violence in order to attain Home Rule for Ireland. Became President of Nationalist Party in 1877. In 1879, he approved the Land League, and his involvement led to imprisonment in 1881. Parnell welcomed Gladstone's Home Rule Bill, and continued his agitation after its defeat in 1886. A year later, however, his reputation suffered from an unfounded accusation in *The Times* of involvement in the murder of Lord Frederick Cavendish, Chief Secretary to the Lord Lieutenant of Ireland. Parnell's career was ruined when he was cited as co-respondent in a divorce case in 1890. For fear of losing Gladstone's support, Parnell's party deposed him. He died of rheumatic fever at the age of 45.

1874 Ireland had been 'sorted', opinion in much of Ireland was that the Union had failed and that Home Rule, in some form, was the only way forward for Ireland.

The Act that was perhaps to have most effect on Irish opposition to Union was the 1872 Ballot Act. This enabled Irish voters to vote freely for nationalist MPs without fear of eviction by their pro-Union landlords. The result was that, in 1874, a large group of MPs from Ireland committed to Home Rule was elected. The Home Rule Party grew, initially under the leadership of Isaac Butt, who favoured a federal solution to the Irish problem, with substantial devolved power to a Parliament in Dublin. A more dynamic and charismatic leader, Charles Parnell, replaced him by 1880. William Shaw was the leader between Butt and Parnell.

Parnell gave a huge boost to the movement to end British rule over Ireland. Using obstructionist tactics to force the Irish issue to the attention of the House of Commons, he worked closely with the leaders of the Land League to ensure that every method was used, from peaceful protest, through '**boycotting**' landlords, to violence to ensure that land reform was successful. Gladstone put through a major land reform act, in 1881, where most of the objectives were attained. Again, strong pressure had attained the needed objectives. The Roman Catholic Church backed Parnell fully.

After the June 1885 general election, Parnell was in a position where he held the balance of power in British politics and a committed Nationalist held nearly every Irish seat in the House of Commons.

Gladstone produced his first Home Rule Bill for Ireland, in 1886. This was partly in response to the powerful and growing pressure in Ireland. Some historians, such as J. L. Hammond and G. Steele, believe that Gladstone had come to the view that this was the only solution to the Irish problem. Other historians have a more cynical view of Gladstone's motives. A. Cooke and John Vincent, in *The Governing Passion*, and D.A. Hamer, in *Liberal Politics in the Age of Gladstone and Rosebery*, believe Gladstone converted to Home Rule to re-assert his control over a divided Liberal Party. As a result of the introduction of the Home Rule Bill in 1886, Gladstone split the Liberal Party. The action did re-assert Gladstone's leadership over the larger part of the Liberal Party. It also forced Liberal

Boycotting: A term now used to describe people who are shunning, or organisations that are ignoring. Its origins lie in the nationalist agitation in Ireland in the late 1870s and early 1880s led by Parnell. Tenants were frequently evicted during the Great Famine of the late 1870s and their land taken over by others. Those who took over the land from evicted tenants were often treated with extreme hostility and given no help to farm their land. This fate befell Captain Charles Boycott (1832–97), in County Mayo. The Government had to come to his aid, spending far more on protecting him and getting his crops harvested than the crops were worth.

How useful is this photograph as evidence of poverty in Ireland in the 1890s?

A one-roomed peasant's cabin in Donegal, in the 1890s. The large basket is a creel for carrying turf.

Unionists, led by Joseph Chamberlain and Lord Hartington, to support the Conservatives.

Opposition in Ireland suffered a further blow when Parnell became implicated in a divorce case, in 1890. The case alienated the Roman Catholic Church and weakened its support for Home Rule. Gladstone's refusal to work with the Home Rule Party as long as Parnell remained leader, split the Home Rule party in two in 1890. For the whole of the 1890s, the Home Rule party remained divided into pro- and anti-Parnell factions.

Opposition to Home Rule was further weakened in the late 1890s by a series of Conservative reforms, nicknamed 'killing Home Rule by kindness'. Inefficient and corrupt local government was reformed, giving cheaper and better local services. Arthur Balfour, the Irish Secretary, pushed through a decent poor relief system. There was agrarian reform as well. Balfour's nickname was 'Bloody Balfour' on account of his willingness to use **coercion** to deal with any opposition in Ireland. Huge numbers of Irish emigrated to the USA. Taxpayers' money was pumped into education and railways – the former providing opportunity and the latter employment. In Wyndham's Land Act of 1903, the UK Government pumped in over £86 million to help farmers and, indirectly, their labourers. **Cottage industries** were subsidised by the State, and public money was spent on roads and bridges, generating more wealth and employment. The mix of coercion and reform eased opposition to the idea of Union.

The supporters of Home Rule were divided in the late 1890s, and with the Liberals uninterested and the Conservatives following a policy of generosity, backed by ruthless firmness to any disorder, opposition to Union lost steam.

Coercion: Term given to government policy usually involving the removal of civil rights and can include imprisonment without trial.

Cottage industries: Small manufacturing enterprises carried out in the workers' own homes, such as weaving or bootmaking.

10.1.4 Why did opposition to Union grow after 1900 and culminate in war and final independence?

A sense of Irish nationalism continued to grow from 1900 onwards. Some Irish people had sympathised with the Boers in the South African War (1899–1902). The Irish nationalists saw the Boers as another nationalist group that wanted independence from Britain.

In 1905, Arthur Griffith founded the **Sinn Fein Party**. It supported the idea of a dual monarchy between Britain and Ireland, similar to the Empire of Austria-Hungary. Both Britain and Ireland would be self-governing but would share defence and foreign policy. Also at this time, the Irish Republican Brotherhood began to gain support. This was due in part to the nationalist enthusiasm created by the centenary celebrations in 1898 of the 1798 Rebellion.

In addition, a working-class movement with socialist ideas allied with the nationalist groups. They saw the British Liberal and Conservative parties as unlikely to bring about the social reforms they desired.

The demand for Home Rule appeared again after the 1910 general elections (January and December). As a result of these elections, the Home Rulers under Redmond held the balance of power in Parliament between the Liberals and Conservatives. With the passage of the Parliament Act, in 1911, the House of Lords veto on law also came to an end. From 1912, it was no longer possible for the House of Lords to stop Home Rule. It could only delay it for two years. As a result, Unionists in Ireland began to resist Home Rule with demonstrations and armed resistance. The Ulster Volunteer Force (UVF) was created in 1912. The UVF comprised 100,000 armed men. In 1913, nationalists formed the Irish Volunteers to defend

Sinn Fein Party: A radical political party committed to Irish independence and unity.

Nine counties in Ireland in 1921

Paramilitary: Similar to an army in that they use weapons and dress and behave like soldiers, but not the official army of the country.

Home Rule. By 1914, Britain faced the prospect of civil war in Ireland between two armed **paramilitary** groups.

Although Home Rule was passed in 1914 – and met the wishes of most of the Home Rulers – it was postponed until the end of the First World War. Redmond supported the decision to postpone Home Rule. He also supported the First World War policy of the British. However, a significant minority of opinion within the Irish Volunteers felt strongly that fighting for Irish freedom was more important than fighting for Belgian freedom. While many in the North supported the War enthusiastically, many in the South did not. Opposition to the War culminated with the Easter Rising, in 1916. This was organised by the Irish Republican Brotherhood, but also included other nationalist groups. The declaration of Irish independence, which was posted on the front of the General Post Office (GPO) in Dublin contained the names of Patrick Pearse, Thomas McDonagh, Thomas Clarke, Sean MacDiarmid, James Connolly, Eamonn Caennt and Joseph Plunkett.

The rebellion started on Easter Sunday 1916. However, it was badly organised and most of the promised German help failed to arrive. The British Army quickly suppressed it, even though there was clearly some sympathy for the 'rebels' among Irish people.

As was often the case, strong action by the Irish led to rapid concession by the British. Lloyd George, the British Prime Minister, started to negotiate a Home Rule Settlement shortly after 16 'rebel' leaders had been executed. These included the signatories of the Declaration of Independence. They had not died in vain. The Irish Convention of 1917–18 contained representatives of most Irish political groups. However, it made no progress towards a political settlement that would satisfy Nationalists and Unionists. Unionists demanded that the six counties of North-East Ireland should remain part of the UK.

The general election in December 1918 proved to be a turning point in Irish history. Sinn Fein won 73 out of the 105 Irish seats (the Ulster Unionists won 26), and simply opted out of the United Kingdom. They set up their own separate parliament in Dublin and their own government with Eamon de Valera as President.

Guerrilla war: A conflict fought between armies, usually an unofficial armed group (the guerrillas) against an official army.

Passive resistance to British rule soon turned to armed conflict by the summer of 1919. From 1919 to the summer of 1921, a **guerrilla war** developed in southern Ireland between British forces and Irish Volunteers known as the Irish Republican Army (the IRA). Although technically under the control of Cathal Brugha, the real power behind the IRA campaign was Michael Collins, Minister of Finance in the **Dail Government**.

Dail Government: The 'illegal' government set up in Dublin after the 1918 general election.

The Anglo-Irish War (1919–21) was particularly brutal. Lloyd George tried to bring about peace with a Home Rule solution with the Government of Ireland Act of 1920. This aimed to create separate Home Rule parliaments for both the North and the South, but the Republicans in the South rejected it. The war continued until June 1921, when a ceasefire was agreed and treaty negotiations between Republicans and the British Government began. In December 1921, the Irish Republican delegation, under a threat made by Lloyd George of renewed war, signed the Anglo-Irish Treaty. In the Treaty, the Irish accepted a status far removed from an independent Republic. Instead, they accepted **dominion status** within the British Empire, as the Irish Free State. This decision was to split the

Dominion status: A country becomes independent, and rules itself, but retains the British monarchy as formal Head of State. This status was similar to that of Canada.

The four provinces of Ireland in 1921

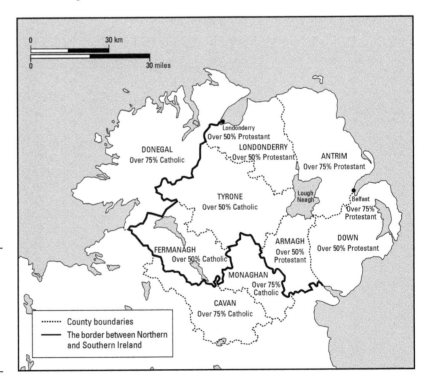

1. How far did opposition to the Union of Britain and Ireland change between 1798 and 1921?

2. Why were some forms of opposition to Union more successful than others (1798–1921)?

Republican movement and cause civil war in the Irish Free State between 1922 and 1923. An issue that caused little debate in the Treaty and in the split that led to civil war was the partition of Ireland. The Irish negotiators believed a boundary commission set up under the Treaty would give so much of North-East Ireland to the Free State that partition would not be possible. When the Boundary Commission reported in 1925, it ensured that the six north-eastern counties (Antrim, Down, Armagh, Tyrone, Fermanagh and Londonderry) stayed outside the Free State as Northern Ireland.

10.2 Theme 2: Who supported the Union?

Key Issues

■ Who were the Ulster Unionists?

■ What were the strengths and weaknesses of the Unionist movement?

■ Assess the nature and extent of Ulster Unionism.

10.2.1 Why did religion become a major issue in Anglo-Irish politics in the 19th century?

10.2.2 Why did Unionism grow in strength after 1870?

10.2.3 What role did the Unionists play in the crisis of 1912–1914?

10.2.1 Why did religion become a major issue in Anglo-Irish politics in the 19th century?

Penal laws: Laws that discriminated against Roman Catholics, forbidding them from holding key offices, for example.

When England moved away from the Roman Catholic Church in the 16th century, Ireland did not. It remained a strongly Roman Catholic country. Protestantism became the religion of the 'alien' British rulers, and the religion of the landed classes, as the 16th and 17th centuries progressed. In the North, mainly in Ulster, much land was removed from Catholics by force. It was given to Protestants from Scotland and England. Those Protestants in the North were also able to gain considerable security of tenure for their land, something that was not allowed to Catholics in the South.

The **penal laws** also meant that Catholics were excluded from the vote, from sitting in the Irish Parliament in Dublin, and from any post of importance in the government or in the legal system. In addition, Roman Catholics had to pay a tax (the tithe) to support the Protestant Church in Ireland. It was hardly surprising that, by 1800, not only was there a strong resentment of Protestants by Catholics, but there was also a strong desire by the Protestants to retain their privileged position.

In the course of the late 18th and early 19th centuries, some of the restrictions on Roman Catholics were removed. They were allowed to vote, and then to stand for Parliament. The deep antagonism between the two religions remained. It was only among highly educated people that there was tolerance and cooperation between the religions. For the most part, there was a deep and mutual loathing.

Protestants formed about 25% of the total population of Ireland, but nearly 60% of the population of the North where they were concentrated. They owned the bulk of the land. Most of the industry of Ireland was in the North as well. It was also in Protestant hands. The 'haves' were Protestant and the 'have nots' tended to be Catholic. Even the famine hit the Catholics of the South much harder than the Protestants in the North.

10.2.2 Why did Unionism grow in strength after 1870?

Unionism: The belief that Ireland had to remain part of the United Kingdom, ruled from London.

Obviously, the Protestants of Ireland viewed the erosion of their privileged position, with emancipation and so on, with concern. When Home Rule, which for them meant Catholic rule from Dublin, became a serious possibility in the 1870s, Ulster **Unionism** (or Orange Movement) became a strong and organised force in the North. It then started to play an important part in British politics.

Hatred of Roman Catholicism and a strong dislike of Fenian violence were important factors in the growth of organised Ulster Unionism. There was also a strong element of rich versus poor in it. The Protestants in the North were very conscious that much of their wealth was dependent on the economic and political link with mainland Britain being maintained. The South may have suffered economically from Union, but the North gained. Many in the North were deeply worried by the land war and the activities of the Land League in the 1870s, and this added to their deep insecurity and sense of fear. Irish nationalists made no attempt to calm the fears of the Protestants, often making it clear that Home Rule would be an opportunity to settle old religious and economic scores.

Ulster Protestants made few attempts to convince Southern Catholics of their willingness to compromise and conciliate, and mutual loathing was the order of the day. The commentator who called it 'tribal warfare' between Catholic and Protestant was not far from the truth.

The rise of the Home Rule Movement in Ireland, the growth of a Home Rule Party in the House of Commons, the election of 16 committed nationalists in Ulster in 1886, and Gladstone's first Home Rule Bill, brought Unionism to a real crisis. The Unionists were aware that they might soon be ruled from Dublin and they would be a minority religion. They also feared that the intolerance with which they treated their Catholic neighbours would happen to them.

Orange: The colour associated with the Protestant cause. It came from the Dutch royal family of Wilhelm III who won the battle of the Boyne, in 1690, against the Catholic James II.

In 1886, the Protestants in the North formed the Loyalist Anti-Repeal Union, determined to oppose the march to Home Rule. They got strong support in England from the rising Tory star, Lord Randolph Churchill, who sensed that Ulster Unionism could be a powerful political weapon to use against the Liberals, as he played the '**Orange** Card'. Like many later Conservatives, Churchill's intentions were more to help the Conservatives and to damage the Liberals, than to bring any Irish 'problem' to an end. Just as Liberals underestimated the strength of Irish nationalism, Conservatives failed to realise the explosive potential of Ulster Unionism and the lengths to which the Unionists would go to prevent Home Rule. They encouraged a force which they were unable to restrain within sensible boundaries.

Unionists' fears subsided after the failure of Gladstone's two Home Rule Bills, but the strength of Unionist feeling did not die. Conservative programmes to ease the economic situation in the South were viewed with hostility in the North and Conservative suggestions for devolution just deepened the Unionist suspicions that the Conservatives were using Ulster for their own political ends.

10.2.3 What role did the Unionists play in the crisis of 1912–1914?

Devolution: A form of home rule, which encourages as much local government as possible, pushing decision making away from the capital to the localities.

In 1905, the Ulster Unionist Council was formed. It was created after Sir Anthony MacDonnell, a civil servant in Dublin, tried to put forward a plan for **devolution** for Ireland. At last, the Protestants in the North had a well-organised and disciplined organisation, which could campaign effectively for their objective of remaining an integral part of the United Kingdom. It was led by James Craig (1871–1940), a man of extreme views and considerable organisational ability. The other key leader of the Unionists was Sir Edward Carson (1854–1935), an outstanding public speaker, but also one prepared to arouse real anger amongst the Unionists and encourage extremist militant behaviour.

When the Liberals introduced the Third Home Rule Bill in 1912, Craig and Carson had behind them a powerful and organised pressure group determined to resist, at all costs, what was seen as a threat to their religion, status, wealth and values. Two hundred and fifty thousand Ulstermen signed the Solemn League and Covenant – a commitment to retain the union, by force if need be. Huge protest marches of over 100,000 Ulstermen were features of the years before 1914, when Home Rule would come into force. In addition, the Ulster Volunteer Force (UVF) was created in 1912. The UVF was an illegal organisation, determined to use force to prevent Home Rule. In 1914, it was involved in gun running on a large scale from Germany, and illegally armed many of its members.

Punch cartoon, 15 April 1914, entitled 'The Fight for the Banner'. John Bull (background left) represents Britain. The person on the left of the banner is John Redmond, leader of the Irish Nationalists. On the right is Sir Edward Carson, leader of the Irish Unionists. John Bull is saying to Redmond and Carson: 'This tires me. Why can't you carry it between you? Neither of you can carry it alone.'

1. What message is the cartoon trying to make about Ireland if Nationalists and Unionists cannot agree?

2. How useful is this cartoon as evidence of the Ulster Crisis of 1912–14?

The UVF was openly encouraged by Conservatives, led by former British Army officers, and advised by ex-Generals of the British Army. Official endorsement seemed to be given to armed rebellion, against the wish of Parliament.

The Conservatives, with their determination to wreck the Liberal Government by fair means or foul, must take a degree of responsibility for the likelihood of civil war in Ireland with their incitement of the Unionists. The incompetence of the British Government was seen over the Curragh Mutiny, when they appeared to tolerate the refusal of British Army officers with family links to Ulster to obey orders they did not like. Those orders might include using force to enforce Home Rule.

Unionism was put on ice in 1914, with the declaration of war. Most of the Unionist volunteers joined up and fought. It was in fact the 36th (Ulster) Division that suffered the worst casualties in the carnage of the first day of the battle of the Somme.

Unionists were, of course, appalled by the 'treason' of the Easter Rising in Dublin in 1916. But, in a way, it helped towards a peaceful solution of the Irish problem in 1922, when North and South separated. Protestant Ulstermen had no wish to be united, even under British rule, with those who seemed to ally with the Germans in the South.

There was no way the Ulstermen could prevent Home Rule. Irish nationalism was far too powerful a force for them to fight on their own, if the British Government stopped trying to prevent it. All they could attain was to keep the North in British hands, using their close links with the Conservative Party and their willingness to fight and cause a serious civil war as key cards. British public opinion was used to fighting wars against those who wished to stop being a British possession. However, it would not tolerate a war against those who wanted to stay.

1. To what extent was the rise of Unionism in Ireland a reaction to the growth of Irish Nationalism?

2. How would you account for the changing fortunes of the Protestant ascendancy in Ireland in the period 1798–1921?

3. Why were the Ulster Unionists unable to prevent Home Rule for the South?

10.3 Theme 3: Change and continuity in the attitude of British governments and parties

Key Issues

- Did the British Government adopt a consistent attitude to Ireland in this period?

- What was the impact of Ireland on the politics of the UK during this period?

- How, and why, did attitudes towards Irish Home Rule change in this period?

10.3.1 Why, and with what results, did Ireland become an ever more divisive issue in British politics, 1798–1922?

10.3.2 What was the impact of Ireland on British politics – from Union to the 1830s?

10.3.3 What impact did Ireland have on British politics from the Famine to 1900?

10.3.4 What impact did Ireland have on British politics, 1906–1922?

10.3.1 Why, and with what results, did Ireland become an ever more divisive issue in British politics, 1798–1922?

Throughout the period between 1798 and 1922, Ireland was a central and usually highly divisive issue in British politics. Ireland cost the English taxpayers millions and thousands of lives were lost. It led to the exclusion from public gaze and ministerial attention of many other important issues. It was always in the headlines, but few ever really analysed why. There was always the assumption that Ireland as an integral part of the UK was of benefit to all. When the possibility of independence for Ireland was raised, few in England could envisage that idea as an acceptable concept.

The same idea had been evident when the United Kingdom 'lost' the American colonies, but to the surprise of many, both the UK and the USA flourished when separated. The UK seemed able to give almost complete independence to Canada, New Zealand and Australia in the 19th century, but not to Ireland. Perhaps it was too close to home, and therefore might be of value to 'enemies'; or possibly the arrogant English felt that although the Irish may not have wanted 'English' rule, they needed it for their own good.

The fact that many leading politicians in the UK owned land in Ireland may have encouraged a proprietary attitude by some. The Marquis of Lansdowne, for example, a key figure in the Conservative Party and its leader in the House of Lords at the time of the crisis over the Third Home Rule Bill (1912–14), owned large estates in County Kerry, and derived considerable income from them. So did many other Conservative peers who felt it necessary to throw out Gladstone's Second Home Rule Bill 'in order to preserve the integrity of the Empire', rather than save their own financial interests.

10.3.2 What was the impact of Ireland on British politics – from Union to the 1830s?

Autonomy: The control or government of a country, organisation or group by itself, rather than by others.

Union, in 1800, was highly controversial. Not only did many in Ireland oppose it as they felt that it would damage Irish interests and reduce what little **autonomy** they had under the old Irish Parliament, but it was also strongly opposed in England. Many in England disliked the extensive use of patronage by Castlereagh and Cornwallis. Commercial interests, always strongly represented in the House of Commons, felt that giving equality to Ireland might damage English commerce. Peers resented the arrival of Irishmen, and many saw it as a concession to both force and Catholicism.

When the second part of the 'deal' – the ending of discrimination against Roman Catholics – was attempted, the King refused. Pitt then felt obliged to resign as he had committed himself to giving the Roman Catholics in Ireland equality with the Protestants. Within months of what had been seen as the solution to the Irish 'problem', it had claimed its first major English political victim – an exceptionally able Prime Minister.

Once the Napoleonic Wars were over, Ireland returned to play a serious role in politics in London. Many issues divided Liverpool's Cabinet between 1812 and 1826, but the most bitter division came over whether Roman Catholics should be allowed to take a seat in the House of Commons. The penal laws were still in existence and there was a deep degree of religious intolerance against Roman Catholics going back to the age of Elizabeth and the Gunpowder Plot of James I. In the eyes of many, Roman Catholicism was seen as the religion of traitors.

After providing a constant source of friction within the Cabinet for more than a decade, the issue of Catholics entering Parliament came to a head in 1828. Wellington and Peel were forced to give in to force. This led to the destruction of the old Tory Party and the rise of the new Conservative Party. Ireland also played a large part in the fact that the Tory Government managed to lose the election of 1830. O'Connell formed a small, but quite powerful, group in the Commons. This led to further reforms for Ireland, which continued to divide English politics.

The tithe wars of the 1830s divided the Whig Government, as the more 'liberal' members were not so enthusiastic for coercion as were the more conservative 'Whigs'. The latter prevailed, and the Irish Coercion Act of 1833 gave the State huge police powers. In 1834, it was a dispute over the Anglican Church in Ireland that led to a major government split. The Prime Minister, Grey, resigned over the issue. Not for the last time was Ireland to be the downfall of a major English politician.

Grey was replaced by Peel, whose Government collapsed in 1835 when the Whigs, Radicals and, of course, the Irish MPs joined together to bring it down. Irish support was critical to the Whigs until 1840. This meant that the Whigs had to take on Irish former issues, such as the Poor Law and education in Ireland, which they would have preferred to avoid as it meant upsetting the more conservative Whigs.

Even the arrival of Peel with a majority Conservative Government, in 1841, did not end Ireland as a divisive issue in British politics. Ireland became an even more important issue. Peel's reform programme for Catholic education, landlord/tenant relations and the franchise was hated by the right of his own party. William Maynooth split his own party and led to the resignation of one of his key ministers, Gladstone.

Peel's Irish reforms are seen as failures. They did not calm Ireland. Also, they led to the split of his party, and his party was out of office until 1874. The Famine led to the repeal of the Corn Laws and massive political disruption. It set the scene for the fragmented politics of the 1846–68 period. Ireland had divided and disrupted British politics on a huge scale, from Union to the Famine.

10.3.3 What impact did Ireland have on British politics from the Famine to 1900?

In the years after the Famine, until 1865, Ireland appeared 'quiet' as far as London was concerned, and was ignored. However, the huge resentment that had built up in Ireland over the Union and the Famine was to place it firmly back on the political agenda. The Fenians used violence from 1865 to 1867. From 1870, Isaac Butt used parliamentary means. Also, Gladstone's decision to 'pacify' meant that Ireland was to dominate British political life from the mid-1860s until 1921. The failure to 'pacify' Ireland then has led to problems up to this day. Ireland was to have a huge impact from 1868 onwards, making and breaking governments, parties and reputations.

The Gladstone Administration of 1868–1874

Ireland played a significant role in Gladstone's Administration. Although much of the work confirmed Gladstone's 'liberalism', it had important side-effects. Many people in Ireland felt that Gladstone was doing too little, too late. In England, people felt he was doing too much. Gladstone's Church Act upset the Anglican Church and those on the right of his party saw his Land Act as an attack on property rights. Unionism as a powerful political, social and religious force came into being at this time, largely inspired by Gladstone's actions. The Whigs, the more conservative elements in the Liberal party, started to view the Prime Minister as a dangerous radical. They looked towards the Conservative Party as their natural home.

Gladstone's Ballot Act created Irish nationalism as a powerful parliamentary force in the election of 1874. To cap it all, Gladstone's Government was defeated in the House of Commons over the Irish

Universities Bill in 1873. He split his party over this issue of supporting 'Catholic' education, and resigned after a motion of 'no confidence' in the Commons over it. Gladstone may have started his Administration with a 'mission to pacify' Ireland, but he not only failed, but also injected a lethal ingredient into British politics.

Disraeli's 1874–80 Administration did not concern itself with Irish issues. Perhaps it should have done, as by 1880 the mixture of Irish nationalism and the Land League was forcing Ireland back on to the British Government's agenda.

Much of Gladstone's Second Administration (1880–85) was dominated by Ireland. The Prime Minister was forced to both coerce and appease Ireland with a tough Coercion Act, the arrest of Parnell, and the passing of the Second Land Act, which again worried the more conservative members of the Liberal Party. His policy on Ireland led to a drift to the Conservatives. After the horror of the Phoenix Park murders, with the killing of the Chief Secretary in cold blood in Dublin, Gladstone's Government collapsed again in 1885, leaving Parnell and the Irish Home Rule Party holding the balance of power in the Commons.

Convinced that Home Rule was the only solution, Gladstone put through his first Home Rule Bill in 1886. This failed, splitting his own party and driving its most talented member, Joseph Chamberlain, into the Conservative Party. This became known as the Conservative and Unionist Party as a result.

English politics was dancing to an Irish tune. Churchill and the 'Orange' card introduced a degree of fanaticism into politics, where consensus and courtesy were replaced by passion and illegality.

The Conservative policy to Ireland in the 1886–92 period was simple. Having won the election largely because of the Liberal implosion over Ireland, the Conservatives largely gave in. After Liberal election victory in 1892, Gladstone introduced his second Home Rule Bill. Although it cleared the Commons, the Lords rejected it and this unconstitutional measure was a precursor of the greater constitutional crisis over the role of the Lords, in 1909. Once again, Ireland had been the causative factor of a major crisis in England.

The Conservative reaction in the post-1894 period demonstrates the remarkable pragmatism of that party. On one hand, there was the ruthless repression of 'Bloody Balfour'; on the other, more radical land reform at a cost to the British taxpayer unimaginable to the Liberals.

London ignored the growth of Irish nationalism in the South. There was neither understanding nor wish to understand. It was a totally reactive policy.

10.3.4 What impact did Ireland have on British politics, 1906–1922?

With the Liberal electoral victory in 1906, Irish aspiration was aroused. However, it was not matched by a favourable Liberal response. An awareness of the Lords' likely reaction was a key factor. After the 1910 elections, the Irish Home Rule Party held the balance of power in the Commons, so they had to be appeased. Needing their support in order to defeat the Lords, Herbert Asquith promised, and then introduced, a Home Rule Bill. Part of the bitter opposition to reforming the Lords lay in the knowledge that Irish Home Rule would follow.

Passage through the Commons was bitter. With senior conservative politicians in London openly inciting the Unionists to armed rebellion, and the King to unconstitutional action, Ireland continued to play a highly damaging role in British politics.

The mismanagement by Asquith of the whole Irish crisis worsened the situation. The problem of the North and the South would not go away, and a 'wait and see' policy was not what Ireland needed. Asquith allowed a situation to arise over the Curragh Mutiny in which officers in the Army were more or less allowed to dictate policy to the politicians. He had to dismiss his Secretary of State for War, Seeley, over the crisis.

The First World War eased the Irish problem temporarily, but it failed to go away. The Easter Rising returned it to the forefront. Again, there were bitter disputes between those in London who wished to coerce and punish, and those who wished to appease. Whether to introduce conscription into Ireland also provoked serious disunity in London and Dublin. Compelling Irishmen to fight for the freedom of others was not easy.

With Lloyd George dependent on Conservative support to remain in power after 1918, he had to heed the grievances and wishes of the Unionists. The Conservatives would not tolerate Ulster being forced to join the South, so partition was imposed on Lloyd George through English political necessity.

The methods used by the **Black and Tans** brought discredit to the British Government. The way in which Sinn Fein simply set up its own parliament and government in Dublin brought ridicule on London. Although the settlement of 1920–22 was the best that was possible in the circumstances, it was a important cause of the downfall of Lloyd George in 1922. Ireland had claimed yet another political victim.

Once the South gained its independence, the Conservatives proceeded to ignore the North. This proved to be a tragic error, as the Protestants embarked on a ruthless policy of discrimination that was to lay a basis for the trouble that exploded in the 1960s, and last to this day.

Black and Tans: Former English soldiers recruited to reinforce the police in Ireland. They could be brutal and often ignored the usual legal methods used by the police.

---

1. What were the attitudes of the main UK political parties to the Unionists?

2. How far did the policies of the two major political parties in Britain – the Whig-Liberal Party and the Tory-Conservative Party – change towards Ireland between 1798 and 1921?

10.4 Theme 4: Change and continuity in the Irish economy

Key Issues

- Which proved to be more difficult for British governments to deal with in Ireland during the period 1798–1921, religious or economic issues?

- How successfully did British governments tackle Irish economic problems, 1798–1921?

- What role did economic issues play in Anglo-Irish history, 1798–1922?

10.4.1 What were the causes of the Famine and what impact did it have on the Irish economy and people?

10.4.2 How did the Irish economy develop after the Famine?

Introduction

The economy of Ireland at the time of the Union was a direct contrast to that of England. There had been major agriculture and industrial change in

England in the course of the 18th century. Mainland UK had become highly productive and wealthy. Ireland had not shared in that rapid and profound economic change. It still had a primarily rural system, with only 20% of the population in towns by 1800. Ireland's agriculture was a **subsistence economy** and there was virtually no heavy industry. The domestic/cottage industries, such as weaving and spinning, were devastated by the massive industrial growth in the UK. Denied the markets that the English had easy access to, and with no sophisticated banking system, a poor transport and communications system, and virtually no local energy source, Ireland could not compete.

There was a substantial population growth in the latter part of the 18th and early 19th century, which put a huge strain on Ireland. This was caused by a lowering of the marriage age, as babies and their mothers were more likely to survive if younger and healthier. Health awareness increased and the Irish staple diet, the potato, was not an unhealthy diet.

The population growth caused problems, with no welfare system and no industrial towns to absorb the surplus rural population, as in the UK. Union, it was hoped, would lead to a sharing of the English markets and a sharing in English wealth – but it did not happen. Economic backwardness encouraged political unrest.

Ireland suffered considerably in the economic downturn after the end of the Napoleonic Wars, in 1815. The serious social and economic division between landlord, tenant and labourer grew; the decline of the cottage industries speeded up and generated even more poverty. The system of land holding discouraged investment in the land, and if a tenant farmer worked to improve land and output, he could find himself being asked for a higher rent as his reward. The tenant farmer was unlikely to get any compensation for improvement to land. So, as long as the rent was paid and the family fed, there seemed little point in trying to generate a profit.

Emigration was the only solution for many, but it was often the solution of the youngest and best. Union did not solve any problems for many Irish people. In fact, it could well be seen to have caused more problems. *Laissez faire* was very much the approach adopted by governments in London when it came to social and economic conditions, and they did not change that approach for Ireland. Behind the political and religious events lay great poverty and deprivation.

Subsistence economy: When most of the economic activity is focused on simply growing enough food for the people that produce it and not for sale at market.

Emigration: Leaving your mother country to live in another country, often far away (e.g. America or Canada).

How far does this illustration explain why Irish emigrants became resentful of British rule in Ireland from the 1850s?

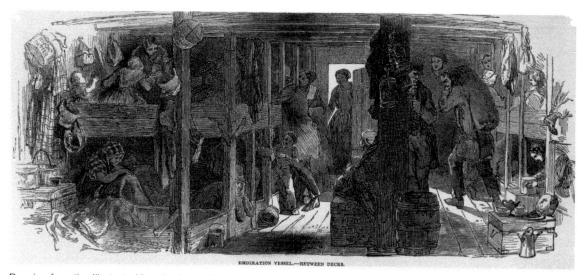

EMIGRATION VESSEL.—BETWEEN DECKS.

Drawing from the *Illustrated London News* of May 1851. It shows the cramped conditions on an emigrant ship.

10.4.1 What were the causes of the Famine and what impact did it have on the Irish economy and people?

Blight: A form of fungal rot.

Emigration in the 1820s and 1830s had not solved Ireland's problems, nor had Ireland shared in the economic progress made in the rest of the UK at that time. Industrial stagnation, land shortage, declining agricultural employment and poor diet were the main features of Irish economic history after 1815. Hungry people supported Daniel O'Connell.

Added to this grim scene, came total disaster by 1845. **Blight** struck the potato crop, which was the staple (basic) diet for the vast majority of the Irish people, especially in the Catholic South. With a very poor population, few economic resources, overpopulation and inefficient system of local government, the blight became a tragedy in months. People started to starve, in their thousands.

Overall, the actual aid given by the rest of the UK was limited. The Government in London had no experience in dealing with such a famine. Also, there was a strong tendency in London to assume that the situation was exaggerated. In addition, with the prevailing *laissez-faire* economic ideas, it was not felt to be part of the role of a government to intervene in such matters.

The Government in London appeared to be more concerned with the implications of repealing the Corn Laws. It was also more concerned about the economic interests of British farmers and political pledges given in the election of 1841 than about actually stopping a large number of UK citizens in Ireland starving to death. Britain was possibly the richest country in the world at the time, with vast resources of money and shipping. It had all that was needed both to buy food and to ship it to Ireland and feed those there.

The English Government seemed to devote itself to academic debates on both the causes and the extent of the problem. It discussed whether public works would actually help or not, and should soup be given out by Protestant organisations with a requirement to convert before the food was consumed.

The governments of both Peel (1841–46) and Russell (1846–52) appeared to be particularly concerned to ensure that Irish landowners paid for Irish poverty, and that the English taxpayer would not suffer for Irish profits. A particularly hard winter in 1848–49 simply increased the death rate. It is estimated that over a million died of starvation or related illnesses in Ireland in this period. Possibly a further million emigrated during or immediately after the famine years, which did not end until nearly 1852.

Given the possible resources at the disposal of a British government, it is perhaps remarkable that there was so little resentment expressed against the Union. What the Government in London had done was too little too late. While the biographers of Peel and Russell might see them as able leaders, with their Bank Charter Acts and calm handling of the Chartist disturbances, viewed from an Irish perspective the fact that a million UK citizens died of hunger, they were clearly less than 'able'.

10.4.2 How did the Irish economy develop after the Famine of 1845–1849?

Much like the economic recovery in Britain in the late 1930s, what recovery there was in Ireland was as much in spite of the actions of Government as because of them. There was no initiative at all from London to ensure that the situation was not repeated. If there had been, then perhaps the IRB and the Land League might not have had little support. After the London government's response, or lack of it, to the famine in Ireland, Union was permanently damned in the eyes of the vast majority of Irish people, both educated and otherwise.

With fewer people (and therefore a less acute land shortage), and the ending of the Corn Laws, Irish agriculture could develop more easily. Smaller-scale farmers still focused on subsistence, and not profit, but larger-scale ones could start to develop livestock and **animal husbandry** for a profit. With most farm prices up, profits were made. Increased rail networks came to Ireland by the late 1850s, making rapid movement of food to towns much easier. Crop rotation, evident in much of Britain by the 1790s, spread to Ireland particularly after the 1860s, as it was easy to see how a cash crop could be developed. Horse power replaced human power, but agricultural machinery did not arrive on a large scale until the 20th century.

Gladstone's two Land Acts brought more peace to the countryside, but they also made it realistic for the tenant farmer to invest, adapt and, above all, improve. Balfour's Land Purchase Act was also vital. In 1899, a Department of Agriculture was set up in Ireland in order to educate farmers (almost a hundred years after a similar organisation was set up in England). The Wyndham Land Act effectively abolished the landlord class in Ireland. By the end of the period, the vast majority of farmers owned the land they worked, and therefore had a vested interest in both its quality and productivity.

The British Government did play a more central role in this area, between 1881 and 1915. In order for the intentions of the Land Act to be implemented, £86.1 million was paid out, and peace and economic justice come to the Irish countryside. Over 4 million emigrated, between the famine and 1914, and that was important to ease social and economic tension.

Industry largely passed Ireland by, except for Ulster. Towns in the South, such as Dublin and Cork, saw a total contrast with England, with the percentage involved in industry actually dropping in Ireland in the 19th century. Linen – the traditional primary industry in Ulster – dropped in importance in the second part of the 19th century, and was replaced by shipbuilding and engineering. The vast proportion of the heavy industry in the North was under Protestant and Unionist control, and it was common for Catholics to be excluded deliberately from any post other than the completely menial. Not only were there religious, social and landholding differences between Ulster and the rest of Ireland, there were major economic differences there as well. Even the retail sector flourished much more in Belfast than in Dublin.

The British Government played no role in the development of industry in Ireland. Railways developed there as **entrepreneurs** felt they could profit from them. The only serious government involvement came in land issues, and that was for political reasons rather than any other. Conservative policy was a reaction to pressure and designed to prevent the perceived evil of Home Rule.

Economic issues played a vital role in Anglo-Irish politics until the 1880s. They fuelled much of the unrest, which occurred both before and after the Famine. Once mass emigration, improved farming and land-holding changes had come in, then economic factors were to play a smaller role in fanning the flames of Irish nationalism.

Animal husbandry: Careful breeding and management of livestock to get better food and animal products (such as wool).

Entrepreneurs: People willing to take risks by investing in new ideas/plans/techniques in business and industry.

Compared with other factors, such as politics, how important were economic issues in bringing about change in Anglo-Irish relations between 1798 and 1921?

10.5 An in-depth study: Gladstone and Ireland, 1868–1894

Key Issues

■ Why was Ireland a major political issue in British politics in these years?

■ How successful was Gladstone in dealing with Irish problems?

■ What impact did Ireland have on the British political system?

10.5.1 Why did Gladstone want to 'pacify Ireland'?

10.5.2 Why was Ireland a major issue again by 1880?

10.5.3 How successfully did Gladstone's Government deal with Ireland between 1880 and 1885?

10.5.4 Historical interpretation: Why did Gladstone convert to Irish Home Rule in 1886?

10.5.5 Why was Home Rule so controversial?

10.5.6 How successful were Conservative policies towards Ireland between 1885 and 1892?

10.5.7 What impact did Parnell and Gladstone have on British–Irish relations?

Framework of Events

1884	Third Parliamentary Reform Act increases the Irish electorate fourfold
1885	Gladstone loses election. Home Rule Party holds balance of power
1886	Gladstone converts to Home Rule
	Salisbury loses office
	First Home Rule Bill fails due to split in Liberal Party
1887	'Bloody Balfour', Crimes Act and Plan of Campaign
	Land Purchase Act
1887–89	'Parnellism and Crime' scandal
1890	Parnell forced to resign from leadership of Irish Home Rule Party. Party splits into pro- and anti-Parnellite factions
1891	Land Purchase Act
	Parnell dies
1892	Gladstone wins office with Irish Home Rule support
1893	Second Irish Home Rule Bill passes House of Commons but is defeated in House of Lords
1894	Gladstone retires from politics.

Overview

O
F all the issues in British politics in the years 1868–94, Ireland proved to be the most controversial and far-reaching in its effects. Ireland was a major issue during Gladstone's first two ministries (1868–74 and 1880–85). In both ministries, Irish issues caused deep divisions in the Liberal Party. Once Gladstone had converted to the idea of Irish Home Rule in 1886, the Liberal Party split on the issue, paving the way for almost 20 years of Conservative dominance in British politics.

The 'Irish Question' involved four interrelated problems: religion, land tenure, law and order, and the political relationship between Britain and Ireland. Ultimately, after 1886, the last problem – in the form of Home Rule versus maintaining the union between Britain and Ireland – became the dominant aspect.

In 1868, Ireland was part of the United Kingdom of Great Britain and Ireland,

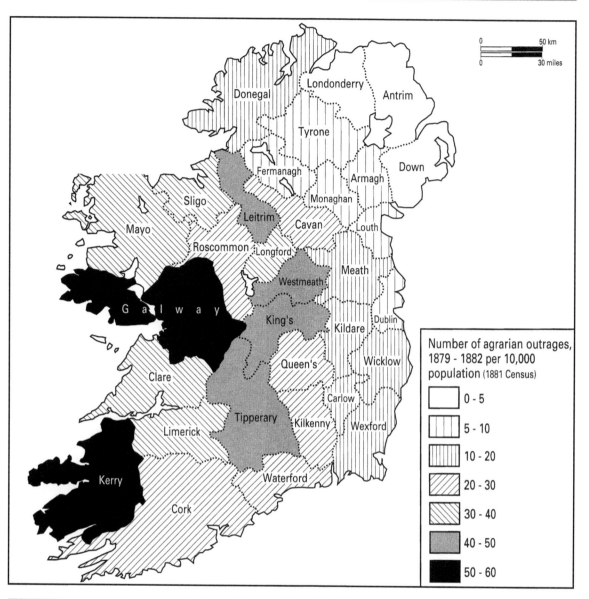

Number of agrarian outrages, 1879 - 1882 per 10,000 population (1881 Census)

- 0 - 5
- 5 - 10
- 10 - 20
- 20 - 30
- 30 - 40
- 40 - 50
- 50 - 60

Ireland at the time of the Land War, 1879–1882

Using the information contained within this chapter, do you think north-east Ireland had little or no land war activism and the west of Ireland had the most land war activism? Give reasons to support your answer.

Anglo-Irish Ascendancy: The social class who dominated Irish society. It comprised members of the Church of Ireland who were the main landowners and who dominated professions such as the law and the armed forces.

as created by the Act of Union of 1800. As a result of that Act, Ireland had lost its own Parliament which had been dominated by the **Anglo-Irish Ascendancy**. In its place, Ireland was given 105 MPs at Westminster and a limited number of places in the House of Lords. On the other hand, the administration of Ireland, in part, continued to be based in Ireland, at Dublin Castle. Departments such as the Board of Works, Education and the Poor Law were based there. In charge of the Irish Administration was the Chief Secretary who usually held a post in the British Cabinet. The monarchy was represented in Ireland by the Lord Lieutenant, who resided in the Vice-Regal Lodge in Dublin.

Between 1868 and 1894, the Irish problem was most closely associated with one British politician, William Gladstone. In all four of his ministries (1868–74, 1880–85, 1886 and 1892–94) Ireland was a dominant, if not *the* dominant issue. Since the 19th century, there has been considerable controversy among historians over Gladstone's motives for his Irish policies. Some historians, such as J. Hammond in *Gladstone and the Irish Nation* (1938), saw his policies as a genuine attempt to address Irish grievances. Others, such as D.A. Hamer in *Liberal Politics in the Age of Gladstone and Rosebery* (1972) and A.B. Cooke and J. Vincent in *The Governing Passion* (1974), have seen Gladstone pursuing policies that had more to do with ensuring Liberal Party unity and his position as Liberal leader than anything directly to do with solving Irish problems. The whole issue of Home Rule is a major area for studying alternative historical interpretations of one of the 19th century's most controversial issues.

An important factor in making Irish affairs occupy centre stage in British politics was the appearance of a new third force in party politics, the Irish Home Rule Party. Founded in 1870 as the Home Government Association the Party, from 1880 under the leadership of Charles Stewart Parnell, played a major role in ensuring Irish affairs were at the top of the political agenda. Throughout the 1880s, Parnell played a central role in British politics, particularly in 1885–86 when he had considerable influence over the creation of the Salisbury Conservative Government in 1885 and the Gladstone Government of 1886.

By 1894, the issue of Ireland in British politics had split the Liberal Party into two camps, Liberals and Liberal Unionists. It had seen the rise and, after 1890, the rapid fall in political stature of Parnell. The Irish issue had also realigned British politics on a pro- and anti-Home Rule basis for a future generation.

10.5.1 Why did Gladstone want to 'pacify Ireland'?

By 1868 Ireland, apart from the north-east area around Belfast, had not experienced an 'industrial revolution'. Most of the population lived in rural areas. In the west of Ireland, subsistence agriculture predominated. Between 1845 and 1849, the country had experienced a disastrous potato famine which had resulted in the deaths of approximately 1 million people and forced a further 1.5 million to emigrate, mainly to Britain, the USA and Canada. For the rest of the century, Ireland experienced a decline in population due to mass emigration. The population fell from 8 million in 1841 to 5 million in 1901. At times, rural areas were affected by unrest between the peasant population (through secret organisations known generally as Ribbonmen), and the landowning classes, the most influential of whom were English or Anglo-Irish nobility. By 1868, the rights of peasants who rented land – tenant right – was a major political issue.

In religion, Ireland was predominantly Roman Catholic (about 80%). Another 10% were nonconformists, situated mainly in north-east Ulster. The remaining population, 690,000 out of 5,700,000 according to the Census of 1861, were Anglicans, members of the Church of Ireland. This was the Established or State Church. This meant that it was supported by the tithe, a tax paid by the whole population, that its bishops were appointed by the monarch and it was controlled by Parliament. Some Church of Ireland bishops also had the right to sit in the House of Lords. This situation caused considerable resentment among both Catholics and nonconformists. This had mainly taken the form of opposition to the tithe. Although this problem had been solved, in part, by an Act of 1836 the established position of a church that was followed by only 10% of the population still caused considerable resentment.

The issues of land and religion both helped fuel Irish separatism. In 1858, the Fenian Brotherhood had been established in the USA with the aim of creating an independent Irish Republic by violent means. Between 1865 and 1868, a series of 'Fenian Outrages' occurred, including an attempted invasion of Canada from the USA (31 May 1866), an attempted uprising in Ireland (March 1867) and terrorist attacks in England at Chester (February 1867), Manchester (September 1867) and in Clerkenwell, London (December 1867).

How successful was Gladstone in dealing with Irish matters, 1868–1874?

Gladstone's aims

In November 1868, Gladstone had fought and won the general election under the slogan of 'Justice for Ireland'. The aim of his Irish policy was simple: 'our purpose and duty is to endeavour to draw a line between the Fenians and the people of Ireland, and make the people of Ireland indisposed to cross it'. He proceeded to introduce a series of proposals designed to encourage the majority of the Irish to accept the union of Britain and Ireland.

The Church Disestablishment Act, 1869

In 1869, the Liberal Government passed the Disestablishment of the Church of Ireland Act. Drafted by Gladstone himself, the Act ended the Church of Ireland's special status as a state church from 1 January 1871. Ecclesiastical courts were abolished and Anglican bishops had to be elected by **diocesan synods**. The property of the Church (valued at £16 million) was confiscated and £5 million was given as compensation to the Church, with £9 million being given to the Poor Law Board for poor relief. In addition, the government grant to the Roman Catholic college for training priests at Maynooth and the grant to nonconformists (the *Regium Donum*) were also abolished.

Diocesan synod: A diocese is an administrative area of the Church over which a bishop has control. A synod is a church assembly where representatives of the parishes within a diocese meet to discuss Church matters.

The proposal aroused strong opposition. Conservatives and Irish Anglicans believed it would weaken the Protestant Supremacy, the union of Church and State, and the rights of property. Benjamin Disraeli, the Conservative Party leader, declared that: 'We have legalised confiscation, we have consecrated sacrilege, we have condoned treason, we have destroyed churches.' Opposition in the House of Lords seemed likely to lead to a constitutional crisis, but the intervention of Queen Victoria ensured that, after minor amendment, the Act was given the Royal Assent on 26 July 1869.

Nevertheless, the Act did remove a major grievance and can be justly regarded as, perhaps, the most successful of Gladstone's Irish policies. The Act also raised hopes among nonconformist Liberals of the Liberation Society who saw it as the first step towards the disestablishment of the Church of England.

The Land Act, 1870

Another major aspect of Gladstone's attempt 'to pacify Ireland' was the Land Act of 1870. Many Irish farmers were 'tenants-at-will', subject to six months' notice, without any right to compensation for any improvements they might have made to the land. In the northern province of Ulster, a land custom (Ulster tenant right) allowed for compensation and the ability of a tenant to sell on his 'interest' in the property, a separate payment from that received by the landowner in rent. During the 1850s and 1860s, an Irish pressure group – the Irish Tenant League – advocated that tenants should benefit from the '3 Fs': free sale, fair rent and fixity of tenure. The Independent Irish Party supported this aim at Westminster in the 1850s.

To avoid setting any precedents for changing property rights elsewhere in the United Kingdom, Gladstone accepted the suggestion of George

Campbell, a former judge in British India. This was to use the tradition of Ulster tenant right as the basis of land legislation. On 15 February 1870, the Land Act duly became law. Ulster custom was extended to the rest of Ireland, given the force of law, ensuring tenants compensation for improvements on eviction for any reason other than non-payment of rent. The 'John Bright' clauses of the Act allowed land purchase by tenants through a government grant of two-thirds of the price.

The Act enraged landowners who saw it as a challenge to property rights. It also fell far short of the '3 Fs' demanded by the Irish Tenant League. The amount of compensation depended upon the size of the farm and could not be more than £250. Fair rent was to be decided by magistrates (JPs) who were, invariably, landowners. From the onset of the agricultural depression in Ireland after 1877, evictions for non-payment of rent became commonplace, particularly in the West. This led to the Land War.

There was also a plan to include government support for the development of Irish railways and economic development for the Irish peasantry, but this was abandoned.

Coercion

The aim of the Church and Land Acts was to bring peace to Ireland and to reduce support for the Fenians. To further this aim, Gladstone released the remaining Fenian prisoners in 1870. With these measures Gladstone hoped that he would be able to prevent any disorder in Ireland where the Habeas Corpus Act was suspended four times between 1866 and 1868. However, due to rural disturbances in Ireland the Liberals found it necessary to introduce coercion. The Peace Preservation Act, in April 1870, and the Westmeath Act, in 1871, strengthened the authority of magistrates to arrest and detain persons suspected of disorder.

Irish Universities Bill, 1873

Unfortunately, the most conspicuous failure in Gladstone's Irish policy was the Irish Universities Bill of 1873, which led, temporarily, to the fall of his Government. Before 1873, Irish university education was limited to Trinity College, Dublin (an Anglican university, founded in 1591, although Catholics could attend from 1794) and the Queen's colleges of Dublin, Belfast and Cork, founded in 1845, by Sir Robert Peel. The Catholic Church objected to Peel's 'godless colleges' because of the lack of religious teaching. They demanded a Catholic university.

In February 1873, Gladstone proposed that the University of Dublin should be separated from Trinity College which, together with the Queen's colleges and a Catholic university, would provide university education. To avoid controversy, religion, philosophy and modern history would not be taught.

The Bill was opposed by supporters of Trinity College. Nonconformists objected to the State endowment of a Catholic university. Catholics opposed what they called 'miseducation'. The Catholic Archbishop of Dublin, Cardinal Cullen, denounced the proposals. Liberals, generally, disliked the 'gagging clauses' against certain subjects.

On 11 March 1873, the Government was defeated by three votes, with only 12 out of 105 Irish MPs voting for the proposal. Gladstone offered his resignation to the Queen, but Disraeli refused to form a minority Conservative administration.

Overall assessment of Gladstone's Irish policy, 1868–1874

Gladstone had removed the most conspicuous example of alien privilege by disestablishing the Church of Ireland. His Land Act was ingenious through its recognition of Irish custom, but it fell far short of what the

Catholic bishops and the Tenant Right League felt was necessary. This helped to fuel the rise of the Irish Home Rule Party.

Gladstone was able to gain the release of the Fenian prisoners in December 1870. However, opposition to the creation of a Catholic university was due to the prevalent anti-Catholicism of the period (increased by the announcement of papal infallibility at the First Vatican Council in 1870 and the accusation of clerical interference at elections in the Keogh Judgement of 1872).

1. Religion, land problems and the desire for Irish separatism all affected relations between Britain and Ireland.

Explain how each of these problems made the Irish Question a major problem.

2. Gladstone planned to 'pacify Ireland' when he came to power in 1868. How successful was he in dealing with Irish problems during his First Ministry?

Gladstone had hoped to forge closer links with Ireland by establishing a permanent royal residence in Dublin, making the Prince of Wales Viceroy. This was suggested on several occasions between December 1870 and 1872. However, it was opposed by the Queen.

The historian F.S.L. Lyons, in *Ireland Since the Famine* (1971), stated:

> Gladstone's Irish legislation, though a long way short of revolutionary, had a symbolic significance far beyond its immediate effects. It signalled a fresh way of looking at Irish problems. It marked a new harmony between English liberalism and Irish Catholicism. Above all, it gave notice that the Protestant Ascendancy was no longer invulnerable.

10.5.2 Why was Ireland a major issue again by 1880?

In contrast to Gladstone, Disraeli and the Conservative Government after 1874 did not place a high priority on Irish affairs. The Chief Secretary for Ireland (Sir Michael Hicks-Beach until 1878 and then William Lowther) did not hold Cabinet rank. There were only minor reforms, such as the 1878 Intermediate Education Act, providing Irish schools with additional funds from the disendowment of the Church of Ireland and the creation of a Royal University of Ireland in 1879.

However, the period is significant because of the rapid rise in political importance of the Irish Home Rule Party and, within that party, of Charles Stewart Parnell.

Why did the Irish Home Rule Party develop so rapidly after 1870?

There had been a number of Irish political groupings at Westminster since the Act of Union, and within the restricted franchise after 1832. During the 1830s and 1840s, 'The Liberator', Daniel O'Connell, had led a small group of Irish MPs, never numbering more than 30. In the 1840s, this group advocated the repeal of the Act of Union and the re-establishment of an Irish Parliament in Dublin. In the 1850s, another 'independent' Irish Party was formed to support the right of Irish tenant farmers and to defend the Catholic Church, but without much success.

Then in 1870, Isaac Butt, a Protestant lawyer who had defended Fenian suspects in court, formed the Home Government Association, campaigning for the right of the Irish people to self-government. This included the control of the Irish executive by an Irish Parliament. Originally a rather conservative association, the body quickly developed into a major focus for Irish nationalism. The Home Rule Party, as it became known, gained several seats in by-elections between 1870 and 1874, usually at the expense of Irish Liberals. Following the 1874 general election, the Party returned 57 MPs to Westminster.

Much has been made of the importance of the Ballot Act of 1872 in helping the rise of the Party. The Act clearly helped prevent landlord intimidation of the relatively small Irish electorate. However, support for the Home Rule Party had already begun to gain momentum, fuelled in part by dissatisfaction with the Land Act of 1870. The Ballot Act merely accelerated the growth of electoral support. Although the Party had made considerable electoral gains by 1874, it suffered from lack of unity and Isaac Butt's indecisive leadership.

In 1875, however, following a by-election victory in County Meath, the Home Rule Party discovered a future leader who would transform the fate of Irish nationalism: Charles Stewart Parnell, a Protestant landowner from County Wicklow.

Parnell's rise to power

Filibustering: The technique of using long speeches and delaying tactics to obstruct legislation.

In 1875, a small group within the Home Rule Party, led by former Fenians Joseph Biggar and John O'Connor Power, began deliberately to obstruct and delay business in the House of Commons through **filibustering**. The aim was to highlight Irish grievances in the hope that Disraeli's Conservative Government would introduce Irish reform. It was to this group that Parnell attached himself and where he rose to be a formidable member of the parliamentary party. In 1876, he defended the Fenians who had attacked a prison van in Manchester in 1867 against claims by the Irish Chief Secretary that they were murderers. This helped Parnell forge links with the Fenian Brotherhood (also called the Irish Republican Brotherhood). Later that year, Parnell was chosen to conduct a fundraising tour among Irish Americans in the USA. He was able to make contact with **Clan Na Gael**, a leading Irish-American group, and its leader, John Devoy. Finally, in 1877, he was chosen as leader of the Home Rule Association of Great Britain. By that date, Parnell had become the 'leader-in-waiting' of the Home Rule Party.

Clan Na Gael: Founded in New York on 20 June 1867 by Jerome Collins and linked to the Fenian Brotherhood. The Supreme Council of the Fenian Brotherhood was recognised by Clan Na Gael as the provisional government of Ireland.

The Land War and the 'New Departure'

As Parnell was rising to political prominence, Irish affairs became a central issue again thanks to a depression in the Irish economy in the 1870s. A succession of wet summers had seen the reappearance of potato blight and famine in parts of western Ireland. The production of potatoes dropped by 75% between 1876 and 1879. Agricultural prices began to fall as a result of the influx of cheap grain from North America. The prices of principal crops declined by £14 million between 1876 and 1879. In Connaught, the poorest and most westerly province of Ireland, matters were made worse by the outbreak of depression in British agriculture with the loss of migrant work on British farms. In these circumstances, landowners began to re-organise their farms into larger units to benefit from lower costs of production. To achieve this, they had to evict tenants. Many of these landowners were Catholic. In 1879, the worst year of the depression, about 1,000 families were evicted, mainly for this reason.

Michael Davitt (1846–1906)
Born in County Mayo, Davitt emigrated to England and was crippled in an industrial accident. He was an early member of the Fenian Brotherhood. Following the failure of the 1867 Fenian rising in Ireland, he became involved in land issues, culminating in the formation of the Land League. Davitt became MP for Meath in 1882.

If Parnell became the focus of Irish nationalist hope in the Home Rule Party, Michael Davitt became the focus of Irish tenant hopes in the agricultural depression. At a meeting in Irishtown, County Mayo, on 19 April 1878, Davitt laid the foundations of what was to become the Land League, a well-organised pressure group which defended the interests of Irish tenants. Influenced by the radical ideas of James Finton Lalor, Davitt wished to see the nationalisation of land. With the development of the Land League came the reappearance of crimes against landlords in the Irish countryside by 'Ribbonmen' – the Land War of 1879–82.

It is against this background that a 'New Departure' in Irish nationalist politics occurred in October 1879. With the support of John Devoy and Clan Na Gael in the USA and the Fenians, Davitt and Parnell formed an Irish nationalist alliance. Parnell became President of the Irish National Land League, which called for lower rents and an end to evictions. Shortly

1. Why did Ireland become a major problem for British politicians in the years 1876–80?

2. Explain why Charles Stewart Parnell became an important figure in Irish politics in the years 1876–80.

after the General Election of 1880, Parnell replaced William Shaw (Butt had died in 1879) as leader of the Home Rule Party. For the first time since Daniel O'Connell's great triumph of Catholic emancipation in the late 1820s, Irish nationalism was united behind an effective, charismatic leader.

10.5.3 How successfully did Gladstone's Government deal with Ireland between 1880 and 1885?

Introduction

By the time Gladstone took office again in 1880, the rural areas of Ireland were becoming ungovernable. Although Disraeli's Government had set up a royal commission to study Irish problems, little had been done to address the underlying causes.

According to historian John Vincent, the Liberal leader did not have a clear policy towards Ireland in 1880 and had hardly mentioned Ireland in his famous **Midlothian campaigns (1879–80)**. Yet during Gladstone's Second Administration, Ireland became the dominant domestic issue.

Midlothian campaigns (1879–80): Political campaigns undertaken by William Gladstone in the 18 months before the 1880 elections. Although they were aimed at winning the Midlothian seat for Gladstone, he used them to launch a nationwide attack on the Disraeli Government – in particular, on issues of foreign policy.

Concession and coercion, 1880–1881

During the period 1880–82, two individuals, apart from Gladstone, played a major role in forging Liberal policy towards Ireland: Parnell and W.E. Forster. In a negative sense, Parnell and the Home Rule Party forced Ireland into the forefront of the political agenda. Through parliamentary obstruction, the Irish brought the House of Commons' business to a standstill. For instance, on 2 February 1881, it took Speaker Brand, on his own authority, to end an Irish filibuster of 41 hours on the Irish Coercion Bill. As a result of Irish obstruction, the rules of debate and voting were changed radically.

The other major influence was Irish Chief Secretary, W.E. Forster (1880–82). Throughout this period, Forster consistently advocated coercion to break the Land League and to end the Land War.

In 1880, Gladstone attempted to pass a Compensation for Disturbance Bill to deal with the issue of eviction, but this was defeated in the House of Lords. In the autumn of 1880, on the advice of Erskine May, Clerk of the House of Commons, Gladstone introduced a new system of Grand Committees into the Commons to deal with English, Scottish and Irish legislation separately. This led to the reorganisation of the Irish government at Dublin Castle.

Forster introduced the most controversial policy following the trial, arrest and acquittal of Land League officials, in October 1880. In February 1881, Parliament passed Forster's Coercion Act [Crimes Act], which became law in March.

In association with the introduction of coercion, Gladstone accepted the recommendations of the Bessborough Commission into Irish land tenure and passed another Land Act in August 1881. This established a land court to fix 'fair rents' for a period of 15 years. In general, during this period of falling prices for agricultural goods, the land court reduced rents by 25% on average. Land Commissioners were also appointed to assist emigration and to advance three-quarters of the purchase money to tenants wishing to buy their farms. Overall, the Land Act gave the Irish peasant the '3 F's. In addition to fair rent, they were assured fixity of tenure and free sale.

The Kilmainham 'Treaty' and the Phoenix Park Murders, 1882

Although the Act helped to redress many of the shortcomings of the 1870 Land Act, Parnell and the Land League still advocated non-payment of rent and boycotted the Land Act, making it inoperable. As a result, in October 1882, Forster had Parnell, John Dillon and other Land League leaders arrested under the Coercion Act and placed in Kilmainham Gaol, Dublin. Forster also declared the Land League 'an illegal and criminal association'. In response, Parnell issued a 'No Rent Manifesto' from prison.

Gladstone, to break what seemed to be deadlock in Ireland, came to an arrangement with Parnell, through an intermediary, Captain O'Shea, in April 1882, without notifying Forster. By the so-called Kilmainham Treaty, Parnell and the other leaders would be released and arrears of rents would be cancelled in return for an assurance from Parnell that the Land War would end. When the 'treaty' was made public, both Forster and the Lord Lieutenant, Lord Cowper, resigned. Both wanted more severe coercion to smash the Land League.

Yet, just at the moment when stability seemed to be returning to Irish affairs, the new Chief Secretary, Lord Frederick Cavendish (a relation of Gladstone), with his Under-Secretary, Burke, were murdered by the Invincibles, a republican organisation, outside the Vice-Regal Lodge in Phoenix Park, Dublin. For a time, Parnell threatened to withdraw from political life.

In response to the crime, the Liberal Government passed a new Coercion Act (The Prevention of Crimes Act) which set up a special tribunal of three judges to try cases without juries. In addition, it gave JPs the authority to detain suspects and declare meetings illegal.

Why did Parnell become the undisputed leader of the Irish national movement by 1885?

During the later years of Gladstone's ministry, Parnell increased his power and influence over the Irish national movement. In October 1882, he reconstituted the Land League as the National League. The emphasis of this organisation was placed on the achievement of Home Rule rather than the nationalisation of land, as advocated by Michael Davitt. The change suggests that Parnell was a moderating, conservative force in nationalist politics. He adopted a political, constitutional path instead of the direct, radical action preferred by Davitt and the Land League.

In 1884, Parnell introduced 'the Pledge' to his party. All Home Rule MPs were now bound to act and vote together in Parliament. This meant that the Irish Party became the most disciplined in the Commons.

In the same year, the Gladstone Government passed the Third Reform Act, which extended the right to vote to labourers. Although this was an important reform in Great Britain, in Ireland it had the effect of enlarging the electorate by a considerable amount. In the general election of 1885, the Irish Party increased its representation to 86 seats – 85 of 105 seats in Ireland and the Scotland Road Division of Liverpool, a constituency with a large Irish immigrant community.

In addition, Parnell's instructions to the Irish Catholic immigrant community in Britain to support the Conservatives is estimated to have cost the Liberals 20 seats. This move was prompted by the suggestion, made by Lord Carnarvon, that the Conservatives might support Home

1. Explain how Gladstone dealt with Irish problems during his Second Administration.

2. 'He did more harm than good to British–Irish relations.'

How far do you agree with this view of Charles Stewart Parnell in the years 1880–85?

Rule. With the Liberals remaining the largest party but with a reduced majority of 86 seats, Parnell and the Home Rule Party held the balance of power in the House of Commons, creating a truly three-party system.

As F.S.L. Lyons stated, in *Ireland Since the Famine* (1971): 'His [Parnell's] creation of a disciplined, efficient and pledge-bound parliamentary party, … by its performance at Westminster, offered a living proof that Ireland was ripe for self-government.'

10.5.4 Why did Gladstone convert to Irish Home Rule in 1886?
A CASE STUDY IN HISTORICAL INTERPRETATION

W.E. Gladstone's decision to 'convert' to the idea of Home Rule for Ireland is, perhaps, the most important political event in the domestic history of Britain in the second half of the 19th century.

Gladstone's conversion split the Liberal Party in 1886 between Gladstonian Liberals (the majority) and Liberal Unionists (93 MPs) led by Lord Hartington (the future Duke of Devonshire) and Joseph Chamberlain. The Liberal Unionists 'crossed' the floor of the House of Commons during the First Home Rule debate and voted with the Conservative opposition, in order to bring down the Gladstone Government. After the 1895 general election, there was a 'merger' of the two parties. It could be argued that from 1846 to 1886 the Whig–Liberal Party dominated British politics. From 1886 to 1905, the Conservatives, with Liberal Unionist support, were the dominant force.

Was Gladstone a genuine Irish reformer?

Since 1886, there has been considerable debate among historians as to why Gladstone took such an important political decision – a decision made more controversial by the manner in which it was announced. Gladstone's son, Herbert, leaked his father's decision to the *Leeds Mercury* in a spectacular newspaper scoop usually referred to as the 'Hawarden Kite', after Gladstone's country home in North Wales.

According to historian J.L. Hammond, in *Gladstone and the Irish Nation*, first published in 1938, Gladstone had decided that Home Rule for Ireland was necessary because it was the logical culmination of his search for a lasting settlement to the problems of British–Irish relations. According to Hammond, Gladstone had declared in 1868 that his mission was 'to pacify Ireland'. During his First Ministry (1868–74), he attempted to solve religious problems (Church Act, 1869), land problems (Land Act, 1870) and the universities issue (Universities Bill, 1873). These were seen by Hammond as part of a coherent programme to deal with Irish affairs.

When Gladstone returned to office in 1880, he continued the work of his First Ministry with more land reform (Second Land Act, 1881). However, he was 'forced' towards the Home Rule solution by the actions of Parnell and the Home Rule Party during the 1880–85 period. By 1886, Gladstone had come to the conclusion that Home Rule was the only conceivable long-term answer to the Irish Question. This traditionalist view sees Gladstone as a politician with a genuine interest in solving what he saw as legitimate Irish grievances and follows a line of argument common to liberal historians as far back as Gladstone's contemporary biographer, John Morley.

Other historians, however, have seen Gladstone's conversion as part of a general development of a Gladstonian philosophy on nationality and not something unique to Ireland. E.D. Steele, in an article entitled 'Gladstone and Ireland' in *Irish Historical Studies* (1970), suggested that Gladstone's support for national self-determination among white, Christian peoples had begun as far back as 1850 after a visit to liberal friends in the Kingdom of Naples. From that date, he became an ardent supporter of Italian unification. This concept was reinforced by his period as High Commissioner to the Greek-populated Ionian Islands in 1858 where Gladstone was appointed after serious rioting against British rule on the island of Corfu. During his time as High Commissioner, he became convinced that union with Greece was the most effective answer to the problem. In the debate on the future of the British protectorate over the islands, in 1863, Gladstone was the main sponsor for the islands' union with the Greek kingdom.

In 1876–77, this view on national self-determination was taken a stage further with the publication of his pamphlet 'The Bulgarian Horrors and the Question of the East'. In it he advocated the granting of independence to the Balkan peoples of the Ottoman (Turkish) empire.

This view was reinforced, according to historian R.T. Shannon, in *Crisis of Imperialism* (1976), when Gladstone visited the Kingdom of Norway-Sweden in 1883, on a summer holiday. In that kingdom, the Norwegians accepted rule by the Swedish King in return for a large measure of home rule. The stability of the kingdom impressed Gladstone, who then began to see Home Rule as a possible lasting solution to British–Irish relations.

After 1885, Gladstone received positive proof that the Irish people desired Home Rule. Following the Third Reform Act of 1884, the Irish electorate increased fourfold and in the subsequent general election of 1885 the Home Rule Party increased its seats to 86. Only north-east Ulster was against Home Rule. Therefore, by July 1886, Gladstone had clear evidence to support the case for Irish Home Rule.

Perhaps the precise timing of the Home Rule 'conversion', in early 1886, can be explained, in part, by James Loughlin's observations in *Gladstone, Home Rule and the Ulster Question, 1882–1893* (1986). According to Loughlin, a major influence on Gladstone's decision was a report on the Irish situation by James Bryce made after the June general election in 1885, entitled 'Irish Opinions on the Irish Problem'. Gladstone, it must be remembered, had visited Ireland just once – in 1877 – and he had to rely on others for direct information concerning conditions in Ireland. Bryce painted a picture of Ireland on the brink of social breakdown. To Gladstone, there was an immediate need to find a solution to Irish problems. Hence his decision to include a land purchase bill alongside the Home Rule Bill in 1886.

Was Gladstone a cynical party politician?

In contrast to these interpretations, a group of historians have seen Gladstone and Ireland from a completely different perspective. They have seen Gladstone's Irish policy as less to do with a genuine attempt to solve British–Irish relations and more to do with the nature of Liberal party politics.

In *Liberal Politics in the Age of Gladstone and Rosebery* (1972), D.A. Hamer claims that Gladstone had been aware of the fractious, coalition nature of the Liberal Party for some time. During the 1866 debate on parliamentary reform, the Liberal Party had split. Robert Lowe led the 'Adullamite' faction against Lord John Russell's Liberal Government. The effect was to allow Lord Derby to form a Conservative Administration (1866–68) which passed its own parliamentary reform act.

Once Gladstone became Liberal leader, he recognised the need to find a rallying cry to unite a political party with a tendency to divide into factions. In the general election of 1868, he used the rallying cry of 'Justice for Ireland'; in 1874, he used the abolition of income tax; and, in 1880, it was anti-Beaconsfieldism. By 1885–86, Gladstone had come to the belief that to prevent the Liberal Party from disintegrating he had to find a strong Liberal theme to unite the Party. Irish Home Rule seemed to fit the bill. According to Gladstone, Ireland had preoccupied his 1880–85 Government giving it little time to pass needed reform at home. Gladstone suggested that once the Home Rule obstruction to the railway line had been removed, the Liberal train of reform was free to move forward.

In *The Governing Passion* (1974), A.B. Cooke and J. Vincent take the more cynical view that Gladstone never expected Irish Home Rule to become law. This now seemed likely with the built-in Conservative majority in the House of Lords and their right of **veto**. They believe that Gladstone converted to Home Rule to 'dish the Whigs' and Joseph Chamberlain in order to regain effective control of the Liberal Party. In 1886, Gladstone was 77 years old and had been an MP since 1832. During his Second Ministry, the Liberal Party had been riven with disputes between aristocratic Whigs and Radicals. Gladstone had seemed to be losing control of his Party. In fact, prior to the June 1885 election, Joseph Chamberlain produced his own unofficial 'Radical Programme' as a manifesto for his wing of the Liberal Party. Once Gladstone 'converted' to Irish Home Rule, Chamberlain and the Whigs left the Party to form the Liberal Unionists. After 1886, although the Liberal Party was smaller it remained under the control of Gladstone until his retirement in 1894.

It would seem that Home Rule could be viewed either from the long-term perspective of British–Irish relations or purely from the viewpoint of British party politics where Gladstone's Irish policy was merely a tool in a game of political tactics to win or to keep political power.

Veto (Latin – 'I forbid'): A negative vote exercised constitutionally by an individual, an institution or a state. It has the effect of automatically defeating the motion against which it is cast.

1. What are the arguments put forward above to support the view that Gladstone wanted to solve the Irish problem?

2. What are the arguments put forward to suggest that Gladstone was more interested in keeping the leadership of the Liberal Party than solving the Irish problem?

3. Explain why historians have disagreed over Gladstone's decision to support Irish Home Rule in 1886.

10.5.5 Why was Home Rule so controversial?

Home Rule had a devastating effect on Liberal Party unity. The issue was responsible for the fall of Salisbury's Conservative Government in 1885 and Gladstone's Liberal Government in 1886. Clearly, it raised many important questions for British politicians.

Superficially, it seems hard to believe why the rather modest Home Rule Bill of 1886 created so much controversy. Under the Bill, Irish MPs would no longer sit at Westminster. This was seen as a blessing to those who had experienced Irish obstruction. Britain would also keep control of defence, finance, posts and trade. So why were so many people willing to oppose Home Rule so vociferously?

Opposition to Home Rule

● Perhaps the strongest opposition to Home Rule came from within Ireland. In north-east Ulster, the population was mainly Protestant. They feared control from a Catholic-dominated, Dublin-based parliament. To them, Home Rule meant 'Rome Rule'. In addition, the economy of north-east Ireland had become industrialised during the 19th century, with linen textile production and shipbuilding predominating.

In many ways, north-east Ireland had more in common, both religiously and economically, with England and Scotland than the rest of Ireland. To the Protestants of Ulster, the Act of Union meant religious freedom and economic prosperity. Aware of these concerns the Conservative politician, Lord Randolph Churchill, visited Belfast in 1886 and his opposition to Home Rule helped to spark off anti-Home Rule rioting there.

● Also, within Ireland, the landowning class and the Protestant Ascendancy were content with the Act of Union. They feared that a Parnellite-dominated Dublin parliament might introduce radical land reform, which might end their privileged position.

● In Britain, a major reason for opposing Home Rule was Home Rule's possible impact on the British Empire. By the mid-1880s, many politicians were beginning to fear that Britain's pre-eminent position as the world's major industrial and imperial nation was coming under threat from nations such as the USA, Germany and Russia. In 1882, John Seeley of Cambridge University delivered a series of lectures entitled 'The Expansion of England', where he suggested that the future of world history lay in the hands of large states such as the USA or Russia. If Britain wished to remain a world power it would have to strengthen its control over the British Empire.

In this political climate the idea of dividing the mother country, the United Kingdom, through Home Rule was seen to weaken not strengthen the Empire. Many saw Home Rule as merely the first step towards the creation of an independent Irish state. Apart from personal dislike of Gladstone, it was Joseph Chamberlain's desire to safeguard the Empire that led him to be a Liberal Unionist.

Support for Home Rule

● In opposition to this view, Gladstone suggested that Home Rule would bring peace to the Irish countryside, thus ending a major cost to the British taxpayer for law and order.

● It would also remove Irish grievances and, therefore, would strengthen not weaken the Empire.

On balance, opponents of Home Rule were more numerous. In 1886, the First Home Rule Bill was defeated in the House of Commons by 343 to 313 votes.

1. What were the reasons why Irish Home Rule was opposed?

2. Why was the issue of Irish Home Rule likely to split the Liberal Party in 1886?

1. What message is the author of this cartoon trying to make about the opposition to Home Rule within Ireland?

2. How useful is this cartoon to a historian writing about the issue of Irish Home Rule?

Should the dog wag the tail, or the tail wag the dog ?

Source-based questions: Irish Home Rule

SOURCE A

1. That … we declare our conviction that it is essentially necessary to the peace and prosperity of Ireland that the right of domestic legislation on all Irish affairs should be restricted to our country.

2. That, in accordance with the ancient and constitutional rights of the Irish nation, we claim the privilege of managing our own affairs by a parliament assembled in Ireland, and composed of the sovereign, the lords and the commons of Ireland.

4. That … we adopt the principle of federal arrangement … leaving to the imperial parliament the power of dealing with all questions affecting the imperial crown and government, legislation regarding the colonies … relations of the empire with foreign states and stability of the empire at large.

8. … no legislation shall be adopted to establish any religious ascendency in Ireland.

From the Proceedings of the Home Rule Conference held in Dublin in November 1873.

SOURCE B

Home Rule will send a quickening stir of grateful life through a discontented land, which has long been rent with civil feuds. It will dress the labourer's face with smiles, lift him in the scale of civilisation, imbue him with the true spirit of human toil. It will educate him and enrich him. It will cover the barren rocks with soil; drain the sterile swamps, people the storm-swept gorges of Ireland's grey hills with beneficent activity and enduring peace.

Joseph Cowan, MP for Newcastle-upon-Tyne. From the Debate on the First Home Rule Bill taken from Hansard, May 1886.

Source-based questions: Irish Home Rule

SOURCE C

In America federalism has developed because existing states wished to be combined into some kind of national unity. Federalism [here] would necessarily mean the breaking up of the nation in order to form a body of states. The vast majority of the United Kingdom, including a million more of the inhabitants of Ireland, have expressed their will to maintain the Union. Popular government means government in accordance with the will of the majority, and therefore according to the principles of popular government the majority of the United Kingdom have a right to maintain the Union. Their wish is decisive, and ought to terminate the whole agitation in favour of Irish Home Rule.

From *England's Case Against Home Rule*
by Professor A. Dicey of Oxford University.

SOURCE D

The core of opposition to the [Home Rule] Bill, and by far the most effective, came from those Liberals who disagreed with Gladstone's policy. It was Mr Trevelyan (Border Burghs) who stressed that the Liberals were not wholly a Home Rule Party. He had resigned from the government because he believed that there could be no intermediate stage between entire separation and imperial control.

From *Home Rule and the Irish Question*
by Grenfell Morton, published in 1980.

1. Study Source A.

What were the aims of the Home Rule Party?

2. Using the information contained within this chapter and in the sources, explain the meaning of the two terms highlighted:

(a) 'religious ascendancy' (Source A)

(b) 'federalism' (Source C).

3. Study Source B.

How, by his use of language and style, does Joseph Cowan suggest that Home Rule would be good for Ireland?

4. Study Sources C and D.

How far do these two sources put forward different reasons why Home Rule for Ireland should be opposed?

5. Study all the sources and use your own knowledge.

How far do these sources explain the reasons put forward for and against Irish Home Rule?

10.5.6 How successful were Conservative policies towards Ireland between 1885 and 1892?

Introduction

A.J. Balfour, the Conservative Irish Chief Secretary 1887–92, stated that 'I shall be as relentless as Cromwell in enforcing obedience to the law, but, at the same time, I shall be as radical as any reformer in redressing grievances.' Balfour did indeed have notable success in both areas.

The Conservatives held power in 1885 and again from 1886 to 1892. They were firmly against Home Rule, but were nevertheless willing to pass reforms which they thought would remove Irish grievances and with them support for Home Rule. Generally called 'Constructive Unionism' or 'Killing Home Rule with Kindness', it combined a policy of land purchase with strong, resolute government.

Land reforms

The policy of land purchase had begun during Salisbury's short ministry in 1885, where the Ashbourne Land Purchase Act allowed tenants an advance of the whole sum needed to buy land, to be repaid over 49 years at 4% interest. In just three years, approximately £5 million was paid out in loans. This Act was followed by further land purchase acts in 1887 and 1891. These increased the amount of money available for tenants to buy their land. By the early 1890s, over £33 million had been made available for land purchase. In these years, the Irish countryside witnessed a quiet revolution as a new class of land proprietor was created.

In addition to land purchase, the Conservatives passed a land act in 1887 that extended the terms of the 1881 Land Act to include 100,000 leaseholders. They also created a new agency, in 1891, called the Congested Districts Board. It aimed to build roads, piers and bridges and to promote local industries in the poorer parts of western Ireland in counties such as Donegal, Mayo, Galway and Kerry, covering an area of 3.5 million acres. In the building of railways alone, 16,000 new jobs were created.

However, Balfour failed to pass an elective local government reform that would have given Ireland county councils along the lines of England and Wales.

Nevertheless, in 1890, when there was a reappearance of the potato blight in western Ireland, Balfour organised an effective relief campaign that prevented the outbreak of famine.

The plan of campaign and coercion

Although the Conservatives passed many significant reforms, Lord Salisbury's Government was still affected by land agitation in the form of the Plan of Campaign, which began in 1886. Under the leadership of John Dillon of the Home Rule Party, tenants were encouraged to bargain collectively for fairer rents on certain chosen estates. If a landlord refused, then the tenants would withhold rent, paying instead into an 'estate fund' to help tenants who might be evicted. This was a new phase of the Land War which had been waged between 1879 and 1882. In response, Balfour introduced the Crimes Act in 1887, which was renewed each year until 1890, to allow magistrates to detain persons suspected of agrarian crimes. Balfour even got Monsignor Persico, a senior Catholic priest at the Vatican, to visit Ireland and report back to Pope Leo XIII. In April 1888, the Pope issued a statement condemning the plan of campaign but the Irish Catholic bishops did little to implement it.

1. How did Balfour plan to bring peace to Ireland?

2. Who do you think was more successful in dealing with Irish problems: Gladstone between 1880 and 1885 or the Conservatives between 1886 and 1892?

Give reasons to support your answer.

10.5.7 What impact did Parnell and Gladstone have on British–Irish relations?

The fall of Parnell

Perhaps the most sensational aspect of British–Irish relations during the Conservative period of government involved Charles Stewart Parnell. In March 1887, *The Times* published a series of articles entitled 'Parnellism and Crime' which suggested that Parnell had been linked to terrorism such as the Phoenix Park Murders. Although Parnell immediately denounced the claims as untrue, it was not until a special commission set up by the Government investigated the matter in 1888 and 1889 that the matter was resolved. In February 1889, the journalist responsible for the letters,

Richard Pigott, admitted under cross-examination that the information against Parnell was false.

No sooner had Parnell survived this storm than he was cited as an adulterer in a divorce case. Although Parnell's liaison with Mrs Katherine O'Shea had existed since 1880, and included the birth of a child, Mrs O'Shea's husband, Captain O'Shea, a Home Rule MP, did not begin divorce proceedings until December 1889. In a period where the public recognition of sexual immorality was seen as a serious matter, the divorce case created a crisis for the Home Rule Party. On 24 November 1890, Gladstone informed the Home Rule Party that unless Parnell resigned as leader he would not be able to maintain Liberal Party support for Home Rule. The following day, in Committee Room 15 of the House of Commons, the Home Rule Party debated Gladstone's ultimatum. The Party split with 45 in favour of Parnell's resignation and 37 against. Although no longer in command of the majority of Home Rule MPs, Parnell returned to Ireland where he fought and lost three by-elections against anti-Parnellites at North Kilkenny, Carlow and North Sligo. Later, in 1891, he contracted pneumonia and died, aged 45, in Brighton on the south coast of England.

Parnell's impact on British–Irish relations

Charles Parnell was known in his own lifetime as 'the uncrowned King of Ireland'. John Dillon, a leading Home Rule MP, stated on 17 February 1886 that Parnell was 'The accredited leader and ambassador of the Irish people'. Parnell stands out as the most influential Irish politician of the period between Daniel O'Connell in the 1820s and 1830s and the Easter Rising of 1916. With the 'New Departure' of 1879 Parnell was able to become undisputed leader of the Irish national movement for over a decade. In that time he was able to make Home Rule a major, if not the major, issue in British politics.

With the passage of the Third Reform Act, 1884, and the introduction of the 'Pledge' among Home Rule candidates, Parnell was able to exert considerable influence in the British party political system. Following the June 1885 election Parnell and his Party held the balance between the Liberal and Conservative parties, creating a true three-party system. Once Gladstone 'converted' to Home Rule, in 1886, Parnell was able to vote out the Conservatives and to support Gladstone's Liberals. However, once Gladstone had become committed to Home Rule, Parnell lost his position as intermediary between the two main parties. From 1886 onwards, the Irish Party was committed to supporting the Liberals.

While some contemporaries may have regarded Parnell's obstructionist tactics at Westminster as the act of an extremist, he was, in fact, a moderating influence on British–Irish relations. Parnell's leadership of the Irish national movement meant that the movement would follow a constitutionalist course rather than the violence of Fenianism. In October 1882, Parnell created the National League from the old Land League and removed Michael Davitt's radical ideas of land nationalisation from its platform. Again in the late 1880s Parnell consistently refused to support openly the Plan of Campaign.

As F.S.L. Lyons notes, in *Ireland Since the Famine* (1971): 'He [Parnell] was not a physical force man, not a separatist, not the leader of any forlorn hope. He was for winning the maximum self-government by the most efficient means and Parliament seemed to him the road by which Ireland could best come at Home Rule.'

Gladstone and Irish affairs: success or failure?

So much has been written about Gladstone and Ireland that a straightforward assessment of his role and his degree of success will, invariably, be debatable. At one extreme of the argument are Liberals such as John Morley who was determined to show Gladstone's commitment to democratic reform. At the other are historians such as John Vincent who, in his 1977 Raleigh Lecture on Gladstone and Ireland, suggested that Gladstone reacted to developments in Ireland on a piecemeal basis without any overall policy. Vincent believed the only consistent and successful Irish policy followed by Gladstone was coercion and repression.

Gladstone did achieve some measure of success in terms of individual aspects of the Irish Question as it existed in late Victorian Britain. In dealing with the religious issue, his Irish Church Act of 1869 – which disestablished the Church of Ireland – did remove a major religious grievance felt by the majority Catholic population. However, with his conversion to Home Rule the thought of a Catholic-dominated Dublin parliament created a Protestant backlash in north-east Ulster that was to cause problems in the future.

In land reform, Gladstone was the first major British politician since Peel to deal with this problem. His Land Acts of 1870 and 1881 laid the foundation for further reforms under the Conservatives in the late 1880s and 1890s. However, his first Land Act, 1870, made little significant change, while his Second Act, in 1881, was virtually stillborn due to the opposition of the Land League. Compared with the Conservative policy of land purchase, Gladstone's efforts were rather modest.

Home Rule will always occupy centre stage in any discussion on Gladstone and Ireland. While Parnell and his Home Rule Party may have pushed for the policy, it was not until Gladstone's conversion to the idea in 1886 that Home Rule became a serious political issue. From 1886 until the First World War, the granting of Home Rule to Ireland became a major Liberal Party policy. In 1886 and again in 1893, Gladstone attempted but failed to pass a Home Rule Bill.

Gladstone's conversion to Irish Home Rule led to a major split in the Liberal Party and to a period of Conservative Party dominance in British politics which lasted until the first decade of the next century. As a political issue, Home Rule was very damaging to the Liberal Party in the short term. In terms of Gladstone's own political career, however, there is some debate as to whether Home Rule was all that bad. By 'dishing the Whigs' and Joseph Chamberlain, Gladstone regained control of the Liberal Party at a time when it seemed likely that he would be forced to retire from politics. Home Rule, far from damaging Gladstone's career, placed him at the forefront of Liberal politics for another eight years until his retirement in 1894, not over Ireland, but over expenditure on the Royal Navy.

1. In what ways did Parnell influence British policy and the British political system during his career?

2. How successful was Gladstone in dealing with Irish problems during his political career?

10.6 An in-depth study: The road to partition

Key Issues

■ Why was Irish Home Rule a major political issue in the years before the First World War?

■ How close was Ireland to civil war in the years 1912–14?

■ How far did the Easter Rising of 1916 affect Anglo-Irish relations?

10.6.1 How successful were the Conservatives in dealing with the Irish Question, 1895–1905?

10.6.2 To what extent did Irish nationalism change in the years before 1914?

10.6.3 Why did Irish Home Rule become a major political issue after 1911?

10.6.4 Why did Ulster oppose Irish Home Rule so strongly?

10.6.5 Historical interpretation: Who was most responsible for the Ulster Crisis of 1912–1914?

10.6.6 To what extent was the Easter Rising a defeat or a victory for Irish nationalism?

10.6.7 Why was Ireland partitioned between 1920 and 1922?

Overview

THE case made by some British historians argues that the British electorate showed little interest in the 'Irish problem' and, after 1895, it seemed that many MPs were willing to follow suit. Up until the passage of the 1911 Parliament Act, which limited the powers of the Conservative majority in the House of Lords, there was no realistic chance of the passage of a Bill that would give Ireland any form of Home Rule. As soon as the Act was passed, Home Rule became a possibility. British politicians returned to the question of Home Rule but found that the Protestant minority in the north of Ireland would never submit to nationalist rule from Dublin. Events from 1912 to 1914 proved that Ireland was again a dominant issue and of central importance to the British political parties. The Liberal Government failed to deal with what turned into a rebellion by Protestant Ulster which almost plunged Ireland into civil war had it not been for the outbreak of world war in 1914. It was identified by historian George Dangerfield as one of three rebellions which marked 'The Strange Death of Liberal England'. By 1914, it not only marked the stubborn defiance of Ulster, but also the rise of Sinn Fein as a nationalist force – a polarisation of politics which ended any hope of a united Ireland and a reconciliation of religious and political differences there. Why did this happen?

10.6.1 How successful were the Conservatives in dealing with the Irish Question, 1895–1905?

Was the Irish question 'off the agenda' in 1895? Lord Salisbury's Government (1895–1902) and later Arthur Balfour's (1902–05) had no intention of introducing Home Rule. They had other preoccupations: Empire, defence, Europe and the 'Condition of England'.

Policy remained steadfast. 'Bloody' Balfour's 1887 Crimes Act still gave the Government wide and severe powers against rural agitators. However, there were developments. Salisbury and Balfour knew well enough that the inequalities in land ownership would bedevil Ireland; a small number of

Anglo-Irish Protestant landlords who owned vast estates deprived the large number of Catholic peasant tenant farmers of land as well as security of tenure. So, in 1896, Balfour encouraged more tenants to buy land from their owners under a scheme that had started in 1885. The policy of 'killing Home Rule with kindness' might satisfy a long-standing cause of Catholic complaint as well as give landlords generous terms for surrendering their land.

This process accelerated dramatically when George Wyndham, the Chief Secretary for Ireland, passed The Land Act of 1903. It provided extra money from the Government in the form of loans. Landlords were paid generously and in cash for releasing all their land so tenants could buy it. The peasants could now become proprietors, borrowing at low rates of interest with 68 years to pay. By 1909, over 300,000 out of 500,000 tenant farmers were purchasing land, which is proof of the scheme's success. In addition, 2 million acres of additional land were acquired and divided among the peasant farmers. Meanwhile, the Government supported efforts to improve standards of farming and encouraged these small producers to join together and sell their produce in cooperatives. There was little doubt that these farmers reaped the benefits of the end of landlordism. Such 'pacification' did blunt the attacks from those who saw land as a continuing grievance.

What do you regard as the most successful policy introduced by the Conservatives between 1895 and 1905? Give reasons to support your answer.

10.6.2 To what extent did Irish Nationalism change in the years before 1914?

As a political force, the Irish Home Rule Party remained split between pro- and anti-Parnellite factions. This division lasted until 1900, when the party reunited under the leadership of John Redmond (leader of the Parnellite faction) and his deputy John Dillon (who led the anti-Parnellite faction). Nationalism, though, was beginning to take different forms. Initially, these were not political; the establishment of a Gaelic League in 1893 encouraged the revival of the Gaelic language, so central to the survival of the culture. The Gaelic Athletic Association was set up to support Irish sports at the expense of anglicised ones such as cricket or tennis. It may be difficult to assess the effects of this 'new nationalism', but it was no accident that the 1890s witnessed the emergence of several writers who argued for the separation of Ireland from Britain. Examples include the socialist and republican James Connolly, and Arthur Griffith who published his own paper, the *United Irishman*, in 1898 to put forward his idea of 'Sinn Fein'

Postcard entitled 'Belfast under Home Rule: making a site for the statue of King John of Ireland'

(a) What message does the cartoon suggest will be the effect on Belfast of the introduction of Home Rule for Ireland?

(b) How useful to a historian is this cartoon as evidence of the Protestant reaction to Home Rule within Ireland?

('Ourselves'). Griffith went on, in 1907, to translate these ideas into a political movement and organisation of the same name, aiming for a form of 'dualism' in Anglo-Irish relations, modelled on Austria-Hungary.

In retrospect, these were ominous signs of future activity. As the Government tried to tackle the land problem, reports of constitutional changes showed more erratic progress. On the one hand, the 1898 Local Government Act enabled new county councils to be elected, further loosening the hold of rural landlords in agricultural areas. A scheme devised in 1904 and 1905 by Sir Anthony MacDonnell, a civil servant, planned to devolve some domestic powers, such as finance, from London to an Irish Council. It was met with such howls of protest from Ulster Unionists that it had to be withdrawn. Although MacDonnell was the prime culprit, George Wyndham was forced to resign and it led to organised opposition from Ulster. In 1905, an Ulster Unionist Council was formed in Belfast to represent and shape the views of opinion in the Protestant north.

How did new Nationalism threaten British rule in Ireland?

10.6.3 Why did Irish Home Rule become a major political issue after 1911?

Did party advantage determine the behaviour of the Liberals and Unionists? In 1906, the Liberals won 401 seats (377 Liberals and 24 'Lib–Labs') and a landslide victory. They were still the party of Home Rule, but there was a lack of urgency, with little need for Irish Nationalist support in the Commons. Both Henry Campbell-Bannerman and, later, Herbert Asquith made no secret of their opinion that they had other matters commanding their attention – primarily social reform and the associated problem of how to deal with the Conservative majority in the House of Lords which insisted on sinking Liberal legislation. Indeed, until the Lords veto had been dealt with, there was no prospect of ever passing a Home Rule Bill. Campbell-Bannerman had made no promises to the Irish, save that he favoured a 'step-by-step' approach that might be less harmful to the Party. Gladstone's twin failures in 1886 and 1893 had left their mark, as did subsequent electoral defeats.

The one early attempt at reform – an Irish Councils Bill in 1907, which proposed to devolve some internal affairs to Dublin – made no headway and was abandoned in the face of considerable opposition. The Chief Secretary to Ireland, Augustine Birrell, was not the man for the job and must bear some responsibility when subsequent events went out of control.

Events in 1909 and 1910 put a different complexion on the Irish problem. The budget crisis resulted in a confrontation with the House of Lords. The results of the two elections fought in 1910 about the issue of their Lordships' veto over the Commons' legislation left the Liberals suddenly reliant on Irish nationalist support. In December, the figures stood at Liberals 272, Unionists 272, Irish Nationalists 84 and Labour 42. John Redmond, the leader of the Irish Nationalists in Parliament, could see the prospect of Irish affairs coming to the fore. So far he had been frustrated by lack of progress as this intelligent, moderate man's resolve to achieve change through democratic, constitutional processes had been tested. It was difficult for Redmond to 'keep the faith' with Parliament, given the growth of 'new' more militant Irish nationalism in the 1890s. Redmond had to be seen to be getting results. However, with the prospect of a Parliament Bill receiving the royal assent, the Lords would only be able to delay Irish Home Rule for two years.

Asquith had not spoken out for Redmond's case, so it is tempting to argue that Asquith's dependence on Irish (and Labour's) support during the passage of the Parliament Bill persuaded the Liberals now to put more energy into Home Rule. Redmond did threaten that 'it will be impossible for us to support Liberal candidates in England' and that this withdrawal of Irish voters 'would certainly mean the loss of many seats'. Conservatives agreed. They were not slow to accuse Redmond of making a 'corrupt bargain', the sole aim of which was to keep Asquith in power. This was a pact they would come to despise as it contributed to the loss of their ability to shape events from the Lords regardless of the wishes of the electorate. Indeed this 'bargain', which they regarded as an abuse of the wishes of British voters, became the justification for some of the Unionists' more irresponsible tactics in 1912 and 1913.

Not all writers agree that Asquith was so dependent on Redmond and the view that the Liberals acted purely out of political opportunism has been challenged. Patricia Jalland's view is that the Liberals could survive without the Nationalists in Parliament, so their adoption of Home Rule was part of a historical 'long-standing commitment' to the cause. In part, it is the case that the Liberals not only had Labour support, but also might count on Redmond not voting with the opposition. Redmond knew the only chance of progress was with the Liberals, which made his threats sound a little emptier than he no doubt intended. Whatever the arguments, Asquith did go ahead with proposals for Home Rule.

In April 1912, he introduced his Home Rule Bill.

The Home Rule Bill

This provided for an Irish parliament which had the facility to pass some limited laws of its own. However, final authority, particularly over finance, defence and foreign affairs was retained at Westminster, in the imperial parliament to which Ireland could send 42 MPs. Ulster would then come under the jurisdiction of the new Dublin Parliament. Although this was a moderate proposal, the reaction of the north was predictable – they loathed it.

1. Explain why Asquith was willing to introduce a Home Rule Bill after 1911.

2. How far had John Redmond's position been strengthened by 1912?

10.6.4 Why did Ulster oppose Irish Home Rule so strongly?

The separate identity of Ulster had its roots in the 17th century, when James I and his son Charles I granted large estates of confiscated land to English and Scottish Protestants. These 'plantations' marked out Ulster from the rest of Ireland, which was largely Catholic. There was unlikely to be much common ground between the south's allegiance to Rome and the Presbyterian north with its angry rantings against anything Catholic.

Such divisions became ingrained after The Glorious Revolution of 1688 when James II fled to Ireland and carried on the fight against Protestant William III. William's defeat of James' Catholic forces at the battle of the Boyne, in 1690, continues to cast its shadow over Ireland today. It was a defining moment that cemented the bonds of loyalty between the Protestants, who were concentrated in the northern provinces, and Britain.

Economic trends underlined this as Belfast developed into a manufacturing and trading centre, which saw its future prosperity in commerce with rapidly industrialising Britain rather than the poor, agricultural south. The thought of an antagonistic Dublin government under Home Rule ruling all Ireland, which might use tariffs against British competition, angered Belfast's shipbuilders and linen manufacturers. This would be a Dublin government that would be dominated by nationalists.

Neither was there any prospect of religious tolerance. There had been a steady influx of Catholics from the south, who migrated north during the 19th century in search of jobs and wages. But the religious divisions in the north stirred John Morley, the Liberal politician, to comment on the 'spirit of bigotry and violence for which a parallel can hardly be found … in Western Europe'. It was Parnell's Nationalism and Gladstone's conversion to Home Rule through the introduction of his 1886 and 1893 Bills which provoked defensive measures from Ulster's Protestants. They recognised the need to defend the union from Nationalist Catholics, claiming that 'Home rule is Rome rule'. The legacy of William III was kept alive by the Orange Order, which pledged itself to the union. Unionist clubs sprang up to feed other organisations such as the Ulster Defence Union or the Loyalist Anti-Repeal Union. Lord Randolph Churchill, the Conservative MP, opposed Gladstone's 1886 attempt at Home Rule. In a move that he calculated would do his personal ambitions no harm, Churchill visited Belfast and declared that 'Ulster will fight, and Ulster will be right'.

Gladstone's 1886 Bill also caused his Ulster MPs to abandon the Liberals and join the Conservatives who were ready to embrace the Ulster unionist viewpoint. The new alliance of Conservatives and Liberal Unionists won a majority of constituencies in the north in the 1886 election. Any more attempts at Home Rule would be unable to ignore Ulster's voice. After the defeat of the 1893 Home Rule Bill and the subsequent triumph of the Conservative-Unionists, Irish voices were more muted. Ulstermen relaxed. The Nationalists waited for better times; perhaps after the publication of the Home Rule Bill?

1. What do you regard as the main reason why many Ulstermen opposed Home Rule? Give reasons to support your answer.

2. What evidence might support the view that the 1912 Home Rule Bill stood little chance of success?

10.6.5 Who was most responsible for the Ulster Crisis of 1912–1914?
A CASE STUDY IN HISTORICAL INTERPRETATION

Asquith's failure to treat Ulster as a separate case was, in part, a result of his lack of understanding of the problem and an unwillingness to accept how serious Ulster's opposition might become. Nevertheless, the signs were clear. In September 1911, 50,000 Ulstermen were told by Sir Edward Carson that Home Rule was a conspiracy and that, if it were passed, then they would have to take over the 'government of the Protestant provinces'.

Carson was Liberal Unionist MP for Dublin University. His skills were recognised on becoming the Solicitor-General firstly for Ireland, then for England. He was a strong personality, committed to the Union, and so determined to organise resistance to the Bill that some historians have speculated on how far Carson was willing to go. Would he have resisted the Government by force to ensure Ulster's exclusion? Nicholas Mansergh and J.C. Beckett argue that he may well have done so, although both Robert Blake and Graham Dangerfield see Carson as a lawyer and constitutionalist who would probably shrink from open insurrection.

The same cannot be said of Captain James Craig, MP, who was keen to implement his well-laid plans for Ulster's self-government (through the Ulster Unionist Council) and ultimately armed resistance.

Sir Edward Carson (1854–1935)
Carson trained as a lawyer. His powerful leadership of the Irish Unionists involved getting more than 250,000 Protestants to sign a covenant declaring undying opposition to Home Rule. Carson also set up the Ulster Volunteer Force, in 1913. During the First World War, he served as Attorney General and, later, as a member of Lloyd George's War Cabinet.

- In 1912, there was clear evidence that Protestant volunteers were being drilled and trained in what became the Ulster Volunteer Force. It may have lacked arms but certainly not organisation, as its Commanding Officer was Lieutenant-General Sir George Richardson who had served in India before retiring from the British Army.

- Both Craig and Carson were present when 100,000 Ulstermen marched in military formation through Balmoral (part of Belfast) a day or so before Asquith rose in the House of Commons to introduce his Bill.

- In September 1912, 'Covenant Day' was marked by more parades and demonstrations and the signing of the 'Solemn League and Covenant' by, in the end, just short of half a million men and women. It proclaimed them 'loyal subjects of his Glorious Majesty King George V', who would use 'all means necessary to defeat the present conspiracy to set up a home rule parliament in Ireland. And in the event of such a Parliament being forced upon us we further and mutually pledge ourselves to refuse to recognise its authority.'

- To that end the Ulster Unionist Council continued to make contingency plans to run the province's government if Home Rule was passed. Finance seemed no problem as the Anglo-Scottish landowners and the businessmen of Belfast contributed freely to the campaign.

All this activity continued under the gaze of Asquith's Government, which signally failed to take any firm action against Ulster's leaders.

What was happening in Parliament?

It was in Parliament that the Ulstermen were receiving fierce support from the Unionists. Their leader since 1911, Andrew Bonar Law, had grown up in Ulster where he would have listened to the sermons delivered by his father who was a Presbyterian minister. He understood Carson's views and lent his support. Bonar Law stood with Carson at Balmoral in April 1912, taking up the cause with enthusiasm. Three months later at Blenheim Palace, home of the Duke of Marlborough, Bonar Law apparently supported the use of any means to resist the forcible inclusion of Ulstermen in a single Ireland: '… if an attempt were made to deprive these (Ulster)men of their birthright – as part of a corrupt parliamentary bargain – they would be justified in resisting such an attempt by all means in their power, including force … if such an attempt is made, I can imagine no length of resistance to which Ulster can go in which I should not be prepared to support them'. Was this an irresponsible call for armed resistance?

To Bonar Law's defenders, it was entirely just to encourage disobedience and insurrection when the Government seemed intent on sweeping aside the civil rights of a minority. This was a minority that was part of the Empire and wished to maintain their constitutional position as loyal citizens of the King. During one of the debates, Bonar Law asked MPs if they believed that 'any Prime Minister could give orders to shoot down men whose only crime is that they refuse to be driven out of our community and deprived of the privilege of British citizenship?' Bonar Law's background also reflects a real commitment to the Union.

To Bonar Law's detractors, however, his was a reckless approach which reflected the impotence felt by Unionists after the passage of the Parliament Act now they could only use the Lords to delay legislation. Any strategy was justified if it would bring about a general election they believed they could win on the issue of defending the Empire and the union. Some historians, such as Professor Buckland, also recognise that as Ulster was the Home Rule Bill's '**Achilles heel**', there was much political advantage to be gained from attacking Asquith's inadequate response to the Ulster problem; political opportunism governed the Party's response.

If Bonar Law's 'Grammar of Anarchy', as Asquith called it, has much to answer for, then so do the Liberal leaders for their slow response. In June 1912, an attempt to amend the Bill by excluding four of the Ulster counties came to nothing. Historian K.W. Aikin claims that 'a favourable opportunity was lost', and the crisis deepened. In the House of Commons, Asquith found it difficult to make himself heard as each side traded insults. Indeed, the Prime Minister seemed incapable of grasping how dangerous

Andrew Bonar Law (1858–1923)
Born in Canada, Bonar Law made his fortune in Scotland as a banker and iron-merchant before entering Parliament in 1900. He was elected Leader of the Opposition in 1911, before becoming Colonial Secretary in Asquith's coalition government (1915–16). He was Chancellor of the Exchequer (1916–19) and Lord Privy Seal (1919–21) in Lloyd George's coalition. He was asked to form a Conservative Cabinet in 1922, but had to resign on health grounds.

Achilles heel: The weakest spot. Achilles was a Greek hero whose right ankle bone was damaged by fire. It was replaced by one taken from a giant who was a particularly fast runner. Achilles became a fast runner but his right heel was always his weak point. A different version of the myth tells of Achilles' mother, Thetis, dipping him into the river Styx to make him invulnerable. Only his heel, which she held him by, remained vulnerable.

the situation was. Historians such as Robert Blake generally agree that Asquith's profound respect for, and faith in, the constitution meant that he found it difficult to come to terms with the ferocity of the opposition both inside and outside Parliament. The Budget crisis was evidence of that. Then, as now, Asquith looked for a settlement that might be achieved through established parliamentary channels.

Did he share Redmond's view that Carson was bluffing? Unfortunately, Asquith never looked like dealing with the Ulster threat – all he offered was a policy of 'wait and see'. It failed to give any direction or purpose to government actions. Jenkins, Asquith's biographer, argues that since there was precious little prospect of finding an answer to the Ulster problem in 1912, there was merit in giving time for passions to cool. Certainly, there was no sign of compromise in Parliament. Carson wanted all Ireland, not just Ulster, to remain inside the Empire. Redmond was aware that Sinn Fein extremists would never accept a clause which excluded Ulster from a united Ireland – a view shared by Joe Devlin, leader of the Ancient Order of Hibernians and the Nationalists in the north.

In the event, 'wait and see' made matters worse. The Ulster Volunteer Force (UVF) continued to march and drill. If it indeed was an illegal organisation, then nothing was done to stop their preparations. By January 1913, the Bill had concluded its passage through the Commons only to be rejected by the Lords in an ill-tempered and hostile atmosphere.

More in hope than expectation, King George V was dragged into the crisis when Bonar Law suggested that he should veto the Home Rule Bill and call an election. Party leaders visited Balmoral during September 1913 to listen to the King's anxieties about the threat of Ulster violence and pleas for compromise. As a result, there were talks between the party leaders. Oddly, it was Carson who seemed more willing to accept a settlement; but his insistence that Ulster be defined as the nine northern counties, at least three of which had Catholic majorities, meant that Redmond would reject the proposal. Asquith could not afford to ignore this; neither could Bonar Law ignore the diehards in his own Party who would fight to the last in defence of the Union.

Meanwhile events were moving into a more dangerous phase. Dublin History Professor John MacNeill had long campaigned for a Nationalist force to be formed in the south. In November 1913, the Catholic Irish Volunteers were set up with 200,000 men in support. Aiken notes that it was set up 'neither to fight for Home Rule nor to fight the Ulster Volunteers'. Potentially, it could be seen as another paramilitary force that could arm itself like the UVF; in which case, it was a step closer towards civil war.

Would the British Army be in a position to stop civil war, if it broke out?

How serious was the 'Mutiny' at the Curragh?

The position of the British Army in Ulster was now called into question as many of its officers were Ulstermen. Field Marshal Frederick Roberts, a respected figure, had his roots in Ulster. So did the Director of Military Operations at the War Office, General Henry Wilson, who managed to keep Bonar Law informed, behind the scenes, of the Army's plans. Would they suppress their countrymen if Home Rule was forced upon them? There was talk among Conservatives that the Annual Army Act should be amended to prevent the Army being used in such a way, against Ulster, unless a general election had taken place. This was dangerous, if not irresponsible, talk and Arthur Balfour warned Bonar Law that others may draw 'a perilous moral from the precedent'. At a time of social unrest led by **Suffragettes** and trade unions, as well as a perilous foreign situation, could Army discipline be relied upon?

Suffragettes: The name given to women who took an active, militant view towards the campaign for votes for women. Activities such as assaults on politicians and burning mailboxes were intended to highlight their case. The most notable Suffragettes were the Pankhursts. Suffragettes were a separate group from the Suffragists – who also wanted votes for women but aimed to achieve this through peaceful persuasion not direct action.

In March 1914, rumours spread that the UVF might try to seize arms. This prompted Churchill and Seeley, the Secretary of State for War, to order reinforcements into key positions in the north to protect munitions dumps. These operations and Churchill's decision to move destroyers to a position just off the coast, followed by a speech in which he said that he thought it was time to 'put these matters to the proof', made the Government's posture appear provocative. Seeley, displaying remarkable lack of judgement, apparently told the Commander-in-Chief in Ireland, General Sir Arthur Paget, that any officer who had a home in Ulster could 'disappear' from duty when the troops were being moved north and deployed. However, anyone else who stayed only to refuse to obey orders would be dismissed. Paget should never have reported this arrangement to his officers. He nevertheless did so, and in such a way that, on 20 March 1914, another Ulsterman, General Sir Hubert Gough, told Paget that he and 57 cavalry officers would resign rather than fight in Ulster. This was a 'mutiny' of sorts and could hardly have come at a worse time.

The way the crisis was handled exposed even more incompetence. Asquith had to abandon the military operations, admitting that it would lead to strikes among about half of the officers in the army. Gough and the others were told to report to the War Office – where they met Seeley and Sir John French. Gough was able to extract assurances that the Army would not be used to crush Ulster's political opposition to the Home Rule Bill.

Asquith faced a barrage of protest. Gough's lack of allegiance had been rewarded rather than punished and there was widespread bitterness from those officers who had maintained their loyalty. Seeley and French were forced to resign and Asquith took over the War Office himself. As if to set the seal on such an embarrassing incident, the UVF had armed itself within weeks. In a highly successful operation, which took place between 24 and 25 April, 35,000 rifles and millions of rounds of ammunition were landed at Larne and distributed without the Government getting to know about it. In these circumstances it is difficult to defend such a catalogue of errors from the Government which had let things drift, from the Army High Command and particularly from the Unionists who had done so much to encourage a climate of disobedience. Historians are undecided as to whether a military solution might have forced Carson to back down; such a solution was now beyond the Government's grasp.

Nevertheless, Asquith was still discussing with Lloyd George the possibility of changing the Home Rule Bill. His Amending Bill would allow the people of any county in Ulster to vote in favour of exclusion from Home Rule for a period of six years. Carson fumed, calling it 'a stay of execution for six years'. The House of Lords rejected it and inserted a clause, which would permanently exclude all of Ulster. This would never be acceptable to the Government but they persevered. A conference held at Buckingham Palace on 21 July 1914 brought the party leaders together. No agreement was reached on the exact area of Ulster to be excluded and the Conference broke up before they could even talk about the issue of how long Ulster might be left out of Home Rule. The Amending Bill had to be dropped.

Within two days, the danger of armed violence seemed to increase when the Nationalists tried to smuggle in arms of their own at Howth, near Dublin. This time, unlike at Larne, the police stepped in – a point not lost on the Irish Volunteers. The British troops returned to Dublin via Bachelor's Walk where trouble broke out; three Volunteers were killed and over 30 wounded.

Had Asquith let things drift deliberately? If so, the combination of 'wait and see', which relied on the Parties arriving at an unlikely consensus, and diehard Unionist resistance encouraged by Bonar Law, had brought Ireland to the brink of civil war. An altogether different war now intervened.

1. Which of the following do you regard as most responsible for the Ulster Crisis of 1912–14?

(a) Herbert Asquith, the Prime Minister

(b) Sir Edward Carson

(c) Andrew Bonar Law.

Give reasons to support your answer.

2. Why do you think historians have disagreed over who was most responsible for the Ulster Crisis of 1912–14?

10.6.6 To what extent was the Easter Rising a defeat or a victory for Irish nationalism?

On 4 August 1914, Britain declared war on Germany. The Home Rule Bill was passed and became law, although it would not be put into effect until the war had ended. John Redmond, leader of the Home Rule Party, was pleased as everybody's expectations were that they would not have to wait too long – after all, the troops would be 'home for Christmas'. In this context, Redmond's patriotic call to arms was not too costly; the nationalist Irish Volunteers would prove their loyalty and would defend Ireland from German attack. He even suggested that 'it would be a disgrace if young Ireland confined their efforts to remaining at home to defend the shores of Ireland from an unlikely invasion …', so they might fight 'wherever the firing line extends …'. Certainly, 169,000 volunteers supported Redmond, but not all Nationalists were as enthusiastic, as it was becoming obvious that Allied offensives were stuck in the mud of Flanders.

How long, then, would Home Rule be delayed? There were suspicions that Carson (who joined the Cabinet in 1915) and the men of Ulster (who were allowed to create the Ulster Division) were receiving special treatment. More extreme nationalists saw the chance to exploit Britain's wartime weakness and a breakaway group of 11,000 men, led by John MacNeill, formed themselves into the Irish Volunteers. The rest stayed loyal to Redmond and now called themselves the National Volunteers.

Professor MacNeill was a knowledgeable and enthusiastic campaigner for Gaelic rights and an independent Ireland. However, he found himself overshadowed by more extreme elements who disliked the war and who were willing to die for the revolutionary cause. Some members of the Irish Republican Brotherhood encouraged sacrifice, the symbolic spilling of blood. James Connolly, who placed his Irish Citizen Army at the disposal of the revolution, asked if Ireland would ever be a free nation under the Home Rule Bill. If a free nation was one which could control all its domestic and foreign affairs, then the answer was 'no, most emphatically NO!' Nothing but complete separation would please the extreme nationalists.

Dublin during the Easter Rising, 1916

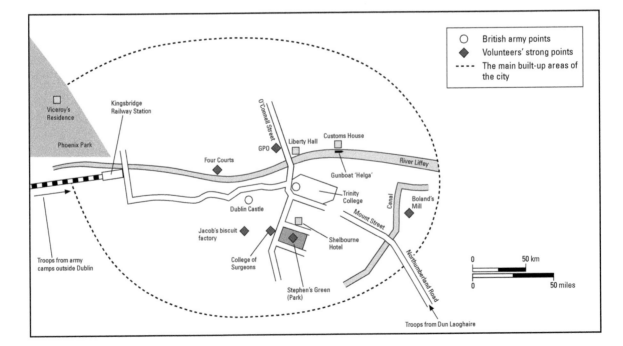

The scene in the General Post Office, Sackville Street, Dublin, 23 April 1916

Does the photograph above reflect the level of destruction caused to Dublin by the Easter Rising?

Give reasons to support your answer.

Patrick Pearse prepared plans for a rising. In all, seven men signed the Proclamation of an Irish Republic: Patrick Pearse, James Connolly, Thomas Clarke, Thomas McDonagh, Sean McDermott, Joseph Plunkett and Eamonn Caennt. These plans were drawn up in so much secrecy that Professor MacNeill did not get wind of them, as he disapproved of what they were doing. MacNeill countermanded Pearse's order for a muster of Volunteers on Easter Sunday, the day before the rising began. Sir Roger Casement, once a British Consular official and fervent Irish nationalist, was sent to gain support and arms from Germany. His shipment was prevented from landing and he was captured, only to be hanged later for treason. Nevertheless, the rising was to go ahead, without any real chance of success.

Easter Monday, 23 April 1916, was chosen. It was a quiet day and 1,600 rebels entered Dublin, occupying the General Post Office and other key buildings. Pearse declared a new Irish republic had been born. If this was the case, it would be short-lived. The rebels were not only outnumbered by the Police and the Army, but also no one came to their aid. MacNeill prevented Volunteers from outside Dublin taking part. The general public in Dublin itself looked on with indifference or disapproval. British reinforcements did the rest. On 29 April, amid scenes of devastation, the Irish rebels surrendered. They had lost 450 men dead, with 2,500 wounded. One Dubliner (quoted in G. Morton's *The Irish Question*) called this Easter Rising a 'piece of criminal folly'. Another suggested that 'exclusion of Ulster seems to me to be the only hope for an ultimately united Ireland'. These were hopeful signs that the extremists would be condemned and a settlement might be accepted which left out Ulster.

However, once again the Government mishandled and misread the situation. The anti-republican sentiments were let slip by taking oppressive measures, including **martial law** and thousands of arrests. The British had decided to punish this act of treason with repression. General Maxwell executed 16 leaders of the rising. He also introduced martial law. Stories of torture and beatings began to circulate, which infuriated the Catholic south and contributed to an anti-British backlash. Irish folklore had already begun to turn the leaders of the Rising into martyrs. Even across the Atlantic, there was hostility among Irish-Americans against the imprisonment of 75 of the rebels who carried US passports.

Asquith was, yet again, stirred into attempting a negotiated settlement. Lloyd George's solution was Home Rule for the south with exclusion for the six northern counties. Redmond and even Carson approved, but other Unionists and Sinn Fein did not. Historians generally point the finger at the Unionists for blocking this proposal. Whoever was to blame, it delivered two fatal blows: one was to Redmond who lost the initiative to Republicans who now took on the title of Sinn Fein, after the Rising; the other was to any realistic chance of a constitutional settlement. As F.S. Lyons noted, 'the whole constitutional movement was the chief casualty of 1916'. Further proof of this was the failure of more talks in 1917, at the Convention held at Trinity College. This time, Republicans boycotted the Convention and the Ulster Unionists refused to consider any compromise associated with Home Rule.

Sinn Fein, meanwhile, was celebrating four by-election victories, including one by Eamon de Valera who was to become the President of the Irish Republic as well as the head of the Irish Volunteers – a significant concentration of power. Sinn Fein clubs and a membership fast approaching a quarter of a million showed how far they had come from the tiny group which had taken part in the Easter Rising.

In 1918, the Government fared no better. Final German offensives on the Western Front exposed a severe shortage of soldiers and forced the extension of conscription to Ireland after a two-year gap. The Government had been warned about the consequences. Sure enough the protests from all quarters, including trade unions (who organised a one-day strike) and the Catholic Church, were so powerful that the scheme was dropped. The south clearly regarded the Imperial war as something that no longer concerned them. The arrest of some Sinn Fein MPs made no difference.

If confirmation was needed of Sinn Fein's prominent position in Irish politics, then it came in the coupon election of 1918, when they won 73 seats having previously held only seven. Of these 73, 26 were unopposed and another 34 were serving prison sentences. All refused to take their seats at Westminster. The old Irish Party collapsed from 86 seats to six, and four of those were in Ulster. Redmond did not witness this debacle as he had died several months earlier – his Party and the moderate approach had clearly failed, which added to his own sense of disappointment. The Unionists themselves gained 26 seats; the message from Ulster remained the same. A settlement was as far off as ever. The physical separation of Westminster from Sinn Fein, who took up their seats in their own Republican Parliament (the Dail) in Dublin in January 1919, reinforced the suspicion that the south was going its own way.

Martial law: Military law when applied to civilians. Normal civil rights are suspended, allowing the Government to arrest individuals and detain them without trial. Suspects could be tried by military court (without a jury) and given the death penalty if found guilty.

1. What results can you give for the military failure of the Easter Rising?

2. In what sense can the Easter Rising be seen as a victory for Irish nationalism?

3. Why did the more extreme nationalists of Sinn Fein replace the Irish Home Rule Party as the main representatives of Irish nationalism by the end of 1918?

10.6.7 Why was Ireland partitioned between 1920 and 1922?

Subsequent events showed how quickly a circle of revolutionary violence was swallowing Ireland. The Irish Republican Army, which had been formed from the Irish Volunteers, came under the talented military direction of Michael Collins who had fought in the Easter Rising. Violence escalated alarmingly, with attacks on property and policemen. The British Government replied by using ex-soldiers called Black and Tans, who were poorly trained and ill disciplined. They matched the IRA's tactics of intimidation, terror and senseless brutality. During this Anglo-Irish War (1919–21), not only were the existing civil authorities being replaced by Sinn Fein government but also martial law was in widespread use.

Was there any hope of a constitutional settlement? The Government of Ireland Act of 1920 gave separate parliaments and governments to the six Protestant counties of the north and to the 26 counties of the south. However, each would have limited internal powers, akin to those proposed in 1914, with considerable authority retained at Westminster's Imperial Parliament. In the subsequent elections, overwhelming victories by Unionists in Ulster and Sinn Fein in the south signalled rejection of the Act. It never stood a chance of working, and terrorist action continued unabated. So did the talks, driven by Lloyd George's determination to find a settlement. He stuck to the task, and agreement was reached by the end of 1921. The Irish Free State, comprising the southern counties, would gain self-governing dominion status (like Canada); while Ulster would be given the right to drop out of the Free State and remain in the Union. The Nationalists were bitterly divided but eventually agreed and this formed the basis of the 1922 constitution.

Was the partition of Ireland an inevitable product of earlier events?

Source-based questions: The Irish Question

SOURCE A

In the name of God and of the dead generations from which she receives her old tradition of nationhood, Ireland, through us, summons her children to her flag and strikes for her freedom … supported by her exiled children in America and by gallant allies in Europe … We declare the right of the people of Ireland to the ownership of Ireland and to the unfettered control of Irish destinies, to be sovereign … we hereby proclaim the Irish Republic as a Sovereign Independent State, and we pledge our lives and the lives of our comrades in arms to the cause of its freedom …
The Republic guarantees religious and civil liberty, equal rights and equal opportunities to all its citizens … oblivious of the differences carefully fostered by an alien Government, which have divided a minority from the majority in the past …

The declaration of Irish independence, which was read out by Patrick Pearse during the Easter Rising of 1916.

SOURCE B

I admit they are wrong; I know they were wrong; but they fought a clean fight, and they fought with superb bravery and skill … As a matter of fact the great bulk of the population were not favourable to the insurrection, and the insurgents themselves, who had confidently counted on a rising of the people in their support, were absolutely disappointed. They got no popular support whatsoever. What is happening is that thousands of people in Dublin, who ten days ago were bitterly opposed to the whole of the Sinn Fein movement and to the rebellion, are now becoming infuriated against the Government on account of these executions …
We who speak for the vast majority of the Irish people, we who have risked a great deal to win the people to your side in this great crisis of your Empire's history – we, I think, were entitled to be consulted before this bloody course of executions was entered upon in Ireland.

The consequences of the Easter Rising of 1916. This extract is from a speech made in the House of Commons by John Dillon, a Nationalist MP, in May 1916.

Source-based questions: The Irish Question

SOURCE C

Protestant opposition to 'Rome rule' was not eradicated [by the Easter Rising]. If anything, it had been reinforced by the republican 'Easter Rising' in Dublin in 1916 and the violent struggles which followed it. For the Protestants, the rising was proof positive of the treachery of the Catholics who had waited until Britain was occupied in a bloody struggle for democracy and freedom, and then attacked from the rear.

From *The Religion and Politics of Paisleyism: God Save Ulster* by S. Bruce, published in 1986.

1. Study Sources A and B.

What do these sources reveal about the different approaches to the Irish Question from the Irish nationalists?

2. Study Source C.

This source argues that Protestants would see the Easter Rising as an act of 'treachery'. How would the writer of Source A deny that interpretation of events?

3. 'It was the way the British Government dealt with the Rising rather than the Easter Rising itself which was a "piece of criminal folly".' Use Sources B and C and your reading to explain if you agree with this view.

Further Reading

Articles

In *Modern History Review*:
'Britain and Ireland 1880–1921: Searching for the Scapegoat' by Christopher Collins (April 1991)
'Gladstone's Irish Policy: Expediency or High Principle?' by E.J. Feuchtwanger (November 1991)
'Parnell and Home Rule' by Donald MacRaild (February 1993)
Also in *History Review* (formerly *History Sixth*):
'Gladstone and Ireland' by Alan O'Day (March 1990)
'Joseph Chamberlain and the Liberal Unionist Party' by D.J. Dutton (March 1994)
In *The Historian* (Winter 1995) there is an article on Gladstone by Ian Machin.

Texts designed for AS and A2 level students

Great Britain and the Irish Question 1800–1922 by Paul Adelman (Hodder, Access to History Series, 1996)
Home Rule and the Irish Question by Grenfell Morton (Longman, Seminar Studies series, 1980)

More advanced reading

Ireland Since the Famine by F.S.L. Lyons (Weidenfeld, 1971)
Modern Ireland 1600–1972 by R. Foster (Penguin, 1988)
Gladstone 1809–1874 by H.C. Matthew (Oxford University Press, 1988)
Gladstone 1874 to 1898 by H.C. Matthew (Oxford University Press, 1995)
The Irish Question and British Politics by D.G. Boyce (Macmillan, 1988)
The Irish Question 1840–1921 by Nicholas Mansergh (University of Toronto Press, 1965)
Ireland 1780–1914 by S.R. Gibbons (Blackie, 1978)
The Liberals and Ireland. The Ulster Question in British Politics to 1914 by Patricia Jalland (Harvester Press, 1980)
'Irish Unionism' by Patrick Buckland (Historical Association pamphlet, 1973).

Index